Protest in Hitler's "National Community"

Protest, Culture, and Society

General editors:
Kathrin Fahlenbrach, Institute for Media and Communication, University of Hamburg
Martin Klimke, New York University Abu Dhabi
Joachim Scharloth, Technische Universität Dresden, Germany

Protest movements have been recognized as significant contributors to processes of political participation and transformations of culture and value systems, as well as to the development of both a national and transnational civil society.

This series brings together the various innovative approaches to phenomena of social change, protest and dissent which have emerged in recent years, from an interdisciplinary perspective. It contextualizes social protest and cultures of dissent in larger political processes and socio-cultural transformations by examining the influence of historical trajectories and the response of various segments of society, political and legal institutions on a national and international level. In doing so, the series offers a more comprehensive and multi-dimensional view of historical and cultural change in the twentieth and twenty-first century.

For a full series listing, please see back matter.

Protest In Hitler's "National Community"

Popular Unrest and the Nazi Response

Edited by

Nathan Stoltzfus and Birgit Maier-Katkin

berghahn
NEW YORK · OXFORD
www.berghahnbooks.com

First published in 2016 by
Berghahn Books
www.berghahnbooks.com

© 2016, 2017 Nathan Stoltzfus and Birgit Maier-Katkin
First paperback edition published in 2017

All rights reserved. Except for the quotation of short passages
for the purposes of criticism and review, no part of this book
may be reproduced in any form or by any means, electronic or
mechanical, including photocopying, recording, or any information
storage and retrieval system now known or to be invented,
without written permission of the publisher.

Library of Congress Cataloging-in-Publication Data
Protest in Hitler's "national community" : popular unrest and the Nazi response / edited by Nathan Stoltzfus and Birgit Maier-Katkin.
    pages cm
    Includes bibliographical references and index.
    ISBN 978-1-78238-824-1 (hardback : alk. paper) — ISBN 978-1-78533-733-8 (paperback) — ISBN 978-1-78238-825-8 (ebook)
 1. Protest movements—Germany—History—20th century.
 2. Government, Resistance to—Germany—History—20th century.
 3. Dissenters—Germany—History—20th century. 4. National socialism—Social aspects—History. 5. Germany—Politics and government—1933–1945. 6. Racism—Government policy—Germany—History—20th century. 7. Germany—Social conditions—1933–1945.
 8. Germany—Race relations—Government policy—History—20th century.   I. Stoltzfus, Nathan.   II. Maier-Katkin, Birgit
    DD256.7.P76 2015
    303.48'4094309043—dc23
                                                        2015003128

British Library Cataloguing in Publication Data
A catalogue record for this book is available from the British Library

ISBN: 978-1-78238-824-1 (hardback)
ISBN: 978-1-78533-733-8 (paperback)
ISBN: 978-1-78238-825-8 (ebook)

Henry Friedlander at Ingeborg Hunzinger's Memorial to the Rosenstrasse Protest, "Block der Frauen," on January 28, 2009. Photo by Benjamin Friedlander.

This book is dedicated to professor Henry Friedlander, historian and Holocaust survivor, who was writing the preface when he suffered a devastating stroke on February 12, 2009. Although his work did not address dissent systematically, Professor Friedlander's dissertation was on the German Revolution of 1918–19 and his final work, *The Origins of Nazi Genocide*, addressed the limitations that expressions of popular opinion imposed on Nazi "euthanasia." On his final trip to Berlin, just two weeks before his stroke, Henry Friedlander paid a visit to the Rosenstrasse Memorial with his son, Professor Benjamin Friedlander. Henry repeatedly said that the release of Jews from Rosenstrasse only made sense to him when it was seen as the result of protest by their non-Jewish relatives, as he had begun to write: "Germans could do something to oppose the regime. Rosenstrasse was proof of that. This is also what Sybil [Milton] thought. You don't have a big roundup of Jews and imprison some of them because you want to make them take the jobs of the leadership you are now deporting. Some say they did not want to do these Jews any harm. But they were not arresting them to give them an iron cross medal."

Contents

List of Illustrations	ix
Editor's Preface	xi
Introduction: Nazi Responses to Popular Protests in the Reich *Nathan Stoltzfus and Brigit Maier-Katkin*	1
CHAPTER 1. Aspects of German Procedures in the Holocaust *Gerhard L. Weinberg*	10
CHAPTER 2. Women and Protest in Wartime Nazi Germany *Jill Stephenson*	18
CHAPTER 3. The Demonstrations in Support of the Protestant Provincial Bishop Hans Meiser: A Successful Protest Against the Nazi Regime? *Christiane Kuller*	38
CHAPTER 4. The Catholic Church, Bishop von Galen, and 'Euthanasia' *Winfried Süß*	55
CHAPTER 5. The Possibilities of Protest in the Third Reich: The Witten Demonstration in Context *Julia S. Torrie*	76
CHAPTER 6. The "Legend" of Women's Resistance in the Rosenstrasse *Katharina von Kellenbach*	106
CHAPTER 7. Auschwitz, the "Fabrik-Aktion," Rosenstrasse: A Plea for a Change of Perspective *Joachim Neander*	125
CHAPTER 8. The 1943 Rosenstrasse Protest and the Churches *Antonia Leugers*	143
CHAPTER 9. Protest and Aftermath: Placing Protest in the History of Nazi Germany *Nathan Stoltzfus*	177

Afterword: Protest and Resistance *David Clay Large*	209
Appendix 1. The Situation of the "Mischlinge" in Germany, Mid-March 1943 by Gerhard Lehfeldt	223
Appendix 2. Decree Regarding the Removal of Jews from Frankfurt/Oder Factories, February 24, 1943	229
Appendix 3. April 1, 1943, OSS Document Identifying Protest in Berlin with the Interruption of Deportation of Jews	233
Appendix 4. Translated Excerpts from the Diaries of Joseph Goebbels, *Die Tagebücher von Joseph Goebbels*, ed. Elke Frölich (Munich: K.G. Saur)	235
Appendix 5. Excerpts from testimonies of women who protested for their Jewish husbands in response to a request from the Berlin Bureau of Reparations, 1955.	241
Appendix 6. Excerpts of Individual Sections and Paragraphs from Legal Texts and Ordinances (1933–1941)	243
Appendix 7. RSHA Guidelines for Deportation to Auschwitz, Berlin, February 20, 1943	247
Appendix 8. Documents of the SS at Auschwitz from early March 1943 indicating their "pull" for workers from Berlin and their expectation that more working Jews (intermarried) would be sent from Berlin	251
Appendix 9. Documents in response to the Witten Protest and from 1944 indicating Hitler's continuing refusal to use force against "racial" civilians who refused to follow regime guidelines for evacuating bombed areas.	255
Appendix 10. Excerpts from the recent German press representing controversies about public protest by ordinary Germans in the Third Reich.	259
Selected Bibliography	263
Index	267

Illustrations

Figure 6.1a. The *Jüdische Allgemeine*, February 18, 1955, called for all who had resisted and suffered under National Socialism to register at the Berlin Bureau of Reparations, including "the participants in the demonstration march of the "Aryan" wives on Rosenstrasse."   114

Figure 6.1b. In response to the Jüdische Allgemeine's call, more than 60 women attested to the Berlin Bureau of Reparations that they had demonstrated on Berlin's Rosenstrasse for the release of Jews in early 1943, using their own descriptions to describe their actions, including "Demonstrations," "Processions," "Demonstration March."   114

Figure 6.1c. In their own words they also described their collective action of calling out together, "We want to have our husbands back," and of being ordered by the guards to "clear the streets or we will shoot." In postwar interviews Goebbels' Head Deputy, Leopold Gutterer, said that the threats of shooting had been directed at the women, and not at the imprisoned Jews, but that this was not done since this would have caused a yet greater circle of unrest within non-Jewish family circles.   115

Figure 8.1. "Whoever wears this symbol is an enemy of our people." Nazi propaganda instructing Germans on why German Jews were required to wear the Star of David. It marked the Jews identified specifically for deportation, which was illustrated during the Gestapo's "Action to Clear the Reich of Jews," the arrests (dubbed the "Factory Action" after the war) that led to the Rosenstrasse Protest. During the early night hours of March 1, 1943, following the second full day of the imprisonment of intermarried Jews at Rosenstrasse 2-4, about 30 who lived in "privileged" intermarriage and thus did not wear the Star of David, were released while those wearing the Star remained at Rosenstrasse. Eleven days earlier, Berlin's Gauleiter Joseph Goebbels had vowed to deport all persons wearing the Star, once and for all. "I have set for myself a goal to make Berlin entirely free of Jews by the middle or end of March at the latest," he wrote on February 18. "With the final deadline of February 28 they are supposed to be first collected in camps and then deported, up to 2,000, batch-by-batch, day-by-day." Weeks after the release of Jews held at Rosenstrasse 2-4, Goebbels admitted that, because there were still persons wearing the Star, the "The Jewish question in Berlin is still not yet completely solved. A whole collection of so-called 'Geltungsjuden' ['half-Jewish' 'Mischlinge' who were counted as Jews and wore the Star], Jews from privileged intermarriages ["full Jews" according to the Nuremberg Laws who were exempted from wearing the Star], and also Jews from intermarriages ["full Jews" required to wear the Star] are still to be found in Berlin . . . I do not want Jews with the Jewish star running around the Reich capital. Either one must take the Jewish star away and privilege them, or on the other hand once and for all evacuate them from the Reich capital," he wrote on April 18, 1943. Historians who write that intermarried Jews were all "privileged" overlook the regime's careful categorization of intermarried Jews it "privileged" and those it did not. (http://www.calvin.edu/academic/cas/gpa/parole.htm).

Editors' Preface

The purpose of this book is to investigate the influences and the limits of this influence on popular unrest and protest in Hitler's *Volksgemeinschaft*—the "German-blooded" National Community he aspired to create. It focuses on the response of National Socialism to unrest and protest, rather than on the motivation for that protest, taking account of the importance of popular support from the dictatorship's perspective. We would like to thank all authors for submitting and revising their chapters on time, and we are grateful for the extensive work of German-to-English translators, led by Birgit Maier-Katkin and including Colleen Chapman and Paul Natiw. Thanks as well to Maria Foscarinis and Dan Maier-Katkin for their editing suggestions, and to Christopher Griffin for preparing the index. We are grateful as well for the work of Marion Berghahn and the editors at Berghahn books, in particular Mollie Firestone, our copy editor.

Nathan Stoltzfus and Birgit Maier-Katkin

Nathan Stoltzfus is the Dorothy and Jonathan Rintels Professor of Holocaust Studies at Florida State University and the author or editor of numerous books and articles, including *Resistance of the Heart: Intermarriage and the Rosenstrasse Protest in Nazi Germany* (W.W. Norton, 1996), *Social Outsiders in Nazi Germany,* co-edited with Robert Gellatlely (Princeton, 2001), *Shades of Green* (Rowman & Littlefield, 2006) co-edited with Christof Mauch and Douglas, *Weiner and Nazi Crimes and the Law*, co-edited with Henry Friedlander (Cambridge, 2008).

Birgit Maier-Katkin is Associate Professor of German at Florida State University. Her research focuses on 20th and 21st century literature and culture. She has published numerous articles on transnational literature, German exiles, as well as Jewish writers among them the essay "Ruth Klüger: Reflections on Auschwitz." *Historical Reflections/Réflexions Historiques* 39.2 (Summer 2013): 57-70. Her book, *Silence and Acts of Memory* (2007), examines Anna Seghers's exile work and explores literature's contribution to the representation of historical memory as well as its impact on cultural identity.

Introduction
Nazi Responses to Popular Protest in the Reich

Nathan Stoltzfus and Brigit Maier-Katkin

This book seeks to show that popular mobilizations of protest have a place in the histories of Nazi Germany. The term "protest" does occur in existing histories, but identifies a very broad array of actions. In this book, protest is defined as a heightened form of social unrest by the "German blooded" Volk within the Reich, that was public and cooperative but spontaneous or loosely improvised, and caused the regime to respond. Popular dissatisfaction and its most strident form of street protest have posed a fundamental departure point for histories of the East German dictatorship, while it is frequently missing altogether in treatments of the Nazi dictatorship. There are various important reasons for this, and yet at least some of this discrepancy is due to interpretations of the Nazi period which became firmly established before historians were accustomed to considering the function of ordinary persons. Over the decades, histories of Nazi Germany have changed to take the German people into account, but attention has continued to shy away from the rare but compelling popular mobilizations of dissent. This book investigates the history of social dissent in Nazi Germany, focusing on popular protest as its most strident form, to show that it was a specific form of popular behavior within the spectrum of popular responses to the dictatorship. The regime's reactions to this form of protest also provide valuable perspectives for understanding the importance of the Volk for the way the dictatorship consolidated and held power.

Of course there were relatively few incidents of popular protest, not only because of Nazi terror but also because many, many Germans were invested in the belief that Hitler was a rare great Leader. Further, the history of protest is difficult because the records of protest are even more rare than was protest itself. A regime determined to make it appear as though all Germans supported it, was equally determined to minimize any evidence that protest existed and so the sparseness of records about popular protest cannot indicate that there was no significant events of protest, nor does the absence of repression and punishment of ordinary Germans who protested show that the regime was unconcerned about it. Rather, it indicates that this dictatorship had an acute anxiety about maintaining popular morale, which it never attempted to address merely by means of terror. This challenges the perception that protest was merely an aberration, or that the Gestapo always repressed all signs of dissent.

It might be surmised that the regime would have responded to popular protest more firmly, had there been more of it. Terror did preempt most open and organized opposition, and its effectiveness was amplified by popular support for it. But the realization that brute force was not equally well suited for achieving all his goals for the Volk was a key to Hitler's "criminal cunning."[1] The Nazi leadership lived with anxiety about discord among Germans, a concern that reached an apex during war. Jill Stephenson's study, in chapter 2, shows that the incidence of public protests by the Volk, rare as they were, did not decrease during World War II, but increased. Further, the regime continued to appease them, without punishing dissidents and sometimes making concessions, which it considered to be temporary. These protests, Stephenson finds, were largely the initiative of women, the large majority on the home front.

To find the rationale for the dictatorship's appeasement of popular dissidence, it is not necessary to posit some semblance of civil society or elements of a constitutional democracy. Rather, it resulted from Hitler's self-serving beliefs that Germany had lost World War I because of a "stab in the back" rather than military defeat, while keeping in mind the Nazi leader's determination to convince the people that he represented their collective will and interests—the new mass age as appropriated by fascism. The "stab-in-the-back" myth was shared by many Germans and provided the basis for effective Nazi propaganda as well as Nazi domestic policies.[2] Also conducive to Hitler's decisions to make temporary concessions to the Volk as a whole were his wildly unrealistic ambitions to reshape the Volk's attitudes from the bottom up, to form the Nazi *Volksgemeinschaft*—Hitler's National Community.

Working toward his plan to transition his Volk into a Nazi *Volksgemeinschaft* that would serve as a cornerstone for his fantasy of a thousand-year Reich, Hitler deployed a variety of means to consolidate power and diffuse popular dissent. The dictatorship sought to lead the Volk convincingly phase by phase, so that they followed even as the dictatorship substituted new perspectives for long-established values. While some German traditions went hand in glove with the new Nazi policies, Volk dissent, when it expressed stubborn popular habits, could cause the dictatorship to change course on a particular policy in order to mitigate dissent, and shift public appearances into alignment with its claims of popular consensus. The dictatorship sometimes made concessions in the methods or pace at which it pursued its course, as it pushed to align popular attitudes more completely with Nazism, struggling to avoid the violation of popular customs too abruptly. The dictatorship did not view these concessions as defeats but rather as lessons learned about the limits of how fast the Volk could be pushed.[3]

The preemption of social unrest was important because it served the propaganda image that Germans were united behind the Führer, and thus dissent was desperately isolated and suicidal. Ameliorating troublesome popular unrest required what the Führer, along with those who shared his perspective, thought of as methods "appropriate" for any given stage of development in the evolution toward this *Volksgemeinschaft*. Tactics to dispel dissent should not draw further attention to dissent. This is illustrated by the interactions between Volk and dictatorship regarding Nazi "euthanasia," examined by Winfried Süß in chapter 4. Although regime leaders agreed that Bishop August von Galen had committed treason from his pulpit, Hitler prohibited executing or even punishing the bishop because of fears that this would cause the multitudes of the bishop's followers to lose enthusiasm for fighting war, since his dissent represented the opinion of millions around the Reich. The adjustments the dictatorship made to appease popular defiance remained limited to specific policies, although these were sometimes policies that touched on its basic purposes, such as the "racial hygiene" intentions behind "euthanasia." In 1934, the refusal of Protestants in southern Germany to merge with the Reich Church caused Hitler to suspend his dream of unifying German Lutherans within one unit, under a single bishop (see chapter 3 by Christiane Kuller). This frustrated Hitler's drive to directly centralize his control over the churches.

Even as some regime agencies increased their use of terror following the Wehrmacht's debacle at Stalingrad by February 1943, Hitler continued to ameliorate causes of unrest that stemmed from traditional practices; the regime recognized that the people drew strength from these customs to fight the war. Dissent, when expressing the sentiment of masses, remained a compelling concern for the Führer, even during the war. The weight of popular opinion when it was expressed across society, is documented in July 1943, as German fear of defeat deepened with the Wehrmacht's debacle at Kursk, its final major offensive on the Eastern Front: a state prosecutor set aside the trial of a woman who had said the Nazi "big wigs" sat at home rather than fighting on the front—in contrast to the Soviet commissars. Antagonistic expressions "and jokes deriding the state—even about the Führer—have increased substantially," one SD report noted, so that singling out just this one woman for punishment would raise difficulties.⁴ The courts did begin to issue harsher sentences for certain crimes, and the military executed tens of thousands of soldiers, most for defeatism. At the same time, Hitler sought to ingratiate the dictatorship with the home front, proffering the Nazi Party and in particular its National Welfare Organization as the best ally of the German Volk, as the people struggled to withstand Allied bombings. As Gerhard Weinberg writes in chapter 1, Hitler remained willing to make compromises for as long as he thought Germany might still win the war (and his perception that winning was possible—even into 1945—rested in part on his self-satisfying observation that there was no uprising on the home front this time as there had been in 1918).

Julia Torrie examines a popular protest in October 1943 for which regime records survive, in chapter 5. According to an SD account, a disciplined protest by several hundred women in the Ruhr city of Witten caused official consternation but was not punished. This Witten protest of women, gathered to express their limited dissent with one orderly and common voice, was followed by somewhat more disorderly mass dissent in the nearby cities of Lünen, Bochum, and Hamm. The women's Rosenstrasse protest, earlier in 1943, began as spontaneous acts by individuals, but over the course of a week it grew, at least at times, into a collective action. As the Gestapo attempted to drive the protesters away, but backed down after each threat without harming them, the protesters began to hope that their desperate efforts to do something might have an impact. Few documents directly about this protest survived the regime's desire to minimize evidence concerning such dissent, but Joachim Neander and Antonia Leugers, in chapters 7 and 8, have placed these events in the context of other reports in order to get as close to what happened as possible.

Of course the dictatorship could not allow its subjects to think they had methods for influencing the regime, any more than it wished to publicize news of popular protest. In early November 1943, reflecting on the Witten-area protests several weeks earlier, Goebbels mulled the question of whether to resolve the matter with force: "One dare not bend to the will of the people in this point [evacuations]," he wrote, but had rather "dam up" the stream of returning evacuees with "appropriate measures." If "friendly cajoling" (*guetliches Zureden*) could not stop the wild evacuees, he continued, "then one must use force . . . Should we toughen our stance where we have been soft up until now, then the will of the people will bend to the will of the state. Currently we are on the best path to bending the will of the state to the will of the people . The state may never, against its better insight, give in to the pressure of the street."⁵ Giving in to the street was increasingly dangerous, wrote Goebbels, because each time this happened the state lost authority and in the end would lose all authority.

Yet as Torrie argues, public popular protest prevailed in the case of Witten, since the state wished to maintain willing support from the Volk as a whole. In January 1944, Hitler ruled that the methods to procure civilian cooperation with the regime's evacuation programs that had led to the Witten protest was not "appropriate," and banned Gauleiters, the reigning Nazi officials in geographic segments of the Reich, from using them. In Hitler's calculations, even the soft coercion of manipulating the distribution of food rations to procure compliance was not the most productive method. "The Führer believes that the goal we aim for can be reached particularly through propaganda activities that once again bring before parents' eyes quite graphically the dangers their children face," Goebbels told the Gauleiters.[6] Thus Hitler's recommended means for keeping the Volk in line with the leadership on evacuations had not changed since his orders on the same matter early in the war. In late July 1944 Bormann and Himmler issued a joint declaration stating that "the use of coercive measures" to prevent evacuees from returning "continues to be seen as inappropriate," although forcible evacuations might be possible in some urgent situations. Following this, Martin Bormann confirmed yet again in October that coercion was not to be used against "wild returnees"—Germans disregarding regulations—or to prevent evacuees to return home without permission.[7]

***

While expressing defiance, the Germans investigated here were uninterested in provoking a violent response from authorities, even as they showed that they believed in their dissent strongly enough to risk expressing it in public. Thus this book does not include incidents like the demonstrations of Catholic Youth activists in Vienna during October 7 and 8, 1938, which attacked a sentry of Hitler Youth and was immediately crushed.[8] It also does not encompass important acts of conspiratorial resistance like the White Rose. A study of collective and mass defiance against Nazi fanaticism by the Jehovah's Witnesses, however, might have found a home within these pages had we found an author to write it.

While it focuses on the dictatorship's response to unrest in its various forms, this book does not focus on advancing arguments that forms of unrest that the regime appeased constitute resistance. David Clay Large, an expert on the massive resistance historiography, does identify the protests as resistance, and he also briefly discusses them in the context of the "bottom-up" and "top-down" paradigms for explaining the nature of Hitler's power. The focus here is on the regime's perspective, as it responds to popular unrest in ways it thinks will best manage the Volk's attitudes toward their dictatorship, sometimes bending to the Volk will for the moment, to sustain authority in Volk opinion, as the surest way forward to victory in the end.

This study does argue for supplementing the categories of Volk response to the dictatorship that are already commonly found in studies of the Third Reich. It casts popular protest as one form of behavior that can be found within the spectrum of actions already identified between perpetrators (*Täter/in*) and resistance aimed at overthrowing the regime itself (*Widerstand*). In chapter 8, Antonia Leugers points to Detlev Peukert's identification of popular protest as an escalated level of resistance beyond "non-conformity," and "refusal," but less than "revolution." Although incidences of popular unrest that altered the regime's course at the time were unusual, they represent a specific type of behavior that enlarges our recognition of types of behaviors, particularly defiance. Nazi officials themselves documented specific Nazi responses to specific popular protests, defining opposition in a broad range of categories.

Scholarship on open, mass dissent in Nazi Germany has frequently focused on discovering what motivated "ordinary Germans" to take the risk. Or it examines protest without studying the way the regime calculated its responses. For example, the case of Bishop Meiser and the mass, public defiance among southern German Protestants in 1934, as Kuller points out here, has been studied as religious rather than political history. Historians have worked valiantly to create a field of milieu studies, in order to unearth signals about why certain persons and communities had a capacity for expressing opposition publicly, and together. Fine social-cultural studies are done on local conditions and attitudes as a way of understanding the people's stand in the face of the dictatorship, and the wall of society that appeared to be backing it.[9]

This concern about motivation for opposition has often overlooked the rich documentation on dissent from the dictatorship's perspective, even as opportunities for oral history to investigate such questions have become as scarce as contemporaneous documentation of popular motivation. Because decisions about how best to lead the Volk forward when dissent erupted publicly was so important, the dictatorship's response to it is best found by examining the actions of Nazi leaders at the highest levels—in Berlin, as well as in the capitals of regions ruled by Nazi Gauleiters and Governors.

In the summer of 1941, Bavarian Governor (*Statthalter*) Franz Ritter von Epp summarized the dismay of National Socialism when the Volk expressed themselves collectively in public opposition to a Nazi Party policy. Statthalter Epp complained bitterly about the widespread brouhaha caused by the decree of Munich Gauleiter and Bavarian Culture Minister Adolf Wagner to remove crucifixes from schools, in this heavily Catholic province. Epp accused the Catholic Church of going on the offensive by using Nazi tactics, and compared its mobilization of opinion and public assemblies with the methods the party used to extend its own support. Wagner, Epp said, "has provoked demonstrations, school strikes, and unrest in the entire province. . . . Much worse, the inner devastation of the people and with it the erection of a front of psychological resistance has remained." Wagner's real role as a responsible domestic leader during wartime, chided Epp, was to preserve morale on the home front "during the hardships of war and [to avoid] unnecessary strains on that morale since, as every participant in the First World War was aware, morale at home could lift or depress morale at the Front."[10]

The Bavarian governor did not suppose that brute force to implement the decree was the means for maximizing Nazi support and power at the moment, as it was becoming clear that the Reich had seriously underestimated Soviet resistance to its invasion. The hypothesis that the regime was especially sensitive to popular attitudes during war is explored only briefly in these pages; Winfried Süß, an expert on Bishop August von Galen's opposition to Nazi "euthanasia," has viewed public protest as more influential when the regime's prestige was weakened due to its failures to live up to its haughty claims.[11] The Gauleiter of the region that included Bishop August von Galen's diocese demanded that Galen be executed for treason during the late summer of 1941, proposing that this could be done at a moment of German war victories, which would be cheered on so loudly that the jubilation would overshadow Galen's "removal."[12]

One popular protest, until recent decades an obscure narrative, has become a source of contention. The protests by gentile wives for Jewish family members on Berlin's Rosenstrasse in the late winter of 1943, more than any other event, has opened discussions on popular street protest in Nazi Germany. Antonia Leugers has refuted arguments that the churches were the rescuers of intermarried Jews, and in these pages as well, Joachim Neander has added considerable evidence in support of previous arguments that the regime intended to deport as many intermarried Jews as possible during what it called the "Entjudungaktionen," or the "Elimination of Jews from German Territory" beginning February 27, 1943 (dubbed the "Factory Action" after the war).[13] They find that the interpretation that the non-Jewish women had nothing to do with the fate of their Jewish family members imprisoned at Rosenstrasse 2-4 (because the regime did not intend any harm to these Jews at this time), does not correspond with the sources. Katharina von Kellenbach, in chapter 6, relates the impulse to deny that the protesters had any influence to the fact that Rosenstrasse protests were initiated and carried through by women. Evidence that the regime planned to deport intermarried Berlin Jews who wore the Jewish Star of David in March 1943, is examined in chapter 9 by Nathan Stoltzfus.

In Germany as in countries around Europe the interpretation of the national past is seen as crucial to contemporary national identity and cohesion. Indeed, according to a French historian, "the progress of historical studies is often a danger for national identity," and West Germany's first chancellor, Konrad Adenauer, was willing to include Nazis in the new democracy. "Too much memory [about Germany's recent past] would undermine a still fragile popular psyche," it was said.[14] As the West German community became increasingly sturdier, the implication goes, repression was necessary in increasingly smaller proportions.

As countries across Europe denied reality in favor of a sheltering amnesia, Germans plotted an exemplary confrontation with their past, relative to others. Still, as the history of popularly mobilized protest illustrates, not all of the Nazi past has been integrated. Karl Jaspers, Germany's philosopher of German guilt, wrote that "political tact may at times exact silence" and also that silence "for a short time" may be justified "to catch one's breath and clear one's head," although "we must guard against evasion . . . silence as an act of combat."[15]

Still today, challenging frontiers remain.[16] While the methods and inquiries characterizing the study of the Nazi dictatorship have often led the way in the approaches to the study of twentieth-century tyrannies, the study of popular protest lags, despite the Nazi dictatorship's peculiar need for popular adulation. This book seeks to create a further context for the examination of the Nazi leadership's perspective, through a study of the limited popular protests that occurred during the Third Reich, and the implications this has for the current national memory. It was not Nazi terror alone that made it so dangerous. Together with an ideology that did not change, the dictatorship's capacity to rely on a range of tactics other than terror, moving quickly to improvise ways to sustain and build its movement among the Volk of the Reich, increased the tactics it had for exercising dominion beyond those of terror.

Notes

1. The phrase is from Karl Jaspers, *The Question of German Guilt* (New York: Fordham University, 2001 [orig. 1947]), 48.
2. Timothy Mason, "The Legacy of 1918 for National Socialism," in *Social Policy in the Third Reich: The Working Class and the National Community*, ed. Timothy W. Mason and Jane Caplan (Providence, RI: Berg, 1993), 19–40.
3. For similar reasons of deal making, the dictatorship also reached compromises in foreign policy and even in the destruction of European Jews. In some respects Hitler had to "temporize and compromise" to achieve his dictatorship in 1933, but that "had the advantage of making the revolution appear less abrupt." Gerhard L. Weinberg, *Hitler's Foreign Policy 1933–1939: The Road to World War II* (New York: Enigma Books, 2005), 26. For illustrations of the dictatorship's compromises related to foreign policy in the genocide of European Jews see Gerhard L. Weinberg,

Germany, Hitler, and World War II: Essays in Modern German and World History (Cambridge: Cambridge University Press, 1995), 236–241.
4. Heinz Boberach, *Meldungen aus dem Reich, 1938–1945: Die geheimen Lageberichte des Sicherheitsdienstes der SS*, 17 vols. (Herrsching: Pawlak Verlag, 1984), July 8, 1943, vol. 14, 5445–5447.
5. Joseph Goebbels, *Die Tagebücher von Joseph Goebbels*, ed. Elke Fröhlich, Part 2, vol. 10 (Munich: K.G. Saur, 1998), November 2, 1943, 222. Julia S. Torrie, *"For Their Own Good": Civilian Evacuations in Germany and France, 1939–1945* (New York: Berghahn Books, 2010), 107–108.
6. Goebbels to all Gauleiters, January 28, 1944, in Torrie, *For Their Own Good*, 110.
7. See Appendix 9, Himmler and Bormann's order of July 29, 1944, from a document from the Baden interior minister, August 21, 1944, and Bormann's confirmation of this order on October 12, 1944, to the Gauleiter's representative in Essen. Julia S. Torrie, *For Their Own Good*, 111.
8. Evan Burr Bukey, *Hitler's Austria: Popular Sentiment in the Nazi Era, 1938–1945* (Chapel Hill: University of North Carolina Press, 2000), 102–103.
9. See for example, *Katholisches Milieu und Widerstand Der Kreuzkampf im Oldenburger Land im Kontext des nationalsozialistischen Herrschaftsgefüges*, ed. Maria Anna Zumholz (Berlin: Lit Verlag, 2012).
10. Quoted in Ian Kershaw, Popular Opinion and Political Dissent in the Third Reich, Bavaria 1933-1945 (Oxford: Oxford University Press, 1983), 353.
11. Winfried Süß, "Dann ist keiner von uns seines Lebens mehr sicher:" Bischof von Galen, der katholische Protest gegen die "Euthanasie" und der Stopp der "Aktion T4", ed. Martin Sabrow, Skandal und Öffentlichkeit in der Diktatur. Göttingen 2004, 102-129, here 106-107.
12. Meyer to Bormann, August 13, 1941, in Beth Griech-Polelle, *Bishop von Galen: German Catholicism and National Socialism* (New Haven, CT: Yale, 2002), 88.
13. Joachim Neander, "Die Auschwitz-Rückkehrer vom 21. März 1943," and Antonia Leugers, "Der Protest in der *Rosenstraße* 1943 und die *Kirchen*," in *Berlin, Rosenstraße 2-4: Protest in der NS-Diktatur. Neue Forschungen zum Frauenprotest in der Rosenstraße 1943*, ed. Antonia Leugers (Annweiler: Plöger, 2004), 47–80, 115–143.
14. Ernst Renan, quoted in Tony Judt, *Postwar: A History of Europe Since 1945* (New York: Penguin, 2005), 803.
15. Jaspers, *German Guilt*, 3, 11.
16. The transformation of perspectives on the Holocaust has remained limited by a historiography that remains comparatively bounded by traditional postwar points of view. Dan Stone, "Holocaust Historiography and Cultural History," *Dapim Journal: Studies on the Holocaust, vol.* 23, No. 1 (2009): 52–68.

Chapter 1

Aspects of German Procedures in the Holocaust

Gerhard L. Weinberg

There are two important aspects of the procedures and policies followed by the Germans during the Holocaust that are frequently not sufficiently taken into account as people look back on those terrible events. The first is that the Germans were feeling their way forward into uncharted territory and had to develop procedures, both social and mechanical, in order to implement a policy of systematic murder that was new—but that we see in retrospect. The second aspect was their expectation, until the very last months of the war, that they were going to win the war and therefore could safely afford to draw back a little in the face of specific difficulties on the assumption that after military victory, whatever had been temporarily conceded could be easily fixed as originally desired. We know that the Allies both held together and won the war, but even an allegedly intelligent man like Albert Speer did not recognize that Germany would lose until January 1945.[1]

While Hitler had called for the extermination of all Jews to a cheering audience in Munich as early as April 1920,[2] action toward that goal was not feasible until after he had taken over power in Germany and initiated persecution of Jews in a steadily increasing way. He began a process of systematic as contrasted with individual killing in 1939 with the handicapped in the "euthanasia" program. It was in that process that some Germans, operating in accordance with his orders, experimented with implementing procedures. How do you determine who fits and who does not fit into the category of individuals who are all to be killed? How do you collect those to be killed from their current locations? How do you kill quickly huge numbers of individuals? How do you dispose of enormous numbers of corpses? How do you recruit and train people to kill others all day long, six days a week, for months on end? In all these areas that we see in retrospect, the Germans had to experiment and figure out how to proceed. While they began with the systematic killing of babies with supposed major defects, the severely handicapped, the very old, the mentally ill, and other categories that changed from time to time, it was the results of this experimenting and finding what appeared to be the most efficient ways to operate that would subsequently be applied in a number of ways to Jews beginning in the summer of 1941.[3] Before turning to that topic, there is a specific development in the so-called euthanasia program that needs to be mentioned because of its relevance to what happened in the Holocaust. The government discovered in 1940–1941 that there was substantial opposition to the euthanasia program. A few prominent members of the Catholic and Protestant clergy spoke out, and there were several local riots when buses came to collect prospective victims. The British obtained a copy of a sermon Bishop von Galen had preached on the subject, made copies, and dropped them in leaflets. As casualties on the Eastern Front mounted in the summer of 1941, the idea that severely wounded German soldiers would be killed by their own government was not thought good for morale at the front or at home. So the program was officially halted but in reality continued in a decentralized way for the rest of the war (with severely wounded veterans of both world wars included). Those who believed in the "stab-in-the-back" legend were always very concerned about morale at home and figured that this was the way to continue the program without public uproar. And those who had stimulated an uproar would be taken care of after victory.[4]

In the first stages of killing Jews, the procedure adopted under the circumstances that the Germans expected was to bring the killers to the victims. Since the expectation was that the German army would proceed very rapidly through precisely that portion of the Soviet Union that had the densest settlements of Jews, three sets of organizations were established to engage in killing on a massive and rapid scale, the Einsatzgruppen of the SS, the battalions of the Order Police, and the units attached to the Kommandostab Reichsführer-SS. Somewhere between forty and fifty thousand men were expected to be able to slaughter the hundreds of thousands of Jews living in the area the army was expected to seize and in fact did seize. In view of this apparent success in the military operation and the obvious willingness of the army to cooperate in the murder process, Hitler decided by the end of July 1941 to extend the killing program to the rest of German-controlled Europe (and subsequently to the rest of the world).

It should be noted that this extension immediately brought with it a significant change in procedure that was adapted to what were considered the practical and political needs of the time: the victims would be taken to the killers instead of having the killers brought to the victims. And with too many of the killers developing psychological and other problems from the endless round of killings, including suicides and other drastic effects, the Germans began to work on other killing methods such as gas vans and the establishment of killing centers where large numbers of Jews could be murdered without so much strain on the killers.

This is not the place to review these developments in detail, but they illustrate the key point made earlier, namely that the Germans were moving in new directions and were quite prepared to experiment and make changes and adjustments along the way. One important field of adjustment was geographic and one was family related. It was in both of these that the assumption of a German victory in the war has to be factored in for any understanding of the adjustments made in the expectation of reversal at a later date.

The most dramatic adjustment of a geographic kind was that concerning Finland. Knowing the basic structure of Finnish society and government, the Germans never even asked for Finnish citizens of the Jewish faith to be turned over for killing. As a result, a tiny number of Finnish Jewish officers and men served on the northern segment of the Eastern Front alongside German officers and men. In the case of Bulgaria, the Germans were allowed to take the Jews from the portions of Yugoslavia and Greece that they had allotted to Bulgaria and to move them to the killing centers. When the Bulgarian government, however, refused to turn over the Jews from pre-1939 Bulgaria, the Germans backed off. This was hardly because they wanted to spare these Jews but because it made more sense to wait until the war was won, and the victorious Germany could then insist, as in the case of Finnish Jews, on getting them to kill. When at the Wannsee Conference it was assumed that the Jews of several European neutrals would be killed, that also was based on the belief that a victorious Germany could easily dictate to any country not occupied and/or annexed that the price for continued independence, at least for a while, was the surrender of the Jewish inhabitants for killing.

In this connection it is worth noting that although Hitler had authorized the killing of the Jews in the German-occupied portion of Greece in early October 1941,[5] no such killing program was started for more than a year as the majority of Greek territory was occupied by Italy. In the hope that the whole country could be emptied of Jews at the same time, the Germans waited for Italian acquiescence, eventually gave up on that prospect in early 1943, and proceeded to murder most of the Jews in their own zone of occupation. Subsequently they did what they could to extend the killing program to the rest of the country after the Italian surrender of September 1943 appeared to provide them with the opportunity to do so. As is well known, the efforts to persuade the Hungarian government to turn over the country's large Jewish population for killing failed until the Germans occupied the country militarily in March 1944 and initiated a systematic killing program there.

There are several other instances of such geographical adjustments during the war. The critical point that has to be understood is that the Germans were moving forward toward their goal of a world without Jews but held back or drew back from time to time because practical political or military considerations suggested to them that it was best to postpone doing so until circumstances changed or victory in the war removed all constraints. Obviously the successes of the Allies in halting German advances, whether in the West, the East, or the South, constrained the project of killing the world's Jews; but even within the area under German direct or indirect control those in charge at times found it expedient to hold back.

The second field of activity in which the Germans made adjustments was that of family relationships. In this there were two types: the people of mixed ancestry, what the Germans called Mischlinge, and those Jews married to non-Jews. In both cases, the government was concerned about the possible morale implications on the home front among the non-Jewish relatives that by definition would be present in both types of situations. The Mischlinge would have non-Jewish relatives and the intermarried Jews would have not only their non-Jewish spouses but the relatives of those spouses as well. For a leadership that was convinced of the truth of the legend that collapse of the home front had led to the loss of World War I, there was always extreme sensitivity to home front morale. It is impossible to exaggerate the extent to which essentially false memories of the end of World War I dominated thinking in German governmental and military thinking in World War II. A recent detailed study of the General Friedrich Fromm, the military commander on the home front for most of World War II, underlines the way in which this was the case.[6] Repeatedly measures of mobilization inside Germany were postponed because of the fear that there might be unwelcome repercussions on civilian morale. Instead of acting on the reality of a German World War I home front more solid than that of any other major belligerent in that conflict, the regime of the Third Reich held back on the basis of its devoted belief in the legend that it was the collapse of the home front that had brought about defeat.

There is a substantial literature on the endless internal debates within the Nazi hierarchy about how to treat those of mixed ancestry, about the types of persecution inflicted on these victims of the regime, and on the way those who survived had experienced the events of the time.[7] Few who have dealt with this issue ask the basic question: Why would a regime that was quite willing to slaughter people by the hundreds of thousands not end the interminable discussions by murdering the approximately 72,000 Mischlinge in Germany? Obviously there was no lack of either will or ability to implement such a decision had it been made. In the face of the killing of vast numbers of able-bodied Jews and the willingness to kill or let die literally millions of Soviet prisoners of war, it can hardly be the need for the labor service to which Mischlinge were condemned that restrained the regime's hand. It was the constant concern about home front morale, in this case on the part of the non-Jewish relatives and friends of the Mischlinge, which held back those who would have preferred to kill them. And in this holding back, there was the assumption that victory in the war would make the next step possible under circumstances in which the enormously higher status of the regime would easily override any minimal objections that non-Jewish relatives and friends might be moved to voice.

The Jews who had non-Jewish spouses were basically in a similar situation. They could be and were persecuted in a number of ways; but it was concern about the morale implications among the non-Jewish spouses and especially their non-Jewish relatives that held back the regime from the most drastic step. Since from the regime's perspective, these spouses had committed an especially horrendous act, one might at first have thought that their reactions and worries and those of their relatives would carry the least weight with the makers of policy. Yet here was the converse of the way in which the imposition of something called "social death," which had been imposed on Germany's Jewish community in the years 1933–1939, could and did leave most non-Jewish Germans indifferent to the fate of their Jewish neighbors as they were hauled off to death from 1941 on.[8]

By definition, these Jews, on the other hand, were tied to their spouses who, in turn, had families and friends who in many cases had not abandoned them because of their marriage to a Jewish person. The issues raised by this situation for the regime and the impact of the regime's policies on the intermarried families have been reviewed well in Nathan Stoltzfus's book, *Resistance of the Heart: Intermarriage and the Rosenstrasse Protest in Nazi Germany*.[9] The point relevant to the issue under review is that under the circumstances of the time, the regime found it expedient to back off.

The German public in January–February 1943 was shocked by the crushing of the German Sixth Army in Stalingrad. Here was a military disaster that could not possibly be minimized or concealed, and the Nazi leadership, especially Hermann Göring and Joseph Goebbels, took major steps to rally the German people and encourage them to devote themselves to even greater efforts in pursuit of victory. This was not a good time to have a riot in the country's capital. The thousands of Jews engaged in forced labor in armaments factories in the Berlin area could be and were shipped to killing centers in German-occupied Poland without any protest or other form of disturbance. Whether these Jews were assigned to forced labor and subsequently murdered, or killed there on arrival, was a matter of indifference to the wider society of the area. But in those same days, the collection by the police of Jews living in mixed marriages promptly provoked a demonstration by their spouses. As it became obvious over several days that this form of uproar could not be quickly and easily stilled, the arrested individuals were released.

In view of the expectation of victory in the war, there was no incentive for the regime to do anything that might have serious repercussions on home front morale. Those released could easily be gathered up again after victory, and any spouses and relatives who did not like it could either acquiesce or join their spouses on the journey to a killing center. The broader concern about home front morale would no longer restrain the regime's hand. It was as a result of this concern during the war and the expectation of victory that both in Berlin and elsewhere in Germany, Jews living in both what were called "privileged marriages" (where the wife was Jewish and the children had been baptized) and the "non-privileged" (where the man was Jewish and/or the children had not been baptized) in a substantial number of instances survived the war.

There is a further development in regard to this issue that at least in this author's opinion sheds light on still another aspect of the Nazi regime and the Holocaust that is too often ignored. In the last weeks of the war, in January, February, and March of 1945, there was a renewed effort to collect Jews in mixed marriages who had hitherto survived though persecuted in innumerable ways. This is most famously illustrated by the situation in Dresden where the famous diarist, Victor Klemperer, escaped such a last-minute roundup of Jews married to Christians only because of the disruption caused by the Allied air raids on the city.[10] This set of efforts by the Nazis needs to be seen in the context of the vested interest that the killers developed in the killing programs of the regime. In the years when the war appeared to be going well for Germany, participation in the murder programs could satisfy ideological preferences and pave the way to promotions, medals, loot, and wonderful careers in the postwar era. In the face of the realization of imminent defeat, continued participation in the killing programs was vastly safer than the obvious alternative assignment: the front where one faced not unarmed, frightened, and undernourished victims but well-armed soldiers of the Allies. That under these circumstances there would be a desperate search for victims to justify avoidance of a much more dangerous employment should not surprise subsequent observers as much as it sometimes has. Collecting and guarding those Jews deported in early 1945 or herding them in lengthy death marches from one camp to another was obviously preferable to the vastly more dangerous alternative assignment awaiting those involved in these activities. And in the imagination of Heinrich Himmler and at least some of his immediate associates like Walter Schellenberg, there was always the possibility of utilizing any Jews still alive in early 1945 in schemes for a separate peace with the Western Allies or a safe future for themselves if for no one else.

In all efforts to understand and relate in a meaningful fashion the events of a terrible era, it is essential to keep in mind that both those in charge and those at the daily implementing end had their own ideas and beliefs and assumptions, and that they acted on the basis of these, even if they were completely evil and/or mistaken. People always act on what they know and believe, not what later observers know and believe. And when people try to accomplish something novel, they are obliged to experiment as they move toward their unprecedented goal. Only with these realities in mind can the subsequent observer understand how developments that at first appear unfathomable came to take place in the way that they actually occurred.

Gerhard L. Weinberg is the William Rand Kenan, Jr., Professor Emeritus of History at the University of North Carolina at Chapel Hill. A lifelong student of World War II, the Holocaust, and Nazi Germany, Weinberg is the author of eleven books, including the 1,200-page epic study *A World at Arms: A Global History of World War II*. Among his many honors, is the reception in 2009 of the Pritzker Prize for lifetime achievement.

Notes

1. Alfred Mierzejewski, "When Did Albert Speer Give Up?" *The Historical Journal* 32, no. 2 (1988): 391–397.
2. Hitler's talk on April 6, 1920: "Wir wollen keine Gefühlsantisemiten sein, die Pogromstimmung erzeugen wollen, sondern es beseelt uns die unerbittliche Entschlossenheit, das Übel an der Wurzel zu packen und mit Stumpf und Stiel auszurotten." Eberhard Jäckel, ed., *Hitler: Sämtliche Aufzeichnungen 1905–1924* (Stuttgart: Deutsche Verlags-Anstalt, 1980), 119–120.
3. Henry Friedlander, *The Origins of Nazi Genocide: From Euthanasia to the Final Solution* (Chapel Hill: University of North Carolina Press, 1995).
4. Beth A. Griech-Polelle, *Bishop von Galen: German Catholicism and National Socialism* (New Haven, CT: Yale University Press, 2002), 88.
5. Hildegard von Kotze, ed., *Heeresadjutant bei Hitler 1938–1943: Aufzeichnungen des Majors Engel* (Stuttgart: Deutsche Verlags-Anstalt, 1974), 11.
6. Bernhard R. Kroener, *"Der starke Mann im Heimatkriegsgebiet," Generaloberst Friedrich Fromm, Eine Biographie* (Paderborn: Schöningh, 2005).
7. Beate Meyer, *"Jüdische Mischlinge": Rassenpolitik und Verfolgungserfahrung 1933–1945* (Hamburg: Dölling und Galitz, 1999); James F. Tent, *In the Shadow of the Holocaust: Nazi Persecution of Jewish-Christian Germans* (Lawrence: University Press of Kansas, 2003).

8. Marion A. Kaplan, *Between Dignity and Despair: Jewish Life in Nazi Germany* (New York: Oxford University Press, 1998).
9. (New York: Norton, 1996).
10. Victor Klemperer, *I Will Bear Witness: A Diary of the Nazi Years 1942–1945* (New York: Random House, 1999), 401.

Chapter 2

Women and Protest in Wartime Nazi Germany
Jill Stephenson

There has been much dispute about whether the Nazi regime should be described as "totalitarian." What can be less controversially said is that its leadership aspired to impose totalitarian control. This involved the suppression of all forms of dissent. In the view of the regime, even those who were not members of opposition groups had to be prevented from expressing dissent or criticism of it, its policies, and its officers. Thus the press was censored, and many newspapers were driven out of existence. Radio was under tight state control.[1] Freedom of speech in public, then, was curtailed to the point where it was almost entirely impossible. The major exception was in church, although priests and pastors who expressed views that offended Nazis could find themselves on the wrong end of a fist or boot.[2] Further, freedom of association was banned. The dissolution of the other political parties and of trade unions was an important part of this.[3]

In addition, the Decree of the Reich President for the Protection of People and State, of February 28, 1933, following the Reichstag fire on the previous night, stated that: "Thus restrictions on . . . the right of assembly and association . . . are permissible beyond the legal limits otherwise prescribed."[4] Once again, the only place where private citizens could meet as a group under auspices other than the regime's was at church functions. Even so, this applied chiefly—and, increasingly, exclusively—to the two main Christian denominations: the Roman Catholic Church, which could claim the allegiance of almost one-third of Germans, and the German Protestant Church whose adherents accounted for almost two-thirds of the population of the "old Reich" of 1937. After the annexations of 1938–1940 the balance between the two denominations was nearer fifty-fifty.[5] Smaller sects were viewed with suspicion and hostility by the regime, and in the later 1930s there were strong, but not entirely successful, attempts to extirpate them. The Jehovah's Witnesses were a particular thorn in the Nazis' flesh, given their principled pacifism, and many of them became martyrs to their faith because of their refusal to conform to Nazi demands.[6]

The regime did provide plenty of opportunity for meetings and group activity, through the NSDAP itself and through its affiliates and formations. Membership of these was in some cases more and in some cases less obligatory. Workers were enrolled in the German Labor Front and farmers in the Reich Food Estate. Professional people, such as teachers, lawyers, doctors, lecturers, students, and bureaucrats had their own Nazi-led associations, membership of which was virtually obligatory when the regime was consolidating its power in a time of severe unemployment. For example, with unemployment especially high among schoolteachers, by 1936 some 97 percent of all German teachers had joined the NS-Lehrerbund (Nazi Teachers' Association), which replaced the long-existing professional organizations for teachers.[7]

Young people were encouraged, pressured, and, eventually, compelled to belong to the Hitler Youth, although its membership did not reach the 100 percent desired by the regime. At the beginning of 1939, its membership stood at 7,287,470, or 82 percent of all young Germans aged between ten and eighteen. This was after strong pressure had been exerted but before full compulsion was introduced, in March 1939; even after that, however, evasion was possible by resolute young people.[8] For adults, membership of organizations other than the relevant occupational one was perhaps prudent but not absolutely necessary. To protect promotion prospects and to secure a quiet life, many joined the NS-Volkswohlfahrt (NSV-NS People's Welfare) or the Reich Association for Physical Exercise. In wartime, middle-class women were likely to join the Red Cross so as not to have to become involved in a party agency. Enthusiasts for National Socialism might join the SA or the Nazi women's organization, the NS-Frauenschaft, although their ranks also included opportunists who saw this either as a means of advancement or merely as a way of protecting their job.[9] All of these organizations held regular meetings, and at local party branch meetings, in particular, careful note was made of who was present and who was not.[10]

Group association outside these limits was scarcely possible. This, and the control of the media and publishing that was quickly imposed by the new regime, meant that acts of political opposition or the open expression of opposition or merely critical sentiments were rendered extremely difficult, given the sanctions imposed by regime functionaries where they occurred. The demonstrative use of terror against dissidents was probably the most effective method of censorship. But part of the reason for the absence of overt opposition was "consent," that is, the approval of many members of society for much of what the Nazi regime was doing, especially in terms of the suppression of the political left, socialists, and—above all—communists.[11] Further, the conquest of the depression, and a return to full employment, won the approval of many Germans. Nevertheless, there were those who would have engaged in political opposition had their organizations not been destroyed, and had there not been the prospect of fearsome sanctions.

In spite of all of this, some Social Democrats and Communists, particularly, continued to engage in underground activity.[12] They tended to be picked off by the Gestapo with pitiful ease, but, especially in the case of some communists, their devotion to the cause ensured that terms in jail did not deter them. For example, one young woman in Hamburg emerged from jail in 1935 only to be arrested again in 1936 for "illegal activity"—in her case, producing and distributing anti-regime leaflets.[13] Other women worked in socialist or communist cells, sometimes taking over functions from men who had been arrested. Those who were apprehended were arrested, and some were executed. There were women members of other resistance groups, and some of them, too, were executed for their illegal activity, the best know of these being Sophie Scholl, a member of the White Rose group, associated with Munich University, that distributed anti-regime leaflets in 1943.[14]

However, "resistance"—even something as seemingly innocuous as distributing leaflets —is different from "protest." Resistance implies some kind of political activity—although in Nazi Germany what was "political" was defined broadly indeed, and, as Hans Mommsen says, the Gestapo decided what was, or was not, "resistance."[15] Leaflets criticizing the regime (and especially those calling for its overthrow) were, in Nazi Germany, "political." Organizing any kind of group activity was regarded as a "political" act, because the Nazi party and its formations and affiliates had been assigned a monopoly of group activity. Thus priests who held meetings for a number of young people were in breach of the ban on political activity; women who met in a group in each other's houses for coffee were regarded with deep suspicion because they were believed to be engaging in prohibited organizational activity.[16] What was regarded as objectionable here was repeated group activity, because repeated association, in a group with the same membership, could signify the coalescence of an opposition network.

By contrast, "protest" was generally not either actually political—that is, political in intent—or regarded as political by the authorities. The response of the Nazi authorities to certain kinds of protest—including complaints made in a public place—clearly suggests that, while they regarded it as irksome, they did not regard it as a threat to their overall authority, even when it challenged a policy imposed by the regime, at local level, at least. The Nazi regime, for all its brutality, was consistently anxious to rule with the consent of the mass of "Aryans," and, especially in wartime, as officials repeatedly said, "it is essential not to antagonise people."[17] Nevertheless, Goebbels's view of protest, noted in his diary in November 1943, was that "The state must never, against its own best interests, give way to the pressure of the street. If it does this, it will be even weaker the second time than the first, and gradually lose its whole authority."[18]

"Protest," in the sense in which it is used here, was the expression of opposition to an individual policy and its ramifications, by a group of women gathering in a public place, and being conspicuous in making their complaint—conspicuous to the authorities in their locality. These women's protests were, then, apolitical—in the sense that they neither threatened the regime's existence nor challenged its authority to govern. They merely challenged an individual policy as it affected them. Protest in this sense occurred on a local or regional level, and related to limited—and mostly local—issues only. It occurred chiefly during the war, and it emanated from discontent about personal and/or material issues: sometimes there was a principle at stake, and sometimes there was not, although in most cases the women felt that they, or people on whose behalf they were demonstrating, were victims of injustice. For example, in April 1943 in Dortmund, a group of three to four hundred people, "who were for the most part women," took the side of a soldier, said to be a deserter, who had been struck by an officer who also threatened to shoot the soldier. The mob became so agitated and threatening that the officer had to flee in a tram.[19]

In wartime, the home front's population consisted disproportionately of women, along with older men and youths, as millions of young and middle-aged adult men were conscripted and sent away from home to serve in the armed forces, or to staff new bureaucracies in German-occupied Europe. Women therefore had to bear the burdens of life on the home front, and increasingly they found these oppressive.[20] This was a source of complaint that, at its most acute, developed sufficient momentum to erupt into open protest. For most women in that era, their overriding concern was with family, home, and faith. When the integrity of one of these was threatened in a way that affected a number of women, protest involved a degree of group solidarity and activity—not of a political kind but rather geared toward a limited objective.

By contrast, much of the time, there was an undercurrent of low-level grumbling, in wartime chiefly about the food supply. Although German civilians were protected almost until the end of the war from real privation by goods plundered from occupied Europe—for example, butter and ham from Denmark, grain from the Ukraine, luxuries of various kinds from France—nevertheless there remained shortages, and women stood in food queues and complained, sometimes loudly. Even in the years of German victories (1939–1942), there were complaints and unruly behavior of a kind that we might not expect to find under a rigorous dictatorship. Sometimes, the police had to be brought in to break up brawls or demonstrations in markets or in front of food shops, where long queues became a feature of normal life. Of particular concern to the Nazi regime was the way in which women in food queues made comparisons between their situation and that which had prevailed during the Great War.[21] This was the last thing that the authorities wanted. The Nazis had themselves nurtured the "stab-in-the-back" myth—the myth that German armies in World War I had been betrayed by civilians at home who undermined morale and, ultimately, caused a revolution that sealed Germany's defeat.[22] Now the Nazi leadership found that, in its war—and in spite of pursuing delivery, rationing, and distribution policies designed to avoid shortages—civilians in their victorious country expected to be able to purchase foodstuffs in much the same way, and in much the same quantities, as they had in peacetime. Although the Nazi version of the "stab-in-the-back" myth emphasized the role of "Jews and socialists" in destroying morale at home, the truth was that *women* had lost hope in the "turnip winters" of 1916–1918 and had led demonstrations against food shortages.[23] Therefore, with the specter of the "stab-in-the-back" firmly in mind, the Nazi authorities viewed with great concern the public complaints about difficulties in obtaining sufficient food and other essentials, especially in 1941–1942, and the disorder that accompanied them.

Yet this kind of disorder did not, for the most part, escalate beyond thieving from fields where food grew, the raiding of coal wagons as they stood in rail stations, and fighting at food stores or on trains carrying frustrated shoppers to the countryside to buy direct from farmers.[24] And, importantly, all of this was done on an individual basis, by women trying desperately to feed their families. This was not a matter that generated solidarity—quite the reverse, as women jockeyed with each other for advantage. This kind of grumbling and disorder, therefore, cannot legitimately be regarded as "protest" although it certainly was an open manifestation of discontent. Where it perhaps spilled over into protest was when, in March 1942, in Berlin rumors about a reduction in rations and the failure to distribute extra bread tokens, to compensate for inadequate supplies of potatoes, led to a crowd smashing the windows of the office of the NSV in Barutherstrasse.[25] All of this raised the specter of the "stab-in-the-back," which was undoubtedly a factor in the Nazi regime's response to protest by women where it did occur. In those instances where women protested openly about a limited issue, the regime sometimes backed down, because of its fear of generating sufficient discontent to lead to a new "stab-in-the-back" in its war. Instances of open protest were relatively scarce. They involved a perceived threat to family, faith, or community that seemed so urgent as to galvanize a group of women into protest.

Two prominent instances of protest by women fall into this category, those held in the Rosenstrasse in Berlin and in Ruhr towns, most notably Witten, both in 1943 and both of which form the subject of essays in this volume. There has been much controversy about the Rosenstrasse protest in late February and early March 1943, but there is broad agreement that the "Aryan" wives of Jewish men who had been incarcerated there had no way of knowing what orders had been given or what the outcome would be, and that therefore—fearing the worst—their protest was courageous. It was courageous because it was in defense of Jews—their husbands—in a climate where to try to protect a Jew was regarded by the regime as a serious offence. It seems also to have been effective in having their husbands released, in the context of a long war that was going badly—this was a month after the surrender at Stalingrad—and in which the authorities were deeply concerned about morale and the popular mood. Had protesting "Aryan" women been treated brutally by the police or SS in a public place, there would have been a damaging effect on both morale and the popular mood. The only way of defusing the—for the authorities—disturbing spectacle of women demonstrating in a public place was to release their Jewish husbands.

As Antonia Leugers shows in this volume, there have been problems and disputes over sources for this episode. The Sicherheitsdienst (SD—Security Service of the SS) appears to have had nothing to say about it, and Goebbels, the Berlin Gauleiter (regional NSDAP leader), recorded in his diary merely that "The evacuation of Jews from Berlin has certainly led to many disagreements. Unfortunately, Jews and Jewesses in privileged marriages were at first also arrested, which led to great anxiety and confusion.... The arrest of Jews and Jewesses in privileged marriages has had a particularly sensational effect in cultural circles."[26]

It is clear that, at the time, inaccurate rumor often prevailed over hard information. In summer 1943, a memo found in the papers of Theophil Wurm, the Württemberg *Landesbischof* (state bishop), on the subject of *Mischlinge* (half-Jews) and *Mischehen* (mixed marriages) stated: "Already in Berlin in February 1943 a number of half-Jews were put into trucks along with Jews and taken to the Rosenstrasse, from where they were later released." Wurm himself had written on March 12, 1943, to Reich Church Minister Kerrl to protest that "Recently even those Jews living in mixed marriages with Christian Germans, and in some cases themselves belonging to a Christian church, have been torn from home and work and transported to the east."[27]

The pressures of war included the rationing of food and the evacuation of women and children from bomb-damaged (or bomb-threatened) areas. To try to ensure that rationing worked in an orderly way, the regime decreed that individuals had to be registered in a particular locality, and that only there would their ration cards be valid. They would not be able to buy rationed food outside this locality. It was this policy that tied civilians to Hamburg in summer 1943, even when they heard credible rumors that a massive bombing raid on the city was being planned. These rumors proved to be horribly true in July/August 1943 when "Operation Gomorrah" was unleashed, to devastating effect.[28] Even before that, however, groups of mothers with children had been evacuated from Hamburg to Bavaria, where they were met with a welcome that was less than warm. There were complaints about the women's idleness: they would not help out on farms, and did not need to because of the allowance that they were paid—an allowance that was, in the eyes of Bavarian farm folk, far too generous. Further, it was said that in the evenings they abandoned their children to their unwilling hosts and went out to enjoy themselves.[29] Difficult relationships between evacuees—not only from Hamburg—and hosts, not only in Bavaria, were frequent.[30]

In the early stages of the Allied bombing campaign, the German authorities used persuasion to encourage women and children to leave towns and cities that were actual or potential bombing targets, and some of them went of their own accord. But by 1943, with the bombing of western Germany intensifying, the encouragement became more insistent, not least because the authorities were concerned about the possible effects on public order of large numbers of homeless citizens at large. In Cologne in July 1943, popular anger verged on disorder among the two hundred thousand people rendered homeless by bombing. Many had had to camp out on the banks of the Rhine, with a network of field kitchens as their only source of food, and "people were said to have stormed food shops."[31] Yet some authorities—the Gauleiter, *Reichstatthälter* (regional chiefs of government), and *Reichsverteidigungskommissare* (RVK—Reich Defense Commissioners), three offices frequently held by a single person—were hesitant about using compulsion to effect an evacuation of women and children, in case that, too, caused public disorder. Gauleiter and RVK Wilhelm Murr in Württemberg was one such. After particularly damaging bombing raids on Stuttgart in July 1944, his office launched a huge press campaign to persuade those not in essential war work to leave the city, with headlines such as "Why are you still in Stuttgart?" The decline in the numbers of Stuttgart residents suggests that his heavy-handed persuasion had some degree of success, without provoking public disorder. Nevertheless, in spite of the massive efforts from 1943 to evacuate all of Stuttgart's school children, the rate of their return to the capital was such that in February 1945 one-third of the city's school children were resident there.³²

Some RVKs, however, resorted to compulsion, forcibly evacuating women and children and banning them from obtaining food in their hometown, from which they had been evacuated. This was what gave rise to protests in Ruhr towns in autumn 1943, the most prominent of which was the protest by women in Witten on October 11, 1943. As an industrial town, Witten was a bombing target, and in 1943 its women and children—and those of some neighboring towns—were forcibly evacuated to the safer south. In the case of the Witteners, this meant Baden, in the German southwest. Witten's schools were closed and their teachers evacuated with the families. The authorities did have sense on their side, because, altogether, Witten was bombed 91 times during the war, and some 80 percent of the town was destroyed.³³ But the problem was that the women were aware that women and children from larger and more prominent targets, such as Cologne and Essen, had not been forced to leave home, and, in addition, they disliked the conditions to which they had been evacuated.³⁴ This was by no means unusual: evacuated women from Ruhr towns had little in common with the farming families on whom they were billeted, and they were often made to feel unwelcome by their hosts, who regarded them as lazy, demanding, and promiscuous. The townswomen found living conditions in the "safer" countryside primitive and lacking in the (urban) facilities to which they were accustomed. As bombing began to affect some country areas, especially in 1944–1945, urban women sometimes felt that they would be safer in the towns where there were bomb shelters than in the countryside where there was virtually no protection. There were also often religious differences—in this case, mainly Protestant Witteners were billeted on mainly Catholic peasants.³⁵

The result was that many of the Witten women returned home. But their ration cards, issued in Baden, were not valid in their hometown, and so—because the Witten urban authorities, unlike many others in Gau Westphalia South, were enforcing Gauleiter and RVK Albert Hoffmann's order that returnees were not to receive ration cards in Witten—they could not buy food for themselves and their children. In protest, on October 11, 1943, about three hundred women demonstrated in Witten, in front of the town hall. They blamed the mayor and local party leaders for their plight, and shouted abuse at them. The municipal authorities ordered the police to disperse the women, but the police refused, saying that the women's protest was justified and that withholding ration cards from them had no basis in law. This was not the only instance of this kind of protest about the withdrawal of ration cards in women's hometown. Similar scenes also occurred in the towns of Hamm, Lünen, and Bochum in the same area and in the same period, with women gathering in front of the municipal food office to protest about the failure to issue ration cards to returned evacuees.[36]

The problems in the Ruhr area, most acutely obvious in Witten, derived from the inflexibility of the Nazi Party's regional organization there, and the inflexibility especially of the recently appointed Gauleiter Hoffmann, who had enhanced authority as RVK in his Gau, with special responsibility for evacuation.[37] Other areas, too, experienced the return of evacuees; for example, by October 1943 more Berliners were returning from evacuation than were being evacuated. Yet, while the Berlin authorities deplored this, they did not deny the returnees their ration cards. In Witten, it was evident that some of those responsible for issuing ration cards—in the Food Office—were not following the Gauleiter's instruction to withhold them from returned evacuees. Clearly, what emboldened the women who protested was the knowledge that there were officials who took their side, and the knowledge that this was a local, not a Reich, policy. As they said: "This doesn't come from the top, it's just the mayor here and the local food office or the Gauleiter who are to blame. They think they know what's what, but we'll show them." Yet, the day after the Witten protest the authorities published a notice, both at the ration card delivery office and in the local paper, restating that ration cards would be denied to returning evacuees. The notice added that no ration cards would be delivered to school-age children, even if they had not been evacuated thus far. Such children had to leave the town in order to regain eligibility for food distribution—elsewhere. The demonstrating women adopted another tactic by applying at the employment exchange for work, and once they secured a job they were entitled to a ration card.[38]

As a conciliatory gesture, Gauleiter Hoffmann toured the evacuation reception area in Baden to find out for himself what conditions were like, and what the evacuees who were still there thought about them. In fact, the NSDAP in Baden, particularly in the form of the NSV, had gone to considerable lengths to try to ensure that the evacuees' needs were catered for.[39] Over the ensuing weeks and months there was much discussion in the higher reaches of the regime about how to treat returning evacuees, with some Gauleiter requesting harsher action against them but others favoring a milder approach. As the SD pointed out, there were disadvantages to evacuating wives and children. Occasionally, husbands working in war industry would absent themselves for a week or more at a time, without authorization, to visit their families in the reception areas. If the women were forced back to Baden, the danger was that more husbands would desert their work to visit them.[40] In some places, as the SD reported in November 1943, evacuees' relatives were able to send them ration cards—including the special distributions of food and little luxuries made to inhabitants of bomb-damaged towns and cities—from their home Gau, which distorted the availability of supplies in the reception area.[41] But Hoffmann's neighbor, Gauleiter Alfred Meyer in Westphalia North, was equally determined to enforce evacuation from his battered Gau. On December 15, 1943, he issued an order banning the food offices in Münster and some other towns from issuing ration cards to children under fifteen and non-employed women, causing great unrest.[42] In the end, in late January 1944, Goebbels sent a circular informing all of the Gauleiter that "The Führer has ordered that [you] should refrain from blocking ration cards."

Julia Torrie argues that this result was a success for the protesting women of Witten.[43] It is true that women in Witten (and elsewhere) did protest in public; it is true that the withdrawal of ration cards from returning evacuees—which had been enforced only patchily—was banned. But the causal link between the two remains (as we say in Scotland) not proven. What may have counted for more in Witten was the fact that some of the women's husbands were at home, working as miners. When they joined their wives outside the Food Office, threatening not to go down the mine again until their wives received ration cards, the danger for the war economy of their withdrawing their labor was too great to be ignored.[44] It was also the case that the events in Westphalia North more immediately preceded Goebbels' circular. Nevertheless, the fact that women did protest in front of an official building in Witten about a policy to which they objected without the authorities being able to take retributive action against them is in itself significant. If anything, the refusal of the police to disperse the women was more of a threat to the authorities than was the women's demonstration itself. It was reminiscent of the refusal of the army detachment in Petrograd in 1917 to fire on women demonstrating about the bread shortage, an event that triggered revolution in Russia during a world war.

There can be little doubt that the reason for women's prominence in the protests in Witten and other Ruhr towns was the war, because, while some aspects of these skirmishes with the regime owed much to the specific circumstances of wartime, they took place at a time when millions of men were away from home. The initiative for protest therefore mainly devolved onto the women who remained at home. This can be seen particularly clearly when the issue of religious symbols and religious instruction in schools was at stake, especially in rural areas. Already before the war there had been attempts—notably in Bavaria and Oldenburg in 1936–1937, but also elsewhere—by Nazi functionaries to remove the Christian cross from school classrooms.[45] Protests against this involved both men and women, and in most cases the Nazi functionaries backed down. In another case, in the commune of Waibstadt in Baden, parents kept their children away from school when the crucifix was removed from classrooms.⁴⁶ In the Rhineland, there were mixed responses, but in Trier it was said that this was typical of the way in which the "little Hitlers" arrogated authority to themselves.⁴⁷

In wartime, however, while popular piety was enhanced by anxiety for family members fighting at the front, Nazi anti-clerical policy was radicalized in some areas, particularly in south Germany and Austria. While party leaders endeavored to minimize the significance of religious festivals by decreeing that they should be celebrated on the Sunday following the actual date of the festival, many in rural areas continued to abandon work on the relevant working days to permit their customary religious observance.⁴⁸ In May 1941, the Landrat in Ebermannstadt called the observance by both Evangelical and Catholic rural people of Ascension Day "a concerted demonstration against the official ban" on weekday religious celebrations. He added that this ban was seen as part of a plan to destroy the religious communities altogether.⁴⁹ Churches continued to be well-attended in places such as the Rhineland, where both main denominations were represented. The Confessing Church was said to be increasing in strength there, in Bad Kreuznach not least through word of mouth "propaganda" among women. The police in Neuwied reported that it had been impossible to found a branch of the NS-Frauenschaft (Nazi Women's Group) there because of the strength of the Women's Union, whose leader was the pastor's wife.⁵⁰

This impression seemed to be confirmed when, in April 1941, Gauleiter Adolf Wagner, the Bavarian Minister of Education, issued a decree for the removal of the cross and other religious symbols from school classrooms, and for an end to prayers in school. This renewed attack incensed the deeply devout Catholic population, especially in Bavaria's many rural areas. As a police report from Kreisführer put it, it had been years since any official measure had shattered the population's trust to such an extent. Mayors of villages said that they would rather give up their (unremunerated) positions than cooperate in the removal of crucifixes. One teacher, who was also an NSDAP local branch leader, said that it would be unenforceable in the countryside.⁵¹ In the villages, crowds gathered outside schools to demand the return of the cross. Protests continued throughout the summer—at a time when German forces were invading the USSR—reaching a peak in autumn 1941 with large crowds involved in civil disobedience. This time, mothers led the opposition—visiting local party and civil officials, and threatening to withdraw their children from school until the cross was reinstated in classrooms. If this threat was ignored, a crowd, with women prominent, gathered in a public place where they seemed to the authorities to be a threatening presence. In the end, Wagner had to give way, in the face of popular protest and the advice of his more pragmatic advisers, and the cross was reinstated in schools in Bavaria's many rural Catholic areas.[52] This was a disputed issue also in the Austrian alpine region. A group of mothers in a village near Salzburg wrote to the authorities in the middle of the war to protest against the removal of the crucifix from classrooms and to plead for its return.[53]

Other religious issues created friction between the Catholic Church and the state. The Landrat in Ebermannstadt reported that in April 1942, in the commune of Niedermirsberg, the removal of the church's bells had led to a breach of the peace. Two workers were sent to remove the bells, but the school children set the bells in motion, which summoned half of the village. Some women set about the workers, threatening them and using violence to eject them from the church, and then threw stones at them until they ran away. But on the following day police protection ensured that the bells could be safely removed.[54] The removal of church bells elsewhere was deplored but not resisted in this way. In neighboring Württemberg, however, attempts to replace religious instruction in schools with "weltanschauliche Unterricht" ("ideological training") met stiff resistance from both the Catholic and Evangelical churches, and from mothers who sometimes found themselves under severe pressure from Nazi functionaries to accept "ideological training" for their children. In some areas, however, they were undeterred. In Westerstetten (Ulm district), for example, thirty mothers descended on the town hall to demand their right to choose religious education for their children. Further, they ostracized two teachers of "ideological instruction," to the extent that the two were obliged to take their meals in a neighboring village because no one in Westerstetten would provide them with food. In the same village, the threatened closure of the local convent was abandoned after a public protest by the commune's women.[55]

Ostracism was used elsewhere as a means of protest against those who offended the sensibilities of devout churchgoers. It was a clear demonstration of popular disapproval of those functionaries of party or state who sought to impose policies that were regarded as an attack on the church. From the Tyrol in 1940, the SD reported that "The few National Socialist teachers in agrarian municipalities are practically treated with hostility by the inhabitants, especially when they have quit the church."[56] In Petersberg, in Gau Kurhessen, the local leader of the NS-Frauenschaft denounced the local curate for boxing her nephew's ears, for which assault the curate was sentenced to four months in jail. The whole village refused to have anything to do with her after that, and, as a result, she had to be replaced.[57] The Catholic priest in Erbach (Ulm district) refused in 1940 to marry a soldier home on leave to the daughter of the local Nazi block leader.[58] According to Johnpeter Horst Grill, in some areas of Baden local party leaders who had followed orders to leave the church "became outcasts."[59] In reporting, in February 1943, that the peasants in his area "are almost exclusively unshakably steadfast" in their attachment to religion, the Landrat of Ebermannstadt related the almost complete failure of Waffen-SS recruiters to attract anyone to its ranks because of attempts by the SS to replace Christmas with alternative festivities, as well as unnamed misdeeds in the area committed in 1935 and 1936.[60]

Adolf Wagner in Bavaria, like Gauleiter Hoffmann in Westphalia South, was a zealous hardliner, but, also like Hoffmann, he found that some of those who were meant to enforce his policy were unwilling to do so in the face of public protests by ordinary "Aryan" women. *Kultminister* Mergenthaler in Württemberg similarly found that even some NSDAP members continued to choose religious education for their children instead of "ideological training."[61] The Gestapo deplored the way in which, in some Austrian villages, "even those few individuals who belonged to the party went to church on Sunday, sang in the church choir, and walked in church processions."[62] The self-inflicted problem was that Wagner, Hoffmann, Mergenthaler, and others were trying to enforce in their bailiwicks policies that were more extreme than those being pursued at national level. This is not to suggest that the central government—to say nothing of the Nazi Party's leadership—did not aspire to remove the symbols and, above all, the influence of the churches and did not hope to enforce their evacuation policies. But some of Hitler's ministers, including Goebbels, were sufficiently prudent to realize that during this war was not the time gratuitously to antagonize sections of the "Aryan" population, and that, in the case of "ideological training," Württemberg was not the place. As an official at the Reich Chancellery put it: "To choose Württemberg as a field of experiment would seem to be particularly unsuitable. . . . This can only cause trouble and anxiety in the population, which ought to be avoided in wartime."[63]

Nevertheless, it was in wartime that regime functionaries began routinely to resort to brutality against "Aryans," including some "Aryan" women. This was visible from early in the war when German women who fraternized with prisoners of war or forced foreign workers, usually to the extent of having sexual intercourse with them, were pilloried by local party functionaries. In some localities, they were taken round the neighborhood in a cart with a placard round their neck detailing their offense. Sometimes, and with Himmler's explicit approval, they had their head shaved in a public place, until Hitler—anxious about foreign reactions to this—put a stop to the practice in 1941. They might be roundly abused by party functionaries, although neighbors were generally more reticent. In many cases, all of this preceded a term in prison, for the crime of "polluting their blood." The length of their prison sentence might be anything from a few months to as much as ten years.[64]

The regime's readiness to use brutality against women as well as men escalated, particularly once Germany had been invaded and defeat seemed assured, if not immediately imminent. When people behaved in a "defeatist" manner or protested against defensive measures in the last days of the war, agents of the regime used unprecedented levels of violence against "Aryan" Germans. As Allied armies closed in on Germany in early 1945, Hitler refused to contemplate surrender (or defeat). He and his minions ordered the call-up of younger and younger age groups of boys to serve in the army, the *Volkssturm*, or even the SS. In south Germany, by March 1945 orders were being given for boys born in 1928, 1929, and even 1930 to be conscripted into the military. But the protests of parents (mostly mothers) in some places ensured that this did not take place.[65]

On March 19, 1945, when much of Germany was already occupied by Allied forces, Hitler issued his "Nero decree" which ordered that German soldiers and civilians were to defend every remaining inch of German territory, by which he meant every town, village, and building. This "no surrender" order meant that civilians as well as soldiers had to put themselves in the line of fire, and to sacrifice their homes for a cause that was patently lost. If Germans did not surrender towns, villages, and buildings to the advancing enemy, that enemy would use its firepower to damage and probably destroy them. American and French forces had no hesitation in bombarding towns and villages where resistance was mounted. Both in areas that were already damaged and in those that had escaped bombing, this was a most unpalatable prospect. Yet army officers and SS units were determined to obey Hitler's orders to the last, the latter out of fanaticism and the former often because they feared the consequences of disobeying orders, although there were also fanatics in the officer corps. Sometimes an army unit was already installed in a town or village, and sometimes there was one nearby and available to be summoned by diehards who wanted them to prevent a surrender by citizens. Sometimes a village received a flying visit from an SS troop and had to reverse any measures already taken to dismantle defenses such as anti-tank barriers. This was the case in Leutershausen, in Bavaria, where an SS unit arrived shortly after a group of women had dismantled anti-tank barriers and forced the villagers to reassemble the barriers and prepare a bridge for demolition. The result of SS attempts to defend the village was that American forces used their superior firepower to destroy half of it.

In south Germany, in some of the last areas to be invaded in spring 1945, women were in the forefront of those who could see that trying to defend the last remnants of unoccupied Germany was an insane policy. In commune after commune, women either raised a white flag as the enemy advanced, or else dismantled anti-tank barriers that had been built on the orders of army, party, or SS officers. This was extremely dangerous, and individual women were shot as a result, for "defeatism." For example, in Bad Windsheim, in Bavaria, about three hundred women, with children and a few elderly men, had assembled in the market place to try to persuade the local army commander not to defend the town. The women abused an army spokesman and pulled him from the wagon on which he was standing. An SS veteran was summoned, and he sought out one woman as token ringleader of the group and shot her. Also in Bavaria, in Ochsenfurt a delegation of women descended on the party's office to demand that the local branch leader surrender the town to the advancing Americans. Then some women started to dismantle the anti-tank barriers around the city, sending packing a detachment of armed *Volkssturm* men who tried to prevent them. But the police were brought in and three of the women were arrested. They were saved from the gallows only by the arrival of American forces.[66]

In Sindelfingen (Böblingen district), in Württemberg, several hundred women gathered in front of the town hall to protest against the erecting of a tank barrier that would make the town a target for invaders' artillery. The town had been bombed twelve times since November 1942, because of the presence of a Daimler armament works, and the women wanted to spare it further damage. But the district army commander insisted on defending Sindelfingen.[67] Nevertheless, other women had more success in acting to prevent the attempted defense of their defenseless homes and villages. For example, in Pfullingen (Reutlingen district), a crowd of women said to be "of all classes and ages" gathered in front of the town hall and demanded the opening of anti-tank barriers. The NSDAP local branch leader berated them, for which they attacked him and another Nazi functionary, and then during the night opened the barriers themselves. The teenage soldiers who were commanded to fire on them shot in the air instead. In Gomaringen (Tübingen district), women gathered in front of the town hall to demand the raising of a white flag in surrender to the advancing enemy. The soldiers present refused, so one of the women raised a white flag herself.[68] At the end of the war, ordinary women, and also men, desperate to preserve their homes and villages or towns, repeated this kind of action over and over again. It could succeed only where there were not significant German forces of army, party, or SS, because by this time the party and SS, at least, were ready to kill any who stood in their way, as they did, with men and women alike, including party functionaries who agreed with citizens whose view was that defense against a powerful adversary was fruitless.[69]

No doubt we could devise an argument to show that all these instances of protest demonstrate women's "agency." Yet they acted within closely circumscribed limits, in areas that affected their family, their home, and their faith. There was no sense of there being a political principle at stake, or of acting for the benefit of anyone beyond the family, faith, or community. To that extent, these protests were limited and containable. Goebbels' fear that if the regime should "give way to the pressure of the street . . . it will be even weaker the second time than the first, and gradually lose its whole authority" would not be realized through the limited protest of wives in "mixed marriages" when there were relatively few of these in Germany by 1943. Nor would the Witten women's protest be a model for those in the great majority of places where the political leadership was not enforcing the policy of withholding ration cards from those who returned home from evacuation. Protests on religious issues, particularly in Catholic areas, were and remained a serious irritant, but only where political leaders adopted a confrontational stance. Particularly in wartime, when the consent of the "Aryan" population was regarded as being absolutely essential to an "inner front" to support the fighting front, protest by "Aryans" had to be tolerated over limited issues that caused unrest in a limited geographical area of the country. Using violence against female protesters, particularly, was mostly not an option when they were "Aryan," and when they were the wives of either soldiers or essential workers, until the last desperate days of the war when regime functionaries resorted implacably to that. The police in Witten had the sense to realize that, even if the local political leadership did not. Even when they were the disobedient wives of Jewish men—disobedient in not having divorced non-"Aryan" husbands—they were still "Aryan" women, and violence against them would have undoubtedly generated a hostile reaction among other "Aryans."

What is clear is that protest during the war devolved onto women because of the absence of so many men, mostly at the front, and that protest that resulted in public disturbances was a matter of acute concern to the regime, especially because of the importance of the memory of the "stab-in-the-back" in World War I, when women had been in the forefront of protests against the privations and suffering in 1916–1918. This was a particular source of anxiety for the regime once German forces had invaded the USSR, with the resultant heavy casualties already depressing morale at home, and with women writing to male family members at the front about their discontents, including the anti-clerical campaign. The last thing that the regime wanted was a collapse of morale, either at the front or at home. Long ago, Richard Evans suggested that this reflected the Nazis' knowledge that women could be much more easily provoked into open resistance than men, and their fear that such resistance might have become very difficult to suppress without alienating not only the general populace but also the soldiers at the front.[70]

Allowing for rather loose use of the word "resistance" here, it may be that women who had not experienced the discipline of the workplace or the army in the Third Reich, and who had grown to maturity before socialization in the Hitler Youth became an issue, had fewer inhibitions than men about taking a stand when their essential interests were under attack. Even if the issues were limited, the women who protested were courageous, because perhaps the most terrifying thing about the Nazi state (for "Aryans") was its unpredictability. As the President of the Württemberg Supreme Court said in March 1940, when someone committed a relatively minor offense, he "cannot judge whether he will get away with a fine or whether he is risking his head."[71] In the face of the arbitrary justice that was a hallmark of the Nazi regime, any public protest required a high degree of both determination and courage.

Jill Stephenson is Professor Emeritus of Modern German History at the University of Edinburgh. She has published widely on modern German history, including *Hitler's Home Front: Württemberg under the Nazis* (2006), *Women in Nazi Germany* (2001), *The Nazi Organisation of Women* (1981), and *Women in Nazi Society* (1975). She is also the co-editor with John Gilmour of *Hitler's Scandinavian Legacy* (2014).

Notes

1. Clemens Zimmermann, *Medien im Nationalsozialismus: Deutschland, Italien und Spanien in den 1930er und 1940er Jahren* (Vienna: Böhlau, 2007), 85–94, 129–131.
2. Paul Sauer, *Württemberg in der Zeit des Nationalsozialismus* (Ulm: Sueddeutsche Verlagsgesellschaft, 1975), 177–178; Jill Stephenson, *Hitler's Home Front: Württemberg under the Nazis* (London: Hambledon Continuum, 2006), 150, 239.
3. Jeremy Noakes and G. Pridham, eds., *Nazism 1919–1945: A Documentary History*: vol. 1: *The Rise to Power 1919–1934* (Exeter: Humanities Press, 1983), 167; vol. 2, *State Economy and Society 1933–1939* (Exeter: Humanities Press, 1984), 328–333; Eric Johnson, *The Nazi Terror: Gestapo, Jews and Ordinary Germans* (New York: Basic Books, 1999), 161–194.
4. Noakes and Pridham, *Nazism*, vol. 1, 142.
5. *Statistisches Jahrbuch für das Deutsche Reich*: 1927, 9; 1941/42, 26.
6. Stephenson, *Hitler's Home Front*, 239–242; Hubert Roser, "Widerstand und Verweigerung der Zeugen Jehovahs im deutschen Südwesten 1933 bis 1945," in *Widerstand als Bekenntnis: die Zeugen Jehovahs und das NS-Regime in Baden und Württemberg*, ed. Hubert Roser (Konstanz: UVK, 1999), 44–58; Dietrich von Raumer, "Zeugen Jehovahs als Kriegsdienstverweigerer: ein trauriges Kapitel der Wehrmachtjustiz," in ibid., 182–206.
7. Noakes and Pridham, *Nazism*, vol. 2, 317–318, 336–339, 343–346; Richard J. Evans, *The Third Reich in Power* (New York: Penguin Press, 2005), 266–268,

444; Charles E. McClelland, *The German Experience of Professionalization: Modern Learned Professions and their Organizations from the Early Nineteenth Century to the Hitler Era* (Cambridge: Cambridge University Press, 1991), 217–229.
8. Noakes and Pridham, *Nazism*, vol. 2, pp. 419–421; Dagmar Reese, *Growing up Female in Nazi Germany: Social History, Popular Culture and Politics in Germany* (Ann Arbor: University of Michigan Press, 2006), 238–245.
9. Franz Josef Heyen, *Nationalsozialismus im Alltag: Quellen zur Geschichte des Nationalsozialismus vornehmlich im Raum Mainz-Koblenz-Trier* (Boppard: Boldt, 1967), 255–257, 259; Jill Stephenson, *The Nazi Organisation of Women* (London: Croom Helm, 1981), 149–150, 185.
10. Stephenson, *Hitler's Home Front*, 96–97.
11. Evans, *The Third Reich in Power*, 213ff.
12. Noakes and Pridham, *Nazism*, vol. 2, 590–593.
13. Sybille Baumbach, Uwe Kaminsky, Alfons Kenkmann, and Beate Meyer, *Rückblenden: Lebensgeschichtliche Interviews mit Verfolgten des NS-Regimes in Hamburg* (Hamburg: Ergebnisse-Verl, 1999), 232–238.
14. Jill Stephenson, *Women in Nazi Germany* (London: Longman, 2001), pp. 109–112.
15. Hans Mommsen, "The Political Legacy of the German Resistance: A Historiographical Critique," in *Contending with Hitler: Varieties of German Resistance in the Third Reich*, ed. David C. Large (New York: Cambridge University Press, 1991), 161.
16. Franz J. Heyen, *Nationalsozialismus im Alltag*, 184–185, 188–189; Staatsarchiv Ludwigsburg (StAL), K110, Bü46, "Lagebericht," July 1, 1939, 46.
17. Bundesarchiv (BA), R22/3387, Der Generalstaatsanwalt Stuttgart an den Herrn Reichsminister der Justiz, July 10, 1940.
18. Joseph Goebbels, *Die Tagebücher*, Elke Fröhlich, ed., Part II: Diktate 1941–1945, vol. 10: Oct.–Dec. 1943, 2 November 1943, 222.
19. "SD-Berichte zu Inlandsfragen vom 8. Juli 1943," in *Meldungen aus dem Reich: Die geheimen Lageberichte des Sicherheitsdienstes der SS* (MadR), ed. Heinz Boberach (Herrsching: Pawlak Verlag, 1977), vol. 14, 5448.
20. "Meldungen aus dem Reich (Nr. 372) 1. April 1943," in Boberach, *MadR*, vol. 13, 5046–5048; Hauptstaatsarchiv Stuttgart (HStAS), J170, Bü18, Gemeinde Tomerdingen. See also Martin Broszat, Elke Fröhlich, and Falk Wiesemann, eds., *Bayern in der NS-Zeit. i: Soziale Lage und politisches Verhalten der Bevölkerung im Spiegel vertraulicher Berichte* (Munich and Vienna, 1977), 154–156.
21. StAL, K110: Bü47, "Betr.: Allgemeine Stimmung und Lage," July 15, 1941, 19; Bü48, "Betr.: Allgemeine Stimmung und Lage," September 1, 1941, 36–37. See also BA, R22/3387, Der Oberlandesgerichtspräsident an den Herrn Reichsminister der Justiz, "Betreff: Bericht über die allgemeine Lage," July 3, 1941; "Meldungen aus dem Reich (Nr. 269) 19. März 1942," in Boberach, *MadR*, vol. 9, 3497.
22. Tim Mason, "The Legacy of 1918 for National Socialism," in *German Democracy and the Triumph of Hitler: Essays in Recent German History*, ed. Anthony Nicholls and Erich Matthias (London: Allen and Unwin, 1971), 215–239.
23. Belinda Davis, *Home Fires Burning: Food, Politics, and Everyday Life in World War I Berlin* (Chapel Hill: University of North Carolina Press, 2000); see especially chapters 9 and 10.

24. StAL, K110: Bü37, SD "Lagebericht," January 25, 1940; Bü47, 20, 22–23.
25. "Meldungen aus dem Reich (Nr. 269) 19. März 1942," in Boberach, *MadR*, vol. 9, 3497.
26. Reuth, *Goebbels Tagebücher*, 1911.
27. Gerhard Schäfer, ed., *Landesbischof D. Wurm und der Nationalsozialistische Staat 1940–1945* (Stuttgart: Calwer Verl., 1968), 160–161, 165–166.
28. Joachim Szodrzynski, "Die 'Heimatfront' zwischen Stalingrad und Kriegsende," in Forschungsstelle für Zeitgeschichte in Hamburg (ed.), *Hamburg im "Dritten Reich"* (Göttingen: Wallstein Verlag, 2005), 642; Ursula Büttner, "Gomorrha" und die Folgen: Der Bombenkrieg," in ibid., 616–620.
29. Broszat, Fröhlich, and Wiesemann, *Bayern*, 51, 159.
30. "SD-Berichte zu Inlandsfragen vom 21. October 1943," in Boberach, *MadR*, vol. 15, 5907–5909; Stephenson, *Hitler's Home Front*, 307–10.
31. StAL, K110, Bü55, RSHA, "Meldungen aus den SD-(Leit)-Abschnittsbereichen, 15 July 1943," 14078.
32. Krause, *Flucht vor dem Bombenkrieg*, 162–64, 200. Michael Krause, *Flucht vor dem Bombenkrieg: "Umquartierung" im Zweiten Weltkrieg und die Wiedereingliederung der Evakuierten in Deutschland 1943-1963* (Düsseldorf: Droste Verlag, 1997).
33. See Julia Torrie's essay in this volume.
34. "SD-Berichte zu Inlandsfragen vom 18. November 1943," in Boberach, *MadR*, vol. 15, 6030–6031.
35. Ibid., 6026–6029; Stephenson, *Hitler's Home Front*, 306–307.
36. "SD-Berichte zu Inlandsfragen vom 18. November 1943," 6029–6031.
37. Erich Stockhorst, *5000 Köpfe: Wer War Was im 3. Reich* (Kiel: Arndt Verlag, 1985), 204.
38. "SD-Berichte zu Inlandsfragen vom 18. November 1943," 6030–6031.
39. Peter Hüttenberger, *Die Gauleiter: Studie zum Wandel des Machtgefüges in der NSDAP* (Stuttgart: Verl.-Anst, 1969), 171.
40. "SD-Berichte zu Inlandsfragen vom 18. November 1943," 6033.
41. "SD-Berichte zu Inlandsfragen vom 22. November 1943," in Boberach, *MadR*, vol. 15, 6058.
42. Gerhard Kock, *Die Kinderlandverschickung im Zweiten Weltkrieg* (Paderborn: Schöningh, 1997), 187, 255.
43. See Julia Torrie's essay in this volume.
44. "SD-Berichte zu Inlandsfragen vom 18. November 1943," 6031.
45. Ian Kershaw, *Popular Opinion and Political Dissent in the Third Reich: Bavaria 1933–1945* (Oxford: Oxford University Press, 1983), 205–208; Jeremy Noakes, "The Oldenburg Crucifix Struggle of November 1936: A Case Study of Opposition in the Third Reich," in *The Shaping of the Nazi State*, ed. Peter D. Stachura (London: Croom Helm, 1978), 218–230. See also Ernst Hanisch, "Peasants and Workers in their Environment: Nonconformity and Opposition to National Socialism in the Austrian Alps," in *Germans against Nazism: Essays in Honour of Peter Hoffmann; Nonconformity, Opposition and Resistance in the Third Reich*, ed. Francis R. Nicosia and Lawrence D. Stokes (Oxford: Berg, 1990), 181–182.
46. Johnpeter Horst Grill, *The Nazi Movement in Baden, 1920–1945* (Chapel Hill: University of North Carolina Press, 1983), 339.
47. Heyen, *Nationalsozialismus im Alltag*, 240–255.

48. Broszat, Fröhlich, and Wiesemann, *Bayern*, 140; Hanisch, "Peasants and Workers in their Environment," 178, 183.
49. Broszat, Fröhlich, and Wiesemann, *Bayern*, 148.
50. Heyen, *Nationalsozialismus im Alltag*, 179–180.
51. Broszat, Fröhlich, and Wiesemann, *Bayern*, 150.
52. Kershaw, *Popular Opinion*, 342–354.
53. Hanisch, "Peasants and Workers in their Environment," 181.
54. Broszat, Fröhlich, and Wiesemann, *Bayern*, 157.
55. Stephenson, *Hitler's Home Front*, 249–255.
56. Quoted in Hanisch, "Peasants and Workers in their Environment," 176.
57. BA, NS6/414, "Auszüge aus Berichten der Gauleitungen u. a. Dienststellen—Aktivität der Kirche," April 9, 1943, 13.
58. Christine Arbogast, *Herrschaftsinstanzen der württembergischen NSDAP: Funktion, Sozialprofil und Lebenswege einer regionalen NS-Elite, 1920–1960* (Munich: R. Oldenbourg, 1998), 76. See also Thomas Schnabel, *Württemberg zwischen Weimar und Bonn, 1928–1945/46* (Stuttgart: Kohlhammer, 1986), 418.
59. Grill, *The Nazi Movement in Baden*, 344.
60. Broszat, Fröhlich, and Wiesemann, *Bayern*, 165.
61. Stephenson, *Hitler's Home Front*, 253.
62. Hanisch, "Peasants and Workers in their Environment," 178.
63. Quoted in John S. Conway, *The Nazi Persecution of the Churches* (London: Weidenfeld & Nicolson, 1968), 190.
64. Stephenson, *Hitler's Home Front*, 280–283; Daniela Münkel, *Nationalsozialistische Agrarpolitik und Bauernalltag* (Frankfurt am Main: Campus, 1996), 412–414; Beatrix Herlemann, *"Der Bauer klebt am Hergebrachten": Bäuerliche Verhaltensweisen unterm Nationalsozialismus auf dem Gebiet des heutigen Landes Niedersachsen* (Hanover: Hahn, 1993), 321; "SD-Berichte zu Inlandsfragen vom 24. January 1944," in Boberach, *MadR*, vol. 16, 6279.
65. HStAS, J170: Bü4 (Crailsheim), Gemeinde Honhardt, October 29, 1948; Bü1 (Aalen), Gemeinde Adelmannsfelden, n.d. (October/November 1948).
66. Stephen G. Fritz, *Endkampf: Soldiers, Civilians, and the Death of the Third Reich* (Lexington: University Press of Kentucky, 2004), 116–131; Stephenson, *Hitler's Home Front*, 322–328.
67. HStAS, J170, Bü3 (Böblingen), Sindelfingen, n.d. [October 1948], 1–5.
68. Thomas Schnabel, "Die Leute wollten nicht einer verlorenen Sache ihre Heimat opfern," in Landeszentrale für politische Bildung und Haus der Geschichte (ed.), *Formen des Widerstandes im Südwesten, 1933–1945* (Ulm: Süddeutsche Verlagsgesellschaft, 1994).
69. Klaus-Dietmar Henke, *Die amerikanische Besetzung Deutschlands* (Munich: Oldenbourg, 1996), 784–788; Stephenson, *Hitler's Home Front*, 323–333.
70. Richard J. Evans, "German Women and the Triumph of Hitler," *Journal of Modern History*, Article Accepted for Demand Publication, abstract printed in vol. 48, no. 1 (1976): 38.
71. BA, R22/3387, Der Oberlandesgerichtspräsident an den Herrn Reichsminister der Justiz, "Betreff: Bericht über die allgemeine Lage," March 2, 1940.

Chapter 3

The Demonstrations in Support of the Protestant Provincial Bishop Hans Meiser
A Successful Protest Against the Nazi Regime?

Christiane Kuller

On October 11, 1934, at 12 noon, August Jäger, a close associate of the National Socialist Reichsbischof Ludwig Müller, accompanied by representatives of the political police and Berlin Reich Church (Reichskirche), forcibly broke into the Munich administrative offices of the Protestant Church in the province of Bavaria, deposed Bavarian Provincial Bishop Hans Meiser, and suspended the leadership of the Bavarian Provincial Church. He then divided Bavaria into two separate dioceses, and appointed a new, temporary bishop to each. Hans Meiser, who refused to sign his name to the letter authorizing his own dismissal, was placed under house arrest.

The dramatic events in Munich in October 1934 were the climax in a battle to bring South German provincial churches into line with the policies of the National Socialist regime. For two weeks, from October 12 to 26, 1934, Bishop Meiser was held under house arrest, while August Jäger attempted to set up a provisional administrative organization under the direction of the National Socialist Reichskirche. During this time, a broad protest movement emerged, a movement that church historian Klaus Scholder has described as one of the largest and at the same time most peculiar protest movements of the Nazi era. It was a movement that pushed the regime to the limits of its power.[1] In the end, Hitler himself backed down, rehabilitated Bishop Meiser, and was forced to admit the failure of his earlier church policy.

To date, these events have, for the most part, been investigated in terms of what they meant to church policy. The role Meiser played in the clash around the formation of a National Socialist Reichskirche has been explored numerous times in the research.[2] The following article, in contrast, approaches the topic from a slightly different perspective. The central questions addressed here are how the effects of the protests made themselves felt, how they were perceived by the National Socialist leadership, and what impact Hitler's relenting had on church policy. In addition, the article takes a first step toward investigating the form, organization, and motivations informing the protest against the house arrest of Bishop Meiser. In the second section, the reactions of the Nazi regime and the reasons for Hitler volte-face on Reich church policy are examined more closely. Lastly, the effects of the events in the autumn of 1934 are once more assessed and summarized.

The Demonstrations in Support of Hans Meiser and his German Protestant Church

The protest within the Protestant Church began on 11 October, shortly after the Landeskirchenamt was occupied. In Munich, but above all in Franconia and Swabia, where the majority of the population was Protestant, hundreds of so-called penitential church services (*Bußgottesdienste*) were held, where parishioners protested against the detention of Bishop Meiser and gathered signatures to petition for his release. The collection of petition signatures was quite deliberately carried out by chairs of the parish councils (*Gemeindevorsteher*) and not by pastors. The idea was to make it clear that not the pastors, but the parishioners were protesting. The Bavarian Provincial Church had already taken steps in the summer of 1934 in preparation for such a protest campaign. As a result, when Meiser was placed under house arrest, the planned *Bußgottesdienste* could be launched immediately. The police did not intervene against these services.[3]

A contact of Bishop Meiser also urged pastors to organize "delegations" (*Abordnungen*) to travel to Munich.[4] Such delegations, which gave the protests public visibility outside the immediate confines of the church, has also been prepared well in advance. As early as mid-September 1934, in other words roughly one month prior to the occupation of the Landeskirchenamt, a pastor from the Franconian deanship in Gunzenhausen in the company of two farmers called on the Undersecretary of the Bavarian Reichsstatthalter, von Epp for the first time. This initial conversation was to be followed by a later delegation numbering forty-five members. Meanwhile, however, the Jäger operation had transpired, and the group was turned away. Instead, fifteen Franconian envoys, among them five theologians and three farmers, met in the interim with representatives of the Munich church in order to draw up a written statement to send to the Bavarian Provincial government.

The delegation handed this statement over to Reichsstatthalter von Epp and Prime Minister Siebert on October 20, 1934, asserting that it would be speaking in the name of some sixty thousand mostly farming Protestants. The delegates also tried to call on the Ministry of Education and Cultural Affairs, the Ministry of the Interior, and at the "Braunes Haus," but were turned away. The public also learned of this campaign because the international press was reporting on it.[5] Additional delegations came from Franconia to Munich; among them, one with four pastors and eighteen farmers who sent a telegram to Hitler on the evening of October 22, 1934, that declared it represented the views of seventy-five thousand Franconian farmers.[6]

Although the members of the delegations initially spoke out against mass demonstrations, arguing that these would not reflect the "the character of our faith,"[7] a large demonstration with many participants soon followed. And though the first groups may well have represented tens of thousands, they only arrived in Munich with a few people; however, on October 21, a group numbering more than eight hundred Nuremberg Protestants traveled by special train to Munich.[8] The Protestant press office reported that around six hundred of them pushed their way into the courtyard of the Landeskirchenamt, where they held a church service for Bishop Meiser. On October 22, some members of this group also protested at government offices.

These demonstrations fundamentally altered the character of the protest. Plainly, Bishop Meiser could mobilize hundreds of sympathizers who would air their criticisms publicly outside the confines of the church. The Nazi regime certainly took note of this development. For example, the monthly situation report prepared by the governments of Swabia and Neuburg retrospectively established, "that the vast majority of the Protestant population not only tacitly supported Provincial Bishop H. Meiser and the confessional posture, but was also ready to adopt his position publicly."[9]

Not least, the protest demonstrations in support of Bishop Meiser are evidence that the information policies of the Reichskirche leadership had failed. To put a stop to demonstrations, the Bavarian political police prohibited all rallies; the distribution of Protestant church newspapers, journals, and fliers; as well as "the ringing of church bells as a form of protest" (*Demonstrationsglockenläuten*), initially from October 11 through the following Sunday, October 14, but later also for the subsequent period.[10] To block the church's channels of communication, Jäger had the head of the Protestant press office, Gerhard Hildmann, taken into custody together with Meiser. In their place, independent communications structures were to be set up and expanded. In fact, numerous opinion pieces, propaganda reports, interviews, and instructions from the new church leadership appeared in the press in the days to follow.

August Jäger failed, however, to successfully shut down all of Hans Meiser's channels of communication. Before the Provincial Church offices were occupied, alternative locations with printing equipment had apparently already been set up in a private Munich home and in the Protestant Burial Society (*Begräbnisverein*); this meant that work could go on despite the occupation of the press office and the arrest of its director.[11] In Rosenheim, a coordination center sprang up, from which the "Representative of the Provincial Bishop" (*Beauftragte des Landesbischofs*) could direct opposition to Jäger's provisional administration.[12]

An informal, internal church organization responsible for disseminating news was already in place before those October days of 1934: News was supplied to representatives in Munich, Upper Bavaria, and Swabia by the Seminar for Preachers (*Predigerseminar*); in Northern Bavaria, some businessmen fulfilled this function. These same distribution channels were also used, shortly after the events, to disseminate the news that the provincial church offices had been occupied. According to contemporary witnesses, Oberkirchenrat Thomas Breit, an eyewitness of Jäger's takeover of the offices, dictated a first report on the raid, which was then duplicated the very same night, slipped into hand-addressed envelopes, and distributed throughout all of Bavaria by six candidates in the Seminar for Preachers.[13]

Together with the provincial church council (*Landeskirchenrat*), Meiser had also composed a position statement for the first Sunday after his arrest exhorting Bavarian Protestants not to obey the new church regime. This was read out in many Bavarian parishes during the church service. On October 16, Meiser sent a pastoral letter to Bavarian pastors. In this way, he was able to issue his statement a day before the newly appointed, provisional bishops officially took office.[14] On October 18, the agents of Bishop Meiser distributed a circular with instructions on how to behave toward "the unlawful church governing body" (*unrechtmäßigen Kirchenleitung*).

Although he was under arrest, Meiser did still appear in public in the following weeks. For instance, numerous church services were held in the courtyard of the Landeskirchenamt in the immediate vicinity of Meiser's home, where he would show himself.[15] Furthermore, the Munich Landeskirchenamt and Meiser's home were also the destination for several protest delegations.

After two weeks, Jäger was forced to concede, "at present, it is not yet possible, in every instance, to prevent Meiser or his representatives from communicating in some way with their partisans in the parishes."[16]

An important obstacle hampering the installation of a new, provisional governing body of the church was the Franconian NSDAP, which unexpectedly withdrew from the conflict. The decision of Gauleiter Julius Streicher to stop actively supporting the National Socialist governing body of the church signaled a clear change in how the protest was being framed, and it marked a turning point in the process unfolding in Bavaria.

As of the summer of 1934, the deputy Gauleiter of Franconia, Karl Holz, had been particularly active in fighting the bishop. Holz was the author of a newspaper article entitled "Remove Provincial Bishop D. Meiser," which had appeared on September 15, 1934, in the *Fränkische Tageszeitung*, a month prior to Jäger's campaign to take over the offices of the church.[17] Together with Wolf Meyer-Erlach, a theologian and champion of the "Deutsche Christen," he had orchestrated a mass demonstration against Hans Meiser in September 1934.[18] Holz coordinated police operations against Meiser supporters in Nuremberg during the early days of the takeover of the Landeskirchenamt.

The deputy Gauleiter of the future National Socialist Reichskirche had also become involved for more personal reasons. Breaking up the current Bavarian Provincial Church into two sub-regions would not only have sidelined the old regional church administrative structures, but also would have served the local power interests of the NSDAP. In the course of the reform, Bavaria was to be divided into a southern Bavarian region, in which Protestant Christians constituted 10 percent of the population, and a Franconian region, in which more than half the inhabitants were Protestant. Whereas the ratio of Protestant Christians to Catholics was roughly 1:3 in the old Bavarian Provincial Church, meaning that the Protestant Church was in a minority position, after division, Protestants in Franconia would have formed the majority. In brief, the formation of a Franconian church district represented a significant increase in the relative power of Karl Holz, deputy Franconian Gauleiter, who was also the secretary (*Schriftführer*) of the South German League of Protestant Christians (Süddeutscher Bund evangelischer Christen), an organization close to the NSDAP. Karl Holz envisioned his "Bund evangelischer Christen" playing a powerful role in the future mediation between church, state, and party in northern Bavaria.[19]

That the bringing to heel of the Protestant Church was an important goal of NSDAP authorities at the Nazi administrative district level (*Gau*) can also be seen in the fact that, shortly after Meiser's detention, Hans Schemm, Gauleiter of the Bayerische Ostmark, likewise demanded a third diocese for his Gau—to be named the "Bayerische Ostmark."[20] This plan, aimed at establishing a "Private and Party Church" for Schemm, was never actually seriously considered, but it did show that Schemm, no less than Holz, did pursue his own interests in this conflict—if nothing else.

Yet, barely a week after the occupation of the Munich Landeskirchenamt, the situation was decisively reconfigured: The Franconian Gauleiter Julius Streicher distanced himself publicly from his deputy Karl Holz's involvement in church policy. During a meeting with Nuremberg pastors on October 17, 1934, Streicher declared the NSDAP would henceforth stay out of the conflict. According to Streicher's statement, Karl Holz had "not spoken as a National Socialist, but as a Protestant" in his newspaper attacks against Bishop Meiser in the run-up to the occupation of the provincial church offices. Streicher ordered that henceforth church and party matters were to be kept separate.[21] The grounds for Streicher's pointed retreat presumably lay in his fear that the vast majority of pastors and parishioners supported Meiser, and he was looking for a way to emerge undefeated from the conflict.

With the retreat of the Franconian Gauleiter, the National Socialist Reichskirche lost the NSDAP as a powerful supporter, and it quite concretely lost access to party resources and regional media, which fell silent on questions of church policy in the days to follow. But Streicher's decision also fundamentally rearranged the forces animating church and popular protest. After this, supporters of Bishop Meiser no longer found themselves trapped in a conflict of loyalty between the provincial bishop and the National Socialist way of thinking.

Existing research gives a great deal of weight to the series of interventions from abroad that joined the wave of protests by the Bavarian population.[22] Foreign church representatives had been watching developments in German church policy with heightened attention for some time. After Meiser's arrest, the President of the Ecumenical Council, Bishop Bell of London, promptly spoke up, at the same time also informing Cosmo Lang, the Archbishop of Canterbury. On October 12, 1934, Bell had a conversation with the German representative in London, who in turn raised the alarm with the Foreign Office. Lang delivered an ultimatum to the Reich government: Hitler had until October 24 to resolve the conflict, if possible by dismissing Reichsbischof Ludwig Müller. The Scandinavian and French churches also waited for a reaction from the Nazi Regime. The international church protests received additional momentum from a congress of the Lutheran World Federation in Munich planned for November, a meeting Meiser was slated to attend. By keeping Meiser under house arrest during this congress, the regime would leave itself exposed in the eyes of the international public, something it could ill afford. Thus it happened, during the second half of October 1934, that numerous documents from the Foreign Minister concerning the South German church question crossed Hitler's desk stamped with an urgent note "immediate" (*sofort*).

Decision-making in the "Führerstaat"

As the domestic and international wave of protests burst forth following Meiser's arrest, the Nazi regime came under pressure to act.[23] The magnitude of the protest against the detention of Meiser worried Bavarian governmental authorities. Reichsstatthalter Ritter von Epp and his colleagues feared a revolt of the entire Lutheran Church in Bavaria.[24] Bavarian Prime Minister Siebert saw himself confronted with a "furor protestanticus" which, in his opinion, would not die down any time soon.[25]

Yet in the view of all participants, the decision to lift the house arrest placed on the bishop could only be made by the authority that had imposed it. The former head of the SA Franz von Pfeffer, the lawyer August Jager, the Bavarian Gauleiter Adolf Wagner, and Jakob Beck of the Bavarian political police all attended the planning session that convened in the Munich "Braunes Haus" on October 8, 1934.[26] The Staff of the Deputy Führer under Rudolph Heß was responsible for hosting the session. The government leadership in Bavaria, however, appears only to have learned of the action Jäger took against Meiser and the Provincial Church after the fact. Even the Reich Interior Minister was only informed after the events had already transpired. Consequently, the provincial and Reich ministers also placed responsibility for lifting the house arrest in the hands of Rudolf Heß, and his church commissioner, Franz von Pfeffer. Heß for his part, wanted his decision to depend on whatever stance Hitler adopted. So, the eyes of all participants turned to Hitler.

But the Führer gave no signal there would be a policy change during the first week of Meiser's house arrest. To the contrary, Hitler stuck to the plan to hold a ceremonial swearing-in of the Nazi Reichsbischof Müller, thereby upholding the earlier policy in Bavaria. The dictator appears initially to have left the power to act entirely in the hands of Franz von Pfeffer, and did not occupy himself further with the question. The situation only received new impetus in the second week of the occupation. Immediately before Müller took his oath on October 23, 1934, Hitler decided to change course. First, he postponed Müller's reception—then he cancelled it. Instead, in the early evening of October 25, Hitler sent a telegraph to Bishop Meiser, Bishop Wurm, and Bishop Marahrens inviting them to join him for "consultation." At 5 P.M. on October 25, Reich Interior Minister Frick instructed Bavarian Prime Minister Siebert to try to have Meiser released: Meiser could hardly remain in custody if he had been invited to meet with Hitler.[27] Bishop Meiser's house arrest was lifted the evening of October 26. In a word, Hitler's personal intervention started the process of Meiser's rehabilitation.

How to explain this fundamental change in Hitler's opinion? First, one should note his original position had never been as clear-cut as it may have seemed to some of the participants who took the side of the Reichskirche and the Deutschen Christen. The fact that Pfeffer and Jäger only became active in Munich on October 11, 1934, and not—as Reich Bishop *Müller* had advertised—after the end of the Reich Party Congress in mid-September, suggests that, at this point in time, Müller enjoyed little backing from the National Socialist dictator.[28]

At first glance, it seems Hitler, who based his rule to a considerable degree on plebiscitary consent, bowed to public pressure. In this view, Hitler's decision in favor of Meiser could be interpreted as a move to limit the damage and to end public unrest.[29] Without a doubt, the protests did play an important role. That the demonstrations could have an impact lay, not least, in the specific nature of the conflict.[30] In this instance, the group defending itself was not some small, marginal group that was explicitly excluded from the "people's community" (*Volksgemeinschaft*), such as Jews, or a group in political opposition to the regime, such as Communists. The protest emerged, for the most part, from within the circle of partisans of the Nazi movement, and was shouldered by well-organized participants who had frequently stood in support of the Nazi movement in the past. The protest also had a very concrete objective that was easy to communicate and which many Protestants in Bavaria could quickly relate to: the reinstatement of Hans Meiser. All this intensified the dynamic of the conflict.

Considering the impressive mobilization, one must at the same time stress that the protest, for the most part, cannot be labeled as opposition to the Nazi regime. A necessary awareness of some principled political or moral opposition to the system was lacking.[31] During his house arrest, Meiser himself had encouraged the pastors to do everything they could to suppress "whatever might give the impression that, other than purely ecclesiastical goals, this struggle also had political goals."[32] Here, as again later, the Bavarian Provincial Bishop only targeted his criticism against specific powers within the NSDAP, not against the National Socialist regime as a whole, not to speak of Hitler. Meiser had already taken this posture in conversation with Hitler on March 1934, when he described himself as "our Führer's most loyal opposition."[33] Meiser and his supporters only directed their protest against that part of National Socialist politics that addressed church policy, without otherwise questioning the regime. In this respect, there was no contradiction when National Socialist songs were sung or the Nazi salute was used during the demonstrations held in support of Meiser.[34]

Contemporary observers also diagnosed this ambivalence. Thus in November 1934, the SPD in exile—not uncritically—interpreted the results of the Church Conflict, writing: "This entire history of the Church Conflict makes one thing quite clear: this was no struggle against the system, but rather a struggle within the system for some portion in the rule, power, and spoils of the new authoritarian state! The Church's counter-revolution was subjected to the terror of the church administration wielded against it—but not state terror!"[35] But these words only partly characterize the events of October 1934: the conflict did by all means possess dissident potential, potential that the National Socialist powers-that-be recognized as dangerous. For one, that fact that it was precisely the regime's loyal supporters who closed ranks behind Meiser was highly explosive. Up until then, the majority of the Franconian rural population could always be counted among the National Socialist movement's most reliable clientele. Thus, the events fomented dissatisfaction among the closest followers of the NSDAP. In a letter addressed to the Reich's Interior Minister, Bavarian Prime Minister Siebert stressed that the signatories would "acknowledge only three ideas": the Führer, the Protestant faith, and the soil [Grun und Boden], but they would not relinquish even one of these three things.[36]

Furthermore, the protests took on a dimension threatening to the regime in that they addressed themselves to state and party institutions and consequently held these institutions responsible for solving the problem. Even if, at its core, the protests did not involve conflict with the National Socialist regime, the protesters did expect state authorities to regulate the dispute. To insist on neutrality, an approach Hitler otherwise liked to rely on, or the collapse of state arbitration, would attract public attention to the fact that the regime had failed in this vital question. Thus, an almost paradoxical situation arose: the *Führerstaat*, embroiled in a conflict in which it hardly had an objective interest, was on the verge of being pushed to the limits of its power. In light of this situation, the Bavarian governmental authorities in Berlin pressured the regime to intervene, to settle this matter once and for all.

But the demonstrations alone did not lead Hitler to change his mind. In the beginning, the public rallies do not appear to have made much of an impression on the dictator. Evidently, at first, Hitler took note of the letters he received from the Bavarian Prime Minister Siebert regarding the protest without comment; he thought the reports coming from Bavaria were exaggerated. Apparently, the foreign protests also did not persuade Hitler to change his mind during the first week of Meiser's arrest.[37] It was only their connection with several other factors, which subjected the dictator to pressure at the end of October 1934 because of his church policy, that resulted in a change of opinion.

One may detect Hitler first hesitating on October 19, 1934, when he did not direct the text for the scheduled swearing-in of Reichsbischof Müller along normal administrative channels, but instead held it back, and postponed the reception of the Reichsbischof by two days.[38] Chronologically, this occurred roughly around the same time as the start of the Dahlemer Synod of the "Bekennende Kirche." The Synod, which had moved up the date of its conference in order to be able to protest the swearing-in of

Reichsbischof Müller, hoping in this way to strengthen the resolve of their harried South German co-religionists, convened on October 19–20, 1934. It also spoke explicitly against the Reichsbischof, stated that ecclesiastical emergency law applied, and proclaimed that all current administrative bodies of the Protestant Church were illegitimate. In this manner, the occupation of the Landeskirchenamt in Munich was declared to be unlawful.[39]

One of the first to speak personally with Hitler about the Munich Church Conflict was the Palatine Gauleiter, Josef Bürckel, who met with Hitler in the beginning of the second week of the arrest, sometime around October 22, 1934.[40] Bürckel introduced an additional, significant argument into the conversation: A referendum was imminent in the Saar; critical press reports on violent church politics threatened to upturn unstable public opinion in the run-up to the Saar referendum. Bürckel, who as Gauleiter of the Palatinate was responsible for the Saar referendum, feared far-reaching, negative consequences. In Bürckel's view at the time of this discussion, the National Socialist dictatorship was very poorly informed; research does suggest that until Hitler met with Bürckel, Pfeffer, with Hitler's mandate, had been allowed a free hand.

Hitler seems to have now gathered more information. In any event, on October 24, 1934, he received a report from the Reich Ministry of Justice concerning the trial of Pastor Martin Niemöller. The pastor had brought an action in the Supreme Court of the Reich challenging his dismissal, thereby placing the entire Reichskirche in question. Indirectly, this action also placed the legality of the regime's church policy in Bavaria in question. Should Niemöller win his case, it would become very difficult for Hitler to side with Reichsbischof Müller, since Müller would at that point have been declared illegitimate by a Supreme Court of the Reich. In the end, a signal from the Reich Ministry of Justice concerning Niemöller's impending victory in the trial on Wednesday, October 24, 1934, appears to have provided the final impetus: Hitler at last distanced himself from Müller and cancelled the reception of the Reichsbischof.[41]

Even so, Meiser's invitation by telegraph to meet with Hitler did not mean the measures taken against the Bavarian Bishop were being lifted. The invitation did, however, signal a decisive change in Hitler's posture, and this prompted the Minister of Interior Wilhelm Frick to take action. On October 26, 1934, the house arrest of Hans Meiser was lifted. On October 29, the Bavarian Bishop Meiser and his Wurttemberg counterpart Theophil Wurm paid visits to the Reich Interior Ministry, the Foreign Ministry, and the Reich Minister of Justice Gürtner to negotiate their reinstatement.[42] On October 30, 1934, Meiser, Wurm, and the Hanoverian Bishop Marahrens met with Hitler.[43] By this act, the dictator recognized de facto these three bishops in their offices. On November 1, 1934, Hans Meiser, with reference to Hitler's reception, officially took over the duties of the Bavarian Provincial Bishop.[44]

If contemporaneous news coverage is to be believed, Hitler hardly expressed any interest in Protestant church politics during the reception that occurred at the end of October. After the talks were over, Reich Interior Minister Frick, who had also taken part in the conversation, instructed the following one sentence statement be released in place of the lengthier press release that had been prepared earlier: "The Führer today received Provincial Bishops D. Marahrens, D. Meiser, and Theophil Wurm."[45]

Internally, Hitler described the outcome of the conversation held on October 30 at a Reichsstatthalterversammlung on the next day as follows: "During the brief reception, Bishop Meiser stressed that confession must be free." Hitler added an undisguised threat: "If confession must be free, well then, the State must also be free. The churches, then, should be left to levy church taxes themselves. He had no intention of capitulating to the churches. Unfortunately, he, the Führer, had been given the impression that church governance had been infringed upon by the Reich Church administration and that illegalities may also have arisen in the creation of the Reich Church Constitution. Perhaps, in this instance, more care should have been given to processes already in place at the time. The Reich Bishop should be granted a new grace period to put matters in order. He, the Führer, had thought of creating a strong, unified Protestant church. Evidently, a segment of the clergy did not want this. Now, no doubt, one would soon see countless, different Protestant churches springing up."[46]

Meiser summed up the meeting shortly later in a somewhat more positive light, as follows: "According to Meiser's report, the result of the Führer discussion with the three Bishops of Bavaria, Wurttemberg and Hanover was that the Führer declared the plan for the intended founding of Protestant Unified Reich Church should be considered a failure. The churches should now look themselves to how they came to blows; he did not want to have anything more to do with the matter; he would, however, henceforth allow all Christian confessions to practice freely." Meiser also, however, picked up on the National Socialist Dictator's financial threat.[47]

The Consequences of the Bavarian Church Conflict

As Meiser was one of the bishops who had resisted the incorporation of his Provincial Church into a National Socialist Reichskirche under Bishop Ludwig Müller, the Reichsbischof had to recognize the reinstatement of the

Bavarian provincial bishop as the final defeat for the Reichskirche. Consequently, this meant Müller had lost the power struggle to compel incorporation of all Protestant churches into his organization. Since the planned Reichskirche was one of the National Socialist institutions dominated by the "Deutsche Christen," the "Deutsche Christen" also had to recognize a major defeat in the collapse of these plans. This meant that Meiser's victory not only led to a temporary end to the power struggle between the Provincial Church and Reichskirche, but also brought the "Deutsche Christen" in Bavaria, who had called for open rebellion against Meiser in the autumn of 1934, back to their senses. After this, in addition to the Wurttemberg and Hanover churches, the Bavarian Provincial Church was one of the three remaining "intact" Protestant churches in the German Reich. For one, this meant their original administrative autonomy was maintained. Secondly, the "intact churches" constituted a third power, subsidiary to neither the National Socialist "Deutsche Christen" nor to the resistance group of the "Bekennende Kirche."

The longer term consequences for the further development of the Protestant Church in Bavaria remained ambivalent: On the one hand, institutional integrity offered a certain degree of protection against the influence of racist thinking, as well as much greater autonomy than that enjoyed in many other churches.[48] On the other hand, Meiser adopted the maxim to never attempt anything risky against the regime, and to preserve his "intact" church with all the means at his disposal. One can recognize the Bavarian Provincial Bishop behaving cautiously on many occasions, behavior that historians explain in terms of Meiser's intention to maintain his Church as an integral whole, while integrating as many subgroups as possible. This point has been especially strongly criticized in recent years with respect to Meiser's attitude toward the persecution of the Jews.

Although the "Bekennende Kirche" could consider the reinstatement of the Southern German bishops a success, friction within the organization increased after Hitler's reception of the bishops from Bavaria, Wurttemberg, and Hanover. Given the situation, the fully explainable, but in the last analysis overhasty, resolutions reached at Dahlem urging all Protestant communities to adopt a uniform stance either for or against the "Bekennende Kirche" placed heavy burdens on the unity of the "Bekennende Kirche."[49] The acknowledged, constitutional, "intact" provincial churches could hardly allow themselves to be reconciled with the "broken" provincial churches, where the "Bekennende Kirche" had to assert its administrative claims more or less illegally on the basis of emergency law through *Bruderräte*.[50] Hans Meiser also increasingly distanced himself from branches of the "Bekennende Kirche" existing within the "broken" churches.

Given the initial strong engagement of the Franconian Gau officials in the conflict, Meiser's reinstatement also meant a vote against the interests of regional party functionaries. Meiser's rehabilitation must have seemed a particularly bitter affront to Franconia's acting Gauleiter, Karl Holz. Even if Gauleiter Julius Streicher and then later his deputy, Karl Holz, gave way and attempted to interpret the end of the conflict in their own way, in the eyes of contemporary observers—especially in Franconia—the NSDAP had suffered a heavy loss. As background reports of the district governors reveal, those weeks in October changed the relationship between the population and the NSDAP in Franconia.[51] The esteem for Hitler, on the other hand, who had disciplined party fanatics who had presumably been acting on their own, was strengthened.[52]

Moreover, by attacking the Bavarian Provincial Church, the Reichskirche leadership had also overridden governmental agencies at the Reich and Provincial levels. The arrest of Meiser and the forceful measures taken in the Landeskirchenamt over the heads of the responsible governmental organizations was an affront committed by the Reichskirche administration against the Reich Interior Minister[53] and the Bavarian provincial government, in particular against Bavarian Prime Minister Siebert, who sympathized with Hans Meiser, as well as Reichsstatthalter Ritter von Epp, who had initially kept himself neutral only to then protest against the drastic steps taken against Meiser.[54]

Given the state's machinery of power, Hitler's decision in favor of Meiser can therefore also be seen as a massive loss of power and reputation for the Reichskirche administration and the Staff of the Deputy Führer. This meant the NSDAP's influence over church affairs had fundamentally shifted and, to a large extent, collapsed. Franz von Pfeffer was stripped of power on October 25; August Jäger resigned his offices on October 29, 1934, and completely vanished from the stage of church politics. Reichsbischof Müller emerged from the conflict as a repudiated man. At the same time, one can also discern a shift of agency away from the NSDAP to the state administration. Thus, the Reich Interior Minister, who had earlier been reluctant to reach a decision for days on end, suddenly and without consulting Rudolf Heß permitted the measures against Meiser to be lifted, once Hitler's invitation to Meiser became known.

The Bavarian Church Conflict in the autumn of 1934 reverberated beyond the areas of conflict immediately concerned. After all, it involved one of the very few public protests during the Nazi era where the regime ultimately backed down. Even if, in addition to the protests, a series of other factors played a significant role in the internal decision-making process as presented, contemporary observers must have formed the impression that, in this instance, a large section of the population had protested against the National Socialist effort to Nazify of the Protestant Provincial Church and that the outcome had reflected the protestors' demands. Regardless of whether, from today's perspective, one can reconstruct a chain of causality or not, the coincidence of protest and outcome had an effect. Long into the postwar era, the Church Conflict became a central locus memoriae (*Erinnerungsort*) of the Bavarian Protestant Church's resistance to Nazi rule.[55]

The SPD-in-exile immediately ascribed large importance in this sense to the Church Conflict of the fall of 1934. In an SPD report from October and November 1934 we find: "Let the old church leadership make their peace as well—whatever occurred worked, and the appearance of a struggle continues to work its effects. As in any struggle, this one also produced its own, distinctive ideology, its own concept of freedom, its own proclamations against tyrants, its sacrifices, and its own combative stance before which the actual issues receded."[56] No doubt this effect was what the regime most feared and responded to. Thus, in the beginning of November, Reich Interior Minister Frick forbade all publications in the secular and clerical press, pamphlets, and leaflets to broach the subject of church conflict.[57] The regime tried in this way to play down the consequences of the church conflict and to ban church political questions from public discussion.

For a long time, the National Socialist rulers harbored a deep suspicion on all questions touching on Protestant church politics. At the same time, the conflict made it unmistakably clear to many church representatives that their hope that the ascent of their own church could be tied to the rise of the new National Socialist Germany had been in vain.[58]

Christiane Kuller received her Ph.D. in Modern European History from Ludwig-Maximilians-University Munich in 2001. She subsequently worked as an Assistant Professor at LMU Munich, researching Aryanization and financial policy in Nazi Germany. Her recent book, *Bürokratie und Verbrechen: Antisemitische Finanzpolitik und Verwaltungspraxis im Nationalsozialistischen Deutschland* (Habilitation), published in 2013, was awarded the Fraenkel Prize 2012. Since 2013 she has been Professor for Contemporary History at the University of Erfurt.

Notes

1. Klaus Scholder, *Die Kirchen und das Dritte Reich*, vol. 2 (Berlin: Ullstein, 1985), 376.
2. Cf. Carsten Nicolaisen, "' . . . unseres Führers allergetreueste Opposition'. Hans Meiser als bayerischer Landesbischof im Kirchenkampf 1933–1945" in *Hans*

Meiser (1881–1956): Ein lutherischer Bischof im Wandel der politischen Systeme, eds. Gerhart Herold and Carsten Nicolaisen (Munich: Claudius Verlag, 2006), 32–52; Siegfried Hermle, "Spielräume kirchenleitenden Handelns—Marahrens, Meiser, Wurm im Vergleich" in *Spielräume des Handelns und der Erinnerung: Die Evangelisch-Lutherische Kirche in Bayern und der Nationalsozialismus*, eds. Berndt Hamm, Harry Oelke, and Gury Schneider-Ludorff (Göttingen: Vandenhoeck & Ruprecht 2010), 120–151; Helmut Baier, "Landesbischof Meiser und sein Umfeld. Netzwerke kirchenleitenden Handelns" in the same Vol., 99–119.

3. Cf. Paul Kremmel, *Pfarrer und Gemeinden im evangelischen Kirchenkampf in Bayern bis 1939: Mit besonderer Berücksichtigung der Ereignisse im Bereich des Bezirksamts Weißenburg in Bayern* (Lichtenfels: Kommissionsverlag Schulze, 1987), 366–368.
4. Letter of Helmut Kern, October 11, 1934, Landeskirchliches Archiv Nürnberg (LAELKB), Kreisdekan Ansbach 1/15/9. The letter arrived in the Bavarian Chancellary by way of the Nuremberg Chief of Police, Benno Martin, so the demonstration trains, which were to arrive a few days later in Munich, were no surprise to the Bavarian State Government.
5. Cf. Kremmel, *Pfarrer*, 392.
6. Kremmel, *Pfarrer*, 394.
7. Delegation statement from October 19, 1934, LAELKB, Personen XXXVI, 41.
8. Photos of the demonstrators in Armin Rudi Kitzmann, *Mit Kreuz und Hakenkreuz: Die Geschichte der Protestanten in München 1918–1945* (Munich: Claudius Verlag, 1999), 267.
9. Monthly Report of the Swabian and Neuburg Government, November 9, 1934, Geheimes Staatsarchiv München (GStAM), MA 106673, cited by Helmut Baier, *Die Deutschen Christen Bayerns im Rahmen des bayerischen Kirchenkampfes* (Nuremberg: Verein für Bayerische Kirchengeschichte, 1968), 155.
10. Radio announcements of various Bavarian police departments, printed in: Baier, *Deutschen Christen*, Dok. XXXX. 415 f.
11. Anne Lore Bühler, *Der Kirchenkampf im evangelischen München: Die Auseinandersetzung mit dem Nationalsozialismus und seinen Folgeerscheinungen im Bereich des Evang.-Luth; Dekanates München 1923–1950* (Nuremberg: Verein für Bayerische Kirchengeschichte, 1974), 85, based on personal communications with Gerhard Hildmann.
12. Baier, *Deutschen Christen*, 138.
13. Kremmel, *Pfarrer*, 366.
14. On October 17,1934, the ecclesiastical superintendents officially assumed their duties. Report of the Bayerischen Kultusministeriums, October 20, 1934, GStAM, MA 107291, cited in Baier, *Deutschen Christen*, 139.
15. There are only two photographs of Meiser taken probably around the time of his house arrest. The police apparently attempted to limit such images. Compare the Nachlass of Kurt Horn im LAELKB, whose camera was confiscated. Thanks to Jürgen König for this information.
16. Letter of Jäger to Pfarramt Gustenfelden, October 23, 1934, KK A 4/298, cited in Baier, *Deutschen Christen*, 138n 66.
17. Front page of *Fränkische Tageszeitung*, September 15, 1934.

18. Scholder, *Kirchen*, 358. The rally, contrary to the expectations of the organizers, became a declaration of loyalty to the Bishop.
19. Strictly confidential letter, "Süddeutscher Bund Evangelischer Christen" to Müller, October 22, 1934, cited in Baier, *Deutschen Christen*, 157.
20. Hans Schemm's position on dividing the Bavarian Church is in "Bayerische Ostmark," October 15, 1934, printed in: Baier, *Deutschen Christen*, Document XXXXIV, 417–419.
21. Concerning the meeting of October 17, 1934 and the corresponding order of Streicher of October 19, 1934, cf. Baier, *Deutschen Christen*, 147–149, and Kremmel, *Pfarrer*, 378f.
22. Cf. for example Kurt Meier, *Kreuz und Hakenkreuz: Die evangelische Kirche im Dritten Reich* (Munich: Deutscher Taschenbuch Verlag, 2001), 72–75, and John S. Conway, *The Nazi Persecution of the Churches 1933–1945* (London: Basic Books, 1968), 100; Ernst C. Helmreich, "The Arrest and Freeing of the Protestant Bishops of Württemberg and Bavaria, September–October 1934," *Central European History* 2, no. 2 (1969): 159–169.
23. Cf. Baier, *Deutschen Christen*, 128–173.
24. Vermerk of the Bavarian Ministerpräsident about the meeting with Reichsstatthalter on October 22, 1934, in *Dokumente zur Kirchenpolitik des Dritten Reiches*, vol. 2 (Munich: Kaiser Verlag, 1975), 185–190, citation, 190.
25. Citation, Siebert to Frick, October 15, 1934, printed in: *Dokumente zur Kirchenpolitik* II, 182f., and from October 20, 1934, cited in Scholder, *Kirchen*, 375f.
26. Scholder, *Kirchen*, 372.
27. Observations of Siebert, October 25 and 26, 1934, printed in *Dokumente zur Kirchenpolitik* II, 192f.
28. Baier, *Deutschen Christen*, 127.
29. Ian Kershaw, *Hitler*, vol. 1, *Herkunft—Aufstieg—Machtentfaltung 1889–1936*. (Munich: Taschenbuchverlag DTV, 2002), 723.
30. Cf. Ian Kershaw, *Public Opinion and Political Dissent in the Third Reich: Bavaria 1933–1945* (Oxford: Clarendon Press 2002), 174–176.
31. Scholder, *Kirchen*, 376; Kershaw, *Public Opinion*, 176.
32. Hans Meiser, *Kirche, Kampf und Christusglaube: Anfechtungen und Antworten eines Lutheraners*, ed. Fritz and Gertrude Meiser (Munich: Claudius-Verlag, 1982), 3; citation in Nicolaisen, *Opposition*, 44–46.
33. See Heinrich Schmid, *Apokalyptisches Wetterleuchten: Ein Beitrag der evangelischen Kirche zum Kampf im "Dritten Reich"* (Munich: Verlag der Evangelisch-lutherischen Kirche in Bayern, 1947), 62; Compare also notes of Meiser from March 13, 1934, in *Dokumente zur Kirchenpolitik* II, 79–81, where the citation is given as the formulation of Hitler.
34. Kershaw, *Public Opinion*, 177.
35. Deutschland-Bericht by the Sopade Nr. 7, October and November 1944, printed in *Deutschland-Berichte der sozialdemokratischen Partei Deutschlands (Sopade) 1934–1940*, 1934, ed. Klaus Behnken, 7. Edition (Frankfurt am Main: Zweitausendeins, 1989), 619–719, 717–19.
36. Citation from the letter of Siebert to Frick, October 15, 1934, printed in *Dokumente zur Kirchenpolitik* II, 182f.

37. Scholder, *Kirchen*, 376, 378.
38. Reichsinnenministerium to Lammers, October 18, 1934, BAB, R43 II/163, cited by Scholder, *Kirchen*, 379.
39. Scholder, *Kirchen*, 379, 394.
40. Ibid., 363, 395.
41. Ibid., 397.
42. There are only very sparse and patchy records of the journey from Meiser. Cf. eds. Hannelore Braun and Carsten Nicolaisen, *Verantwortung für die Kirche: Stenographische Aufzeichnungen und Mitschriften von Landesbischof Hans Meiser 1933–1955*, vol. 1 summer 1933 to summer 1935 (Göttingen: Vandenhoeck & Ruprecht, 1985), 347, n 65.
43. Report in "Völkischen Beobachter" Nr. 304, October 31, 1934.
44. LAELKB, Meiser 26, Cf. Helmut Baier and Ernst Henn, *Chronologie des bayerischen Kirchenkampfes, 1933–1945*, (Nuremberg Verein für Bayerische Kirchengeschichte, 1969), 93.
45. Gerhard Besier, *Die Kirchen und das Dritte Reich*, vol. 3: *Spaltungen und Abwehrkämpfe 1934–1937* (Berlin: Propyläen Verlag, 2001), 21.
46. *Akten der Parteikanzlei der NSDAP. Rekonstruktion eines verlorengegangenen Bestandes. Regesten*, vol. 1 eds. Helmut Heiber with Hildegard von Kotze, Gerhard Weiher, Ingo Arndt and Carla Mojto (Munich: Saur, 1983), 66f.
47. Report of Meiser to Siebert, November 2, 1934, printed in: *Dokumente zur Kirchenpolitik* II, Nr. 67/34, II.
48. Ibid.
49. Scholder, *Kirchen*, 394.
50. Nicolaisen, *Opposition*, 46 f.
51. Kershaw, *Public Opinion*, 178.
52. Ian Kershaw, *Der Hitler-Mythos. Führerkult und Volksmeinung* (Stuttgart: Deutsche Verlagsanstalt, 1999), 103.
53. Cf. Günter Neliba, *Der Legalist des Unrechtsstaates Wilhelm Frick: Eine politische Biographie* (Paderborn: Schöningh, 1992), 134.
54. From the Bavarian government, only Gauleiter and Minister of the Interior Adolf Wagner was involved in the operations.
55. Cf. Harry Oelke, "Kirchliche Erinnerungskultur im evangelischen Bayern: Landesbischof Hans Meiser und der Nationalsozialismus" in *Spielräume des Handelns und der Erinnerung: Die Evangelisch-Lutherische Kirche in Bayern und der Nationalsozialismus*, ed. Berndt Hamm, Harry Oelke, and Gury Schneider-Ludorff (Göttingen: Vandenhoeck & Ruprecht, 2010), 205–236.
56. *Sopade-Bericht 7*, 718.
57. Heinrich Hermelink, *Kirche im Kampf: Dokumente des Widerstands und des Aufbaus in der evangelischen Kirche Deutschlands von 1933 bis 1945* (Tübingen: Wunderlich, 1940), 190; Baier and Henn, *Chronologie*, 93.
58. Kershaw, *Public Opinion*, 179.

Chapter 4

The Catholic Church, Bishop von Galen, and "Euthanasia"

Winfried Süß

The subject of the church and its role in the murder of the sick under National Socialism is a broad field of research. It remains undisputed that the Christian churches emphatically condemned the mass murder of mentally handicapped human beings and protested in various ways against the Nazi "euthanasia." The subjects of controversy, however, are the participation of church-run institutions in the health-care policy of the National Socialists, the cooperative and collaborative relationships between church and dictatorship, the motive for church cooperation, and the timing and the impact of the church protests. Especially with regards to Catholic Christians, these topics are embedded in the discussion of the relationship between the church and the Nazi dictatorship, which has been ongoing for many years and has recently focused on the war years.[1] In comparison to the debate about the attitude of the Catholic Church toward National Socialism and the murder of the Jews, which is often waged with great passion but sometimes with a quite limited benefit for research, an analysis of the patterns of behavior exhibited by Catholic Christians when facing the murder of the sick seems more important to me. An analysis which understands governance as a function of social interactions can yield information about the functional mechanisms of a dictatorship supported by plebiscites, about the conditions of communication in a public sphere deformed by dictatorship and about the opportunities and limits of socially rooted protests against the actions of this dictatorship.[2]

The contribution of both Christian churches was substantial and crucial to the functioning of public health in Nazi Germany. It is therefore only possible to insightfully discuss the topic of the Catholic Church and "euthanasia" if we do so against the background of its position within the German health-care system. This position was based on traditions, patterns of behavior, and institutions of Christian charity, which reach back far into premodern times and had mostly found their institutional form in Germany during the course of the nineteenth century. Nazi rule and its internal and external war, Catholic patterns of behavior and institutions were positioned within a new context for which they were neither created nor prepared for.

Doubtlessly the contribution of both Christian churches toward German public health was immense, particularly during the war years. It included institutional resources, well-established administrative structures and financial means, but especially staff. At the start of the war just under a third of all civilian hospital beds and just under a sixth of all places in the institutions for people with mental disabilities were in Catholic church facilities. During the war between forty and sixty thousand beds for wounded soldiers were placed in Catholic facilities. The eminent importance of the churches becomes even clearer when looking at the non-physician staff, which was not only employed in the church's own institutions, but also in nursing care and the economic facilities of state and municipal hospitals. Of the approximately two-hundred thousand nurses in the German Reich, about ninety-five thousand belonged to the Catholic Caritas and about forty-five thousand to the Protestant Diakonie.[3] Put bluntly: Without the church's contribution to health-care the National Socialist war could hardly have been waged for six years.

Church-run institutions were closely intermeshed with the state welfare system regarding personnel and finances. This led to strong interdependencies. For instance, on the one hand church-run hospitals and military hospitals were able to work particularly cost-effectively, but on the other hand charitable monastic orders depended, among other things, on the economic benefits of providing health-care in order to subsidize other charitable areas of activity. Against this background the Catholic Church involved itself in the health-care sector mostly voluntarily. However it is not possible with deduce that the Catholic Church was in general agreement with National Socialism, to the health-care policy of the "Third Reich," or with the war unleashed. The involvement of the church in the health-care sector was based on patterns of behavior with roots far back in the pre-modern period. This includes a self-conception that saw service to the sick as an important part of religious practice. This charitable task of the churches was not put in doubt by the radical change in health policy after the National Socialist takeover. It even gained additional meaning: From the point of view of the churches (under increasing pressure after 1933) involvement in the health-care sector was one of their core areas of social activity, providing them with influence and legitimacy. For this reason the churches had an existential interest in preserving these important positions of influence.

Against the backdrop of such thinking the Catholic hierarchy was ready to adapt to the maxims of Nazi health-care policy to a considerable degree:

In the case of forced sterilization, the theological condemnation of this practice in the Papal encyclical Casti Conubii (1930) prevented any direct forms of cooperation. This resulted in an interdiction for Catholic physicians and nurses to take part in the preparation and the carrying out of sterilizations, a ruling that the Catholic bishops once again confirmed after the adoption of the "Gesetz zur Verhütung erbkranken Nachwuchses" (Law for the Prevention of Hereditarily Diseased Offspring) in July 1933.[4] In practice the general ban was avoided by the use of broad interpretations. In particular the definition of the term "prohibited participation" remained unclear and was left to the discretion of the individual bishops. Even though the bishops left no doubt as to their (in principle) strong opposition, they ultimately accommodated themselves with the practice of forced sterilizations and allowed Catholics to take part in them to an extensive degree. Otherwise the concern was that the church would lose important positions of influence in the health sector.[5] This gap between moral theological theory and health policy practice resulted in large scale insecurity among Catholic physicians and nurses regarding the behavior expected from the church and even the Nazi regime got the impression that the leadership of the Catholic Church in Germany was ready to come to an arrangement regarding this question.

With the beginning of the war new motives gained importance in the involvement of the church. Even if the Catholic bishops reacted in a reserved manner regarding the outbreak of the war, the fundamental pattern of patriotic loyalty predominated. Under the circumstances refusal to participate in the war was inconceivable to a large majority of Catholics, especially since any suspicions of national unreliability were to be avoided. In providing resources toward the care of wounded soldiers, Catholic Christians were also able to connect with nationalist legitimization models from World War I. This nationalism was mixed with a strong dose of anti-Bolshevism. This is evident, among other things, in the sermons of the bishop of Münster, Clemens August Graf von Galen: Within one and the same pastoral letter he both attacked the fundamental principles of the National Socialist *Volksgemeinschaft* (peoples community) ideology as well as praying "with a warm heart" for the "full-scale success" of the "struggle of the German army against godless Communism."[6]

During the course of the war another motive moved to the foreground: Now it was about preserving the institutional integrity of church-run organizations by moving parts of them into a Wehrmacht hospital or a civilian auxiliary hospital to protect them from the grasp of the Gestapo and the Nazi Party. The repercussions of this strategy on the patients in the sanatoriums and mental institutions were ambivalent and partially quite dangerous. On the one hand many mentally handicapped persons were thus able to receive places in a church-run institution where the living conditions and the chances of survival were usually better than in state psychiatric institutions. On the other hand the inclusion of a military hospital always entailed a worsening of the living conditions as auxiliary hospitals were usually set up in the best rooms available, leaving only the remainder of the buildings for the psychiatric patients to huddle together in. Finally, the admittance of patients from elsewhere into a Catholic institution could serve, among other things, as a trigger for patient transfers that ended in the "euthanasia" program and thus in death for mentally handicapped persons.

Clearly the relationship between the churches and the Nazi public health service is only imperfectly described by the term "cooperation," if only because the Nazi potentates were quite ambivalent about the involvement of the church. While the contribution of the church toward war health-care was emphatically called upon by the Nazi regime, National Socialist health politicians viewed charitable monastic orders as unwelcome competition. These institutions needed to be forced out in order to take away their legitimacy, which arose from the fact that they were taking part in the care of the sick. The key position occupied by the churches in the nursing field and especially in war health-care was thus soberly included into the planning of the Nazi regime. Its measures were mostly directed toward the goal of a total mobilization of all forces for the war, even if this came at the price of temporary concessions regarding the autonomy of church-run institutions. In this situation the churches and the Nazi regime were thus simultaneously competitors and cooperative partners. Accordingly, they inserted their partially convergent, partially divergent interests into their collaboration. Against this background, the relationship between the Catholic Church and the Nazi health service can be described as antagonistic cooperation.[7]

From the point of view of the churches, cooperation ended exactly at the point where health-care policy turned into the extermination of life. Here the position of the church was clear. In the case of the Catholic Church this included the strict condemnation of abortions on eugenic and racist grounds. Such abortions had been conducted in the German Reich on the mentally handicapped since 1934 without a legal basis and since 1943 increasingly also on pregnant forced laborers. According to the Catholic Church, abortions were considered as "the killing of human life."[8] Any participation was "strictly forbidden by divine law" according to the inculcation of Munich's Cardinal Faulhaber toward the nuns of his diocese. Unlike in the case of forced sterilizations, the leadership of the Catholic Church was not willing to compromise on this matter, even if this entailed the loss of Catholic positions in the health-care system. Cardinal Bertram, who otherwise attempted to reach compromises with the regime, told the Reich Ministry of the Interior, in no uncertain terms that the threat of withdrawing Catholic nuns from the hospitals could "not make an impression"[9] in this matter.

Any participation in the National Socialist "euthanasia" program was just as strictly forbidden. Since spring 1940 the bishops had reliable information from a number of sanatoriums and care institutions for people with mental disabilities that many of the transferred patients were dead within a short period of time. In the summer of 1940 the outlines of a systematic campaign of murder became visible and from fall 1940 onward the bishops possessed detailed information on the process flow of "euthanasia."[10] The churches and their charitable organizations were decisive for the assembly and dissemination of verified information about the murder of the sick, for they were the only organizations still to possess channels of communication independent of the regime in which dispersed regional information could be collected, summarized, and put together to form an overall picture. In the summer of 1940 the Bishops' Conference forbade "Catholic Health Facilities to actively participate in the movement of its patients in order to exterminate so-called unworthy life."[11] This meant that any assistance to the transfer of the sick from the sanatoriums and care institutions was forbidden, especially especially marking patients, administering tranquilizers, or traveling with transports. According to the detailed instructions of the bishops, only so-called "labors of love, which only aim at the spiritual and bodily well-being of the sick" were exempt.[12]

The position of the Catholic Church hierarchy toward the Nazi "euthanasia" murder of the mentally ill was clearly negative. But the way of defending the handicapped remained disputed within the Catholic hierarchy until the end of Nazi rule. Yet opposition to this program of eliminating what in Nazi lingo was "life unworthy of life" did not at first result in open protest or even institutionally supported resistance by the Catholic bishops. For some time individual bishops had posed the question of whether the statements of the bishops were only supposed to cover Catholic concerns or whether they must not push more broadly for the protection of the inherent "god-given original rights and freedoms"[13] belonging to every person within the National Socialist area of control. For a long time only a minority of bishops were in favor of this extension, which was especially advocated by Bishop Galen of Münster.[14] Only late in the war, as it became apparent that Germany could lose, were the bishops able to agree to such an encompassing mandate; this was done in the famous Decalogue pastoral letter of September 1943. Additionally there were considerable differences of opinion among the Catholic bishops about what forms of opposition should be taken to the Nazi regime. While Cardinal Bertram and other, mostly older bishops chose the traditional form of articulating protests to authorities by letter even in the case of the "euthanasia" murders, Bishop Konrad von Preysing of Berlin and Bishop von Galen advocated conducting the conflict between the church and the Nazi regime more publicly. However von Galen's influence within the community of the bishops was not large since he was one of the youngest members of the Bishops' Conference and was considered a theological lightweight.[15] Additionally the (historically formed) high value ascribed to united action by the bishops worked against quick changes of course regarding such a fundamental question, since it required compromise necessary in order to include the bishops with the lowest readiness to engage in conflict. Individual bishops and even the Fulda Bishops' Conference had intervened repeatedly with the Reich government since the summer of 1940 by several letters in order to stop the murders, without receiving a reaction. In July 1941 the Fulda Bishops' Conference finally reacted with a joint public pastoral letter. However it was so vaguely formulated that it was hardly recognizable as dissent, and thus it carried little influence. For this reason it also did not resonate much among the population.

In July and August 1941 the bishop of Münster took a different path. In a series of three sermons carefully referenced to each other in language and leitmotivs, Clemens August von Galen turned against the dictatorship's harassment of Catholic institutions, the limitations on the practice of religion, and the encroachments on church-owned property. In the third sermon given on August 3, 1941, in the Lamberti Church in Münster / Westphalia he decried "euthanasia" with drastic words and described it as murder. The bishop told his audience that "many unexpected deaths of the mentally ill" were being "caused intentionally" and sharply turned against "the terrible doctrine . . . which intends to justify the murder of innocents" and "in principle enables . . . the violent killing . . . of the incurably sick."[16] Subsequently he described the consequences resulting from the National Socialist practice of making the right to life of the sick dependent on their use to the *Volksgemeinschaft*. "If," von Galen said in the conjunctive mood, "one applies the tenet . . . that one may kill an 'unproductive' fellow human being, then woe to us all when we become old and decrepit! . . . woe to our good soldiers,"[17] who return home wounded.

What motivated the bishop to seek a public confrontation with the regime precisely during the summer of 1941? The immediate trigger was the imminent removal of mentally ill patients from the Marienthal mental institution near Münster. Von Galen protested exactly at the moment the murder of the sick reached his Diocese. This reaction fits with what we know about how he saw his role as a bishop. Von Galen understood his office as a bishop as a sentinel position and "as an annunciator and defender of the legal and moral order desired by God which confers original rights and freedoms on every individual"[18]; he felt he had a calling "to boldly stand in for the authority of law" when evil reached his diocese. However we also know that von Galen was unhappy about the reaction of the Catholic Church leadership to the murder of the sick. The bishop of Münster had been advocating no longer "contenting oneself . . . with ineffective paper complaints"[19] and had instead called upon his fellow bishops to make the conflict public. He asked his colleague Bishop Wilhelm Berning of Osnabrück the question whether the church could continue taking the responsibility for leading the defensive struggle "in the present almost passive manner," especially since the regime was interpreting restraint as weakness. Von Galen emphasized that until then his trust in the "experience and virtue" of the older bishops had prevented him from pushing ahead in this question of an "escape into the open," and that he would "soon no longer be able to calm" his conscience "with such arguments 'ex authoritate.'"

Galen already had some experience with public protests. Previously, in 1936, in a memorandum for Cardinal Secretary of State Eugenio Pacelli, he had advocated "stepping into the public sphere at every opportunity" to "protest openly against every new infringement of the rights and the freedom of the Church."[20] He had successfully practiced this form of confrontation which had mobilized the Catholic milieu in 1936–1937 during the Oldenburg crucifix struggle and had inflicted a painful defeat on the Nazi regime. Galen's series of sermons in July/August 1941 was not spontaneous but had been carefully prepared by the bishop and his staff.[21] There is some evidence that von Galen also took his protest into the public sphere because he had realized that, due to the hardline position of Cardinal Bertram, no decisive and public protest of the Bishops' Conference against "euthanasia" would materialize.[22]

Since a number of points addressed by the bishop in his sermons concerned encroachments against the Catholic Church it has been argued that the protest against the "euthanasia" murders had not actually been his main aim. The decisive motive had been concern that large-scale confiscations of Catholic institutions by Himmler's Gestapo would occur in Münster and its environs under the pretext of the necessities of war. The protest against "euthanasia" had thus mostly been self-protective of his own catholic milieu.[23] But von Galen did not understand his protest as an explicitly "Catholic concern."[24] Secular and ecclesiastical rights and liberties were co-referential and insolubly linked to each other for the bishop. Further von Galen had already advocated extending the mandate of the church to general questions of human rights since the early 1930s. This distinguishes him markedly from the majority of the bishops who advocated a defensive position on the basis of the Concordat in order to primarily protect Catholic concerns.[25]

In his series of sermons von Galen emphasized that Catholic concerns and important interdenominational grievances were interrelated, and he connected them with the objections against the murder of the sick. He developed a position opposite that of National Socialist morality which declared the welfare of the individual subordinate to the interests of the *Volkskörper* (the organism of the people as a whole). He demanded no less than a return to a social consensus in which core norms of the National Socialist *Volksgemeinschaft* would have no place: the rule of law, basic rights of the individual founded in natural law, and a profession of Christianity. Even if von Galen excluded open resistance against the regime, his sermons challenged the moral foundations of Nazi rule to such a degree that faithful Catholics hardly retained any room for maneuver regarding forms of cooperation with the regime. The conflict was about fundamental questions. In this sense von Galen's protest far exceeded Catholic concerns in the strict sense and was directed against the basis of National Socialist rule.

The speed by which von Galen's sermons reached their readers is remarkable. By the end of September the Gestapo estimated that they could be found "in all sections of the population and in diverse regions"[26] of the German sphere of influence—literally from Africa up to the Arctic Circle, where they caused unrest among the soldiers.[27] Von Galen's protest also met with vivid interest among the Allies: in October 1941 reports were circulating in the British government about the "extraordinarily courageous and outspoken sermons" of the "Catholic Niemöller" from Münster.[28] The sermons probably reached President Roosevelt's desk in February 1942.[29]

The sermons first circulated among Westphalian Catholics closely connected to the church. Individual copies passed from hand to hand among trusted friends. As early as September 1941 the Gestapo had indications that von Galen's sermon against the murder of the sick was also circulating among the Protestant population.[30] Often the texts were passed on by Catholic priests by request of their Protestant colleagues. The intact communication networks of the Catholic Church and its milieu organizations were particularly decisive for regional and super-regional distribution in the days immediately after the sermons were delivered. The sermon texts did not reach many priests through official church channels, arriving instead from "sources unknown."[31] Unlike Episcopal pastoral letters, the reading of the "euthanasia" sermon during services was not made obligatory. It took place, partly by order of rural Deaneries, and partly on the initiative of the parish priests reacting to requests from the congregation.[32] The spread of protest against "euthanasia" were thus propagated in many ways: Through the spoken word, from the pulpit to selective public of church services, in copies of the sermons that were being passed on secretively, and as part of the discourse within the Catholic milieu that stabilized the prevailing worldview against the murders. The content of the sermons soon seeped into the general public from its source in the Catholic milieu, the "*Gemeindeöffentlichkeit*"[33] (the public sphere of the parish), by way of situational contacts such as at the workplace and in the air raid shelter. This was very risky in cases where the transmission of the texts left the safety zone of trustworthy social contacts, as is attested by more than thirty related Gestapo cases though the end of 1941.[34]

Small groups with a strong Catholic bent produced small print runs, mostly by way of typewritten carbon copies, which they circulated within the milieu communication networks of the family and among acquaintances.[35] The main burden of duplication was born by groups that had formed under the protection of the parishes. Some of these groups were based on the networks of the spectrum of elitist Catholic youth groups that had been pushed into illegality, for instance the *Sturmschar*; others were recruited among altar boys and parish youth groups. Often these groups would meet up in chaplain and vicar residences, i.e. at the centers of life of the young clergy.[36] Therefore the Catholic protest against the murder of the sick was also an act of rebellion by youth against the National Socialist dictatorship.

Apart from small-scale forms of text distribution along trusted communication lines, more anonymous forms of dissemination such as postal dispatch and leaving copies of the sermons in trains also possessed a certain importance. They made the sermon texts known outside of Westphalia. Another path of distribution probably underestimated so far was the transmission of the sermons to members of the Wehrmacht through army postal service letters, the secret dispersion of the texts in field hospitals, but also distribution through persons on home leave who sometimes had been explicitly asked to acquire copies of Galen's sermons by their units.[37] From the second half of October 1941 onward, the Allies made the texts of Galen's sermons known in Germany by leaflets and radio. However, since information about the National Socialist murder of the sick was already widely disseminated in the German population at this stage, these new sources of information supported and strengthened existing popular knowledge.[38]

The communication networks of the Catholic milieu thus contributed decisively to the dissemination of the sermon texts. Rudiments of a situational alternate public sphere can be discerned here that successfully undermined the communication monopoly of the Nazi dictatorship and generated solidarity at the edge of the Catholic milieu in persons from other segments of the population. This finding is remarkable as newer social history research has presupposed that the Catholic milieu eroded and lost cohesion during the dictatorship. Even in places where the milieus remained intact as spaces for retreat from general society, the perspective of experiential history shows that they remained part of German society as a whole and could thus not escape being touched by the political and cultural changes of Nazi rule. The capability of the Catholic milieu to mobilize resistance against the Nazi dictatorship has thus been rated quite reservedly by recent scholarship. Detlef Schmiechen-Ackermann, for instance, argues that the price that had to be paid for the consolidation of the core milieu was the increasing driving out of Catholics closely affiliated with the church from the general public, so that any potential resistance hardly possessed any opportunities to unfold openly.[39] Such findings should be complemented by a more dialectic point of view. This emphasis on the general trend of a decreasing integration of the Catholic milieu should be complemented with greater attention to its persistent capability to mobilize and inquiries into the specific contexts of Catholic mobilization.

As for the impact of Bishop von Galen probably no other protest action against the Nazi regime created such a stir: von Galen's third sermon had a particularly strong impact. It evoked tumultuous protests among the congregants in the Lamberti Church.[40] The sermon also drew considerable attention beyond the city limits of Münster. When was read out in the churches of the diocese in the following weeks it caused a dramatic loss of reputation for the regime, which was especially directed against the Nazi Party. According to a letter written to the military district command, "hope and belief in the blessings of the Party" were melting away "like snow in the sun" since the "euthanasia" crimes became known.[41] Leaflets and anonymous letters drew unflattering comparisons between National Socialist Germany and Bolshevist Russia and called for passive resistance in the name of the bishop.[42] Circulating rumors positioned the bishop in direct opposition to the representatives of the National Socialist repressive apparatus. Misconceptions continued to persist which placed the popular bishop beside the Wehrmacht as a representative of traditional morals and which suspected an alliance of the church and the military against National Socialism.[43] According to another rumor the Gestapo had to leave empty-handed when they wanted to arrest the bishop after he donned his vestments.[44] All of this points to persistent mobilization against the regime.

The sweeping super-regional effect of a series of sermons in a West German provincial town demands an explanation. It would be too simple to identify disclosure, the element most typical of scandal, as the sole reason for the effectiveness of the sermons, since the series of judicial and administrative reports clearly show that the secrecy enacted by the regime had already been threatened for some time. Information about the "euthanasia" program had seeped into the population by summer 1940 and was widely dispersed by early 1941 at the latest.⁴⁵ The majority of the German population opposed the "euthanasia" program. While there were isolated consenting statements,⁴⁶ even loyal Nazi Party members felt as if "the ground was being taken away beneath their feet"⁴⁷ according to a high-ranking functionary in the Nazi Women's League—the murderous event simply seemed too horrible.

Still, protests from the population against "euthanasia" remained rare exceptions, aside from a few critical statements by courageous physicians and lawyers as well as petitions by desperate relatives.⁴⁸ This cannot only be explained by the systematic terror of the regime against dissenters, but rather by the specific nature of the information about "euthanasia," for knowledge about the murder of the sick was selective and often without any discernible contexts. Additionally this information was distributed very unequally throughout the population. Networks of devout Christians played an important role in the collection and dissemination of such tidings. Their information mostly stemmed from second- or third-hand reports, i.e. they were rumors and therefore belonged to an uncertain and quite inconsequential category of information. This also explains why earlier church protests did not result in consequences similar to those of von Galen's sermons, for his sermon on August 3, 1941, was not the first public protest against "euthanasia." Previously a number of priests and at least one Catholic bishop, Wilhelm Berning of Osnabrück, had protested during services that "the protection of human life"⁴⁹ was no longer being honored in Germany. And even von Galen himself had made an addition in a pastoral letter by the German bishops in which he voiced the suspicion that numerous deaths among psychiatric patients had been induced intentionally.⁵⁰ But all this resulted in hardly more than short-term local reactions among churchgoers. Therefore the question has to be addressed as to which special conditions were responsible for the fact that the protest of the bishop of Münster reverberated so strongly.

An important hint can be found in an analysis of the rumors circulating about the bishop of Münster after the sermons. Even though these rumors were only loosely connected with historical facts, they still point toward the decisive effect of the sermons. Von Galen's protest against "euthanasia" polarized the German population, parts of which became estranged from the regime. He initiated discussion processes that questioned the National Socialist model of a structured public sphere limited to passive consent. Such reactions were by no means only approving. While some praised the "manfulness"⁵¹ and "courageous appearance"⁵² of the bishop, who "despite all dangers had the courage to express what has been strongly depressing all upright and devout people in Germany for a long time,"⁵³ others reacted with incredulous amazement and outrage about a Catholic bishop who was "committing sabotage against the work of the Führer"[54] and yet remained unpunished.

Such discussion processes were hardly reconcilable with the National Socialist ideal of a politically structured *Volksgemeinschaft*. They also had a strong delegitimizing effect on core areas of National Socialist social policy. In the long term the public face of the Nazi regime lost a lot of its luster. An artisan from Paderborn, for example, asked who would be interested in a generous reform of the pension system that was announced for the time after the end of the war if the future beneficiaries had to expect to be killed before receiving anything.[55] Trust in the health service in particular suffered a deep crisis from the disclosure of the murder of the sick from which it did not recover until the end of the war. Von Galen's protest thus exerted its effect less via the disclosures typical of scandal, but rather mostly by awakening the topic of "euthanasia" from a phase of latency. Probably the most important and long-lasting effect of his sermon was the removal of the discursive taboo from the murder of the sick. By openly denouncing the state crime of "euthanasia" without any counter-reaction from the regime, he created the space for a more extensive debate of the topic in the general population. A widespread opinion held that, if the bishop "was not arrested for his utterances, then every German is entitled to speak about the matter."[56]

It is also important that the series of sermons was addressed to a population open to criticism due to the events of the war. Apart from the alarming news from the Eastern front, heavy air raids in North and West German cities, and the displeasure at the confiscation of monastic institutions in the Catholic part of the population shaped public opinion.[57] This had to appear threatening to an elite leadership that relied on repeatedly reestablishing a plebiscitary consensus between the regime and the population. Goebbels thus expected "a not only materially, but also psychologically critical winter."[58]

The special explosiveness of the episcopal protest in this situation was based on the fact that von Galen linked the outrage about the failure of the regime in the management of the repercussions of the air war and the uproar about Himmler's attack of the Catholic cloisters with his opposition to the murder of the sick. In this manner three event complexes were merged into one scandal in the perception of the population: A government no longer capable of guaranteeing the security of its citizens, an administration acting without legal foundation, a health system turning its purpose on its head by killing patients. Against this background something seemed even more ominous than the killing of the sick—namely, its potential enlargement, which would not only affect the isolated group of mentally handicapped persons in the sanatoriums and mental institutions, but potentially any German. This was a fundamental difference between the transfer of psychiatric patients and the deportation of Jews, which large segments of the population faced with indifference. That the old, invalids, and the war wounded were endangered by "euthanasia" was only hinted at in the conjunctive mood by the bishop. It was precisely this possibility only hinted at by the bishop in the conjunctive mood, which opponents and adherents of the regime perceived as a statement of fact—this is what stuck in their heads as the essence of the sermon. This was expressed in an SD report, which summarized the sermon in its concise heading, "Bishop of Münster—Killing of Wounded Soldiers."[59] This shift of emphasis exacerbated the explosiveness of the protest from the pulpit decisively by tying motives of opposition due to a worldview with a concrete protest event, which was hard to justify even within the context of National Socialist values.

Galen's public protest posed a challenge to the dictatorship. In the eyes of the National Socialist rulers the bishop had crossed a line with his sermons. In mid-August 1941 Joseph Goebbels dictated angrily into his diary that the bishop of Münster had "given an impertinent and provoking speech" and had claimed "that our Euthanasia endeavors extend so far that wounded persons no longer usable for practical work are being murdered by us."[60] He considered von Galen's "herding services for the enemy" a "Dolchstoß [stab] in the back of the fighting front" and "a crime ripe for the state prosecutor." Yet von Galen was not brought to justice; on the contrary: Hardly three weeks after the fiery sermon by the bishop of Münster Hitler ordered a stop to "Aktion T4" and thus ended the first phase of mass murder of adult psychiatric patients.

There has been a long dispute in scholarship as to whether there was a direct connection between von Galen's sermons and the discontinuation of "Aktion T4."[61] However available evidence shows that there is a causal connection.[62] Four suppositions were the basis for the decision to end the program, suppositions that partially relied on misperceptions by the Nazi regime. The first, probably decisive misperception was that the National Socialist leadership understood von Galen's series of sermons as the beginning of a "confrontation at any price"[63] and classified early indications of a targeted dissemination of the texts as an indication of a new conflict strategy with which the Catholic bishops were reacting to Himmler's attack on the cloisters.[64] As shown above this was quite probably a misinterpretation. The unrealistic thinking about their enemy exhibited by the Nazi regime saw the Catholic Church as more cohesive and more ready for opposition than it actually was. This miscalculation had far-reaching repercussions. It not only increased the political costs of attempts to coerce von Galen considerably, but also changed the perspective of the conflict decisively by connecting it with policy toward the church. Rather than a diffuse unrest among the population due to the murder of the sick, the regime feared a long-term conflict founded on milieu organizations, controlled by the church hierarchy, and waged by way of the communication channels of the church—ergo not only through the scandal's own momentum, but also through its channelisation by a countervailing power. A second miscalculation was that the political decision-makers assumed that von Galen had described the killing of soldiers wounded in battle as fact rather than as a possibility, for a Gestapo report had mixed up the indicative and the conjunctive mood and had ascribed to von Galen the literal claim that "mental patients, other sick persons and invalids"[65] as well as war-wounded persons were "being transported away . . . to be killed." Thirdly they reckoned that a dissemination of the accusations was not preventable, even if the Gestapo made every endeavor to arrest the propagators of the sermons. Fourthly they were certain that the population believed the statements of the Catholic dignitary.[66] It was clear that the Gauleiter of Münster could not decide the matter by himself and that the Reich authorities and Party offices concerned with propaganda and church policy as well as ultimately Hitler had to be consulted.

In the process of decision-making, the horizon of expectations of the political leadership which was shaped by these misinterpretations as well as the regime's need for legitimization limited the options for action available to the Nazi rulers. Against this background the option to arrest von Galen and banish him from his diocese, similar to what had been done during the Kulturkampf of the nineteenth century, was raised by a number of offices, but was finally rejected. After lengthy discussion the proposal of the Party Chancellery to charge the unruly bishop in a show trial and sentence him to death was also dismissed, even though initially Hitler had apparently considered "making an example" of this disorderly bishop.[67] Goebbels did not consider either measure promising, for if violence was exercised against the bishop, especially the death penalty, the outbreak of a fundamental conflict would have to be expected which would not only bring the Westphalians but also large segments of Catholic Germany into open opposition against the National Socialist state. Hitler's propaganda minister calculated coolly that, at the moment, the regime could not prevail in a "tooth and nail struggle,"[68] while it would be easy to settle the whole matter after a successful conclusion of the war. For this reason Goebbels tried to convince Bormann and Himmler to suspend anti-church measures for a limited time and not let the conflict with the bishop escalate. In this way he sought to secure the potential legitimacy and resources offered by churches loyal to the political system for the regime and simultaneously gain more influence on matters of church policy.[69]

The propaganda minister also saw little promise in the option of meeting the sermons of the bishop with a propaganda campaign since in the meantime it seemed near impossible to generally deny the murder of the sick. Here von Galen's protest had decisively curtailed the communication strategies available to the regime. A public rebuke of the allegation that brain-damaged soldiers were being murdered just like mentally handicapped persons would have required informing the population about the main features of "euthanasia" and subsequently developing a nuanced argumentation that would have clearly distinguished between the actual murder of the sick, which the regime considered justifiable, and the alleged murder of soldiers, which even in the eyes of the regime was unjustifiable.[70] It is characteristic that the regime only made use of propaganda in this matter very sparingly. Counter-propaganda mostly took place in closed Party meetings, but even here Goebbels' foot soldiers had to experience that the audience debated the pros and cons of "euthanasia" and protested when accusations were personally addressed at the bishop or posed counter-questions "which got the speaker into real trouble."[71]

In a number of conversations with Goebbels and with Heinrich Lammers, the chief of the Reich Chancellery, Hitler had to recognize that one of the fundamental prerequisites of his risk calculation in the implementation of "euthanasia" no longer applied, for he had expected that the murder of the sick would be organized "without the public . . . being informed about it"[72] and that the public would "not be disturbed . . . by [occasional] leaked tidings." The church protests unequivocally showed the dictator that the veil of secrecy over the murder of the sick had been torn and could no longer be repaired. They also demonstrated that "euthanasia" could not be the subject of a consensus in wide segments of the German population and that the regime had to expect further resistance from the Catholic Church in this matter.[73] Thus only a third option remained for the dictatorship: In order not to endanger the unity of the population during the war against the Soviet Union, on August 19, 1941, Hitler decided in future to reduce the psychological "burdens of the war . . . to a minimum."[74] A few days later he ordered the cessation of both the *Klostersturm* as well as "Aktion T4."

The history of the impact of von Galen's sermons shows us that a protest strategy relying on an alternate public sphere could be successful in a "consensus dictatorship"[75] since time and time again it relied on the plebiscitary establishment of consensus between the regime and the population. Von Galen's public protest forced the Nazi rulers to act in cases in which church protests had previously been ignored or had been suppressed administratively. The regime did not recognize the legitimacy of the protest, but left the accuser untouched and quietly removed the visible part of the scandal. In this way the clockwork of extermination was stopped for more than a year and the murder program for adult psychiatric patients, which so far had claimed more than seventy thousand lives, was interrupted before it returned to the sanatoriums and mental institutions in a better disguised form. From this point of view the protest of the bishop of Münster achieved more than any other protest action against the Nazi dictatorship. For a decisive moment he was able to limit the political room for maneuver of the Nazi regime severely and endanger the social basis of its reign. From the contemporary point of view Hitler's decision to discontinue "euthanasia" was, however, less far-reaching than it may seem from today's perspective. The regime reacted to a competing worldview that had demonstrated its ability to mobilize its adherents with a partial withdrawal and a tabling of the conflict—from the perspective of a leadership that considered "final victory" to be within its grasp in the summer of 1941, it was not a price too large to pay for the undisturbed mobilization of the German population for the campaign of conquest in the East. And it has to be emphasized that the success of Bishop von Galen's protest was only possible due to the concurrence of many attendant circumstances. Others paid for their objection to "euthanasia" with Gestapo confinement and even their lives—for instance, four clergymen from Lübeck who had disseminated the sermons of Bishop von Galen and were sentenced to death by the *Volksgerichtshof* in 1943.[76]

Winfried Süß is senior research fellow and project director at the Center for Contemporary History in Potsdam. He has taught as assistant professor at the University of Munich (1999–2005), as a guest professor for comparative welfare state research at the University of Göttingen (2012–2013), and as a guest professor for Modern European History at the University of Wuppertal (2013–2014). Süß is co-editor of the peer-reviewed journals *Beiträge zur Geschichte des Nationalsozialismus* and *Zeitschrift für Sozialreform/Journal of Social Policy Research*. His books include *Der "Volkskörper" im Krieg: Gesundheitspolitik, medizinische Versorgung und Krankenmord im nationalsozialistischen Deutschland 1939–1945* (Munich 2003), *Das "Dritte Reich": Eine Einführung*, edited with Dietmar Süß, 3rd ed. (Munich 2009), and *Soziale Ungleichheit im Sozialstaat: Großbritannien und die Bundesrepublik im Vergleich*, edited with Hans Günter Hockerts (Munich 2010).

Notes

1. For an overview of the current state of research, see Christoph Kösters, "NS-Vergangenheit und Katholizismusforschung: Ein Beitrag zur Erinnerungskultur und Zeitgeschichtsschreibung nach 1945," *Zeitschrift für Kirchengeschichte* 120 (2009): 27–57; Karl-Joseph Hummel and Christoph Kösters, eds., *Kirchen im Krieg:*

Europa 1939–1945 (Paderborn: F. Schöningh, 2007). Translated from the German by Giles Wesley Bennett.
2. Cf. Alf Lüdtke, ed., *Herrschaft als soziale Praxis: Historische und sozial-anthropologische Studien* (Göttingen: Vandenhoeck & Ruprecht, 1991).
3. Cardinal Adolf Bertram to the Reich Chancellery, July 8, 1939, Archiv des Deutschen Caritasverbandes [Archive of the German Caritas Association], Freiburg (ADCV), 357+544, 01; Statistics about the war effort of the Catholic Church in Germany, August 12, 1943, in Ludwig Volk, ed., *Akten Deutscher Bischöfe über die Lage der Kirche 1933–1945*, vol. 6: *1943–1945* (Mainz: Matthias-Grünewald-Verlag, 1985), 125.
4. Ingrid Richter, *Katholizismus und Eugenik in der Weimarer Republik und im Dritten Reich. Zwischen Sittlichkeitsreform und Rassenhygiene* (Paderborn: F. Schöningh, 2001).
5. Pfaffenbüchler to Faulhaber, May 3, 1934, Archiv des Erzbistums München und Freising [Archive of the Archbishopric of Munich and Freising], Munich (AEM), Faulhaber Papers, 8381.
6. Pastoral letter by von Galen, September 14, 1941, in Ludwig Löffler, ed., *Clemens August Graf von Galen: Akten, Briefe, Predigten 1933–1946*, 2 vols. (Mainz: Matthias-Grünewald-Verlag, 1988), vol. 2, 907.
7. Winfried Süß, "Antagonistische Kooperationen: Katholische Kirche und nationalsozialistische Gesundheitspolitik" in Hummel and Kösters, *Kirchen*, 317–341.
8. Faulhaber to the Superior General of the Sisters of Mercy/Munich, January 28, 1944, AEM, Faulhaber Papers, 8384.
9. Bertram to the Reich Minister of the Interior, March 6, 1943, AEM, Faulhaber Papers, 8384.
10. Galen to Bertram, July 28, 1940, in Ludwig Volk, ed., *Akten deutscher Bischöfe über die Lage der Kirche 1933–1945*, vol. 5, *1940–1942* (Mainz: Matthias-Grünewald-Verlag, 1983), 78; Report by Neuhäusler, late October 1940, ibid. 235–237.
11. Excerpt from the protocol of the Fulda Bishops Conference, August 20–22, 1940, ADCV, 732.27.
12. David to the Cloister Commissioners and Superiors General of the monks and nuns active in the sanatoriums and mental institutions of the Cologne Archdiocese, August 31, 1941, ADCV, 732.27.
13. Pastoral letter by the German Catholic Bishops, June 26, 1941, in Volk, *Akten Deutscher Bischöfe*, vol. 5: 1940–1942, 466.
14. Cf. e.g. Galen's Memorandum, July 31, 1937, in Ludwig Volk, ed., *Akten Kardinal Michael von Faulhabers*: vol. 2: 1935–1945 (Mainz: Matthias-Grünewald-Verlag, 1984), 385.
15. On von Galen's position among the German bishops see Maria Anna Zumholz, "Clemens August Graf von Galen und der deutsche Episkopat 1933–1945" in *Clemens August Graf von Galen: Neue Forschungen zum Leben und Wirken des Bischofs von Münster*, ed. Joachim Kuropka (Münster: Verlag Regensberg, 1992), 179–220; for newer summaries of research on Galen cf. Thomas Flammer, Barbara Schüler, and Hubert Wolf, eds, *Clemens August von Galen: Ein Kirchenfürst im Nationalsozialismus* (Darmstadt: Wissenschaftliche Buchgesellschaft, 2007); Joachim Kuropka, ed., *Streitfall Galen: Studien und Dokumente* (Münster: Aschendorff, 2007).

16. Löffler, *Galen-Akten*, vol. 2, 876.
17. Ibid., p. 878.
18. Sermon, July 13, 1941, Löffler, *Galen-Akten*, vol. 2, 848.
19. Von Galen to Berning, May 26, 1941, in Löffler, *Galen-Akten*, vol. 2, 838.
20. Memorandum by von Galen for Cardinal Secretary of State Pacelli, March 1936, quoted in Hubert Wolf, *Clemens August Graf von Galen: Gehorsam und Gewissen* (Freiburg i. Br.: Herder, 2006), 103.
21. Next to the homilist Adolf Donders it was mostly Galen's Cathedral Chaplain Portmann who provided ideas. Wolf, *von Galen*, 113f.
22. The possibility that von Galen had previously discussed his step into the public sphere at least with some of the bishops is suggested by Archbishop Gröber's request for Faulhaber "to direct his attention to the situation in Münster and make sure that there would be unity among the Bavarian bishops in case of action against Münster." Gröber to Faulhaber, July 30, 1941, AEM, Faulhaber Papers, 3360.
23. Beth A. Griech-Polelle, *Bishop von Galen: German Catholicism and National Socialism* (New Haven, CT: Yale University Press, 2002), 59f., 78.
24. Sermon, July 13, 1941, in Löffler, *Galen-Akten*, vol. 2, 849.
25. Heinz Hürten, "Katholische Kirche und Widerstand" in *Widerstand gegen den Nationalsozialismus*, ed. Peter Steinbach and Johannes Tuchel (Berlin: Akademie Verlag, 1994), 182–192, 187–189.
26. Report by the Inspekteur der Sipo und des SD, August 20, 1941, in Joachim Kuropka, ed., *Meldungen aus Münster 1924–1944: Geheime und vertrauliche Berichte von Polizei, Gestapo, NSDAP und ihren Gliederungen, staatlicher Verwaltung, Gerichtsbarkeit und Wehrmacht über die politische und gesellschaftliche Situation in Münster* (Münster: Verlag Regensberg, 1991), 542.
27. Hermann L. to the episcopal press office in Münster, May 15, 1991, Bistumsarchiv [Episcopal Archive] Münster (BAM), von Galen Collection, 77; Burgard to Portmann October 16, 1945, BAM, Portmann Papers, A 16.
28. Notes on the situation of the church in Europe, October 31, 1941, Public Record Office London, Inf. 1/760, Roman Catholic Section.
29. William J. Donovan, Memorandum to the President, February 19, 1942, National Archives Washington, RG 22 M 1642, Roll 22.
30. Report by the Inspekteur der Sipo und des SD, September 24, 1941, in Kuropka, *Meldungen*, 545.
31. Deanery Dinslaken to Portmann, September 21, 1945, BAM, Portmann Papers, A 16.
32. Hüntmann to Portmann, November 4, 1945, BAM, Portmann Papers, A 16.
33. Detlef Schmiechen-Ackermann, "Katholische Diaspora zwischen Rückzug und Selbstbehauptung in der NS-Zeit: Überlegungen zum Verhältnis von Milieubildung und Widerstandspotentialen am Fallbeispiel von Hannover," *Geschichte in Wissenschaft und Unterricht* 49 (1998): 462–476, 471.
34. The figure only includes indications that can be dated exactly and explicitly relate to this topic as derived from the Meldungen wichtiger staatspolizeilicher Ereignisse of the Reichssicherheitshauptamt, Institut für Zeitgeschichte, Munich (IfZ), MA/442/1 and as well as from Ulrich Hehl, *Priester unter Hitlers Terror: Eine biographische und statistische Erhebung.* (Mainz: Matthias-Grünewald-Verlag, 1998).

35. Gertrud H. to the episcopal press office in Münster, May 3, 1991, BAM, von Galen Collection, 77; Maria L. to the episcopal press office in Münster, May 11, 1991, BAM, ibid.
36. Havixbeck Parish to Portmann, November 17, 1945, BAM, Portmann Papers, A 16.
37. Deanery Ibbenbüren to Portmann, October 16, 1945, BAM, Portmann Papers, A 16.
38. Reichssicherheitshauptamt, Meldungen wichtiger staatspolizeilicher Ereignisse, November 5, 1941, BAB, R 58, 195; transcription of the BBC lunch program by the Deutsche Nachrichtenbüro, October 19, 1941, appendix to the Report by the Gauleitung Westfalen-Nord, October 1941, in Kuropka, *Meldungen*, 553.
39. Schmiechen-Ackermann, "Katholische Diaspora," 462–476.
40. Hildegard B. an die Bischöfliche Pressestelle Münster, July 24, 1991, BAM, Sammlung von Galen, 77.
41. Franz Bergmann (pseudonym) to the chief of staff of the general command of the VI Army Corps, September 8, 1941, Bundesarchiv-Miliärarchiv Freiburg, RW 14, 11.
42. Letter to the police president in Münster, copy in the weekly Report by the Inspekteur der Sipo und des SD, August 14, 1941, Report by the Inspekteur der Sipo und des SD, August 21, 1941, in *Eugenik, Sterilisation, Euthanasie. Politische Biologie in Deutschland 1895–1945*, ed. Jochen-Christoph Kaiser, Kurt Nowak, and Michael Schwartz (Berlin: Buchverlag Union, 1992), 285f.; copy of a leaflet common in the Gau Cologne Aachen in November 1941, BAB, R 55, 978.
43. Parish of Vreden to Portmann, October 29, 1945, ibid.
44. Wüster (Kreisamt für Rassenpolitik Göttingen) to the NSDAP-Kreisleitung Göttingen, October 21, 1941, Niedersächsisches Hauptstaatsarchiv [Central State Archive] Hannover, Hann. 310-I/O/120.
45. Cf. Kurt Nowak, "Widerstand, Zustimmung, Hinnahme: Das Verhalten der Bevölkerung zur 'Euthanasie,'" in *Medizin und Gesundheitspolitik in der NS-Zeit*, ed. Norbert Frei (Munich: R. Oldenbourg, 1991), 235–252, 241f.
46. SD-Leitabschnitt Cologne to the Reichssicherheitshauptamt, Amt III, June 19, 1941, Nordrhein-Westfälisches Hauptstaatsarchiv [Central State Archive] Düsseldorf, RW 34, 30.
47. Elsa von Löwis to Ms Buch, November 25, 1940, IfZ, Nuremberg Documents, NO-001.
48. Franz-Werner Kersting, "Ärzteschaft und NS-'Euthanasie' im Kontext des Galen-Protestes" in Joachim Kuropka, ed., *Clemens August Graf von Galen: Menschenrechte—Widerstand—Euthanasie—Neubeginn* (Münster: Regensberg, 1998), 205–220.
49. Sermon by Berning in Rulle, June 8, 1941, in Klemens August Recker, *"Wem wollt ihr glauben?" Bischof Berning (1877–1955) im Dritten Reich* (Paderborn: Schöningh, 1997), 287.
50. Konrad Repgen, Die deutschen Bischöfe und der Zweite Weltkrieg, *Historisches Jahrbuch* 115 (1995): 411-452, 431f.
51. Hecking to Portmann October 17, 1945, BAM, Portmann Papers, A 16.
52. Anonymous letter from the Rhineland, August 27, 1941, BAM, GV, Neues Archiv, A-024.

53. Anonymous letter from Münster, August 24, 1941, BAM, GV, Neues Archiv, A-024.
54. Witthage to Portmann, November 21, 1945, BAM, Portmann Papers, A 16. The report recounts the discussion of a non-local female Party member with Westphalian Nazi Party members.
55. Report by the SD-Hauptaußenstelle Bielefeld, September 9, 1941, in Kaiser, Nowak, and Schwartz, *Eugenik*, 288.
56. NSDAP-Kreisleitung Tecklenburg to the Gauleitung Westfalen-Nord, August 15, 1941, StAM, Kreis- und Ortsgruppenleitungen, 125.
57. Some representative examples: Report by the Inspekteur der Sicherheitspolizei und des SD, July 17, 1941 in Kuropka, *Meldungen*, 211f. Report by the Inspekteur der Sipo und des SD, July 24, 1941, in Kuropka, *Meldungen*, 531.
58. Joseph Goebbels, *Die Tagebücher von Joseph Goebbels*, ed. Elke Fröhlich, Part 2: *Diktate 1941–1945*, 15 vols. (Munich: K.G. Sauer, 1996), entry for August 8, 1941, vol. 2/1, 195.
59. Overview of reports by the SD-Abschnitt München to the Reichssicherheitshauptamt, Abteilung III B 3; Zentrum zur Aufbewahrung historisch-dokumentarischer Sammlungen (RGVA), Moscow, 500/3/763.
60. Goebbels, *Tagebücher*, August 14, 1941, vol. 2/1, 232.
61. Michael Burleigh and Beth Griech-Polelle contest this connection or at least relativize it strongly; Griech-Polelle, *Bishop*, 93; Michael Burleigh, *Death and Deliverance: "Euthanasia" in Germany 1900–1945* (Cambridge: Cambridge University Press, 1994), 180.
62. For a detailed reconstruction of the decision-making see Winfried Süß, *Der "Volkskörper" im Krieg: Gesundheitspolitik, medizinische Versorgung und Krankenmord im nationalsozialistischen Deutschland 1939–1945* (Munich: Oldenbourg Wissenschaftsverlag, 2003), 127–151.
63. Report by the Inspekteur der Sipo und des SD, July 7, 1941 in Kuropka, *Meldungen*, 533.
64. Note by Tießler for Bormann, August 13, 1941, in Heinrich Portmann, *Der Bischof von Münster: Das Echo eines Kampfes für Gottesrecht und Menschenrecht* (Münster: Aschendorff, 1946) 195.
65. Mittendorf, report on von Galen's sermon given on August 3, 1941, August 4, 1941, in Löffler, *Galen-Akten*, vol. 2, 883; Goebbels, *Tagebücher*, August 23, 1941, vol. 2/1, 298 f.
66. Walter Tießler, *Licht und Schatten oder: Schonungslose Wahrheit*, MS, undated, p. 141, IfZ, ED/158.
67. Goebbels, *Tagebücher*, August 19, 1941, vol. 2/1, 266.
68. Goebbels, *Tagebücher*, August 18, 1941, vol. 2/1, 254.
69. Hans Günter Hockerts, *Die Goebbels-Tagebücher 1932–1941*. "Eine neue Hauptquelle zur Erforschung der nationalsozialistischen Kirchenpolitik" in *Politik und Konfession*, ed. Dieter Albrecht and Hans Günter Hockerts, et al. (Berlin: Duncker & Humblot, 1983), 359–392, 382–387.
70. Tießler, *Licht und Schatten*, vol. 2, p. 141, IfZ, ED, 158.
71. Extract from the Borghorst parish chronicle 1945, BAM, Portmann Papers, A 16.

72. Interrogation of Brandt, protocol of the Nuremberg Doctors' Trial, February 4, 1947, IfZ, MB 15/20, fol. 2426.
73. Statement by Lammers, March 21, 1961, 5, Zentrale Stelle zur Verfolgung von NS-Verbrechen [Central Office of the State Justice Administrations for the Investigation of National Socialist Crimes], Ludwigsburg, Aussagensammlung, Euthanasie, Ordner La-Lh.
74. Goebbels, *Tagebücher*, August 19, 1941, vol. 2/1, 264.
75. Cf. Frank Bajohr, "Die Zustimmungsdiktatur. Grundzüge nationalsozialistischer Herrschaft in Hamburg," in Forschungsstelle für Zeitgeschichte in Hamburg (ed.), *Hamburg im "Dritten Reich"* (Göttingen: Wallstein, 2005), 69–121.
76. Cf. Isabella Spolovjnak-Pridat and Helmut Siepenkort, eds., Ökumene im Widerstand. Der Lübecker Christenprozess 1943 (Lübeck: Schmidt-Römhild Verlag, 2006).

Chapter 5

The Possibilities of Protest in the Third Reich
The Witten Demonstration in Context

Julia S. Torrie

In a November 1943 report on current events and their effect on women's mood, the *Sicherheitsdienst* (SD) transmitted the following information to the Third Reich's highest authorities: "On 11 Oct. 1943 about 300 women *demonstrated* in Witten in order to take a public position against the measures that had led to the refusal to hand out ration cards. It came to shameful displays, so that the city authorities of Witten saw themselves compelled to *call in the police to re-establish order*. These, however, refused to step in, as the women's demands were fair and there was *no legal basis* for the refusal to hand out ration cards to returned citizens.[1]" As the SD reported, some three hundred citizens (mainly women, but also some men) had taken to the streets in the *Ruhrgebiet* town of Witten. They were angry about evacuation rules, and in particular, about a recent decision to deny ration cards to evacuees who returned to their home cities prematurely. According to the SD, demonstrations like the one at Witten had taken place in front of municipal food offices in nearby Hamm, Lünen, and Bochum in the same period.

Initially, the regime responded by trying to tighten its grip on wayward evacuees, but within four months of the protests, Hitler himself had interceded to prevent ration cards from being denied to evacuees who returned home without permission.[2] More women and children were able to remain in the cities, and the regime improved programs to help working fathers visit their evacuated families. Ultimately, the public action in Witten and elsewhere convinced policy-makers that coercive measures could not be used to separate families and control civilian evacuations. More broadly, it confirmed that in some circumstances, public protests could make the leaders of the Third Reich change their minds.

The present chapter traces the course of the Witten demonstration, explores its causes, and suggests reasons for its success. Like other instances of popular protest in the Third Reich, particularly the Rosenstrasse protest and the Bavarian crucifix campaign, events at Witten show that even a relatively spontaneous, small-scale protest was taken seriously by National Socialist leaders. As late as the turn of the years 1943 and 1944, popular opposition led to changes in policy. Certainly, these protests are not identical or equivalent, but the Witten demonstration shares features with other notable instances of non-compliance in the Third Reich. Comparison with these events helps explain how and why they challenged National Socialist authority. Factors such as the underlying motivation for the protests and their objectives, who protested, and differences of opinion about how to respond among the upper echelons of Reich leadership contributed to the success of all three movements. Events at Witten confirm that in an authoritarian context, any public grouping of citizens constituted a threat to the government. Protests did not need to be particularly "explicit" to be effective.[3]

Responses to popular non-compliance in the Third Reich show that while the state relied on terror, it was also remarkably sensitive to public opinion. Although historians focusing on Hitler's pervasive terror system as well as those arguing for broad German complicity with his regime have downplayed public protests, albeit for rather different reasons, protests both remained possible, and an effective way to pressure the government.

Popular support for the Third Reich and protest were two sides of the same coin. Terror was not implemented blindly, and the regime was subtle enough to modify its direction in response to public outcry. For the most part, Hitler acted with the support of Reich citizens and gained strength from their widespread approval for such measures as the persecution of the Jews, or the pursuit of an aggressive war after 1939. But when, as at Witten, on the Rosenstrasse, or in Bavarian schools, there were clear signs that the population was not prepared to go along with government policies, Hitler and his advisors backed off. Some of the coterie of leading men, perhaps Goebbels in particular, were more sensitive to popular opinion than others, but protesters ably exploited the leadership's reliance on popular support and the importance it placed on an image of unity without dissent.

The Witten protest has been noted by many historians, but rarely studied in depth. Since it is less well-known than either the Bavarian crucifix campaign, or the Rosenstrasse protest, some additional background will help set the protest in context. The major source of information about events at Witten is the SD-report quoted above, and many details remain unclear.[4] Initially, historians viewed the protest as either a sign of women's disapproval for National Socialist policies, or as a manifestation of workers' opposition, specifically.[5] More recently, they have given more weight to the protest's immediate causes and context, recognizing that it was directed at civilian evacuation measures. In his work on children's evacuations, for instance, Gerhard Kock links the event to parents' disapproval of the regime's attempts to make the evacuation of their offspring compulsory.[6] Gerhard Sollbach follows a similar line of reasoning, reconstructing events surrounding the protest with material from the city archives of the *Ruhrgebiet*.[7] Olaf Groehler's *Bombenkrieg gegen Deutschland*, on the other hand, connects the incident to workers' rejection of evacuations because they found it difficult to pay the extra costs these measures entailed.[8] Building on previous scholarship, my research emphasizes that family ties motivated the protesters, who succeeded because their protest was the most visible sign of much wider popular disapproval for draconian evacuation measures.

Existing analyses focus on the protest itself, and since they examine its aftermath only briefly, if at all, they fail to recognize that the Witten demonstration actually led to changes in policy. Evacuees' public display convinced Reich leaders of the depth of popular disgruntlement. Once it was clear that coercive evacuation policies might undermine people's support for the war effort, the authorities acted quickly to moderate them. Like the opposition of the Rosenstrasse women to the imprisonment of their husbands, Witteners' public opposition to specific evacuation measures convinced policymakers that it made no sense to maintain a hard line that ran counter to popular sympathies.

At the time of the Witten demonstration, there were over three million civilian evacuees in Germany.[9] Allied aerial bombing had increased significantly through the summer of 1943, marked by the fire-bombing of Hamburg, and the so-called Battle of the Ruhr from April to June. Witten, like its neighbors, lived from heavy industry and coal mining, and the city housed important facilities for Ruhrstahl AG, Mannesmann, and Deutsche Tafelglas (DETAG). By the end of the war, Witten had been attacked ninety-one times, and the downtown area was destroyed to about 80 percent.[10]

Faced with escalating air war, some Germans left endangered areas independently, while others, particularly children and women, were evacuated by the state. They moved into temporary quarters in the south and east of the Reich, areas less easily reached by Allied bombers. Although many evacuees settled in well after an initial adjustment period, by mid-fall 1943, it was clear that at least an equally large group were unhappy in their billets.[11] Viewing a winter far from home with trepidation, disgruntled evacuees began returning home spontaneously, clogging the country's over-stretched transportation networks, and flouting government regulations that required them to stay in the reception areas.[12] In some regions, as many as a third of all evacuees returned home without permission.[13]

The previous spring, in anticipation of violent bombing over the summer, the Ministry of the Interior had brought together evacuation guidelines developed since the beginning of the war.[14] Among other things, the rules now assigned specific reception areas to evacuees, putting an end to the earlier practice of *Freizügigkeit*, which had allowed evacuees who paid their own expenses to go wherever they liked. Residents of Westfalen-Süd, the Gau encompassing Witten, Bochum and Dortmund, would be sent to Baden, the Sudetenland, or Pomerania.[15] A letter from Secretary of State Wilhelm Stuckart to Propaganda Minister Goebbels in April 1943 described this change as an attempt to regulate evacuees' movements to minimize the organizational and practical problems caused by their rapidly increasing numbers.[16] At the same time, the inflexible interventionism of the Spring circular set the tone for evacuation policy through the summer and fall of 1943, when, for the first time, Hitler's regime was faced with truly large-scale evacuations.[17]

Such a vast population movement gave rise to many problems. Big city evacuees had a hard time adjusting to sometimes primitive conditions in rural Germany, and they were viewed suspiciously by the locals. For several reasons, Germany favored long-distance evacuations, which tended to exacerbate problems caused by regional differences. Strangers from the northern and western parts of the Reich found it difficult to get along with fellow-citizens in the south and east, with whom they might share neither customs, dialect, nor religion. Many evacuees felt unwelcome in the reception areas, and when the weather turned cold, or bombing in their home areas decreased temporarily, they went home.[18]

In time, the question of whether or not evacuations could be made compulsory became pressing. The Witten demonstration was essentially about this issue, for the government sought greater control over evacuations than the population was willing to accept. In 1939 and 1940, evacuations to clear Germany's border zones had been compulsory by virtue of military necessity, and the regime subsequently used coercion for some local evacuations resulting from air raid damage—for instance, when a house was rendered uninhabitable, or when there were unexploded bombs in the neighborhood. But in most cases, the situation was less clear-cut, and policy-makers wavered about whether or not civilians could be forced to undertake an evacuation.

In his April 1943 letter to Goebbels mentioned above, Secretary of State Stuckart summarized the regime's position, stressing that, "The question of evacuation . . . has always been treated from the viewpoint of a voluntary measure."[19] However, he also explained that with growing numbers of evacuees, disorderly evacuations threatened to overwhelm local officials. Through the summer and fall of 1943, the regime tried to implement stricter policies, but by early 1944, it had become clear that excessive controls on evacuation were not worth the trouble they caused. The Witten demonstration precipitated this realization, making evacuees' displeasure impossible to ignore, and pushing the government to change its policies.

But why did unrest crystallize at Witten? On the face of it, a relatively small city like Witten was unlikely terrain for a successful protest, yet certain features of the city combined to foster unrest.[20] The evacuation program for Gau Westfalen-Süd, including Witten, had ballooned when the "Battle of the Ruhr" began. Sent mainly to Baden, rather than the other possible reception areas for Westfalen-Süd, Pomerania, and the Sudetenland, Witten residents were accommodated in the rural and pious Black Forest, where the locals treated them as an alien, corrupting influence. Worse, in early June 1943, Party leaders in Baden announced that, although the evacuees had been told they could return home after three months, now their stay would "*be increased by another quarter year. They will remain in the existing billets.*"[21] Requests to return to the *Ruhrgebiet* would be denied. Back in Witten, the director of the city's schools was told at the end of June that all children would be evacuated in later July, and schools closed to ensure the order was carried out.[22]

Similar measures were being enacted across the Reich, and even as increasing numbers of people were sent away, more and more returned of their own accord from the reception areas. By October 1943, the number of Berliners returning home outpaced those willing to be evacuated. The same was true of other urban centers, particularly those of the *Ruhrgebiet*.[23] Witten evacuees were surely frustrated by the prolongation of their stay, especially once the Allies appeared to be shifting some of their energy away from the Ruhr.[24] Local officials pointed out, however, that the cities were still not safe, and destroyed structures could not be rebuilt immediately.[25] The *Reichsbahn* was overstretched, and women and children were not, in the view of the regime, economically "necessary" at home. Evacuations must continue.

The regime employed several methods to keep evacuees from returning home prematurely.[26] One was to close schools in the home district. School closures gave the regime a legal basis to argue that parents were neglecting their duty to educate their children if they brought them back to the city.[27] The second method was to prohibit evacuees from purchasing train tickets to vulnerable urban zones. Party officials negotiated with the train service so that its agents would refuse to sell tickets to evacuees unless they could show they had permission to leave. Tellingly, while the *Reichsbahn* was fairly cooperative with regard to policing evacuated children's movements, its agents generally refused to treat adults the same way. The head evacuee liaison officer of Westfalen-Süd in Baden, Spratte, reported that, "In one district it has . . . been possible to block the train tickets of women who are leaving without permission. This would naturally be the most desirable situation, but it is unfortunately not realizable in all districts." Spratte concluded that since the *Reichsbahn* would not cooperate, other means of enforcement would have to be found.[28] The final method used was to deny ration cards to so-called "wild" returnees. Gauleiter Hoffmann of Westfalen-Süd imposed this measure on July 26, 1943, and within less than three months it had led to the Witten protest.[29]

The trouble was that despite Hoffmann's order, evacuees continued to return, to the point that in early September, the SD found that, "In some reception towns about a third of the evacuees has left the assigned quarters, and has either moved elsewhere, or returned home."[30] A few days later, liaison officer Spratte expressed his frustration about the "mania of our women" to return home even when it was not safe.[31]

Soon, official frustration and the sense of powerlessness exhibited by Spratte and others led to a radicalization of policy and propaganda. In mid-September, the *Ruhrgebiet*'s largest wartime daily newspaper, the *Westfälische Landeszeitung (WLZ)*, described disobedient evacuees in almost criminal terms as *Schädlinge* (pests), claiming that they were "sabotaging the measures to protect our children, the most valuable possession of our people."[32] National Socialists called certain types of criminals *Volksschädlinge* (pests on the body politic), and an ordinance from the beginning of the war specified that this group included, for instance, those caught plundering the houses of bomb victims, or thieving during a blackout. Both could be subject to the death penalty.[33] Although labeling unwilling evacuees "Schädlinge," was not quite as harsh as "Volksschädlinge," it nonetheless implied that their behavior was subversive and damaged the war effort.

Still, some local functionaries turned a blind eye on "illegal" returnees, suggesting that they disapproved of Hoffmann's enforcement measures. Sympathy with the evacuees was troublesome, and on October 9, Hoffmann complained that his order not to issue ration cards "is not only not sufficiently observed by individual citizens, but also not carried out everywhere with the necessary energy by the responsible government offices."[34] Measures to compel evacuations by closing schools were not being enforced either, and Spratte reminded local officials of the procedures they were to follow.[35]

Two days later, three hundred people (mainly women and children, though some men also participated) gathered in front of the Witten city hall to express their anger about the denial of ration cards. Faced with a public demonstration, the police refused to act. Both they and Witten's angry citizens knew that no law had been passed to legalize Hoffmann's order, and that the measure violated all popular sense of justice. One protester argued, "Let's just wait and see whether I get no food for the children. I can certainly leave my children where I want to. After all, they're still *my* children." Another insisted that, "Those people from the food offices should first show me the law that says the children have to go away. If there's no law about it, and there isn't, then no one can ever take my ration cards away from me." Still a third claimed that, "If I'm gone, then my child should be gone too, and not toil alone in the world. We'll stay together . . . they can't just do whatever they want with us, it's still *voluntary*." Most bitter of all was the comment that if the situation did not change, "They might as well just send us to Russia right away, point a machine gun at us and get it over with."[36]

Nonetheless, the municipal government maintained its hard line, and in the short-term, Witten's "wild" returnees resorted to a ruse to recover their eligibility for sustenance. The women applied for work in essential industries, claiming that they had made arrangements for childcare, even when this was not the case. Taking a job reaffirmed their importance to the urban community, and they were again able to obtain rations. Most importantly, they were no longer targeted for compulsory evacuation, and could stay at home with their families.[37] Employment that had initially seemed difficult or unappealing to many German women precisely because of their family responsibilities now became the lesser of evils.

"Wild" returnees were a serious problem all over the Reich, yet apart from smaller incidents reported by the SD at Lünen, Bochum, and Hamm in the same period, disturbances like that at Witten do not seem to have occurred elsewhere. Why? Several factors made Witten fertile ground for dissent. For one thing, the town's evacuees were sent to Baden, where, observers suggested, the local inhabitants were particularly unwelcoming.[38] In addition to typical regional and urban/rural differences, Badeners tended to be Catholic, whereas Witten had many Protestants, so religious tensions were likely high.

Witten was also a mining and steel town, about half of whose residents had traditionally voted Socialist or Communist.[39] With a population of 73,500 in 1939, it was medium-sized, with a close-knit working-class community. Olaf Groehler has pointed out that in Berlin, dissatisfaction with evacuations, as measured by "wild" returns, was greatest in working-class neighborhoods. He concludes that working-class families returned home more often because they found running two households too expensive.[40] Class and lack of means might therefore have contributed to the Witten protest, but neither the SD-reports, nor evacuees' own letters suggest that evacuees were particularly worried about their finances.[41] Evacuees' allowances were available to those of lesser means and the sources show that it was not Witteners inability to afford two household that made them return home; rather, it was that in their particular circumstances, two households made no sense.

The position of many *Ruhrgebiet* women was exceptional among evacuees, for their husbands were not soldiers, but workers, tied to their jobs in essential industries regardless of the bombs. By late September 1943, as the weather cooled and temporary quarters grew less comfortable, these evacuees started worrying about winter. Articles in the *WLZ*, evacuees' letters, and reports of liaison officers in the reception areas show that evacuated women were not only concerned about their own situation, but also, perhaps to a greater degree, about the husbands they had left behind. The *WLZ* suggested that workers' wives must be asking themselves, "What will it be like . . . if we stay in the reception areas over the winter, and our men come home in the evenings—often soaking wet—and find a cold apartment?"[42] Responding to a telephone call from Goebbels' staff about "wild" returns on the day after the Witten demonstration, Westfalen-Nord's representative in Gau Salzburg reported that, "The highest percentage of the returnees are mothers from the industrial area [i.e. the *Ruhrgebiet*]. The main explanation used . . . is that the men at home cannot cater for themselves alone, or cannot manage with their [ration] tickets."[43] Even if, as commentators suspected, husbands fed their spouses' anxieties by writing "whining letters" about their inability to master household tasks and asking their wives to return to the city, the fact remained that it was difficult for *Ruhrgebiet* men to manage a home while working full-time.[44]

Added to the sheer impracticality of running two households, homesickness and frustration at being separated from one's loved ones became important causes of the Witten protest. The SD-report of November 18 (which devoted ten of its thirteen pages to the evacuees' situation) listed as the first reason for their unhappiness, "*The ripping apart of the family* without the possibility of visits, with all of its accompanying phenomena, [which] is, over the long-term, seen as an intolerable situation not only by the men, but also by their wives." Workingmen claimed they missed their families so much that it took all of the joy out of their work. The SD worried about "the *sexual problem*" and the long-term effects of separating spouses, which tended towards a "decay of marriages." They also noted that "separation from the children is designated as an especially heavy, and therefore over the long-term unbearable, burden."[45]

The evacuees' unease thus crystallized around family ties, but what made them move from displeasure to action? It seems that a strong sense of solidarity, perhaps fostered by the independent stance of one particular individual, was crucial. Many Witten mothers and children ended up in the small Black Forest town of Donaueschingen, where they were accompanied by Wilhelm

Reeswinkel, the principal of Witten's Protestant school.[46] Reeswinkel served as informal spokesman for the group, organized activities for them, and drew the ire of the official liaison officer from Westfalen-Süd, who complained that Reeswinkel would not cooperate with Party programs for all evacuees, and acted "with his Witteners as a 'state within the state.'"[47] Although the Party offered Reeswinkel the job of town liaison officer for Donaueschingen, he turned it down, presumably because this would have compromised his position. It seems likely that Reeswinkel acted as a kind of moral authority, helping make the Witten evacuees both more aware of their own rights, and more willing to stand up for those rights against the regime.[48]

The Witten demonstration was not "resistance" of a formal kind. According to the SD-report, the protesters' complaints were directed at local authority figures, and they drew a conscious distinction between what they saw as local abuses, and the government in Berlin: "This doesn't come from the top, it's just the mayor and the local food office, or the Gauleiter who are to responsible for this here. They think they know what's what, but we'll show them." The SD noted more generally that, "Most women [stand behind] the Führer himself."[49]

Instead, the Witten protest exemplified small-scale dissent or opposition.[50] In some ways, it was a kind of bread riot, harkening back to the subsistence crises of earlier eras, or to demonstrations during World War I and the early Weimar years.[51] Though the protest was not the result of a food shortage as such, it certainly concerned the population's right to eat, since without ration cards, the "illegally" returned evacuees could not feed themselves and their children. Like a typical bread riot, the action took place in a central public space, the *Rathausplatz*, then called *Adolf-Hitler-Platz*. The focus of the protest was the municipal food office, where ration cards were distributed.[52] The protesters who laid claim to this important public space were motivated by a naïve sense of justice and values offended, similar to that of earlier subsistence riots.[53]

At the same time, however, the protest cannot be dismissed as an accident resulting from sheer naïveté. The Witteners were surely aware of the danger of demonstrating, yet felt so strongly about their position that they were prepared to take considerable risks to oppose government policies. Claiming that they would rather face the bombs than return to their assigned quarters in southern Germany, they had already contravened evacuation regulations and travel restrictions by boarding trains back to the vulnerable Ruhr. This choice put them at odds with the authorities, and could easily have cost them their lives due to Allied bombing. At home, observers reported to the SD that Witten's women, rendered furious by the authorities' refusal to modify the regulations, "were capable of anything, without the slightest restraint or concern about the consequences."⁵⁴ The SD recognized that the evacuees' disapproval was more than a passing whim, commenting that, "the *negative attitude* of broad segments of the population toward *the evacuations* could not be more clearly indicated than by the . . . stubbornness with which people were trying to sabotage official measures to carry out evacuations."⁵⁵

Within this wider context of opposition to coercive evacuations, it is difficult to ascertain whether the Witten demonstration was spontaneous or planned in advance. In describing the similar, but smaller protests in Hamm, Lünen, and Bochum, the SD suggested that trouble had arisen spontaneously as disgruntled citizens queued to receive ration cards. Apparently, "during the hours of waiting," queuing women "exchange[d stories of] their experiences in the reception areas and at the same time the wildest claims [were] made."⁵⁶ It would not have taken much to provoke open protest. In an unrelated incident in Dortmund-Hörde in July 1943, a group of three to four hundred civilians, mainly women, had attacked an officer who was attempting to apprehend a Flak soldier for lackluster saluting. This event appeared to be entirely unplanned, and underlines the potential volatility of war-weary *Ruhrgebiet* crowds.⁵⁷

As Jana Leichsenring's attempts to trace the involvement of the Hilfswerk beim Bischöflichen Ordinariat Berlin in the Rosenstrasse protest confirm, it is difficult to do more than hypothesize about the degree to which popular protests are organized.⁵⁸ However, the Witten demonstration involved about three hundred participants, and it may have been somewhat better planned than the other nearby events mentioned by the SD. Without documents recording the participants' side of the story, one cannot be certain, but the SD-report describes the protest as an attempt to "*force*" the authorities to deliver ration cards to returned evacuees.⁵⁹ Using the verb "demonstrieren" to describe the event, the report says that the women had demonstrated in order "to take a public position against the measures that had led to the refusal to hand out ration cards."⁶⁰ This wording, emphasizing that the demonstrators sought to take a public stance on particular measures, suggests that although the protest may have been spontaneous, it was certainly perceived as serious, thoughtful dissent by the SD. The SD's report, in turn, was read by the Reich's highest authorities, so this treatment of the protest, contrasting starkly with Spratte's view that returns from the reception areas were an irrational female "mania," surely added weight to the evacuees' claims.⁶¹

But why did the demonstration succeed? The evacuees' persistence, and the authorities' realization that events at Witten represented just the tip of an iceberg of anti-evacuation feeling, helped insure that the protesters' voices would be heard. The specific composition of the crowd at Witten was also important, and demonstrators' arguments about family unity were difficult to counter. Furthermore, Reich leaders knew there was no legal basis for denying citizens their ration cards, and there were growing disagreements among the Gauleiter and state bureaucrats about how to respond to the upheaval. More generally, the wartime context made it difficult to ignore the protest's potential impact on morale.

Particularly in wartime, the composition of the protest was crucial to its success. A regime based on mass support, such as Hitler's, could not afford to alienate its citizens by using excessive force against members of the *Volksgemeinschaft*, "Aryan" women like the Witteners who were supported by their worker and soldier relatives. The SD reported specifically that the women had protested with small children and babes-in-arms, and that in some cases, miners had taken the place of their wives in the line-up for ration tickets. The men insisted that they would not return to work until they had secured ration cards for their families.[62] *Ruhrgebiet* workers' wishes even gained "support from important people in industry, who explain[ed] that it [lay] in the interest of morale and the productivity of the workers to arrange for the workers to have their wives and children back here soon as possible."[63]

As the crowd's composition confirms, family concerns were central to the protest. Attempts to make civilians conform to evacuation regulations threatened values for which people claimed they were willing to die. As one protester put it, "Let them come to me. My children won't leave, and if I have nothing to eat, then I can croak [*verrecken*] alongside them."[64] Protesters' arguments about family unity were echoed elsewhere in the Reich, and it was difficult for the authorities to respond effectively. During a meeting to encourage families in the Prenzlauer Berg area of Berlin to evacuate their children, parents were told that, "children are not just the property of their parents, but like the soil tilled by the farmer, they are also the property of the state." At this point, "a soldier got up and, without saying a word, left the meeting."[65]

Since the National Socialists had stressed the strength and value of the family from the outset, it was hardly credible for the authorities to argue in 1943 that parents were less conscientious if they allowed their children to be evacuated half-way across the Reich to live with strangers, than if they tried to keep the family together in the city despite the risks. In the January 1944 circular that marked the regime's move away from forcible measures in evacuation, Goebbels implicitly recognized how awkward it was to punish citizens for wanting to be with their loved ones. He told the Gauleiter not to fine parents for the class days their non-evacuated children missed when schools in the home cities had been closed. "The Führer," Goebbels emphasized, "is of the opinion that other ways and means must be found to move these fellow-citizens, too, to evacuate their children." Goebbels added: "The

Führer believes that the goal we aim for can be reached particularly through propaganda activities that once again bring before parents' eyes quite graphically the dangers their children face."[66] Instead of punishing parents and spouses for wanting to keep their loved ones close by, Hitler and Goebbels tried to exploit familial concern to motivate additional departures from endangered cities.

The absence of a legal basis for denying ration cards also fed into the decision not to pursue a harsher line against returned evacuees. On the one hand, the absence of a law about the matter did not stop Gauleiter Hoffmann from refusing to issue ration cards to Westfalen-Süd's "wild" returnees. It is quite possible that without the Witten protest, he would have continued in this course regardless of its tenuous legality.[67] On the other hand, given the Third Reich's fondness for sham legal justifications, it seems probable that if Hoffmann and others had sought to expand the policy, or to maintain it over a longer period of time, legislation would have been passed to "legalize" the procedure after the fact. The absence of a law was a weak point, something both Witten's citizens, and the local *Schutzpolizei* exploited, the former to justify their protest, the latter to explain their failure to intervene. Because public demonstrations were forbidden by an early National Socialist law, the *Schutzpolizei* had a pre-existing legal basis for intervening in the demonstration.[68] Yet they chose not to intervene, citing the absence of a law regarding ration cards to explain their actions and to cover themselves against charges of softness. The absence of a law gave them a convenient loophole, when in fact, according to the SD-report, the policemen failed to intervene because they thought the evacuees' claims were fair.[69]

Even more significantly, the lack of legal basis for denying ration cards made the president of the regional court (*Oberlandesgerichtspräsident*) in Hamm, who was responsible for the Witten area, uneasy. His quarterly report of December 1943 commented on the large numbers of evacuations being undertaken and underlined that over time an extraordinary number of evacuees, including children, returned home without permission. The court president spoke of thousands of people, and pointed to the specific problems this caused for the exercise of justice in his area. As the Court President was aware, Westfalen-Süd's Reich Defense Commissioner (*Reichsverteidigungskommissar*) Gauleiter Hoffmann had refused to hand out ration cards to evacuees who returned to the Gau without permission and "There have been some wild scenes at the food offices, [of which] one has already preoccupied the courts."[70] In this context, Hoffmann's policy was problematic because the lack of legal foundation made it hard for judges to rule effectively on cases resulting from the denial of ration cards. The court president was no dove on evacuation issues—in the same report he recommended withdrawing custody from parents who refused to evacuate their children—but he *was* concerned about the difficulties of enforcing a policy without a solid legal footing. The degraded state of justice in the Third Reich is evidenced by the fact the court president did not actually demand a law be passed before he would defend the denial of ration cards. Rather, he was dismayed to find that although he had asked Hoffmann, "to at least share with me copies of his orders, [he had] not yet received them."[71] As in the case of the Nazis' "euthanasia" program, the absence of even the appearance of a law made it difficult to justify reprehensible policies to the German people.[72]

The impact of the Witten demonstration was thus increased by the family unity arguments protesters used, and the fact that ration cards were being denied without any legal basis. The demonstration also occurred at a time when air war and its consequences were the most important domestic issues facing the Reich. As responses were debated at the highest levels of the government, Goebbels, Himmler, and Bormann initially sought to clamp down on undisciplined evacuees. Other voices, from the state bureaucracy and among the Party Gauleiter, spoke in favor of moderation. Accompanied by huge numbers of "wild" returns across Germany, the Witten demonstration helped tip the balance toward lenience and persuasion, not force, at a critical juncture.

The demonstration caught the authorities' attention immediately. On the day after it occurred, Goebbels' staff telephoned the reception Gaue to ask about ways "to direct the 'wild' returns of the mothers from the reception areas."[73] Three days later, Gauleiter Hoffmann embarked on a several-day trip to Baden to meet with evacuees and discuss their difficulties in "open conversation."[74]

Rather than abating, the wave of 'illegal' returnees grew, and it began to unnerve the Reich's high authorities. In early November, Goebbels reacted harshly, writing:

> We must try . . . through appropriate measures, to dam this flood of returning evacuees. If this is not achievable through well-meaning persuasion, then coercion must be used. It is not true that coercion does not lead to the desired result. . . . Nothing has been felt of this [coercion] yet, and the Volk knows perfectly well where the soft spot of the leadership is, and will always know how to exploit it. If we harden the spot where we have thus far been soft the Volk will bend to the will of the State. At the moment we are on the way to bending the will of the State under to the will of the Volk . . . The state must never, against its own best interests, give way to the pressure of the street. If it does this, it will be even weaker the second time than the first, and gradually lose its whole authority.[75]

Though Goebbels mentioned "well-meaning persuasion," coercion was at the heart of his reaction, which defended a forceful response to popular protest. His comments seem emblematic of the regime's hard-nosed approach, suggesting that policy-makers saw the Witten demonstration and on-going returns in the context of a larger undermining of the state's authority, and had little intention of compromising.

On November 6, Goebbels hosted a meeting of various secretaries of state to discuss evacuation issues.[76] He made no specific reference to the Witten demonstration in his diary, but comments on November 21, 1943, show he had read the SD-report describing the incident, and he confided the same day that, "the most difficult domestic policy issue we face is that of the flood of returning evacuees." Goebbels reiterated that the free flow of people across the Reich overtaxed the transportation system and risked destabilizing the food supply as the authorities struggled to make winter provisions available to evacuees and urbanites alike.[77] A forceful reaction seemed essential, and a few days later, Goebbels wrote that although heavy bombing in Berlin had already served to decrease "wild" returns there, together with Himmler he had worked out a plan "following which significant pressure will be exercised on the evacuees after all, partly through tightening how we organize transportation, and partly also through pressure on food delivery."[78] At this point, perhaps in response, Gauleiter Meyer of Westfalen-Nord began denying ration cards to "illegal" returnees in Münster and other major cities of his Gau.[79]

Martin Bormann too supported a hard line, for Goebbels reported in mid-December that he had received a letter from the Party chancellor suggesting more rigorous air war measures, including the forcible evacuation of women and children from heavily-populated urban centers. "All of a sudden [Bormann] is taking a position here that I had already proposed months ago," Goebbels announced, confirming that he had favored a no-compromise approach to evacuations for a long time, and continued to do so.[80]

Two days later, Goebbels again underlined the degree to which air war and evacuations preoccupied the government—"domestically, we are busy almost exclusively with air war,"—and complained that each Gauleiter seemed to want to retain "safe" areas of his region for the local urban population, neglecting completely the needs of cities like Berlin or the heavily populated Ruhr that had too little safe hinterland to absorb threatened civilians.[81] Bombing and evacuations remained crisis issues over Christmas 1943, Goebbels noting in January that 2,650 Reich citizens had been killed by air raids in December alone, and that the total since 1939 was now an "extremely alarming" 102,000.[82]

Evacuations were essential to save lives, and since strict discipline seemed to be the only way to avoid throwing transportation and food systems into disarray, Goebbels, Himmler, and Bormann all initially favored an inflexible approach. However, the Witten demonstration raised the stakes, and particularly by early January 1944, the tide of opinion was turning. On January 14, Goebbels noted in his diary that, "Various Gauleiter have called for legal measures against returning evacuees. For the time being, I turn down such measures, for another whole group of Gauleiter are against them. It is impossible to achieve consensus with regard to this question, and since every Gauleiter does what he thinks is best, a decision from the Führer [*eine Führerentscheidung*] must be obtained."[83] A note of doubt had crept in about the advisability of coercion, and Goebbels observed that not all Gauleiter thought it wise. As in other cases of conflict within the party leadership, the Führer would decide. Ten days later, Goebbels visited Hitler's headquarters in East Prussia, and over lunch, the decision was made.[84] Goebbels noted shortly thereafter that he was still very busy with air war, and that "based on Hitler's instructions I am issuing a detailed circular to the Gauleiter that announces a series of the Führer's orders." The circular appeared the following day, informing the Gauleiter that, "The Führer has ordered that [you] should refrain from blocking ration cards."[85]

In November and December 1943, Goebbels, Himmler and Bormann all thought harsher measures were the only way to stem the flow of "wild" returnees, yet by late January, the regime had reversed its position completely. Given that the Witten demonstration took place in mid-October, why did it take so long for leaders to change their minds? In part, this was simply due to the slow march of bureaucracy in wartime, perhaps exacerbated by the Christmas season. In addition, although colder weather and the approach of Christmas had encouraged many evacuees to return home, by early January the situation had probably calmed down somewhat on its own, which favored a less panicked, more reflective reaction on the part of the Reich's highest officials. Above all, the additional breathing room likely allowed the leadership to reconsider the risks associated with widespread popular disapproval for draconian evacuation measures, and to take notice of the growing split among the Gauleiter that Goebbels mentioned on January 14.

It is clear that while some regional party leaders requested harsher action against disobedient evacuees, others favored a mild approach. Until now, each had acted according to his own preferences locally, and the public was aware of resulting inconsistencies. As the Witten demonstrators argued, "This doesn't come from the top, it's just the mayor and the local food office, or the Gauleiter who are responsible for this here."[86] Such disagreements were hardly new, moreover, for there had been debate about how to react to "wild" returnees since at least April 1943, when the idea of denying ration cards was first contemplated. When Stuckart wrote to Goebbels about the need to control evacuations more at that time, he reported that the treatment of evacuees by various government offices "is rather too harsh as opposed to too considerate." Stuckart believed that coercive measures should be weighed carefully and, "the denial of all ration tickets necessary to support life would mostly work itself out against innocent family members."[87] In July 1943, Gauleiter Grohé of Cologne-Aachen also criticized the policy of forcing evacuees into specific reception areas. Highlighting people's unwillingness to leave the cities, he contended that, "The conclusion from this must be that one only evacuates what one must evacuate, and that one does not pressure anyone to leave his home area if it is at all possible to provide him with even the most humble shelter."[88]

In his circular informing the Gauleiter that ration cards must no longer be denied to returned evacuees, Goebbels referred to these differences of opinion and the resulting inconsistency specifically, pointing out that "While carrying out measures to prevent evacuees' undesired returns . . . difficulties have arisen from the fact that this question is not resolved uniformly for the whole Reich. Individual regions have defended themselves against these returns by blocking ration cards. Because the borders [between regions] often run right through built-up areas, different practices have often arisen in the same communities."[89] Though inconsistency was partly a sign of what Goebbels saw as each Gauleiter's "egotism,"[90] it was also evidence of an on-going power struggle between moderates and hard-liners in evacuation matters. The existence of this fault-line gave the Witten demonstration added impact.

If the demonstration profited from existing divisions, it probably also aggravated them. Nathan Stoltzfus has argued that displays of people who disagreed with the authorities "could open up or exacerbate differences among the leadership," and that "the regime made concessions when it calculated that the support it could thus maintain was more valuable than the implementation of its policies and goals."[91] The Witten demonstration certainly polarized attitudes, as witnessed by Goebbels' vitriolic musings about bending the Volk to the will of the state. However, as widespread disapproval for evacuation policy became clearer and the risk of provoking another demonstration more obvious, a moderate viewpoint was able to prevail.

Combined with other factors, one final detail may have tipped the balance in favor of moderation in January 1944. In late December 1943, Gauleiter Hoffmann—Goebbels' second-in-command in the Reich Inspection of Civilian Air War Measures (Reichsinspektion der zivilen Luftkriegsmaßnahmen), and the man responsible for denying ration cards to returned evacuees in Westfalen-Süd—fell seriously ill. Hoffmann was a hard-liner on evacuation issues, close to both Himmler and Bormann, who also favored a clamp-down. When Hoffmann became incapacitated, Gauleiter Grohé of

Köln-Aachen, an equally committed National Socialist from earliest days, but more flexible regarding evacuation, replaced him as Goebbels' advisor on air war issues.[92] The turn toward greater flexibility can be dated from this period, for Grohé disapproved of the use of coercion in evacuations. He downplayed "soft" considerations like family ties, and insisted instead on the danger that poor civilian morale, exacerbated by evacuations, might present to the war effort.[93] Grohé believed that the best way to secure good morale at home, and by extension at the Front, was to leave people where they were, instead of evacuating them all over the Reich.[94]

The fact that the instructions to refrain from blocking ration cards appeared over Goebbels' signature, not Hitler's, raises the question of who actually decided not to use force against returned evacuees—Goebbels, or the Führer himself—and to what extent the two men were of one mind on this issue. Comments in Goebbels' diary suggest that Hitler's initial position on evacuation issues, like that of Goebbels, was hard-line. After speaking to Hitler about school closures in December 1943, Goebbels wrote that, "Here, the Führer shares my opinion . . . that when schools are evacuated, no classes should take place in the affected city . . . because otherwise the mothers will return with their children, and depending on the aerial situation we would end up repeating the evacuation process a dozen times per year, something the Reichsbahn is not in a position to do."[95]

As Goebbels changed his mind on evacuation issues, so too did the Führer. Although for lack of other sources we rely on Goebbels' assertions alone, there is no evidence that Hitler objected to the softening of policy that Goebbels suggested in January 1944. Goebbels made no bones about the fact that he saw himself as Hitler's main advisor in air war matters, and had a good deal of influence on Hitler. Goebbels noted in his diary on January 14, 1944, that although a decision from Hitler was necessary to quell infighting among Gauleiter about evacuation issues, "I am convinced that the Führer will issue his orders entirely in the way that I suggest [*ganz in meinem Sinne*]."[96] There is no reason to doubt this assertion; indeed, the shift in policy regarding "wild" returnees appears to have been Goebbels' decision primarily, brought forward for Hitler's approval in late January. Had the two men disagreed, Goebbels would have noted in his diary (as he typically did) that he had succeeded in convincing the Führer of the merits of his point of view. Instead, he simply remarked that he had discussed responses to air war with Hitler, and was about to issue a circular to the Gauleiter.[97] Still, the Führer's imprimatur was necessary to give the change force, and for this reason Goebbels underlined repeatedly in the circular of January 28, 1944, that the decisions he laid out were those of Hitler himself. He reiterated this information specifically in the sentence ordering the Gauleiter to "refrain from blocking ration cards."[98]

It is not surprising that Goebbels should play such a significant role in determining the regime's response to the Witten demonstration. The minister of "people's enlightenment and propaganda" acted as a kind of public relations officer for the Third Reich. He was particularly sensitive to protests like that at Witten, and inclined to favor a compromise solution if he believed it could be achieved. Moreover, because of its potential to undermine morale, Goebbels took a special interest in air war. At precisely the same time, in late 1943, that he reflected on the larger problems air raids posed for the Reich, he was made painfully aware of their local and personal implications when Berlin (the city of which he was Gauleiter), suffered a series of heavy raids that killed over 3,700 people, and rendered 450,000 homeless. Goebbels' own residence in Hermann-Göring-Strasse was badly hit, and his mother and mother-in-law in the Moabit neighborhood lost their homes.[99] Events in Berlin apparently gave the impetus for the creation of the Reich Inspection of Civilian Air War Measures, created on Hitler's initiative on December 21, 1943, and put directly under Goebbels' leadership.[100] The Reich Inspection's primary objective was to oversee air raid protection and disseminate knowledge about effective responses across the Reich. All of this confirms that air war was *the* most important domestic issue in the later fall of 1943, and a man of Goebbels' status and ambitions saw great potential in this field of action.

It has been suggested that despite Goebbels' desire to gain control over civilian air war measures, "he never achieved total control over this area" essentially because he was always competing with other figures, like Himmler or Göring, who were responsible for specific air raid protection measures like fire-fighting and civil defense proper.[101] Certainly, Goebbels did not control every aspect of Germany's responses to aerial invasion, but this was not his intention, nor would it have aligned with the pre-existing structure of air raid responses in Germany. Bunker-building, fire-fighting and air raid protection in the strictest sense had always been treated as separate issues from evacuations and programs to assist civilians after air raids. Until 1940, many voices in Germany (including, most vocally, Göring's) had claimed that only extremely limited civilian evacuations would be necessary.[102] When evacuations proved inevitable, they were a new field of action into which the National Socialists expanded reluctantly, and which did not share the high profile given air raid protection.[103] However, once air raids began to affect millions of Germans, Goebbels saw a niche for precisely the kind of propaganda-based leadership he was best placed to offer. There can be no question that the regime's response to the Witten demonstration was ultimately the result of Goebbels' own deliberations. More generally, the propaganda minister was able to influence Hitler's decision-making significantly, particularly on questions that were at the intersection of popular opinion and war.

The turn away from forcible evacuation precipitated by the Witten demonstration was a lasting one. Within four days of the disturbance, long before any written change in policy, Gauleiter Hoffmann had travelled to Baden to meet with evacuees. He talked to numerous displaced civilians and their hosts, attempting to regain their confidence by promising new measures to ensure the coal supply, repair winter clothing, and divert evacuees with "cultural leisure activities" from their home regions. Hoffmann also pledged to expand assistance for evacuees' menfolk left alone in the *Ruhrgebiet*.[104] In December, two separate Interministerial Air War Damages Committee newsletters informed members about specific measures undertaken locally to keep in touch with evacuees and prevent "wild" returns.[105] Communication was emphasized at every level, both so that the government could obtain detailed knowledge of evacuees' problems, and to give evacuees the sense that their leaders were concerned about their welfare. The Reich Inspection of Air War measures carried on this work on a large scale, visiting six Gaue in January 1944 alone.[106] The decision not to deny ration cards to returned evacuees was therefore also the culmination of a process of popular pulse-taking on evacuation issues that began in response to the unrest at Witten. Under Goebbels' leadership, this pulse-taking continued until the end of the war, helping to ensure that evacuees could make their concerns known without having to resort to a public demonstration. Evacuations never again became the explosive issue they were in the late fall of 1943.

In time, as Germany lost control over its own airspace and bombing affected the whole country, "wild" returns decreased. Himmler and Bormann reiterated the general decision not to use force in preventative evacuations in July 1944.[107] In October the same year, Bormann repeated Hitler's specific order not to deny ration cards to prematurely returned evacuees. In response to a telegram from the acting Gauleiter of Essen, Bormann noted that Hitler had decided earlier that year that forcible measures could not be used against returning evacuees, and emphasized that, "The reasons for his decision at that time are still relevant today." Instead, the authorities should try to limit returns by exercising restraint in giving evacuees permission to travel, and by using propaganda in the reception areas to inform evacuees about the dangers that awaited those who returned to vulnerable cities.[108] Although Reich leaders continued to find the population's refusal to do as it was told frustrating, after the Witten protest, the Third Reich never again moved as close to sanctioning widespread forcible measures against civilian evacuees.

Clearly, the protest at Witten changed evacuation enforcement. Comparison with other instances of popular non-compliance in the Third Reich, such as the Rosenstrasse protest and the Bavarian crucifix campaign, sets it in a wider context and draws out factors that helped such protests gain the authorities' attention. Together, these events confirm that popular protests were treated as serious, thoughtful dissent by Reich leaders, and had the force to alter policies.

All three protests were "single-issue" campaigns with limited and thus achievable objectives.[109] Protesters were not trying to overthrow the regime, but rather, to challenge specific measures they found unjust. Inconsistencies in policy application by party authorities encouraged the protesters, who were predominantly women.[110] Although non-conforming individuals like Wilhelm Reeswinkel may have played the role of catalysts, protests developed spontaneously, with little or no formal organization, and grew until they became an embarrassment to the regime. The protesters were related to both soldiers at the Front and workers at home, and their membership in the "national community," made it difficult for the authorities to crack down on their opposition. Local officials often sympathized with the protesters, and particularly in wartime, the importance of women and other civilians' morale made it unwise to ignore their demands.

In all three cases, family feelings were instrumental motivators of protest. In Bavaria, the crucifix campaign was primarily religiously motivated, but family concerns nonetheless contributed to the action, for most of the women protesting were "mothers of schoolchildren" concerned about their children's religious education.[111] At the Rosenstrasse, protesters' love for their incarcerated spouses or other relatives was clearly behind the action, as Nathan Stoltzfus has ably shown. At Witten, the desire for family unity was the key reason evacuees returned without permission from the reception areas. The fact that in all three cases citizens were opposing policies that affected their family members broadened public sympathy for the protesters, and made it hard for the regime to respond with force. National Socialists, who had propounded the strength and unity of the family for years, found it difficult to fault people for wanting to assist their loved ones. Moreover, since family feeling was something anyone might share, these protests reasonably represented the tip of an iceberg of broader popular opposition that the regime strove to limit as much as possible. Witteners were far from being the only "wild" returnees in Germany, and the women of the Rosenstrasse not the only intermarried wives. It seemed important to nip protest in the bud, before it could spread to other potentially disgruntled citizens.[112]

Another similarity between the three protests was the fact that the authorities initially hoped to bully the protesters into compliance by continuing, or hardening their policies. The day after the Witten protest, for example, the authorities published a notice at the ration card delivery office and in the local paper re-stating that ration cards would be denied to returning evacuees. The notice added that no ration cards would be delivered to school-age children, even if they had not been evacuated thus far. Such children must leave the city in order to regain eligibility for food.[113] In the crucifix campaign, some local party representatives continued to remove crucifixes from schools after the Bavarian Gauleiter, Wagner, had quietly issued a decree telling them to desist. Goebbels and other important figures also sought to react with force at first.[114] Twenty-five Rosenstrasse detainees were deported to Auschwitz before most were returned to Berlin when it became obvious that their spouses' protests would not stop.[115] In all three cases, the first reaction was to try to "harden" the spot where the state had been "soft", as Goebbels had put it. Ultimately, however, the regime's leaders, and perhaps Goebbels above all in his role as "public relations" and propaganda specialist, actually gave way to "the pressure of the street."[116] In full recognition of the fact that this might weaken the state's authority, they decided that more could be gained from acceding to protesters' limited demands, than from using terror to repress "ordinary" Germans' dissent.[117]

In all three cases, popular protests altered the course of Reich policies. Of all the factors contributing to their success, the mainly female crowds of *Volksgemeinschaft* members, the widespread public sympathy, and the fact that the protests brought to light (and surely raised the stakes in) disagreements about appropriate courses of action at the Reich's highest levels were probably the most important. Particularly in the absence of contemporary documents recording the participants' side of the story, it may be easy to dismiss these protests as accidental, their success as luck. Certainly, none came close to threatening Hitler's dominance, but this was not their intention. They were directed at specific policies, which they successfully changed. The very rarity of such protests underlines the courage required to undertake them, and they confirm that the flipside of widespread popular support for most of Hitler's policies was that when the costs of rigidity became too high, even the Third Reich was responsive to popular opinion at its core.

Julia Torrie is Associate Professor of History at St. Thomas University. She completed her doctorate at Harvard University in 2002. Her current research focuses on modern German-French interchanges, especially in the context of wartime social policies, military occupations, and popular protest. Her book, *For Their Own Good: Civilian Evacuations in Germany and France, 1939–1945,* appeared with Berghahn Books in 2010.

Notes

1. Emphasis in the original, SD-report, November 18, 1943 (BA: R 58/190).
2. Hitler's decision is detailed in a letter from Goebbels to all Gauleiter, January 28, 1944 (BA: R 55/447).

3. To justify his recent dismissal of the Rosenstrasse protest (the reversal of an earlier stance that emphasized the importance of the protest), Richard Evans writes that "there had never been any intention of sending these particular [intermarried] Jews east for extermination, and the crowd [that gathered in the Rosenstrasse] had not engaged in any kind of explicit protest." Richard J. Evans, *The Third Reich at War* (New York: Penguin, 2009), 271–272. Cf. Richard Evans, "Wives Against the Nazis," *The Sunday Telegraph* (London), available at http://www.chambon.org/rosenstrasse_evans_en.htm (last visited April 15 2015). While other chapters in this volume deal more specifically with debates surrounding the success or lack thereof of the Rosenstrasse protest, my objective here is to underline that the Rosenstrasse protest was not the only popular protest in the Third Reich, and that even protests that were not especially "explicit" could alter government policies. Rather than rehearsing the debate about what "real" resistance is, or what popular opposition might have achieved had it been more widespread, I seek to explore why, within the larger context of consent for the National Socialist regime, protests like those in Witten and on Berlin's Rosenstrasse struck a nerve. For additional discussion of resistance (*Resistenz*), opposition, and dissent, as well as the Rosenstrasse protest specifically, see Martin Broszat, *Nach Hitler: Der schwierigen Umgang mit unseren Geschichte*, ed. Hermann Graml and Klaus-Dietmar Henke (Munich: R. Oldenburg, 1986), 68–91; Christof Dipper, "Schwierigkeiten mit der Resistenz," *Geschichte und Gesellschaft* 22 (1996): 415; Neil Gregor, "Politics, Culture and Political Culture: Recent Work on the Third Reich and its Aftermath," *Journal of Modern History* 78, no. 3 (2006): 665; Wolf Gruner, *Widerstand in der Rosenstraße: die Fabrik-Aktion und die Verfolgung der "Mischehen" 1943* (Frankfurt am Main: Fischer, 2005); Ian Kershaw, *The Nazi Dictatorship: Problems and Perspectives of Interpretation*, 3rd ed. (New York: Routledge, 1993), chapter 8; Antonia Leugers, ed., *Berlin, Rosenstraße 2-4: Protest in der NS-Diktatur: Neue Forschungen zum Frauenprotest in der Rosenstraße 1943* (Annweiler: Plöger, 2005); Jill Stephenson, "Resistance and the Third Reich," *Journal of Contemporary History* 36, no. 3 (2001): 507–516; Nathan Stoltzfus, *Resistance of the Heart: Intermarriage and the Rosenstrasse Protest in Nazi Germany* (New York: W.W. Norton, 1996), 258–278; Nathan Stoltzfus, "'Third Reich History as if the People Mattered': Eine Entgegnung auf Christof Dipper," *Geschichte und Gesellschaft* 26, no. 4 (2000): 672–684.
4. The report is published in Heinz Boberach, ed., *Meldungen aus dem Reich: Auswahl aus den geheimen Lageberichten des Sicherheitsdienstes der SS 1939–1944* (Berlin: Luchterhand, 1965), 451–453. Since sources for the demonstration are scant, historians rely on the SD-report (BA: R 58/190). Attempts by the working group on women's history in Witten (Arbeitskreis Frauengeschichte Witten) to contact eyewitnesses to the demonstration failed. The absence of accounts from participants is problematic, though my focus is primarily on how the regime perceived the event and responded to it, rather than on Witteners' own view of their action.
5. Richard Evans, Martina Kliner-Lintzen, and Sybil Milton viewed the protest as a sign of women's discontent, though Evans has linked it more directly to evacuations in recent work; Detlev Peukert and Wolfgang Werner interpret it as workers' opposition. Richard Evans, "German Women and the Triumph of Hitler," *Journal of Modern History* 48, no. 1 (1976); Evans, *The Third Reich at War*, 452;

Martina Kliner-Lintzen, "Rathaus Witten: Unmut oder Widerstand?," in *Wittener Frauengeschichte(n): Dokumentation anläßlich einer frauengeschichtlichen Stadtrundfahrt*, ed. Beate Brunner and Martine Kliner-Lintzen (Witten: Laube, 1990); Sybil Milton, "Women and the Holocaust: The Case of German and German-Jewish Women," in *When Biology became Destiny: Women in Weimar and Nazi Germany*, ed. Renate Bridenthal, et al. (New York: Monthly Review Press, 1984), 319; Detlev Peukert, *Ruhrarbeiter gegen den Faschismus: Dokumentation über Widerstand im Ruhrgebiet 1933–1945* (Frankfurt am Main: Röderberg, 1976), 310; Wolfgang Franz Werner, *'Bleib übrig!': Deutsche Arbeiter in der nationalsozialistischen Kriegswirtschaft*, ed. Hans-Joachim Behr et al., vol. 9, *Düsseldorfer Schriften zur Neueren Landesgeschichte und zur Geschichte Nordrhein-Westfalens* (Düsseldorf: Schwann, 1983), 272.

6. Gerhard Kock, *"Der Führer sorgt für unser Kinder . . .": Die Kinderlandverschickung im Zweiten Weltkrieg* (Paderborn: Schöningh, 1997), 186–187.
7. Gerhard E. Sollbach, "'Mütter—schafft eure Kinder fort!': Kinderlandverschickung im Ruhrgebiet während des Zweiten Weltkriegs," *Geschichte im Westen* 13 (1998).
8. Olaf Groehler, *Bombenkrieg gegen Deutschland* (Berlin: Akademie-Verlag, 1990), 275.
9. The Reich Statistics Office reported 3.29 million evacuees on October 18, 1943 (BA: R 3102/44).
10. Heinrich Schoppmeyer, *Über 775 Jahre Witten: Beiträge zur Geschichte der Stadt Witten* (Meinerzhagen: Meinerzhagener, 1989), vol. 2, 75; Wilfried Beer, *Kriegsalltag an der Heimatfront: Alliierter Luftkrieg und deutsche Gegenmaßnahmen zur Abwehr und Schadensbegrenzung, dargestellt für den Raum Münster* (Bremen: H. M. Hauschild, 1990); Norbert Krüger, "Die Bombenangriffe auf das Ruhrgebiet im Frühjahr 1943," in *Ueber Leben im Krieg: Kriegserfahrungen in einer Industrieregion: 1939–1945*, ed. Ulrich Borsdorf and Mathilde Jamin (Reinbek bei Hamburg: Rowohlt, 1989), 91–92.
11. SD-report, November 18, 1943 (BA: R 58/190)
12. The train system was overburdened due to military exigencies, and of course also because of ongoing deportations of Jews and others. The authorities placed a temporary ban on all non-essential trips in the Reich between December 15, 1943, and January 3, 1944. Joseph Goebbels, *Die Tagebücher von Joseph Goebbels*, ed. Elke Fröhlich, part 2, *Diktate 1941–1945*, vol. 10, *October–December 1943*, ed. Volker Dahm (Munich, K.G. Sauer, 1994), November 6, 1943, 240; December 4, 1943, 418; Raul Hilberg, *Sonderzüge nach Auschwitz*, vol. 18, *Dokumente zur Eisenbahngeschichte* (Mainz: Dumjahn, 1981).
13. SD-report, September 9, 1943 (BA: R 58/188).
14. Circular, April 19, 1943 (StAM: NSV 648: 2).
15. The first two reception areas are noted in the Ministry of the Interior circular of April 19, 1943. A more detailed plan, July 1, 1943, adds Pomerania (StAM: NSV 648:2).
16. BA: R 1501/1415; Meeting of welfare officials at Mülheim/Ruhr, minutes, April 30, 1943 (StAM: NSV 642); Oberregierungsrat Fischer, "Umquartierung der Bevölkerung vor und nach Luftangriffen," *Deutsche Verwaltung* 21, no. 5 (1944): 116.

17. From 3.29 million evacuees on October 18, 1943, the number had increased to 3.34 million in January 1944, and it continued to rise. No national statistics appear to have survived for the period before autumn 1943, but evacuation programs clearly expanded enormously through summer and fall 1943 (BA: R 3102/44).
18. On the problems associated with evacuations, see Julia S. Torrie, *For Their Own Good: Civilian Evacuations in Germany and France, 1939–1945* (New York: Berghahn Books, 2010), especially chapter four.
19. Letter from Stuckart to Goebbels, April 1943 (BA: R 1501/1415).
20. Nathan Stoltzfus has argued that protests must be "sufficiently large and public" to succeed, which might tend to rule out rural areas and small cities. Stoltzfus, *Resistance*, 271.
21. Emphasis in the original, Gauleitung Baden: NSV, Circular Nr. 71/43, June 4, 1943 (GLAKHE: 465d/908). These individuals were initially sent south as part of a short-term NSV "holiday" program for women and children subjected to aerial bombing. In August, the NSV in Baden declared that women with young children from Witten and neighboring cities "do not count anymore as people who have been sent to take a cure [*Verschickte*], but as evacuees." This change in status implied a more permanent displacement. NSV Kreis Schlettstadt note to NSV Ortsgruppen, August 2, 1943 (BA: NS 45/104).
22. Whole school classes were evacuated from early summer 1943. Kock, *Kinderlandverschickung*, 214; Wilhelm Reeswinkel, "Wittener Kinder in der Kriegsheimat," *Jahrbuch des Veriens für Orts und Heimatkunde in der Grafschaft Mark* 56 (1953): 122.
23. Groehler, *Bombenkrieg*, 274.
24. Civilians felt the "calming of the aerial situation" spoke against evacuation. SD-report, November 18, 1943 (BA: R 58/190).
25. Westfalen-Süd representative in Baden, Spratte, Circular, September 14, 1943 (GLAKHE 465d/907); "Wichtige Mitteilung zur Umquartierung," *WLZ*, October 4, 1943.
26. I have focused on sanctions used to keep Westfalen-Süd evacuees in Baden, though similar methods were tried elsewhere. Evacuees who returned home, regardless of the reason, were no longer eligible for the evacuees' allowance, but since their expenses presumably decreased, too, this was not a powerful incentive to stay in the reception areas (BA: R 1501/1419).
27. Kock, *Kinderlandverschickung*, 186, 220–225.
28. Circular Nr. 4, August 31, 1943 (GLAKHE: 465d/907).
29. Hoffmann became Westfalen-Süd's Gauleiter in June 1943, but had performed the duties associated with this position from January that year. Hermann Weiß, ed., *Biographisches Lexicon zum Dritten Reich*, 2nd ed. (Frankfurt am Main: S. Fischer, 1998), 238. His decision regarding evacuees is recorded in a letter from October 9, 1943 (StAM: Gauleitung Westfalen-Süd, 16). Head liaison officer Spratte informed local liaison officers in August 1943 of Hoffmann's decision that, "Evacuees who return to the endangered or destroyed cities without sound reasons shall be issued no ration cards by the food offices responsible." Hoffmann quoted in Spratte circular, August 31, 1943, (GLAKHE: 465d/907).
30. SD-report, September 9, 1943 (BA: R 58/188).

31. Spratte's view of returns as irrational female behaviour was not unusual. Spratte, Circular Nr. 5, September 14, 1943 (GLAKHE 465d/907).
32. The WLZ was also made available to *Ruhr* evacuees in the reception areas. See GLAKHE 465d/907; "Evakuierte!: Der Feind sucht euch zu treffen! Weshalb keine Marken für Rückkehrer?" *WLZ*, September 18–19, 1943; "Wichtige Mitteilung zur Umquartierung," *WLZ*, October 4, 1943.
33. Robert Gellately, *Backing Hitler: Consent and Coercion in Nazi Germany* (Oxford: Oxford University Press, 2001), 49, 183.
34. Hoffmann to local officials responsible for evacuation measures, October 9, 1943 (StAM: Gauleitung Westfalen-Süd, 16); Sollbach, "Mütter," 155.
35. GLAKHE 465d/916.
36. Emphasis in the original, SD-report, November 18, 1943 (BA: R 58/190).
37. SD-report, October 18, 1943 (BA: R 58/190). Hoffmann's letter, October 9, 1943, spelled out the "loophole": "Those women who commit themselves freely to work service in their hometown can . . . return to their residences, but on condition that their school-age or younger children remain evacuated" (StAM, NSDAP Gauleitung Westfalen-Süd, 16). Spratte's circular October 20, 1943 (GLAKHE: 465d/907) emphasizes that women who agreed to take a job were welcome to return home.
38. SD-report, August 19, 1943 (BA: R 58/187).
39. Between 1920 and 1933, the SPD and KPD won about 50 percent of Witteners' votes in Reich elections. Even in the election of March 5, 1933, the SPD had 27.6 percent and the KPD 15.7 percent, for a total of 43.3 percent. Centrist parties claimed another 13.9 percent of the vote, leaving 42.8 percent for the Right. 34.2 percent went to the NSDAP. Schoppmeyer, *Über 775 Jahre Witten*, 64.
40. Groehler, *Bombenkrieg*, 276. On workers' protest in the Third Reich, see note 5 above and Ulrich Herbert, "Arbeiterschaft im 'Dritten Reich': Zwischenbilanz und offene Fragen," *Geschichte und Gesellschaft* 15 (1989); Klaus Witsotsky, *Der Ruhrbergbau im Dritten Reich: Studien zur Sozialpolitik im Ruhrbergbau und zum sozialen Verhalten der Bergleute in den Jahren 1933 bis 1939*, vol. 8, *Düsseldorfer Schriften zur Neuern Landesgeschichte und zur Geschichte Nordrhein-Westfalens* (Düsseldorf: Schwann, 1983).
41. Rather the opposite seems to have been true, for correspondents from the reception areas often complained that evacuees had too much money. One missive cites a Witten miner who apparently told his wife he had plenty to live on at home, so she should be able to "put together a considerable trousseau" with the surplus from her allowance. Letter from Artur S., August 26, 1944 (BA: R 1501/1419). For evacuees' own letters, see BA: R 55/591; BA: R 55/592; GLAKHE 465d/910.
42. "Wer heizt für den heimkommenden Mann? Niemand wird frieren: Die Nachbarn helfen," *WLZ*, September 29, 1943, 5. *Luftkriegsschädenausschuß*, Bulletin Nr. 37 summarizes problems associated with cooler weather, September 8, 1943 (StAM: NSV 648:1). The National Socialist party thought neighbors might assist, but local women already had enough to do; moreover, the idea of anyone else coming into their homes to help their husbands sent evacuated wives into jealous paroxysms. SD-report, November 18, 1943 (BA: R 58/190).

43. Westfalen-Nord's evacuation representative in Gau Salzburg, report on evacuation, October 30, 1943 (STAM: NSV 649: 2).
44. An NSV representative in Baden felt that evacuees' husbands should "show a little more discipline and a soldierly bearing and not constantly write whining letters, or threaten 'if you don't come, you'll see what I do.'" Letter, October 30, 1943 (GLAKHE 465d/916); see also StAM: NSV 1159.
45. Emphasis in the original, SD-report, November 18, 1943 (BA: R 58/190). A school authorities' report on Esseners in Swabia and Tirol, July 12–22, 1943, also cites homesickness for family members as a main cause of "wild" returns (Stadtarchiv Essen: 45/4035). Earlier in the summer, officials in Baden had complained about the number of parents traveling *to* the reception areas to visit their children—another family-motivated type of non-compliance that the regime tried to discourage. Spratte to NSDAP Ortsgruppenleiter in Hüfingen, August 3, 1943 (GLAKHE 495d/916).
46. It is not clear exactly how many Witteners were sent to Donaueschingen. Reeswinkel claimed to be responsible for seventy women and children from his school. Statistics from August 1943 show there were 1,947 evacuees from Westfalen-Süd in the town, but do not give their origins more specifically. In August 1943, there were a total of 77,653 Westfalen-Süd evacuees in Baden (GLAKHE: 465d/914).
47. Since letters about Reeswinkel refer to him as "Herr," not "Parteigenossen," he was not a Nazi party member. His own letters suggest that he had a strong traditional sense of morality and "honour." Reeswinkel was not popular with Westfalen-Süd's representative in the district from at least October 1943. District representative Jaeger to Westfalen-Süd's representative in Baden, Fischer, March 10, 1944 (GLAKHE: 465d/919, and correspondence in GLAKHE: 465d/916). Reeswinkel wrote about the Witten evacuations after the war, but without mentioning his own role or the protest. Reeswinkel, "Wittener," 118–146.
48. On March 3, 1944, Jaeger wrote that "apparently in many instances, . . . the [Witten] women turn to [Reeswinkel] with their questions about vacations [i.e. trips home], and possibly leave following his advice, without my permission" (GLAKHE: 465d/919). Perhaps the same had been true the previous fall. At the Rosenstrasse, Margarethe Sommer of the Hilfswerk beim Bischöflichen Ordinariat Berlin may have played a motivating role similar to that of Reeswinkel. Jana Leichsenring, "Wurde der Protest in der Rosenstraße . . . organisiert?," in *Berlin, Rosenstraße 2-4: Protest in der NS-Diktatur: Neue Forschungen zum Frauenprotest in der Rosenstraße 1943*, ed. Antonia Leugers (Annweiler: Plöger, 2005), 81–114.
49. SD-report, November 18, 1943 (BA: R 58/190). Cf. Ian Kershaw, *The Hitler Myth: Image and Reality in the Third Reich* (Oxford: Oxford University Press, 1987), 102–104, 211–212.
50. Following Ian Kershaw, I refer to low-level activity like the Witten demonstration as opposition or dissent, terms more satisfactory than *Resistenz* essentially because the latter suggests more formal, principled opposition to the regime than was manifested at Witten. Kershaw, *Nazi Dictatorship*, chapter 8.
51. On food-related protests in World War I, see Belinda J. Davis, *Home Fires Burning: Food, Politics, and Everyday Life in World War I Berlin* (Chapel Hill: University

of North Carolina Press, 2000). Kliner-Linzen and Milton refer to the demonstration as a kind of bread riot, while Evans notes similarities between this kind of "women's protest" and those of peasants. Evans, "German Women," 40; Kliner-Lintzen, "Rathaus Witten," 319; Milton, "Women and the Holocaust," 45. Cf. Karen Hagemann, "Frauenprotest und Männerdemonstrationen: Zum geschlechts-spezifischen Aktionsverhalten im großstädtischen Arbeitermilieu der Weimarer Republik," in *Massenmedium Straße: Zur Kulturgeschichte der Demonstration*, ed. Bernd Jürgen (Frankfurt am Main: Campus, 1991).

52. The location of the demonstration is not completely clear, but it likely took place in front of the municipal food office, which in a small city was probably inside the city hall. See SD-report, 18 Nov. 1943 (BA: R 58/190); Kliner-Lintzen, "Rathaus Witten," 45.
53. One might point to Barrington Moore's conclusion that the desire to revolt stems from a popular perception that the governors are not "playing fairly"; that they have broken the social contract. Barrington Moore, *Injustice: The Social Bases of Obedience and Revolt* (White Plains, NY: M.E. Sharpe, 1978), 509–510.
54. SD-Report, November 18, 1943 (BA: R 58/190).
55. Emphasis in original. SD-Report, November 18, 1943 (BA: R 58/190).
56. SD-Report, November 18, 1943 (BA: R 58/190).
57. Intriguingly, both this protest, and the one at Witten, took place on a Monday. This may have been a coincidence, but it is also possible that ration card delivery and the need to attend to urgent weekday errands brought crowds of women together in public spaces on Mondays, making this a likely day for protest. Events in Dortmund-Hörde are recounted in SD-report, July 8, 1943, cited in, "Der Führer darf das gar nicht wissen: Aus den Stimmungs-Analysen des nationalsozialistischen Sicherheitsdienstes von 1939 bis 1943," *Der Spiegel* 51, December 15, 1965, 83, available at http://www.spiegel.de/spiegel/print/d-46275329.html (last visited 22 Oct. 2015).
58. Leichsenring, "Berlin," 81–114.
59. Faced with the authorities' refusal to deliver their cards, the SD reported, "Die betreffenden Frauen hätten jedoch versucht, die Aushändigung der Lebensmittelkarten *zu erzwingen*." Emphasis in original. SD-report, November 18, 1943 (BA: R 58/190).
60. SD-report, November 18, 1943 (BA: R 58/190).
61. Davis emphasizes that a sympathetic police reaction and press coverage treating women's claims as rational and legitimate helped further the demands of Berlin's "women of lesser means" during World War I. Davis, *Home Fires*, 99ff.
62. SD-report, November 18, 1943 (BA: R 58/190).
63. SD-report, November 18, 1943 (BA: R 58/190).
64. SD-report, November 18, 1943 (BA: R 58/190).
65. SD-report, February 10, 1944 (BA: R 58/192).
66. Letter from Goebbels to all Gauleiter, January 28, 1944 (BA: R 55/447).
67. Even after the January circular publicizing the Führer's decision, ration cards were denied to "wild" returnees on a small scale in certain localities, as in Münster (Gau Westfalen-Nord) in September 1944. Kock, *Kinderlandverschickung*, 187n 171.
68. Stoltzfus, *Resistance*, 15.

69. SD-report, November 18, 1943 (BA: R 58/190).
70. Oberlandsgerichtspräsident Hamm to Reichsminister der Justiz, quarterly report, December 6, 1943 (BA: R3001/alt R 22/3367).
71. Oberlandsgerichtspräsident Hamm to Reichsminister der Justiz, quarterly report, December 6, 1943 (BA: R3001/alt R 22/3367).
72. Ian Kershaw notes that some who objected to the National Socialist "euthanasia" program were not opposed to the program *per se*, but found the absence of a law to back up the policy disturbing. Ian Kershaw, *Popular Opinion and Political Dissent in the Third Reich: Bavaria 1933–1945* (Oxford: Oxford University Press, 1983), 336–337, 340.
73. This call (a "Rundruf") is mentioned in a report on evacuation by Westfalen-Nord's evacuation representative in Gau Salzburg, October 30, 1943 (STAM: NSV 649: 2), which summarizes the content and dates it specifically to October 12, 1943.
74. "Gauleiter Albert Hoffmann bei den Umquartierten in Baden: Neue Maßnahmen der Versorgung und Betreuung," *WLZ*, October 16–17, 1943, Nr. 242, 1; "Der Gauleiter brachte die Grüße der Heimat: Buntes Mosaik von seinem Besuch bei den umquartierten Frauen und Kindern in Baden," *WLZ*, 22 Oct. 1943, Nr. 247, 3.
75. Goebbels, *Tagebücher*, vol. 10, November 2, 1943, 222.
76. Goebbels, *Tagebücher*, vol. 10, November 7, 1943, 248.
77. Goebbels, *Tagebücher*, vol. 10, November 21, 1943, 330.
78. Goebbels, *Tagebücher*, vol. 10, November 26, 1943, 362.
79. Meyer imposed the restriction on December 15, 1943, Kock, *Kinderlandverschickung*, 186.
80. Goebbels, *Tagebücher*, vol. 10, December 12, 1943, 465.
81. Goebbels, *Tagebücher*, vol. 10, December 14, 1943, 475.
82. Goebbels, *Tagebücher*, vol. 11, January 23, 1943, 144.
83. Goebbels, *Tagebücher*, vol. 11, January 14, 1944, 88–89.
84. The meeting took place on January 24, 1944, and was described by Goebbels the following day. Goebbels, *Tagebücher*, vol. 11, January 25, 1944, 165.
85. BA: R 55/447 and Goebbels, *Tagebücher*, vol. 11, January 27, 1944, 182.
86. SD-report, November 18, 1943 (BA: R 58/190).
87. BA: R1501/1415. Interestingly, the denial of ration cards had already failed in February 1943 as a disciplinary measure against civilians in occupied France, where, despite German orders, French officials refused to deny ration cards to workers who did not want to return to their jobs in heavily bombed Lorient. Regardless of its failure in occupied France, where popular opinion presumably mattered less to the German authorities than in the Reich itself, Gauleiter Hoffmann went ahead with the same controversial disciplinary measure at home. On the situation at Lorient, see General Delegation of the French Government in the Occupied Territories to Direction of (French) armistice services, note, February 2, 1943 (Archives Nationales, Paris: 41 AJ/356); Robert Gildea, *Marianne in Chains: In Search of the German Occupation 1940–45* (London: MacMillan, 2002), chapter 3.
88. "Bericht des Gauleiters Grohé über die Luftangriffe in den letzten Wochen," July 22, 1943 (BA: R 3001/2328).
89. Letter from Goebbels to all Gauleiter, January 28, 1944 (BA: R 55/447).

90. Goebbels, *Tagebücher,* Volume 10, December 16, 1943, 482.
91. Stoltzfus, *Resistance,* 270, 14.
92. Goebbels, *Tagebücher,* vol. 11, January 12, 1944, 77.
93. "Bericht des Gauleiters Grohé über die Luftangriffe und ihre Folgen im Gau Köln-Aachen in den Monaten Januar und Februar 1943," March 5, 1943 (BA: R 3001/2308).
94. "Bericht des Gauleiters Grohé über die Luftangriffe in den letzten Wochen," July 22, 1943 (BA: R 3001/2328).
95. Goebbels, *Tagebücher,* vol. 10, December 20, 1943, 514–515.
96. Goebbels, *Tagebücher,* vol. 11, January 14, 1944, 88.
97. See Goebbels's account of his meeting with the Führer, January 24, 1944. Goebbels, *Tagebücher,* vol. 11, entries for January 25, 1944, 165, and January 27, 1944, 182.
98. Letter from Goebbels to all Gauleiter, January 28, 1944 (BA: R 55/447).
99. Goebbels, *Tagebücher,* vol. 10, November 24, 1943, 344–345.
100. Goebbels, *Tagebücher,* vol. 10, November 25, 1943, 354; ibid., November 26, 1943, 362. Goebbels had already been in charge of the Interministerial Air War Damages Committee (Interministerieller Luftkriegsschädenausschuß) since the previous January. Richard Evans suggests that events in Kassel, where the local NSDAP leader failed to provide effective leadership during a major bombing on October 22, 1943, spurred the creation of the Reich Inspection, but Goebbels himself emphasized the Berlin experience, and stressed the need to prepare other cities to endure the same intensity of bombing as the capital. Evans, *The Third Reich at War,* 453.
101. Evans, *The Third Reich at War,* 453.
102. On the history of evacuations in Germany prior to 1939, see Torrie, *For Their Own Good,* chapter one.
103. Peter Fritzsche, *A Nation of Fliers: German Aviation and the Popular Imagination* (Cambridge, MA: Harvard University Press, 1992).
104. "Gauleiter Albert Hoffmann bei den Umquartierten in Baden: Neue Maßnahmen der Versorgung und Betreuung," *WLZ,* October 16–17, 1943, Nr. 242, 1; "Der Gauleiter brachte die Grüße der Heimat: Buntes Mosaik von seinem Besuch bei den umquartierten Frauen und Kindern in Baden," *WLZ,* October 22, 1943, Nr. 247, 3.
105. LK-Mitteilung Nr. 68, December 6, 1943 (R 55/447); LK- Mitteilung 77, ca. December 22 or 23, 1943 (StAM: NSV 650).
106. Letter from Goebbels to all Gauleiter, January 28, 1944 (BA: R 55/447).
107. Himmler and Bormann's order (July 29, 1944) is cited in a document from the Baden Interior Minister, August 21, 1944 (GLAKHE 465d/1529).
108. Martin Bormann to Acting Gauleiter Schlessmann, Essen, October 12, 1944 (StAM: NSV 650). Schlessmann may well have contacted Bormann for clarification after ration cards appeared to be being denied in nearby Münster in late September (see note 67).
109. Kershaw, *Popular Opinion,* 356; Stoltzfus, *Resistance,* 260; Leugers, *Berlin.*
110. Kershaw, *Popular Opinion,* 345, 349–350; Stoltzfus, *Resistance,* 201.
111. Kershaw, *Popular Opinion,* 349.

112. Cf. Stoltzfus, *Resistance*, 245, 261–262.
113. SD-report, November 18, 1943 (BA: R 58/190).
114. Kershaw, *Popular Opinion*, 343.
115. Stoltzfus, *Resistance*, 232, 243–244; Joachim Neander, "Die Auschwitz-Rückkehrer vom 21. März 1943," in Leugers, *Berlin*, 118–119, 139.
116. Goebbels, *Tagebücher,* vol. 10, November 2, 1943, 222.
117. Stoltzfus, *Resistance*, 245; Kershaw, *Popular Opinion*, 357, cf. 339.

Chapter 6

The "Legend" of Women's Resistance in the Rosenstrasse

Katharina von Kellenbach

In 1996 Nathan Stoltzfus called the weeklong vigil of non-Jewish women in Berlin in March 1943 who demanded the release of their interned Jewish husbands a "singular incident of mass German protest against the deportation of German Jews."[1] His book stimulated considerable academic as well as popular media interest and occasioned numerous articles, commemorative events, and documentaries, as well as a movie. This sudden popularity may have provoked the scholarly backlash, which has begun to refer to what Stoltzfus calls an "open confrontation . . . on the Gestapo's very front step"[2] as a "legend."[3] Wolf Gruner was the first to question Stoltzfus's history and conclusion that "mass public protest was the most powerful form of civilian opposition."[4] A review of Wolf Gruner's thesis in the *Spiegel* (2002) begins by calling the street protests in the Rosenstrasse a "miracle," then an "alleged miracle," and finally a "legendary event" in the course of three paragraphs. In their recent publications, Richard Evans (2009) and Saul Friedländer (2008) have adopted the designation "legend" for interpretations that claim that the protest interrupted Gestapo plans for deporting intermarried Jews interned at Rosenstrasse.[5] I approach this topic as a religious studies scholar, for whom "miracles," "legends," and "myths"[6] are a stock-in-trade, though I am acutely aware that these designations are considered devastating judgments among historians.

The tone and acrimony of the debate suggests that there is more going on than a scholarly dispute over historical evidence. I will leave the evidentiary basis of these discussions to the historical experts who are contributing to this volume. Instead I want to comment on the mechanisms and the ease with which women's presence in history can be relegated to the realm of legend. I will argue that this demotion of women's protests to a "legend" stands in a long tradition of denigration of women's agency in the patriarchal world of history, religion, and politics.

I want to begin these reflections on the interplay of gender, history, and legend with a historical digression into the first century C.E. where another group of women suddenly come into public view under a cross. The New Testament is not only a religious text concerned with miracles and legends, but also a historical document that allows scholars to reconstruct the lives and aspirations of ordinary folk in a colony of the Roman Empire in the first century, such as fishermen, carpenters, prostitutes, and tax collectors. It is remarkable to find historical reference to the struggles and stories of uneducated men in the countryside of Galilee. It is even harder to find written references to the lives of women. Like most other ancient texts written by men, the Gospel accounts ignore the existence of women for the most part. Narrative emphasis is put on twelve men who gather around Jesus of Nazareth and travel with him from the Galilee in order to attend the Passover festivities in Jerusalem. The story of Jesus's arrest, interrogation, and eventual execution at the hands of the Roman authorities moves dramatically through the gradual abandonment by his male disciples. One disciple betrays him, others fail to stay awake during the night vigil, and Peter denies him three times. Suddenly in the hour of despair, and attested in all four canonical as well as in several non-canonical Gospels, a group of women comes into view. We learn of their existence only at the very end of Jesus's ministry and astoundingly are informed that they had been there all along: "There were also many women there, looking on from afar, who had followed Jesus from Galilee, ministering to him, among them were Mary Magdalene, and Mary the mother of James and Joseph" (Matthew 27:55).[7]

This single, tantalizing sentence breaks the dominant narrative focus on the male band of brothers who allegedly made up the early Jesus movement. Why do these first-century Jewish women move into public view only during the crucifixion, a time of violence and repression? I would argue that this story is one instance among many throughout history where women moved into focus as public (and therefore political) actors at the height of government repression, often in response to the brutalization of loved ones at the hands of the state.

In patriarchal societies, women are not considered political or religious agents. They are relegated to the private realm of the family where they are supposed to care for loved ones within the confines of the home. They are supposed to be invisible. Their devotion and dedication is not perceived as a political act or a reflection of religious conviction but as a sign of personal commitment and emotional attachment. As the Jesus movement was targeted for religious subversion and political sedition, only the women remained able to move about in public. Fearing for their lives, the male disciples dispersed into hiding. At this point, the women, who had been in the streets traveling with the twelve disciples all along, move into the public eye—for the first time. And just as quickly, they disappear from the story again. The hidden brethren dismiss their testimony about Jesus's empty tomb as "an idle tale [that] they did not believe." (Luke 24:11). Their public standing in emergent Christian communities was curtailed and their personal authority undermined, most notably in the case of Mary Magdalene who was slandered as a prostitute. In subsequent historical reconstructions of early Christianity, these courageous and committed women would again be ignored and relegated to the background of the private sphere.

A more recent example of a similar dynamic is the story of the Argentine Mothers of the Plaza de Mayo. Like the women of Berlin's Rosenstrasse and Jerusalem's Golgotha, these women took to the streets at the height of repression and violence. As mothers of *disappeared* sons and daughters, these women decried the deceptions and despotic cruelty of a military dictatorship at a time of fearful silence when all public protest had become impossible. While the women of the Rosenstrasse acted on authority of their marital status and in defense of the institution of marriage, the Argentine women invoked the symbol of motherhood to oppose governmental authority. They rebutted the ideological dehumanization of their children as *terrorists*, just as the Berlin women opposed the anti-Semitic demonization of their husbands. Furthermore, in each instance, these women refuse to submit to the government's logic of absolute control, as Marguerite Guzman Bouvard has argued in *Revolutionizing Motherhood*: "The military junta, as well as the police and security forces still active today, believed that it is possible to exercise total control of the population and that power is based on physical force. The Mothers proved otherwise, blatantly expanding the interstices of control."[8]

In each of these cases, the women faced derision and ridicule. While the New Testament dismisses the women's witness as "idle tales" (Luke 24:11), the Argentine women were smeared as *"Las Locas,"* the Crazy Ones.[9] Scorn and mockery are common strategies, not limited to particular times or governments. They serve to undermine the credibility of women and to "keep them in their places—that is, marginal and invisible."[10] In the following, we will explore whether the scholars who have begun to call the history of the Rosenstrasse a "legend," wittingly or unwittingly stand in this (patriarchal) tradition of disdain.

The work of feminist scholarship "begins with hearing silence."[11] In the face of the near-universal absence of women's voices and experiences, feminist scholars developed a "hermeneutic of suspicion."[12] Approaching history with a "hermeneutic of suspicion" means to question the pervasive absence of women from the world of religion, politics, art, philosophy, and science, and to operate on the basis of an assumption that women make up more than fifty percent of humanity. As half of humankind, women have participated and impacted all historical events even if sacred, secular, legal, political, and literary texts do not mention their existence. Feminist historical scholarship using the hermeneutics of suspicion has been able to substantially expand the knowledge base of politically, religiously, and scholarly active women. But women's moral agency, political participation, and religious subjectivity remain contested and concealed—in history, as well as in the contemporary world. Gerda Lerner, scion of women's history in the United States, concluded her *tour de force* of the history of feminist consciousness in the Western world: "For 1200 years, in sporadic, intermittent and often pathetically ineffective ways, women struggled to counteract the trend and to leave, as men did, traces of their names and actions in the historical record. Yet, in the face of patriarchal hegemony over culture, the leaving of 'traces' and even the collection of sources was utterly insufficient to affect the way History was being written and being taught."[13]

The erasure of women from the historical record serves the disempowerment and marginalization of women in contemporary politics. History is a vital battleground on which communities construct meaning. As a scholar of religious studies, I am very aware of the power of narratives to anchor and authorize current aspirations for meaning and identity. The very term religion (*re-ligio*) means to "tie" or "bind back" contemporary communal concerns into a more or less ancient past. Religious as well as secular political communities tell and retell stories from the past. As long as history remains the domain of strong men, kings, and military leaders, the lives of ordinary men and women will be considered of little consequence. By expanding history to include the lives of peasants and slaves, their emancipation and empowerment becomes more likely and relevant. This is the simplest and most basic justification for "social history," "women's history," or "black history."

The events in the Rosenstrasse turned women's private care for their husbands from a hidden "resistance of the heart" into public acts of resistance against Nazi policies. Like the Jewish women under the cross and the Argentine Women on the Plaza del Mayo, these women understood themselves to be ordinary women, compelled primarily by personal attachment. They acted as wives and mothers and congregated in the streets of Berlin in the spring of 1943 precisely because they could not be classified as members of any particular political movement. They were not organized and did not represent particular institutions (i.e. the churches) or political parties (i.e. the Communist Party). Their public presence extended and exposed women's care that ordinarily occurs in private. Although the daily struggle to nurture and protect the lives of family members is usually not considered a political or religious act, it is in fact, always political.[14] But most chroniclers take women's work for granted when documenting the serious business of religion, politics, and history. It is only under certain political circumstances that the care of women bursts onto the public stage.

Stoltzfus breaks with two disciplinary conventions that tend to marginalize women in history: first, he interprets women's presence in the streets as an act of solidarity that had political consequences for the Nazi state. Second, the voice and experience of these women is given weight by Stoltzfus's use of interviews and unpublished sources, including diaries and letters. His critics have jumped on his reliance on oral history. Historian Richard Evans delivers such an authoritative verdict in a footnote of his 2009 monumental *The Third Reich at War:* "For the legend in its classical form see Nathan Stoltzfus, *Resistance of the Heart* . . . (relying heavily on oral history interviews)."[15] Without further comment or critical analysis, Evans dismisses Stoltzfus's reading primarily for its reliance on "oral history." His assessment is patently wrong and fails to engage the substantial written documents that have convinced other reviewers of the evidence that the protest mounted by women was successful in securing the release of their Jewish husbands.[16] Arguments over the merits of empirical evidence are part of the scholarly process. But those who have recently discredited the Rosenstrasse as a legend tend to ignore the written record and disguise their dismissal on the basis of methodology. Such principled objections to oral history serve to solidify the marginalization of women whose voices and experiences are habitually overlooked by the keepers of official records.[17] Scholars who insist on textual authority and "hard evidence" of written records exacerbate the irrelevance and invisibility of women.

Wolf Gruner's dissertation research, under the direction of Wolfgang Benz, initiated the reconsideration of the weeklong detention of intermarried Jewish men, women, and children in the Rosenstrasse 2-4. His thesis rests on two main arguments: first, he questions the recollections of eyewitnesses on whom Stoltzfus bases his conclusions and maintains instead that the designation of the assembled family members as a "demonstration" is an overstatement and exaggeration. He maintains that in the absence of written documents such as police reports or newspaper accounts and in light of various inconsistencies among different eyewitness accounts one may only call these street gatherings a "silent protest."[18] Second, Gruner cites written Gestapo orders and SS deportation guidelines to argue that the street protests could not have lead to the release of the arrested men because their deportation had not been intended. Although the incarcerated men were in fact released, Gruner maintains that this occurred in accordance with prior government plans and not in response to any street disturbances. The women themselves may have thought that they got their men released from prison, but in factual reality they did not.

Saul Friedländer concurs with Gruner's conclusion that the protesters' demeanor and intentions as well as the nature of the gathering in the Rosenstrasse have been inflated. Friedländer accepts Gruner's thesis of a "silent protest"[19] and describes the crowd gathered in front of the building in the Rosenstrasse in the following way:

> [S]cores of spouses, other relatives, and friends did gather on the opposite sidewalk and at times called for the prisoners; they mainly waited for information or tried to get food parcels into the building. Such unusual gatherings certainly demanded a measure of courage, but they were relatively modest and completely nonaggressive. They did not bring about the release of the detainees, as deportation had not been planned at any time for these Jews. The event turned into legend, however: A demonstration of thousands of German women brought about the liberation of their Jewish husbands. It is an uplifting legend, yet a legend nonetheless.[20]

A "gathering" on the "sidewalk" of people waiting patiently for information cannot claim to be a "demonstration." The "spouses" and "relatives" (note the non-gendered term) were "modest" and "non-aggressive." While "modest" and "non-aggressive" are feminine traits, "non-violent" conduct is masculine behavior that implies politically strategic mode of behavior. A crowd of women hardly appears as a political gathering, which leads Richard Evans to conclude that "the crowd had not engaged in any kind of explicit protest."[21] While Gruner and Friedländer grudgingly admit that the women's weeklong and vociferous presence in the streets required "a measure of courage," the language is designed to contest the "legend": This was not a non-violent action but a "non-aggressive" gathering, those assembled were not women but "relatives," it should not be called a "protest" but be merely considered a "crowd," the women were not calling out and demanding the release of their husband but waited meekly, passively, and silently.

Subtly, the terminology in this retelling reinscribes normative gender expectations, which incidentally the women themselves might have shared with later historians. In her analysis of resistance in women's literature, literary critic Leigh Westerfield notes that it is one of the "characteristics of women's narratives . . . that they frequently represent the illegal activity of females not as an organized means to a clearly defined political end or as a defence of social and cultural ideals, but rather as a spontaneous gesture of help for victims of Nazi repression and persecution . . . the modest terms in which women have couched descriptions of female resisters' experiences have more to do with dominant cultural and social expectations that demand a weak and passive demeanor of women than with a realistic assessment of what women actually accomplished as opponents of Nazism."[22] "Modesty" is one such term that appears both in Friedländer's description as well as the women's self-assessment. Ruth Andreas-Friedrich was an exception. A participant and eyewitness of the events in the Rosenstrasse, her diary published in 1947 as *Schattenmann: Schauplatz Berlin— Tagebuchaufzeichnungen 1938–1945*[23] "does not tone down these events in which the women defy social prescriptions of feminine submissiveness; rather she characterizes the women as 'masculine' in their toughness and their unbreakable spirit. The author bluntly names the action 'rebellion.'"[24] Ruth Andreas-Friedrich defied gendered expectations of female modesty by claiming courage, fighting spirit, and heroism, a portrayal that invites suspicions of sensationalism and exaggeration.

Gruner puts quotation marks around the word "diary"[25] and dismisses her journal entries on the events in the Rosenstrasse as "not entirely authentic, but written shortly after the end of the war."[26] "Most extant reports," he maintains, "were recorded decades later and sometimes more than half a century after the events."[27] The possibility of hindsight embellishment and faulty memory disqualify the credibility of these reports. Gruner questions such recollections of eyewitnesses and points to inconsistencies and contradictions by comparing different oral accounts: someone saw machine guns, others didn't; some maintain that the street was closed and the tram diverted, others didn't; some heard loud rhythmic shouting, others heard only low-voiced grumbling and murmured demands, some put the number of protesters in the thousands while others remembered a much smaller gathering. Such differences in eyewitness recollections can be accounted for by the weeklong duration of the protests. Over the course of a week, the crowds fluctuated as did the police presence. Sometimes people chanted and sometimes they complained quietly, at some points police charged with weapons while at other times they withdrew during a weeklong tug-of-war. But for Gruner the paucity of "written evidence" undermines the reliability of eyewitness accounts as he makes his case for a postwar "legend:" "Without contemporary written sources," he maintains, "it is impossible to come to historically verifiable conclusions" concerning the number of participants, the lengths, the strengths of their demands, the level of threat by the police and SS, their demeanor, etc.[28]

Gruner has himself been criticized for inconsistent and flawed use of written documents.[29] On the one hand, he asserts the supremacy of written records in order to undermine the credibility of eyewitnesses but on the other hand, he disregards documents that contradict his thesis.[30] To pick only one example of such a strategy: he maintains that the silence in Berlin's major daily newspapers and their failure to report about protests and street disturbances in the Rosenstrasse proves that the crowd was small and contained to the sidewalks.³¹ But such a conclusion based on contemporary press reports ignores common sense knowledge of the well-oiled censorship and propaganda machinery of the Nazi state. We know of no repressive regime in recent memory that has allowed its own or the international press to report freely on street protests. Gruner withholds at least one written contemporary report that was prepared by Gerhardt Lehfeldt in mid-March 1943 and delivered to Protestant Bishop Wurm and Catholic Bishop Bertram. In this report, Lehfeldt provides detailed information on the arrest of intermarried Jewish partners. He also relates a summons received by two Swedish reporters who were specifically told by officials in the propaganda ministry to refrain from reporting about "certain actions in Berlin . . . in the coming days . . . in their newspaper." ³² If foreign reporters were explicitly prohibited from reporting, one may safely assume that Berlin newspapers were kept under tight control.

The *Jüdische Allgemeine*, Februrary 18, 1955, called for all who had resisted and suffered under National Socialism to register at the Berlin Bureau of Reparations, including "the participants in the demonstration march of the "Aryan" wives on Rosenstrasse." In response to the *Jüdische Allgemeine*'s call, more than sixty women attested to the Berlin Bureau of Reparations to demonstrating on Berlin's Rosenstrasse for the release of Jews in early 1943, using their own words to describe the numbers of women present and their actions, including "Demonstrations," "Processions," and "Demonstration March." In their own words they also described their collective action of calling out together, "We want to have our husbands back," and of being told to leave and threatened with weapons.

The pervasive use of censorship and tactical deception by the Nazi regime means that written records must also be subjected to critical analysis. Historians should not give greater credence to a Gestapo incidence or contemporary newspaper report that could only be released with prior approval by the propaganda ministry than to recollections of surviving participants. Documents written by state actors reflect the perspective of perpetrators and should not automatically be considered more reliable. While the Nazi state left copious amounts of written documentation, its victims struggled to leave spotty clues and often failed despite heroic and desperate attempts to leave traces of their struggles. But for Gruner "many recollections of survivors," who "were interviewed decades later," were contaminated by earlier newspaper accounts published shortly after the war.³³ While eyewitness testimony is susceptible to hearsay, can be shaped by media discussions, and may be influenced by various cultural pressures,

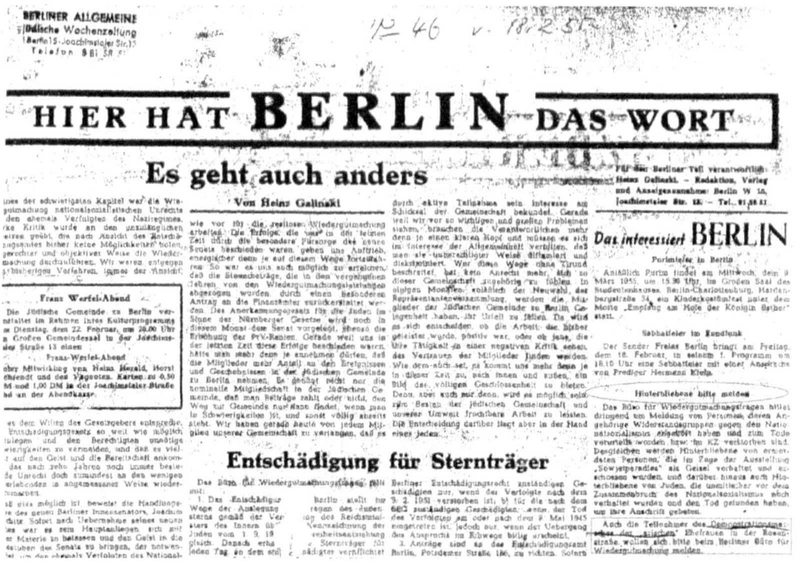

BERLINER ALLGEMEINE
Jüdische Wochenzeitung
Berlin 15, Joachimstaler Str. 13
Telefon 91 58 ..

HIER HAT BERLIN DAS WORT

Es geht auch anders

Von Heinz Galinski

Franz-Werfel-Abend

Entschädigung für Sternträger

Das interessiert BERLIN

Purimfeier in Berlin

Sabbatfeier im Rundfunk

Hinterbliebene bitte melden

Figure 6.1a. The *Jüdische Allgemeine*, February 18, 1955, called for all who had resisted and suffered under National Socialism to register at the Berlin Bureau of Reparations, including "the participants in the demonstration march of the "Aryan" wives on Rosenstrasse."

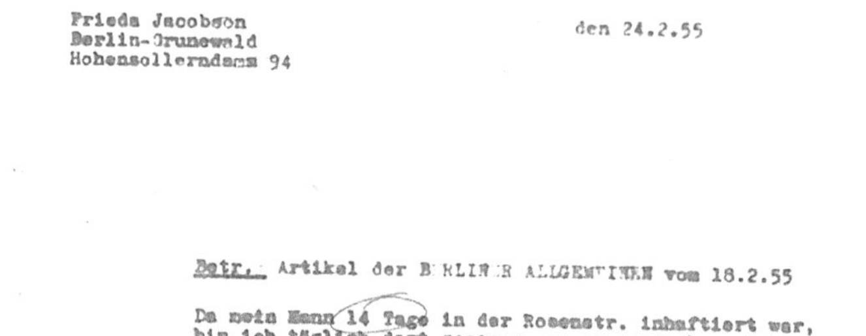

Frieda Jacobson
Berlin-Grunewald
Hohenzollerndamm 94

den 24.2.55

Betr.: Artikel der BERLINER ALLGEMEINEN vom 18.2.55

Da mein Mann 14 Tage in der Rosenstr. inhaftiert war, bin ich täglich dort gewesen, um zu versuchen, Lebensmittel hineinzuschmuggeln, und ist es mir auch einige Male mit Hilfe der Ordner gelungen, etwas durchgeben zu können.

Besondere Demonstrationen unternahm ich mit hunderten von anderen Frauen, am 1. Sonntag nach der Einlieferung in der Rosenstr. mit

Frau

Figure 6.1b. In response to the Jüdische Allgemeine's call, more than 60 women attested to the Berlin Bureau of Reparations that they had demonstrated on Berlin's Rosenstrasse for the release of Jews in early 1943, using their own descriptions to describe their actions, including "Demonstrations," "Processions," "Demonstration March."

```
Gertrud Blumenthal                 Berlin-Steglitz, den 6. März 1955
                                   Mühlebornweg 24

        Bezugnehmend auf Ihre Rundfrage in der "Berliner Allgemeinen"
        teile ich Ihnen mit, daß ich mich meinerseits im Jahre 1943
        an Demonstrationen in der Rosenstraße beteiligt habe, da auch
        mein Mann inhaftiert war.
           Nachdem wir Demonstranten durch Gestapoleute mit Pistolen be-
        droht wurden, stieben wir erst auseinander, um uns kurze Zeit
        danach wieder zu sammeln und weiter zu demonstrieren.
           Ich hoffe, Ihnen mit diesen Angaben gedient zu haben und
        zeichne,
                                   mit Hochachtung
                                   gez. Gertrud Blumenthal
```

Figure 6.1c. In their own words they also described their collective action of calling out together, "We want to have our husbands back," and of being ordered by the guards to "clear the streets or we will shoot." In postwar interviews Goebbels' Head Deputy, Leopold Gutterer, said that the threats of shooting had been directed at the women, and not at the imprisoned Jews, but that this was not done since this would have caused a yet greater circle of unrest within non-Jewish family circles.

historians can (and do) take measures to distinguish fact from fiction. The testimony by former protesters in the Rosenstrasse rests on sufficient written primary source material to be taken seriously.

Gruner's second basis for challenging the "legend" concerns the street protests' ultimate outcome or success. No deportations, so goes Gruner's argument, had been planned by the Nazi authorities, and therefore, the protests did not contribute to the eventual release of the interned men, nor to the return of thirty-five men who had already been deported to Auschwitz. And Saul Friedländer reiterates this position: "deportation had not been planned at any time for these Jews," and therefore the street "gathering" did not accomplish their release. Instead, the women's patient vigil had no effect on the authorities who were meticulously performing racial identity checks and proceeding with their original plans of reassigning (slave) labor postings. Richard Evans's assertion that "there had never been any intention of sending these particular Jews East for extermination" seems downright reckless in light of what we know about the Holocaust. The contention that the only case of public street protests should coincide with the only, or one of the few, cases in which the Nazi state had no intentions of deporting a group of Jews arrested during an *Aktion* of mass arrests and deportations known as *Entjudung des Reichgebietes Aktion* borders on a miracle. The point of the challenge seems to be that the women's actions were futile. They could have just as well stayed at home and waited patiently for the "registration" and "reassignment plans" of the Gestapo to work. And in the long run, they accomplished nothing, as their actions did not stop the deportation and extermination of European Jews.

The dismissal of the Rosenstrasse as a legendary protest may be indicative of political changes and the decline of women's political activism. The decline of feminist street activism (at least in the Western world) seems to justify a revision in the history of women's resistance. In 1976 Richard Evans acknowledged:

> Nazis' knowledge that women could be much more easily provoked into open resistance than men, and their fear that such resistance might have become very difficult to suppress without alienating not only the general populace but also the soldiers at the front. . . . The Nazi authorities kept a particularly close watch on the morale of women during the war; and they paid close attention to the maintenance of food supplies, whose inadequate provision during the First World War had led to violent disturbances, invariably led and carried out by women, as early as the spring of 1916. Nevertheless, similar outbreaks took place during the Second World War. On 11

October 1943, for example, a series of riots took place in Hamm, Lünen, Bochum and Witten in the Ruhr, in which the wives of miners were said to have played a particularly prominent part. In Witten, some 3000 women were reported to have staged a demonstration violent enough to oblige the authorities to command the police to disperse them. Even more remarkably, the police refused to carry out their orders, declaring that the women's cause was a just one.... All this was, of course, a facet of the continued resistance of Catholic women to the Third Reich. Yet it also demonstrated once more that many of the Nazis' policies had the effect of undermining or breaking up the family unit which Nazi ideology declared the aim of the Third Reich to preserve.[34]

It is puzzling that Evans considered women's protests politically efficacious in 1976 but warns against elevating "this incident [the Rosenstrasse] into a rare public protest that had secured the internees' release"[35] in 2008. Twenty years after the women's liberation movement, the possibility that mere women might have forced the Nazi state into a tactical retreat appears less reasonable. The gender of the protesters is one subtext. The power of the state and its receptiveness to pressures from the street is another. In 1995, Wolf Gruner suggested that acknowledgment of success in the Rosenstrasse carries "the danger to dramatically underestimate the rule of the NS-regime." The Rosenstrasse protest, he maintained, was "obviously not the cause for the release of the Jews" because the assumption "that such demonstrations could have hindered the deportation plans of the RSHA certainly do not hold up within the historical context."[36] The possibility that spontaneous and seemingly uncoordinated street presence of mere women might defy an all-powerful state appears to be unthinkable.

But comparison to other instances of women's protest to military dictatorships suggest the opposite: it is precisely in moments of overwhelming powerlessness and despair, at times when most other political activism has ceased and resistance seems impossible that women mobilize in the streets. As Jo Fisher observes in the case of Argentina: "After their success in stamping out all organized resistance of working-class and political organizations, the military dismissed as laughable the suggestion that a group of women could pose any threat to their position. In reality the sudden appearance of the Mothers in Plaza del Mayo had provoked serious difficulties in the seemingly impenetrable apparatus of military rule."[37] It is precisely the "unreasonable" and hence unpredictable behavior of women that is capable of defying military dictatorships. The most recent example of women's "impulsive" and uncontrollable appearance in the streets comes from Liberia where women forced the warring factions of Liberia's bloody civil war into peace negotiations and eventually, President Charles Taylor from power.[38] As "apolitical" agents, such women defy the logic of violence and power. They take to the streets out of sheer desperation, compelled by moral obligations arising from their gendered roles as mothers and wives. Philosopher Sara Ruddick coined the term "women's politics of resistance" to refer to women "who take responsibility for the tasks of caring labor and then find themselves confronted with policies or actions that interfere with their right or capacity to do their work. In the name of womanly duties that they have assumed and that their communities expect of them, they resist."[39] Such resistance is not motivated by the likelihood of success and is not assessed by its "degree of effectiveness,"[40] but is rooted in maternal obligation. Marguerite Guzman Bouvard characterizes the politics of the Argentine Mothers of Plaza del Mayo: "These women provide us with an alternative model of political action based upon familial and community responsibility rather than upon individual goals. As the Mothers confront the government . . . they explode the myths that the private sphere is isolated from and irrelevant to the political system and that middle-aged and elderly women are powerless."[41]

While the Latin American mothers as well as the Liberian women eventually mastered the arts of political organizing in order to advance their agendas in the political realm (such as the election of the first female African president, Ellen Johnson Sirleaf), the initial impulse was rooted in a private politics of care taking. The women of Berlin did not transcend that initial impulse. Their protests lasted only one week and failed to create a community that might have sustained defiance at later times when their husbands were threatened again by deportation. But they are a testament to the Nazi state's inability to adequately anticipate or contain dissident groups of women who failed to submit to totalitarian power and authoritarian ideologies of dehumanization. Mere wives and mothers may be the only ones capable of confronting a state when "real" political actors can do so no longer.

While gender is one subtext in the debate surrounding the Rosenstrasse, definitions of resistance and the role of non-violent protests is another. In her critical review of Margarethe von Trotta's film *Rosenstrasse,* Beate Meyer detects three projections "of contemporary hopes, utopias and myths onto the historical material," [42] namely "non-violence, feminism and morality," which were nurtured by the women's movement of the seventies and eighties but have "little to do with the historical material."[43] She objects particularly to the "emphasis on non-violent resistance" which she refers to repeatedly as "utopian." Her choice of words seems to indicate that non-violence has never been and will never be realistic, effective, or successful but rather should be considered a political fad among the well-fed and complacent in democratic societies like West Germany during the eighties. She opposes any impression that "apparently non-violent protests or civil disobedience formed in the Rosenstrasse, which forced the NS regime to its knees."[44] In part, the discussion over the "success" of the protests in the Rosenstrasse masks an underlying controversy over the validity of non-violence as either effective or "utopian" form of resistance. Meyer returns to categories of resistance developed by German historians in the eighties that distinguish between (1) non-conformity, (2) refusal (*Verweigerung*), (3) protest, and (4) resistance, defined as "general criticism of the system."[45] Needless to say the women's public street vigils in the Rosenstrasse merely advance to stage 3 (protest), but not to stage 4 (resistance), a category presumably reserved for more manly missions of military and political organizing (such as the aristocratic resistance of July 20, 1944, the communist underground, or partisan activities). As Carol Gilligan has pointed out, women's inability to measure up to man-made developmental stages and categories of excellence has a long and eminent tradition in philosophy, theology, psychology, literature, art, etc.[46] Certainly, the women of the Rosenstrasse did not gather in clandestine meetings to issue political communiqués against Nazi anti-Semitism, but the ease with which their street activism is dismissed as "utopian," "apolitical," and "ineffectual" is breathtaking. Their refusal to submit quietly to the arrest, internment, and planned deportation of their Jewish husbands shattered the regime's conceit of complete control and their fiction of people's acquiescence and consent to the Final Solution.

The story of hundreds of non-Jewish women who took to the streets of Berlin to demand the release of arrested family members remains a historical fact. These women set a model of civil courage (*Zivilcourage*[47]) and of civil disobedience by refusing to accept the decrees of a totalitarian state. Their detained loved ones were not deported as feared but discharged from prison. Numerous written documents verify that their non-violent vigils were efficacious in securing the release and return of detained family members.[48] Their claim to have won a rare (though temporary) victory against a ruthless regime remains historically legitimate. The significance of their actions is not measured by their outcome but by their repudiation of the state's projection of limitless power and control. The women of Berlin stand in a long tradition of mothers and wives who congregate under crosses, outside prison walls, and on public plazas braving swords, guns, and tanks. While non-violent action may not be able to stop a machinery of destruction running at full speed, the women's non-cooperation set a sign that moral obligations of care endure despite state repression.

Let me end these reflections on Friedländer's classification of the events in the Rosenstrasse as an "*uplifting* legend." Since Theodor Adorno's *dictum* that there can be no more poetry after Auschwitz, scholars have insisted that the systematic murder of millions and the destruction of European Jewish cultures must be documented and embraced as a "discourse of ruin." Famously, Lawrence Langer has warned against excavating "from the rubble of mass murder a piece of testimony to support his or her philosophy or system of belief or critical point of view."[49] In the face of six million Jewish dead, the survival of the few and occasional "gestures" of "sharing and support or even of self-sacrifice . . . feed the legends on which the myths of civilization have been built."[50] Langer has eloquently opposed the temptations of the "vocabulary of redemption and salvation"[51] and cautioned against "our own need to plant a life-sustaining seed in the barren soil that conceals the remnants of two-thirds of European Jewry."[52] Similarly, philosopher Lynn S. Arnault castigates American popular representations of the Holocaust for providing "a happy ending . . . [that] leave us with the optimistic belief that cruelty brings out the good in people."[53] This "will to redemption," she argues, is ultimately rooted in Christian notions of redemptive suffering and the "redemptive longing" "that good eventually triumphs against evil, thereby restoring meaning and purpose to our lives."[54] By qualifying the history of the Rosenstrasse as an "uplifting legend" Friedländer seems to suggest that its retelling feeds such deep desires and generates lessons of hope, faith, and defiance in the midst of horror and degradation.

In the name of historical truth, we are asked to dismiss as "legends on which the myths of civilization have been built," those events which instantiate enduring relationships of love, acts of care, and gestures of humanity. In the words of Lawrence Langer, the Holocaust should enter global consciousness as a "warrant for futility"[55] and serve as a permanent reminder of the powerlessness of individuals to resist "radical evil" imposed by majorities and implemented by agents of the state. It is certainly true that our world in general, and the Holocaust in particular, are crushed by death, suffering, and destruction. But are we really better off disregarding "triumphant moments exhibiting the resilience of the human spirit, the resourceful will, the intrepid mind, the resolve to survive Nazi oppression"[56] as wishful thinking? Such moments, I would submit, are never entirely absent and can never be totally extinguished. While the insistence on confronting the devastation of the Holocaust without flinching is valid, the categorical negation of faith, hope, and love in the name of empirical correctness and historical accuracy is not.

It is understandable but regrettable that scholars are rapidly relegating women's protests in the Rosenstrasse to the realm of myth and legend. These events run into three powerful suspicions prevalent among intellectuals: cultural skepticism of women's political agency, misgivings over the value of non-violent action, and concerns over romantic and/or heroic misconstructions of the history of the Holocaust. Indeed, the memory of the Holocaust must be guarded against false heroism and sentimentalized tales confirming the victory of good over the forces of evil (so prevalent in the Hollywood version of reality). Nevertheless, responsible scholarship does not allow censuring events that attest to the presence of moral principles and responsible politics, however marginal or seemingly inconsequential these events may be. The events in the Rosenstrasse exemplify the power of ordinary women to disrupt politics as usual by asserting the primacy of love and care over fear and terror. This may just be a history on which the myths of civilization can be built.

Katharina von Kellenbach is Professor of Religious Studies at St. Mary's College of Maryland. Her areas of expertise include feminist theology, interreligious dialogue, and Jewish-Christian relations in a post-Holocaust world. Previous publications include *Anti-Judaism in Feminist Religious Writings* (New York: Oxford University Press, 1994) and *The Mark of Cain: Guilt and Denial in the Lives of Nazi Perpetrators* (New York: Oxford University Press, 2013).

Notes

1. Nathan Stoltzfus, *Resistance of the Heart: Intermarriage and the Rosenstrasse Protest in Nazi Germany* (New York: W.W. Norton, 1996), xxv.
2. Ibid., xxv.
3. Richard Evans, *The Third Reich At War* (New York: Penguin, 2009), 271; Saul Friedländer, *The Years of Extermination: Nazi Germany and the Jews, 1939–1945* (New York, Harper Collins, 2008), 425. Both are citing Wolf Gruner, *Widerstand in der Rosenstraße: Die Fabrik-Aktion und die Verfolgung der "Mischehen" 1943* (Frankfurt am Main: Fischer, 2005). "Die Fabrikaktion und die Ereignisse in der Berliner Rosenstrasse," *Jahrbuch für Antisemitismusforschung* 11 (2002).
4. Stoltzfus, *Resistance*, 259.
5. See footnote 3; See also Richard Breitman et. al., *U.S. Intelligence and the Nazis (Cambridge: Cambridge University Press, 2005), p. 42, n. 55.*
6. Ulrich Gutmair, "Mythos Rosenstraße," *Netzeitung*, September 24, 2003, http://www.netzeitung.de/wirtschaft/255682.html (accessed June 5, 2010).
7. Mark 15:40; Luke 23:49; John 19:25.
8. Marguerite Guzman Bouvard, *Revolutionizing Motherhood: The Mothers of the Plaza de Mayo* (Wilmington, DE: Scholarly Resource Book, 1994), 243.
9. Jo Fisher, *Mothers of the Disappeared* (Boston: South End Press, 1989), 52–71.
10. Guzman Bouvard, *Revolutionizing Motherhood*, 244.
11. Judith Plaskow, *Standing Again at Sinai: Judaism from a Feminist Perspective* (New York: Harper & Row, 1990), 1.
12. Elisabeth Schüssler Fiorenza, *In Memory of Her: A Feminist Theological Reconstruction of Christian Origins* (New York: Crossroad Publishing, 1994).

13. Gerda Lerner, *The Creation of Feminist Consciousness: From the Middle Ages to 1870* (New York: Oxford University Press, 1993), 272.
14. Sara Ruddick, *Maternal Thinking: Towards a Politics of Peace* (Boston: Beacon Press, 1989).
15. Evans, *The Third Reich At War*, 271 n. 201.
16. Cf. Ian Kershaw, *Hitler*, vol. 2: *1936–1945, Nemesis* (New York, 2000), 963n. 115; Raul Hilberg, *Perpetrators, Victims, Bystanders: The Jewish Catastrophe, 1933–1945* (New York: Aaron Asher Books, 1992), 132; See also Evans's earlier review "Wives Against the Nazis," *The Sunday Telegraph*, November 17, 1996.
17. Gerda Lerner notes that the rise of graduate schools by the end of the nineteenth century aggravated women's invisibility: "Academic History produced by academically trained historians confirmed and solidified the already existing marginalization of women in the historical text." Lerner, *The Creation of Feminist Consciousness*, 270.
18. Gruner, *Widerstand in der Rosenstraße*, 139–156.
19. Ibid., 139–156.
20. Friedländer, *The Years of Extermination*, 425. Evans (*The Third Reich at War*, 271) repeats this assessment virtually verbatim:
    > Following the decision to begin deporting Jewish munitions workers in Germany and replace them with Poles, the police began round up the remaining 'full' Jews and their families in Germany on 27 February 1943 . . . Between 1,500 and 2,000 Berlin Jews who had been arrested had been able to show the police that they were exempted from deportation, mostly because they were married to non-Jewish partners. While the authorities worked out the details of where they were to be sent to work—not in munitions factories any more, for security reasons, but in the few remaining Jewish institutions in the capital, such as hospitals—the internees' wives, relatives and friends gathered on the pavement across from the building at Rosenstrasse 2-4 where they had been detained, waiting for the decision, calling out to them, and occasionally trying to get food parcels into the building. By 8 March 1943 most of the internees had been reassigned to new jobs; the rest followed. The small crowd dispersed. Subsequent legend elevated this incident into a rare public protest that had secured the internees' release; but there had never been any intention of sending these particular Jews east for extermination, and the crowd had not engaged in any kind of explicit protest.
21. Evans, *The Third Reich at War*, 271.
22. Leigh Westerfield, *This Anguish, Like a Kind of Intimate Song: Resistance in Women's Literature of World War II* (Amsterdam: Rodopi, 2004), 94–95.
23. Published in English as *Berlin Underground, 1938–1945* (New York: Henry and Holt, 1947; London, 1948).
24. Westerfield, *This Anguish*, 122.
25. Gruner, "Die Fabrikaktion," 139.
26. Gruner, *Widerstand*, 139.
27. Ibid.

28. "Da zeitgenössische Quellen fehlen, bleiben bis heute die Zahl der Teilnehmer, die konkreten Umstande sowie die Dauer und die Form des Protestes in der Rosenstrasse ungesichert." Gruner, *Widerstand*, 141.
29. Antonia Leugers, "Widerstand /gegen/ die Rosenstrasse. Kritische Anmerkungen zu einer Neuerscheinung von Wolf Grunder," *theologie.geschichte* 1 (2001). http://aps.sulb.uni-saarland.de/theologie.geschichte/inhalt/2006/11.html. Print version: *theologie.geschichte*. Zeitschrift für Theologie und Kulturgeschichte Band 1 (2006), hg. v. Lucia Scherzberg, August H. Leugers-Scherzberg (Verlag Monsenstein und Vannerdat, Münster 2008), S. 131–205. Antonia Leugers, ed., *Berlin, Rosenstraße 2-4: Protest in der NS-Diktatur* (Annweiler: Plöger, 2005).
30. Jana Leichsenring, "Wurde der Protest in der Rosenstraße Ende Februar/Anfang März organisiert? In Leugers, *Berlin*, 81–115.
31. Gruner, *Widerstand*, 143, 143n. 21.
32. Gerhardt Lehfeldt, "Bericht über die Lage von Mischlingen," in Leugers, *Berlin*, 233–238, 238.
33. Gruner, *Widerstand in der Rosenstraße*. 140.
34. Richard Evans. "German Women and the Triumph of Hitler." *The Journal of Modern History* 48, no. 1 (March 1976): 160.
35. Evans, *The Third Reich at War*, 271.
36. Wolf Gruner, "Die Reichshauptstadt und die Verfolgung der Berliner Juden 1933–1945," in *Jüdische Geschichte in Berlin: Essays und Studien*, ed. Reinhard Rürup (Berlin: Edition Hentrich, 1995), 253.
37. Fisher, *Mothers of the Disappeared*, 60.
38. Cf. the recent documentary film *Pray the Devil Back to Hell*, Fork Films, Abigail E. Disney and Gini Reticker (Sausalito, CA: Roco Films Educational, 2008).
39. Ruddick, *Maternal Thinking*, 224.
40. Ibid., 234.
41. Guzman Bouvard, *Revolutionizing Motherhood*, 15.
42. Beate Meyer, "Geschichte im Film: Judenverfolgung, Mischehen und der Protest in der Rosenstraße 1943," *Zeitschrift für Geschichtswissenschaft* 52, no. 1 (2004): 23–36, 36.
43. Ibid.
44. Meyer, "Geschichte im Film," 34.
45. Ibid.
46. On women's inability to measure up in stage models, see Carol Gilligan, *In a Different Voice: Psychological Theory and Women's Development* (Cambridge, MA: Harvard University Press, 1993).
47. Dietrich Bonhoeffer, *Letters and Papers from Prison* (New York: McMillan, 1997), 40.
48. Cf. an American intelligence report from the OSS (predecessor of the CIA) stated that according to a "trustworthy" source a Gestapo action against Berlin Jews in early March 1943 "had to be discontinued some time ago because of the protest which such action aroused." Report from Berne of April 1, 1943, from Allen Dulles, National Archives and Records Administration at College Park, RG 226 (OSS), Entry 134: Washington Registry Office Radio & Cable Files, Box 171, Folder 1079, photographed on p. 90, "Dissent in Nazi Germany," Nathan Stoltzfus, *The*

Atlantic Monthly 270, no. 3 (September 1992): 87–94. See also, a contemporaneous report from Gerhard Lehfeldt from the private archives of Robert A. Graham, titled "Die Lage der 'Mischlinge' in Deutschland, Mitte Maerz 1943," as used by Antonia Leugers and Joachim Neander. See footnote 32.
49. Lawrence L. Langer, *Preempting the Holocaust* (New Haven, CT: Yale University Press, 1998), 7.
50. Lawrence L. Langer, *Holocaust Testimonies: The Ruins of Memory* (New Haven, CT: Yale University Press, 1991), 26.
51. Langer, *Holocaust Testimonies*, 37.
52. Langer, *Preempting the Holocaust*, 58.
53. Lynn S Arnault, "Cruelty, Horror and the Will to Redemption" *Hypatia* 18, no. 2 (2003), 155–188, here 158.
54. Ibid.
55. Lawrence L. Langer, *Admitting the Holocaust: Collected Essays* (New York: Oxford University Press, 1995), 3.
56. Langer, *Holocaust Testimonies*, 35–36.

Chapter 7

Auschwitz, the "Fabrik-Aktion," Rosenstrasse
A plea for a change of perspective

Joachim Neander

A "Little Historikerstreit"[1] about the Rosenstraße Event

The Berlin *Fabrik-Aktion* has become the most spectacular part of the nationwide "De-Judaization of the Reich Territory" raids of 27 February 1943. The "Technical Guidelines for the Evacuation of Jews toward the East," issued by the Reich Main Security Office seven days earlier, on 20 February 1943, exempted from deportation to Auschwitz "for the time being" (*vorerst*) Jews living in "mixed marriages." But in Berlin, about 2,000 of these were rounded up and interned in a building on Rosenstraße 2-4, in the center of Berlin. Wives of the internees gathered in the street, tried to contact their family members within the building, and vociferously demanded their release. The great majority of the internees was, indeed, released on 6 March 1943; some even a few days earlier, and the remaining in the course of the following days.

These facts have never been disputed. Two questions, however, have been answered differently: why were about 2,000 intermarried Jews arrested and kept in detention for about a week, and what was the reason for their release? Until the turn of the twenty-first century, the generally accepted answers were as follows: Like all German *"full* Jews" (according to the 1935 Nuremberg Laws), they, too, were destined for deportation to Auschwitz and were imprisoned at Rosenstrasse to wait deportation, but the public protest caused the Nazi leadership to backpedal and release the prisoners.

This interpretation has been contested by Wolf Gruner since 1997, who concluded that the Gestapo arrested these Jews from "mixed marriages" in order to check their "racial status" and to select from them for work in Jewish institutions. Thus the Gestapo did not intend to deport a single Jew from "mixed marriages," and those who had been arrested and the protest of their wives had no influence on their release whatsoever. Although Gruner had already expressed this opinion in his doctoral thesis, published in 1997, it was given widespread attention when it appeared in the *Jahrbuch für Antisemitismusforschung* in 2002. In the following years, a "Little *Historikerstreit*" broke out, fought in the columns of scholarly and lay journals, as well as on the H-German Website, and culminating in two book publications that appeared on the market in 2005: *Widerstand in der Rosenstraße*, where Gruner expounded his view of the matter at great lengths, and the anthology *Berlin, Rosenstraße 2-4*, where five history scholars defended the "traditional" narrative against Gruner.

As we will see, the demand for workers from Auschwitz at the time of the *Fabrik-Aktion* showed that the regime did intend to deport the intermarried Jews it imprisoned at Rosenstrasse. Under the given conditions, the urgent demand for workers for Auschwitz could only be satisfied by ending the "temporary" exemption from deportation for some intermarried Berlin Jews, so that a considerable number of Jews from "mixed marriages" were to be sent to Auschwitz, too. They were not to be gassed, but put to work as slave laborers.

Historians until now have interpreted the Berlin *Fabrik-Aktion* always from the point of view of the center of power. Crucial in this narrative is the will of the Nazi leadership—Hitler, Goebbels, Himmler—to get rid of the last Jews still living in the Reich and, above all, in its capital. They gave the orders, the Stapoleitstelle issued directives, the Gestapo arrested, the tax office confiscated, the Reichsbahn deported, the women at Rosenstrasse demonstrated. At the receiving end lies Auschwitz with the objects of this *Aktion*. Arriving at Auschwitz, the Jews were selected at the ramp and killed in the gas chambers, or sent to slave labor. Their property was plundered, their corpses burnt, their names erased.

This is the classical one-way outlook from the center toward the periphery—and Auschwitz, indeed, was Reich "periphery."[2]. But this view suffers from an inherent tendency to underestimate the interaction between center and periphery--typical for modern societies with their highly developed division of labor. In the case of Auschwitz, this view overlooks the camp's critical economic function of supplying the German war industries with laborers. Auschwitz was not only a place of mass extermination, but also a center for providing the whole system of Nazi concentration camps with hundreds of thousands of slave laborers—not only Jews, and not only from deportation transports. Together with its sub-camps it was also the biggest Nazi slave labor camp complex itself. The availability of cheap labor—and, until the end of 1943, the camp's location out of range of Allied aircraft—encouraged more and more factories to settle in its vicinity.

Auschwitz was the first concentration camp that lent prisoners—beginning in early 1941—to war vital enterprises. The importance of

Auschwitz within the system of the Nazi concentration camps grew to the same extent as the demand for prisoner workers grew, and its influence on the Inspectorate of the Concentration Camps at Oranienburg also increased. More and more, Auschwitz became a player on its own. This can best be seen by a fact that singled it out from all other Nazi concentration camps: as of the spring of 1942, its "Prisoner Labor" Department gained autonomy as part of the camp administration.[3] Its head, SS-Obersturmführer Heinrich Schwarz, was answerable in technical matters[4] to SS-Obersturmbannführer Gerhard Maurer, head of Office D II, "Prisoner Employment," at the SS-WVHA.

The main work projects of Auschwitz: Birkenau and Buna

From April 1941 until its evacuation in mid-January 1945, the main work projects of Camp Auschwitz had been the expansion of the camp (*Lagerausbau*) and the construction work at the building site of the "Buna" factory. About three miles from the center of the town of Auschwitz and four and a half miles from the main Auschwitz camp, one of the biggest chemical factories of the Reich was constructed. On the banks of the Vistula River, which provided plenty of water, and with a pool of cheap labor and rich layers of coal and limestone in the vicinity, the IG Farben trust planned to produce there synthetic fuel and rubber, both products vital for modern warfare. In an agreement reached in mid-February 1941 with Reich Marshal Hermann Göring, head of the Reich Defense Council, the SS promised "to supply a maximum number of skilled and unskilled construction workers [. . .] The overall demand for construction and installation work at the building site will be between 8,000 and 12,000 men, depending on the speed of completion".[5]

When Reichsführer-SS Heinrich Himmler visited Auschwitz on March 1, 1941, he ordered camp commandant Rudolf Höss to provide ten thousand prisoners for the construction of the Buna factory.[6] At the same time, however, Höss' prisoners had to build the giant sub-camp of Birkenau, initially planned for two hundred thousand inmates, a project with top priority that absorbed nearly the whole prisoner workforce of Auschwitz. So IG Farben Auschwitz had to be content with about one thousand prisoners, who were transported daily from the main camp to the construction site and back again. At the beginning of August 1942, however, camp commandant Höss ordered a "camp blockade" (*Lagersperre*). A spotted fever epidemic was ravaging the camp, and because the German authorities feared it would spread beyond the barbed wire fences, no prisoner was allowed to leave the camp's premises.[7] Seizing the initiative, IG Farben, in October 1942, set up a camp for Auschwitz prisoners about three hundred yards south of the construction site, near the village of Monowice. The new camp was called "Work Camp Monowitz," "Camp IV," or "Buna Camp." At the same time, Maurer from the SS-WVHA (SS Main Economic and Administrative Department) promised to have "about 1,600" prisoners transferred to Auschwitz in the framework of the "de-judaization" of the concentration camps in the Reich's interior ordered by Himmler at the turn of October 1942.[8]

Between October 19 and 24, 1942, a total of 1,003 Jews from the concentration camps Buchenwald, Dachau, Flossenbürg, Natzweiler, Mauthausen, and Sachsenhausen arrived at Auschwitz, along with 499 non-Jewish prisoners from Dachau on October 29. The next day the director of the camp's labor department, *Arbeitseinsatzführer* Schwarz, complained to his superior by wireless message about this "delivery": "The prisoners are in an appalling condition, physically very weak—musulmen.[9] One-third perhaps fit for action after a fortnight of recovery. Employment at Buna absolutely out of question."[10] At the same time, the first eight hundred prisoners selected from the aforementioned "Jewish transports" were transferred to the new Monowitz camp.

The Buna Workforce Crisis 1942–1943

The number of laborers at this camp, however, was still far below the level that Himmler recently had promised to the Reich Marshal and the IG Farben managers.[11] At that time, fewer than 1,400 prisoners were working there.[12] The SS-WVHA therefore began to send more prisoners to Auschwitz to be employed at Buna. On November 29, 1942, for example, a transport of 150 men arrived from Buchenwald, specially announced as "unskilled construction workers." But again SS-Obersturmführer Schwarz had good reasons for complaining: "From the whole transport, 100 prisoners, i. e. 2/3, are fit for work. Learned construction workers—2%."[13]

Buna remained the biggest headache of the prisoner labor departments at Auschwitz as well as at Oranienburg. The subcamp's strength waxed and waned, growing to 3,700 men in December 1942, but decreasing quickly due to the high mortality rate and the selection of those deemed "unfit for work" --: those who had become too weak and sick to work.[14] To achieve a quicker replenishment of the Buna camp, Maurer, on January 11, 1943, slashed the quarantine for the intake of prisoners designated for Buna from six to three weeks.[15]

More importantly, Maurer asked the RSHA for Jews from deportation transports. On January 26, 1943, he informed Auschwitz that "according to a telex from Eichmann's office at the Reich Main Security Office (IV B 4), a total of 5,000 Jews were transferred from Theresienstadt to Auschwitz on January 20, 23, and 26 [. . .] The prisoners are to be employed by the Construction Office and at the Buna works."[16] Buna, however, came away empty-handed. From 5,022 Jews who had arrived from Theresienstadt, only 930 could be selected "for work." They were obviously not fit for the hard physical labor at the Buna construction site and, therefore, "put to the disposition of the Construction Office on February 15, 1943, after having completed quarantine." The remaining 4,092 men, women, and children were "separately accommodated," i.e. murdered in the gas chambers. With brutal frankness *Arbeitseinsatzführer* Schwarz gave the reason in awkward German: "Separate accommodation was necessary due to extreme physical weakness, of the women, because in their majority, they were children."[17]

Stalingrad and its Consequences for Auschwitz

By February 1943 it was clear that Buna's increasing and ever more urgent demand for workers could neither be fulfilled by transfer from other concentration camps nor by deportations from the "Ghetto for the Elderly," the Theresienstadt camp. A new source had to be found, particularly because the workforce situation at Buna was again alarmingly deteriorating. In the beginning of February 1943, the strength of the Buna camp had reached a new low: 1,700 men, from them only 1,450 men deemed "fit for work."[18] Stirred up by this development, Maurer again came to Buna on February 10, 1943, and "promised to make sure that the number of prisoners will soon increase to 4,000, possibly even to 4,500," as the weekly report of IG Farben Auschwitz for the period of time from February 8 to 21, 1943, shows.[19]

At Auschwitz, in the meantime, a situation had developed that threatened to endanger not only the Buna project. News about the devastating German defeat at Stalingrad in the first days of February 1943 had quickly spread through the camp.[20] Outside of the camp everybody also knew about this debacle,[21] and it was not only the "fanatically Polish"[22] population in the vicinity of the camp who celebrated. All over Poland people did not conceal their satisfaction about the blow the Red Army had given to the "German-fascist aggressor."[23] In fact, after Stalingrad, they all were convinced that Germany would lose the war.[24] Most of them believed that the moment of their liberation was no longer far away, and many of them thought about shortening the waiting time.

In light of this new attitude, the many thousand Polish political prisoners, "concentrated" in the true sense of the word at Auschwitz, must have looked especially dangerous to the German security authorities. Polish prisoners comprised the largest national group, and over the course of time had acquired more and more key positions in camp management and services. The camp Gestapo already suspected that a resistance group had formed among Polish prisoners, with contact to underground groups operating outside the camp. Now the shock that Stalingrad had caused among the Germans and the euphoria it had evoked among the Poles led the camp leadership to fear a prisoner uprising with support from outside. As a preemptive measure, six thousand healthy and strong Polish prisoners (i.e. those who would be the most dangerous in an uprising) were to be transferred from Auschwitz and distributed among camps within the Reich.[25] There are no extant documents that directly tell us who made this decision, and when it was made. But from the areas of responsibility among the German authorities it can be concluded that Office Group IV "Gestapo" of the RSHA made the decision, because it was the authority responsible for security in general and for personal matters of the prisoners, including committal, transfer, and release. The decision must have been made also in accordance with Office Group D "Concentration Camps" of the SS-WVHA, responsible for all organizational and economic matters of the camps and, in this case, for the execution of the RSHA decision.

We have also a hint as to the time frame within which the decision was taken. On February 25, 1943, Dr. Enno Lolling, chief physician of the concentration camps and head of Office D III of the SS-WVHA, inquired at Auschwitz about the date "when the quarantine will end for the first transport of the 6,000 Poles there."[26] Since the departure quarantine for Auschwitz lasted at least three weeks, and as the first transports—to Buchenwald and Neuengamme—left Auschwitz on March 10, 1943,[27] those prisoners destined for transfer into the Reich's interior must have begun their quarantine not later than February 17, 1943, and a decision to this effect would have been made not later than a few days earlier.

Docile German Jews to Replace Rebellious Poles

It is inconceivable that such far-reaching decisions directly affecting the employment of six thousand Auschwitz prisoners were made without the participation of Office D II of the SS-WVHA and Department IIIa at Auschwitz, which were responsible for prisoner employment in general and at Auschwitz in particular. Already on October 10, 1942, Labor Deployment Director Schwarz had told the SS-WVHA in no uncertain terms "that a transfer of Polish prisoners to other camps [. . .] is not possible. Such a transfer would lead to a total collapse of all construction work here."[28] And camp extension as well as Buna still had the highest priority at Auschwitz, a fact of which Himmler more than once had reminded commandant Höss. Neither Höss, nor Schwarz, nor Maurer could ever have consented to the withdrawal of six thousand healthy prisoners from Auschwitz—"skilled workers" as they were called in the exchange of telexes, and fully fit for work—if the RSHA had not guaranteed them immediate and equal replacement.

Not later than mid-March 1943, when these 6,000 Poles would have already left the camp, Auschwitz would need about nine thousand qualified workers—six thousand as replacement for the Polish workers, and three thousand to fill Buna up to the strength that Maurer had promised to the IG Farben managers. A telex from D I, the Central Office of Office Group D of the SS-WVHA, signed by the head of D I, Arthur Liebehenschel, and received at Auschwitz (delayed) on March 2, 1943, made it clear where these workers should come from:

> As is known to you, on March 1, 1943, the transports of Jews from Berlin will begin. It is herewith stressed again that in these transports there will be about fifteen thousand healthy Jews, fit for work, who hitherto have been working in the armament industry of Berlin. You have to take care with all means that they will remain suitable for work.[29]

Twenty minutes later a telex from Office D II of the SS-WVHA arrived at Auschwitz:

> Re: Transport of Jewish armament workers from Berlin.
> I am stressing again that the Jewish armament workers, whose transports began yesterday, must remain fit for work at any rate. From the fact that they had been employed in the Berlin armament industry it follows that they are suitable for work. First the Buna camp must be filled up to full strength.
> Signed Maurer, SS-Obersturmbannführer.[30]

The telex shows again the high priority that the SS-WVHA had for the Buna project. The preparations for the withdrawal of the Polish prisoners from Auschwitz took place at the same time as the preparations for the Berlin

Fabrik-Aktion, during the second and third week of February 1943. The functional and temporal connections between the *Fabrik-Aktion* and the transfer of prisoners from Auschwitz into the interior of the Reich point to the fact that the *Fabrik-Aktion* took place within a typical "push-and-pull" constellation[31]: there was a push from Berlin, which wanted to get rid of its Jews, together with a pull from Auschwitz, which needed Jews urgently as slave workers.

In both telexes quoted above it is taken for granted ("as is known to you," "I am stressing again") that Auschwitz had been informed in advance about the timing and expected scale of the *Fabrik-Aktion* in Berlin. This information could have been imparted by the RSHA itself, and must have been done as well by the SS-WVHA, whose Offices D I, D II, and D IV were involved in the *Fabrik-Aktion*: the camp commandant was answerable to D I, to labor deployment director to D II, and the chief of camp administration to D IV. All of them were responsible, administratively and logistically, for the incoming transports.[32] The SS-WVHA, on the other hand, could have received information only from the RSHA, whose Department of Jewish Affairs, IV B 4, under Adolf Eichmann planned and organized the deportations and to which the SS-WVHA had to make known its demand for Jewish labor.

Did the Gestapo Really Never Intend to Deport Jews from "Mixed Marriages"?

In his telex, Liebehenschel indicated that there were fifteen thousand Jews employed in the Berlin armaments industry who were "healthy and fit for work." This figure, however, was no longer relevant, since deportations during January and February 1943 had decreased the number of Berlin armaments workers to about eleven thousand.[33] Regardless of whether the RSHA had promised to deport fifteen thousand, or eleven thousand, or only nine thousand Jewish men and women from Berlin to Auschwitz, numbers of such magnitude could only have been reached by deporting a significant portion of the Berlin Jews living in "mixed marriages."[34]

Of course these figures—along with the upshot that intermarried Jews would have to be sent to Auschwitz as slave laborers to fulfill the promise to the camp and meet its expectations—was known to the RSHA authorities planning the *Fabrik-Aktion* (after all, no other segment of the population was so scrupulously registered and kept under surveillance as the Jews). These authorities also knew that the majority of the eleven thousand Jewish armaments workers living in Berlin on the eve of the *Fabrik-Aktion* were living in "mixed marriages."[35] Thus these authorities had consciously decided to end the "temporary" exemption of intermarried Jews from deportations -- at least to the extent necessary to meet SS-WVHA promises made to fulfill the expectations for slave laborers at Auschwitz.

These considerations, obtained retrospectively from the point of view of Auschwitz, are corroborated by a contemporaneous source from Berlin "The situation of Mischlinge in Germany in mid-March 1943," a report by Gerhard Lehfeldt. Among other things, he writes about the Fabrik-Aktion: "Eichmann reports: The Eastern front urgently demanded 9,000 men for building a wall. He, therefore, had all Jews arrested who still were available, and since there were not enough of them, he had to fall back upon the first-degree Mischlinge, too. [36] It was not a case of deportation, but of employment for work." The "urgency" and the figure "9,000" as well as the remark that the Jews were to be employed in construction work in the East all point to Auschwitz.[37]

An Ad-Hoc Decision by Eichmann and Its Consequences

We do not know when exactly the RSHA guidelines for deportation dated February 20, 1943, were drafted, and if, at that time, the high demand of workforce for Auschwitz (nine thousand men) was already known to the RSHA. As considerations to replace Jewish German workforce by Gentile Poles date back to the end of 1942, it is quite possible that the guidelines were drafted already at the turn of 1943. This would also explain Liebehenschel's mentioning of "15,000" Berlin Jewish armaments workers designated for Auschwitz, and it could support Wolf Gruner's thesis that the RSHA, in the beginning of 1943, had not planned, from the outset, to deport Jews from "mixed marriages."[38]

By mid-February, a week before the guidelines were issued, the situation had already changed: on the one hand, an urgent demand for nine thousand Jewish German workers for Auschwitz had suddenly appeared; on the other hand, the RSHA, in its zeal to make Berlin *judenfrei*, had significantly reduced the number of Jewish armament workers living in the city. When the *Fabrik-Aktion* started in the last days of February 1943, the RSHA had given its word to the SS-WVHA to send (as a minimum) about nine thousand Jewish armaments workers from Berlin to Auschwitz, but only about four thousand "deportable" Jewish workers were still available there.

Eichmann could have told the SS-WVHA that he could not fulfill their needs. Or he could make a quick decision and suspend, for Berlin, the clause in the RSHA guidelines that granted Jews living in a "mixed marriage" from deportation--merely a "temporary" exemption in any case. This makes sense insofar as it would single out the events of the *Fabrik-Aktion* in Berlin as an exception for Berlin[39] in the framework of the "de-Judaization of the Reich Territory" events.[40] The Berlin Gestapo, which led and controlled the Aktion, therefore, arrested only two thousand Jews from "mixed marriages"—as Gruner rightfully remarked, not quite a quarter of the total[41]—and interned nearly all of them separately in the Rosenstrasse building.[42] It was, to quote H.G. Adler, *"ein Vorstoß"* (a trial balloon).[43] The Gestapo would wait and see how the Aryan majority in the city would react. If everything "went well" (in the Gestapo's eyes), as had been the case with all the previous deportations of "unprotected" Jews from Berlin, the Rosenstrasse internees would be deported to Auschwitz as well, with the exception of those few who "knew the right people"[44] or who were needed as replacement for those "full Jews" who were employed in the Jewish institutions and whose names were on the deportation lists. Then it would be the turn of the next batch of Jews from "mixed marriages." Within a short time, Berlin would be, indeed, *Judenfrei*, as Goebbels, the Gauleiter of Berlin, had promised to his Führer.

If, however, any difficulty should appear, the whole procedure could be stopped immediately referring to the exemption clauses in the guidelines for deportation, the blame could be put on some allegedly "over-zealous" subordinate, the arrested could be released, and if "non-deportable" individuals had already been sent to Auschwitz, even a few of them could be called back as an "act of good will." This, in fact, is what did happen.

Transport 35a from Berlin, Rosenstrasse, to Auschwitz

On March 6, 1943, the day when the bulk of the intermarried Jews held at Rosenstrasse were released, twenty-five men were carried away to a railway siding where a deportation train to Auschwitz was waiting for departure. They were crammed into one of the freight cars already occupied by Jews from the 35th Berlin transport. The train left Berlin in the evening and arrived at Auschwitz on March 7, 1943, early in the morning. Its arrival is documented by a telex from Labor Deployment Director Heinrich Schwarz to Office D II of the SS-WVHA, sent on March 8, 1943.[45] It says, among other things, that a transport (the 35th) arrived on March 7 from Berlin "including 25 Schutzhäftlinge." All these twenty-five were directly sent to the Buna camp. For sake of simplicity, they will be combined in the following as "Transport 35a."

Since they were explicitly mentioned as *Schutzhäftlinge* (prisoners in protective custody) in the Schwarz telex,[46] Wolf Gruner ascribes to them "a different prisoner status," different from that of the ordinary deportees, and draws from this far-reaching conclusions, among other things that they arrived already being *Schutzhäftlinge*. This, however, is highly questionable. Outside the concentration camps, imposing *Schutzhaft* was an individual act. A person became a *Schutzhäftling* if and only if s/he was arrested by the police, which had to file a request to RSHA Office IV C 2 for issuing a *Schutzhaftbefehl* (detention order). It was, admittedly, a mere formality. The Schutzhaftbefehl with the grounds for detention was read to the prisoner.[47] The original remained in the prisoner's file at the police unit (Gestapo or Criminal Police) that had requested its issue, and a copy went, together with the prisoner's personal papers, to the receiving prison or concentration camp. It served, among others, to classify the *Zugang* (arrival) according to reasons for arrest and, in the concentration camps, to determine the color of the triangle s/he had to wear on her/his camp uniform, which, in consequence, determined her/his position in the prisoner society, which, in turn, was of paramount influence on her/his chances of survival.

Now, as we will see, twenty-three participants of Transport 35a were released from Auschwitz after two weeks and came back to Berlin. All who survived the war reported that a *Schutzhaftbefehl* was read to them for the first time after their return to Berlin, and never before. They, therefore, did not arrive as *Schutzhäftlinge* at Auschwitz, contrary to Gruner's assertion. To interpret SS-Obersturmführer Schwarz's remark "including 25 Schutzhäftlinge [. . .] sent for work to Buna" let us look first at what one of the survivors reported after the war.

At the railway siding in Berlin, before mounting the train for Auschwitz, the prisoners turned to the accompanying police officer: "We drew the inspector's attention to the fact that we were living in mixed marriages and that all the others just had been released. He said, What do you want? You will be neither shot nor hanged. You will be employed there where we need you more urgently."[48] This remark corroborates Lehfeldt's account, reporting that Eichmann had told his source "It is not a case of deportation, but of employment for work." We should not forget that these men, as every healthy German Jewish individual between fourteen and sixty-five years, had been forced laborers already for some time. Not they, but the Labor Office in accordance with the Gestapo decided where they had to work. Their transfer to the Buna building site via Auschwitz Main Camp, therefore, could easily be declared to be a simple transfer of workforce from one place of work to another.

But at their new place of work, the twenty-five men from Rosenstrasse would no longer be forced laborers with a certain—though narrowly limited—degree of personal freedom, but inmates of a concentration camp, and as such they had to be assigned to a prisoner category. The documents accompanying them obviously contained the information that they had already been selected as fit for work and that there was nothing special against them. So the Political Department at Auschwitz (the office responsible for personal matters of the prisoners) took them in automatically—and collectively—as *Schutzhäftlinge*, such as it did with all those Jews from deportation transports who were registered as prisoners (and not gassed on arrival). This was, of course, known to Labor Deployment Director Schwarz when he, on March 8, 1943, dispatched his telex to Oranienburg, and nothing more than that is the meaning of his remark quoted above. All further-reaching conclusions, such as those made by Gruner,[49] are devoid of any foundation.

There is, however, another, overlooked, aspect of Transport 35a. Bringing the selection process forward, to Berlin instead of Auschwitz, and treating the commitment of those selected as "fit for work" as a mere transfer of workforce, circumvented the guidelines for deportation. But why was it not done already from the beginning? Transport 35a appears as another "trial balloon," a forerunner of the committal of all German Mischlinge and Jewish partners of "mixed marriages" from their places of work as forced laborers to camps with concentration camp–like living conditions, as ordered by the Nazi leadership in March 1944.[50]

The Unprecedented: Thirty-Five Jews Are Released From Auschwitz

The most remarkable aspect of Transport 35a, however, is that on March 21, 1943, twenty-three of them, together with twelve German Jews from Transports 34 and 35, were released.[51] They returned to Berlin in civilian clothes, this time even in a passenger car and under a "friendly" SS escort. All twenty-three returnees from Transport 35a were married without children, but among the other twelve returnees, we find only three married men, four divorcees, one widower, and three singles (the marriage status of one of the returnees is unknown) , and six of them (but none of the married men) had children.[52] It is difficult to detect a pattern in this set.

On their return, the former Auschwitz prisoners were summoned to the Gestapo, interrogated, and instructed to keep silent about their Auschwitz experience. They were told that they were not allowed to go back to their families nor to their former places of work. What is more, they had to "confess" that they had been engaged in "actions hostile to the state," which served to justify, at this late point, the issue of a detention order. They were committed to the Labor Education Camp at Groß-Beeren, a forced labor camp run by the local

Gestapo with living conditions only slightly better than in a concentration camp. Survivors said that more than a dozen of their group died there. Some were later on transferred to other forced labor camps, but never sent again to a concentration camp. Of the thirty-five Auschwitz returnees, twenty-one definitely survived the war. Eight are documented as having died before the end of the war. The fate of the remaining six is unknown.

Can the fact that thirty-five German Jews from Berlin, deported to Auschwitz in the framework of the Fabrik-Aktion, were released and sent back to Berlin, prove Wolf Gruner's central thesis that the Gestapo never intended to deport them—that only some overzealous subordinate had made a mistake that was corrected later without much ado?[53] Circumstances prove otherwise.[54] It is a rare bureaucrat who voluntarily admits that he made a mistake, or who, without significant pressure from above, corrects it. This holds especially for the secret police in dictatorships. Someone must have exerted pressure on the RSHA, because only it could order the release of even a single concentration camp prisoner. In fact, authorities at the time said that these men were released from Auschwitz on orders from "high authorities."[55]

Were it half-hearted protests from the Catholic Church, as Rainer Decker suggested?[56] Very improbable, as none of these Jews were married to a Catholic, otherwise their name would have appeared in the files of the "Relief Organization at the Bishopric of Berlin." Interventions by employers, as Decker suggested, too? Still more improbable, as none of those Jews were "irreplaceable"—three-quarters of them were employed as unskilled workers, and only one-quarter held a position as a skilled worker. But these, too, could be easily replaced by the Polish workers soon to come, who traditionally had a good reputation in Germany since the days of Polish mass immigration in the second half of the nineteenth century.

The decision to recall thirty-five deported Jews from Auschwitz was a political one, and the pressure exerted on the RSHA to order this could only have come from high above, from political channels, i.e. from the NSDAP leadership in Berlin. And these listened carefully to the morale of the people at the home front, especially in a tense situation such as that which had developed after Stalingrad and the first big air raids over Berlin. The street protests in Berlin, at Rosenstrasse and other places, signaled that they had touched a raw nerve with the arrest of Jews from "mixed marriages." At any rate, it was better for them to backtrack for the moment.

Joachim Neander's latest book is *The German Corpse Factory: The Master Hoax of British Propaganda in the First World War* (Saarbrücken: Saarland University Press, 2013). He is also the author of *Mathematik und Ideologie* (Munich, 1974), *Das Konzentrationslager Mittelbau in der Endphase der* *nationalsozialistischen Diktatur* (Clausthal-Zellerfeld, 1997), and *"Hat in Europa kein annäherndes Beispiel": Mittelbau-Dora—ein KZ für Hitlers Krieg* (Berlin, 2000). He was a regular contributor to PRO MEMORIA (Oświęcim, Poland).

Notes

This chapter is translated from Antonia Leugers's 2005 edited collection, *Berlin, Rosenstraße 2-4: Protest in der NS-Diktatur; Neue Forschungen zum Frauenprotest in der Rosenstraße 1943* (Annweiler: Plöger, 2005)

1. Editors of Die Zeit wrote in an introduction to an article that clashing interpretations about the Rosenstrasse events had caused a "little historians' controversy." "Wer nur den NS-Dokumenten vertraut, verkennt den Widerstand der Deutschen. Anmerkungen zum *Historikerstreit* um die "Rosenstraße." Nathan Stoltzfus, "Die Wahrheit jenseits der Akten," Die Zeit, 34/2003, Oct 30, 2003.
2. "The center-periphery model is a spatial metaphor which describes and attempts to explain the structural relationship between the advanced or metropolitan 'center' and a less developed 'periphery' within a particular country." Gordon Marshall, *Oxford Dictionary of Sociology* (Oxford and New York: Oxford University Press, 1998), entry "Centre-periphery model."
3. Preliminarily as of April 15, finally as of September 23, 1942. See Special Orders issued by the Commandant's Office (Kommandantur-Sonderbefehle) from these days. Archives of the Auschwitz-Birkenau State Museum (in the following abbreviated APMAB), file D-AuI-1/Kommandanturbefehle.
4. In personal, "disciplinary," matters, he remained answerable to the camp commandant. This system of "double subordination" was common in the Nazi state. It opened leeway for personal initiative to the functionary and made the system flexible, but also prone to chaos, especially at the end of the war, when the structures were collapsing.
5. Guidelines for the construction of the Buna works at Auschwitz, February 18, 1941; quoted from Franciszek Piper, *Arbeitseinsatz der Häftlinge aus dem KL Auschwitz*, Oświęcim: Verlag des Staatlichen Museums in (Oświęcim, 1995), 239.
6. Danuta Czech, *Kalendarz wydarzeń w KL Auschwitz*, (Oświęcim: Wydawnictwo Państwowego Muzeum w Oświęcimiu-Brzezince, 1992), 52.
7. Lagersperre also affected the SS crew, whose members were not allowed to enter the town.
8. Letter from SS-WVHA D II/1 to KL Auschwitz, October 5, 1942. Copy in Nachman Blumental, ed., *Dokumenty i materiały—tom I—obozy* (Łódź: Wydawnictwo Centralnej Żydowskiej Komisji Historycznej przy C.K. Żydów w Polsce, 1946), 73.
9. "Musulman" (in German: *Muselmann*, in Polish: *muzułman*) was the camp jargon term for prisoners with the characteristic skeleton-like appearance and utterly indifferent behavior.
10. Radio message from October 30, 1942. APMAB file D-AuI-3a/11 item no. 31982.

11. IG Farben urged Maurer to come to Buna on November 6, 1942 for a special two-day's visit "to discuss then and there the employment of prisoners at the building site." IG Farben weekly report no. 76/77, for the period of time from November 2–15, 1942. APMAB Maurer trial files, vol. 7, 60.
12. On 15 November 1942—1,388 prisoners. Irena Strzelecka and Piotr Setkiewicz, "The Construction, Expansion and Development of the Camp and its Branches," in Wacław Długoborski and Franciszek Piper, eds., *Auschwitz 1940-1945. Central Issues in the History of the Camp*, 5 vols. Translated from the Polish by William Brand. Vol. I: *The Establishment and Organization of the Camp* (Oświęcim: Auschwitz-Birkenau State Museum, 2000): 112–113.
13. Telex to SS-WVHA D II, December 5, 1942. APMAB file D-AuI-3a/16 item no. 31987.
14. Strzelecka/Setkiewicz, *The Construction, Expansion and Development*: 113. .
15. The quarantine on intake should make sure that the newcomer did not bring in contagious diseases. It lasted, as a rule, three to four weeks.
16. Telex from Oranienburg D II to Auschwitz, January 26, 1943. APMAB file D-AuI-3a/32 item no. 32003.
17. Quotations in this paragraph are from a telex, signed "Schwarz, SS-Obersturmführer," from KL Auschwitz to SS-WVHA Office D II, February 20, 1943. APMAB file D-AuI-3a/&% item no. 32119.
18. Bernd C. Wagner, *IG Auschwitz. Zwangsarbeit und Vernichtung von Häftlingen des Lagers Monowitz 1941-1945* (Munich: K. G. Saur, 2000): 333. Figures given were from February 12, 1943.
19. Weekly report no. 90/91 part I. APMAB Maurer trial files, vol. 7 page 63.
20. "It was not difficult to listen to the news broadcast by the enemy. In Auschwitz, there were plenty of radios." Rudolf Höß, *Kommandant in Auschwitz: Autobiographische Aufzeichnungen des Rudolf Höß*. ed. Martin Broszat (Munich: Deutscher Taschenbuch-Verlag, 1963), 151.
21. In the Reich a three days' public mourning was decreed. In occupied Poland, General Governor Frank, on February 4, 1943, had all theater, cinema, and cabaret performances and all entertainment called off for a period of three days. Tadeusz Wroński, *Kronika okupanowego Krakowa* (Kraków: Wydawnictwo Literackie, 1974): 253.
22. Characterized as such in a letter from Höss to Richard Glücks, Inspector of the Concentration Camps, July 12, 1940, quoted in Strzelecka and Setkiewicz, *The Construction, Expansion and Development:* 71.
23. Polish historiography agrees that "Stalingrad" lifted the population's mood and spurred the resistance movement on. See e.g. Andrzej Chwalba, *Dzieje Krakowa. Kraków w latach 1939-1945* (Kraków: Wydawnictwo Literackie, 2002): 258.
24. Höß, *Kommandant in Auschwitz,* 151.
25. This perspective is backed by memories of survivors (Tadeusz Sobolewicz, *Wytrzymałem. Więc jestem* (Katowice: Wydawnictwo "Śląsk", 1986): 145) and generally shared by Polish historians; see e.g. Czech, *Kalendarz wydarzeń*, 359n. 28, 393n. 46. It is also backed by a telex from SS-WVHA Office Group D, signed by its head Richard Glücks, from March 29, 1943, saying that among the 1,000 Poles who were to be transferred from Mauthausen to Buna in the beginning of April

1943, there should be no Poles "for security reasons." APMAB file D-AuI-3a/151 item no. 32205.
26. Telex from Oranienburg, received at KL Auschwitz on February 25, 1943, at 6:45 P.M. APMAB file D-AuI-3a/75 item no. 32129.
27. Telex from SS-WVHA (signed Glücks) to the commandants of Auschwitz and Buchenwald, March 3, 1943: "K.L. Auschwitz transfers 1,000 Polish prisoners to Buchenwald" with handwritten remark: "March 10, 1943, done." APMAB file D-AuI-3a/89 item no. 32143. The same telex was sent to Neuengamme. It bears the same handwritten remark. APMAB file D-AuI-3a/92 item no. 32146.
28. APMAB file D-AuI-3a/9 item no. 31980.
29. The telex was received at Auschwitz at 9:40 P.M. APMAB file D-AuI-3a/85a item no. 172841.
30. Received at Auschwitz at 9:59 P.M. Copy in Blumental, *Dokumenty i materiały*, 108.
31. The "Push-Pull" model of migration theory goes back to Everett S. Lee, "A Theory of Migration," *Demography* vol. 3, no. 1, 1966, pp. 47-57. "Push factors" are negative factors in the home region that "push away" the migrant, that cause or even force him to emigrate. "Pull factors" are positive factors in the target region that attract the migrant, in an extreme case even force him to immigrate. See also Johannes Obergfell, *Mexiko und die Migration* (Berlin: epubli, 2011).
32. If the Jews from the incoming transports, indeed, should "remain fit for work at any rate"—and we should not doubt that this was meant sincerely by Glücks and Maurer—these preparations would take some time, which means, on the other hand, that Auschwitz must have been informed about the forthcoming arrival of the Jews at about the same time when the decision was taken to withdraw the 6,000 Poles.
33. Wolf Gruner, "Die Fabrik-Aktion und die Ereignisse in der Berliner Rosenstraße. Fakten und Fiktionen um den 27. Februar 1943," *Jahrbuch für Antisemitismusforschung* vol. 11, 2002, pp. 137-177, here: 154.
34. If we add up all the men and women who were selected as "fit for work" from the RSHA transports from Germany that arrived at Auschwitz between March 2 and 3, 1943, we arrive at a number of 3,977 individuals. Among them there were about 120 partners from "mixed marriages" and a small number of Mischlinge who, according to the guidelines issued by the RSHA on February 20, 1943, were also exempted on a "temporary" basis from deportation. If we set them aside and calculate generously that two-thirds of the registered prisoners, i.e. 2,500 individuals, came from Berlin (and this would be a lower limit since nearly all other German cities (with the exception of Breslau) were already practically *judenfrei*). and if we take into account that about 1,500 Jewish armaments workers from Berlin who did not live in a "mixed marriage," were hiding, we arrive at a number of about 2,500 + 1,500 = 4,000 "deportable" Berlin Jews who fulfilled the criteria mentioned in the telexes from the SS-WVHA from March 2, 1943: healthy, fit for work without reservations, and employed in the armaments industry. If $X > 4,000$ Berlin Jewish armaments workers were to be deported to Auschwitz, inevitably $X - 4,000$ had to be taken from the pool of those seven thousand Jewish armaments workers who had the "temporary" exemption from deportation according to the February 20, 1943 RSHA guidelines.

35. According to Gruner, *Die Fabrik-Aktion*: 158, about 8,800 Berlin Jews were living, at that time, in "mixed marriages." About 7,000 could have been armaments workers. Together with the above estimated 4,000 "full Jews," they would yield the 11,000 mentioned in Gruner, *Die Fabrik-Aktion*: 154.
36. Gerhard Lehfeldt: Bericht über die Lage von "Mischlingen", [Berlin, Mitte März 1943] in: Antonia Leugers, ed., Berlin, *Rosenstraße 2-4: Protest in der NS-Diktatur. Neue Forschungen zum Frauenprotest in der Rosenstraße 1943*, Annweiler 2005, S. 233-238. Lehfeldt uses the terms "Mischling," "first-degree Mischling," and "mixed marriage" more or less synonymously. In France, a similar procedure was common: if there were less "deportable" Jews available than planned, the transports were filled up with "non-deportable" Jews. Examples in Serge Klarsfeld, *Vichy—Auschwitz. Le rôle de Vichy dans la Solution Finale de la Question Juive en France—1942* (Paris: Arthème Fayard, 1983): 431, 440, 441, 446.
37. We should not over-interpret the words "Eastern front." First, the murder program at Auschwitz was veiled in secrecy. Auschwitz was officially always presented as a "labor camp." Even at the higher echelons only a few persons knew exactly what was going on there. Second, after Stalingrad, it seemed plausible to build a wall against the "Red Flood." It may have been imagined by Lehfeldt's source, maybe by Eichmann himself. At any rate, the direction of the transports—eastward—was mentioned correctly.
38. It would not explain, however, the decision by Berlin Gauleiter Joseph Goebbels in mid-February 1943 that the *Fabrik-Aktion* would make his Berlin Gau *Judenfrei*—meaning that all persons wearing the Star of David, including thousands of intermarried Jews, would have to leave Berlin by the end of March, the deadline he set for himself in his diary on February 18, 1943. Elke Frölich, ed., *Die Tagebücher von Joseph Goebbels*, Part 2, 1941-1945, vol. 7, January-March 1943 (Munich: K. G. Saur, 1996), 368-69.
39. Wolf Gruner, "Ein Historikerstreit? Die Internierung der Juden aus Mischehen in der Rosenstraße 1943. Das Ereignis, seine Diskussion und seine Geschichte," *Zeitschrift für Geschichtswissenschaft I*, 2004, pp. 5-22, here: 15; similarly Gruner, *Die Fabrik-Aktion*: 15, but rejected it at once categorically.
40. There is testimony that, in some instances, all Jews of a town were deported, regardless of their marital status. See, e.g., letter by Hans-Oskar Baron Löwenstein de Witt to the editor of the *Süddeutsche Zeitung*, September 20, 2003, in Antonia Leugers, ed. *Berlin, Rosenstraße 2–4: Protest in der NS-Diktatur: Neue Forschungen zum Frauenprotest in der Rosenstraße 1943.* (Annweiler: Plöger, 2005), 244–245.
41. Gruner, *Die Fabrik-Aktion*: 161.
42. About one hundred Jews from "mixed marriages" were assembled at other places together with the "deportable" Jews and deported from there, too. Joachim Neander, "Die Auschwitz-Rückkehrer vom 21. März 1943," in Leugers, *Berlin, Rosenstraße 2-4*: 138.
43. H. G. Adler, *Der verwaltete Mensch. Studien zur Deportation der Juden aus Deutschland* (Tübingen: JCB Mohr (Siebeck), 1974): 202.
44. Nathan Stoltzfus, *Resistance of the Heart. Intermarriage and the Rosenstrasse Protest in Nazi Germany* (WW Norton, 1996): 73, 120, 247.

45. It was first published 1946 in a collection of documents (Blumental, *Dokumenty i materiały*, 110). Since then it has been reprinted many times.
46. Gruner, *Die Fabrik-Aktion*: 171; Gruner, *Ein Historikerstreit?* : 20.
47. "Aryan" Germans even received a copy for themselves.
48. Report by Günther Rosenthal, no date. Berlin Museum, Jewish Department, file no. DOK87/1/Nr.3. Thanks to Beate Meyer, Hamburg, for providing me with this information.
49. Gruner, *Ein Historikerstreit?*: 20f.
50. James F. Tent, *In the Shadow of the Holocaust: Nazi Persecution of Jewish-Christian Germans* (Lawrence: University Press of Kansas, 2003), 148.
51. Two participants of Transport 35a did not return on March 21; they probably were sick at that time or thought it was better to stay behind. Both, however, survived Auschwitz, and one of them also survived the war. The matter of the "Auschwitz returnees" has been discussed in great detail in Neander, "*Die Auschwitz-Rückkehrer vom 21. März 1943*," in Berlin, Rosenstrasse 2-4 (2005) 115-143.
52. The numbers add up only to eleven, as one member of the "Group of the Twelve" is hitherto totally unknown. Most probably there is still more information in the files of the archives of the Centrum Judaicum, Berlin, to which the "Victims of Fascism" files of the GDR state archives were transferred after the reunification of Germany. The head of the archive, Dr. Simon, however, has denied the author access without giving reasons.
53. Gruner, *Ein Historikerstreit?*: 20.
54. If we look only at the twenty-three returnees from Rosenstrasse, we could possibly begin to agree. They all were married to an "Aryan" partner and therefore, according to the guidelines, exempt from deportation. But what about the eight from the "Group of the Twelve" who were not (or no more, or never) married to anyone, be she Aryan or not, and who therefore had to be deported, according to the guidelines? Why were they also called back? And why were only they and none of the approximately ninety other Berlin Jews from mixed marriages, who were deported during the Fabrik-Aktion, ever released? These questions have been asked since 2005, but until now, they remain unanswered. Neander, *Die Auschwitz-Rückkehrer*: 139–140.
55. Stoltzfus, Resistance of the Heart, 253.
56. Rainer Decker in http://hsozkult.geschichte.hu-berlin.de/rezensio/buecher/2000/dera0500.htm.

Chapter 8

The 1943 Rosenstrasse Protest and the Churches

Antonia Leugers

Had Margarethe von Trotta premiered her feature film *Rosenstrasse* in the year 1990, Wolfgang Benz might have received it with something like the empathic tribute to the Rosenstrasse that he renders in his book of that same year. Benz highlighted the historical events in the Rosenstrasse "as one of the very rare events of public revolt against the regime. . . . Perhaps two hundred wives protested loudly in unprecedented solidarity for days on end on the street in front of the building (where the husbands were held) until the decision to deport the men was reversed and the men were free again. What a stunning success of resistance achieved by a minority that existed at the fringes of Nazi society with almost no rights!"[1]

Yet by the time of the actual film premiere in 2003, Benz did not offer praise but instead harsh criticism, which received immediate media attention. Most of all he questioned the basic assertion that there was any connection between the women's protest and the release of their husbands,[2] citing the research findings of his student Wolf Gruner. Although in his dissertation Gruner primarily focused on forced labor and examines the women's protest only peripherally, he fundamentally reinterpreted the events on the Rosenstrasse,[3] which in turn have been cited by others.[4] Subsequently, Gruner has vehemently defended his claim that Jewish spouses who were living in so-called racial intermarriages were only detained at Rosenstrasse for the purpose of work registration in order to replace Jewish employees at Jewish institutions who were to be deported from Berlin.[5] While Gruner delivers this claim with conviction and resourcefulness, his findings are puzzling in light of the evidence that is available before February 27, 1943.[6] Gruner interprets one particular church source as substantiating his claim, but in fact the contrary is true.

The Importance of the Wienken-Source

In fact, one source[7] already well-known to researchers of Catholicism had to be brought to Gruner's attention in order for him to incorporate it into his argument.[8] On March 4, 1943, Heinrich Wienken,[9] the negotiator (*Unterhändler*) for the Fulda Bishops' Conference, heard from Adolf Eichmann in the Reich Security Main Office (RSHA) that the "non-Aryan Catholics from racial intermarriages who had been detained in Berlin were going to be released."[10] Gruner seems unaware of a source by Nuncio Orsenigo dated March 3, 1943. This source confirmed that the nuncio had reported to Rome on March 3, that even "baptized Jews" or those married to an "Aryan" had been included in the massive arrest of Jews since February 28, 1943. The nuncio alluded to his conversation with someone in the Ministry of Foreign Affairs, who told him that nobody is able to defy the "tangible and rampant violence" of the Gestapo.[11] Thus, Nuncio Orsenigo regarded his attempt to intercede as unsuccessful. However, one day later, on the sixth day of protest by the wives and relatives in the Rosenstrasse,[12] Wienken learned from the RSHA about the impending release of the detained husbands. This information does not substantiate Gruner's claims.

In fact, Eichmann reported that Berlin Jews were going to be sent back to the armament factories, which contradicts Gruner's claim that the objective was to merely remove all Jews from the armament industry.[13] That is presumably why Gruner omitted this sentence, when he cited this report from Eichmann, but reprinted just the part of the document that best served his claims.[14] In addition, claims that the "*Geltungsjuden*" could not be exempted from the guidelines and would be deported to Theresienstadt is not accurate. According to the guidelines issued by the RSHA on February 20, 1943,[15] Jews from "intermarriages" and "*Geltungsjuden*" were to be "temporarily" withheld from deportation. If Gruner's thesis were correct, Eichmann should have specified that people belonging to these categories would only be registered[16]—in which case the expression "released again" would be wrong because one does not "detain" people to register them; instead, such people would be receiving new job assignments and be sent back home. To simplify matters, this information could have been shared with the protesters on Rosenstrasse.

Therefore, Gruner's thesis leaves a fundamental question unanswered: Why were the husbands detained for one entire week while family members protested in fear? Furthermore, why were twenty-five people deported from the Rosenstrasse if there was no intention to deport anyone—a fact which Joachim Neander explicates at length.[17] The detained husbands were released: some were employed in Jewish institutions as replacement personnel, the rest ended up in various low-end service jobs.[18]

While the evidence provided by Gruner about the selection of replacement personnel fits well into the chronology of events, he cannot provide compelling evidence for his claim that from the outset there was never any intention—especially in Berlin—to deport Jews from intermarriages. Indeed, the partially false data received by Wienken provides the basis for the opposite conclusion. Gruner maintains that there were no children under fourteen years of age detained at Rosenstrasse.[19] He seems to be unaware of the fact that children younger than fourteen were present, as established by the extensive investigations of Nathan Stoltzfus and eyewitness reports.[20] Certainly, children would not have been registered for suitable work replacement. They also would not have been picked up from factories but directly from their homes. Some persons wearing the Star of David were also arrested on sight while in public, and imprisoned.

In the RSHA's guidelines from February 20, 1943 "intermarriages" were officially excluded from deportations "temporarily" *(vorläufig)*. However, despite this, not only in Berlin but also in other places such as Hamburg or Frankfurt/Main, persons from intermarriages were actually arrested and later deported.[21] In an ordinance of the Gestapo in Frankfurt/Oder from February 24, 1943, officials were told to act "inconspicuously" concerning persons in "intermarriages." But the Gestapo was allowed to take those Jews living in intermarriages into protective custody who exhibited "impudent behavior" and they could file an order for their internment in a concentration camp. Officials were given liberty to deal with these situations but told to avoid the impression that their actions might be a means to simultaneously and fundamentally solve the "intermarriage problem" once and for all.[22] In a footnote in his dissertation, Gruner correctly identifies this as a "carte blanche"[23] for the officials carrying out this ordinance. Indeed, this interpretation is further substantiated by the fact that a copy of this Frankfurt/Oder ordinance was sent in the form of a transcription by the district administrator from Calau to police administrators. At the end of this memo, he reiterates exactly this segment: impudent behavior could be penalized by detention. Gruner omits this particular passage in his reprint,[24] although this ordinance clearly reveals the actual intent: intermarried Jews were to be included in the "solution of the Jewish question" through inconspicuous operations. Gerhard Lehfeldt also writes of "murder plans"[25] in his report of mid-March 1943 regarding these Jews. The intended imminent inclusion of so-called "protected" persons—according to the RSHA guidelines and the Frankfurt ordinance—into

Figure 8.1. "Whoever wears this symbol is an enemy of our people." Nazi propaganda instructing Germans on why German Jews were required to wear the Star of David. It marked the Jews identified specifically for deportation, which was illustrated during the Gestapo's "Action to Clear the Reich of Jews," the arrests (dubbed the "Factory Action" after the war) that led to the Rosenstrasse Protest. During the early night hours of March 1, 1943, following the second full day of the imprisonment of intermarried Jews at Rosenstrasse 2-4, about 30 who lived in "privileged" intermarriage and thus did not wear the Star of David, were released while those wearing the Star remained at Rosenstrasse. Eleven days earlier, Berlin's Gauleiter Joseph Goebbels had vowed to deport all persons wearing the Star, once and for all. "I have set for myself a goal to make Berlin entirely free of Jews by the middle or end of March at the latest," he wrote on February 18. "With the final deadline of February 28 they are supposed to be first collected in camps and then deported, up to 2,000, batch-by-batch, day-by-day." Weeks after the release of Jews held at Rosenstrasse 2-4, Goebbels admitted that, because there were still persons wearing the Star, "The Jewish question in Berlin is still not yet completely solved. A whole collection of so-called 'Geltungsjuden' ['half-Jewish' 'Mischlinge' who were counted as Jews and wore the Star], Jews from privileged intermarriages ["full Jews" according to the Nuremberg Laws who were exempted from wearing the Star], and also Jews from intermarriages ["full Jews" required to wear the Star] are still to be found in Berlin . . . I do not want Jews with the Jewish star running around the Reich capital. Either one must take the Jewish star away and privilege them, or on the other hand once and for all evacuate them from the Reich capital," he wrote on April 18, 1943. Historians who write that intermarried Jews were all "privileged" overlook the regime's careful categorization of intermarried Jews it "privileged" and those it did not. (http://www.calvin.edu/academic/cas/gpa/parole.htm).

the overall "solution to the Jewish question" is also confirmed in the Gestapo reports about Dr. Gertrud Luckner from Freiburg, who advocated on behalf of Catholics of Jewish heritage.[26]

The Validity of Evidence from Internal Gestapo Sources

Gertrud Luckner traveled extensively between February 22 and March 2, 1943, from Freiburg via Stuttgart, Würzburg, Bamberg, Nuremberg, Eichstätt, and Munich back to Freiburg. The Gestapo kept her under surveillance and subsequently interrogated people with whom she had met on her itinerary. She was arrested on March 24 and transferred to the concentration camp Ravensbrück, where she was detained until 1945. Luckner had requested lists of "intermarriages" and "*Mischlinge*" from Jewish community centers. She did so despite the public announcement of the RSHA-guidelines on February 20, which allegedly protected such people. In his report, Secretary for Criminal Investigation Hans von Ameln notes that on February 24, 1943, Luckner indicated to Johanna Stahl in Würzburg that "at the moment a sizable evacuation was to take place in Berlin."[27] It seems Luckner was aware of plans for a "final action" (*Schlußaktion*) on February 27. She informed Ivan Schwab in Würzburg and Justin Baum in Bamberg, on February 25, that the intermarriage law "has been postponed as of now;" however, "measures against intermarriages and *Mischlinge*" were imminent. Luckner also warned that *Mischlinge* should avoid committing unlawful acts so as not to give the Gestapo any reason to intervene, which shows how well Luckner was informed about the internal implementation of official instructions concerning the so-called solution of the Jewish question.[28] In their final report for the Berlin RSHA, Gestapo headquarters in Düsseldorf wanted to especially highlight the following point about the Luckner case: "it has been confirmed that Luckner maintains contact points in the entire Reich; she personally gets in touch with Jews, intermarried couples, and *Mischlinge*, to notify them of impending actions." Luckner states that one must "in spite of it all count on actions by the Gestapo against intermarriages and *Mischlinge*." Thus it is clear that Luckner was being "closely informed about internal instructions."[29] Without an overt inclusion of "intermarriages" into the guidelines from February 20, 1943, on-site officials were given leeway in their actions, which allowed for either radical approaches or a flexible withdrawal. They were legally authorized to respond to local situations in flexible ways, in order to remove as many intermarried Jews as possible at that time.

Proceedings Against "Intermarriages" and "Mischlinge"

Very rarely were police stations candid about the true goals of the Nazi government; the handling of the "intermarriage" issue in the spring and summer of 1943 in various regions of Germany confirms this. Viktor Klemperer noted on March 14 that an "Aryan" woman comes daily to the cemetery in Dresden to adorn a place with an urn. "Her Jewish husband and her son who was declared a 'Jewish *Mischling*' had been arrested for unknown reasons and a few weeks later were shot during 'an escape attempt.'"[30] Eugen Grimminger was arrested on March 2 for financing the travel and flyer campaign of the "White Rose."[31] He never again saw his Jewish wife, Jenny, to whom he had been married since 1922. On April 10, she was arrested in Stuttgart, brought to the concentration camp Ravensbrück and then to Auschwitz where she was killed on December 2, 1943.[32]

Father Odilo Braun OP, who harshly condemned this procedure,[33] traveled on behalf of the Relief Organization at the Berlin Bishopric, which at the time was chaired by Dr. Margarete Sommer.[34] Sommer retrospectively summarized the developments in August 1943 by describing the various methods employed: since March the relief organization has received news from the individual dioceses "which shows that instead of the generally feared measures—that either had not been put into place or had been even reversed—several districts were now introducing partial actions which enforced the actual separation of intermarriages without legal basis and in a less inconspicuous, yet more radical manner."[35] In Hesse many non-Aryan spouses from intermarriages were arrested one week after the release (due to unusually heated protests) of intermarried non-Aryans who had been apprehended in Berlin at the turn of March. Some were arrested without reason, others without verifiable allegations of the supposed misdemeanor they had committed. Sommer calls these charges "pretenses." "These 'arrested citizens' were kept in large rooms that were divided up in the smallest of cages." For months the aggrieved people were locked up in this way. Sommer continued that: "After having been forced to sign a so-called camp admittance form (*Lagerschein*) to create the impression that they voluntarily had come to the evacuation camp, many of these arrested people were deported. Already two weeks after the first deportation of these unfortunate people, the first death reports arrived. It is reported that with this type of 'criminalization', intermarriages were also to be separated in other German areas."[36]

In the summer of 1943, the Protestant *Landesbischof* in Stuttgart, Theophil Wurm, received an anonymous statement similarly characterizing the situation in Frankfurt am Main: "Radical elements are at work" who "by avoiding any standardization of the law create a concrete situation which aims to finalize the separation of intermarriages through Gestapo intervention. In Frankfurt am Main numerous Jewish spouses of Aryans were detained for months in a police jail and are now brought to a concentration camp, their spouses were never told the reasons for their arrest . . . Also it would be quite hard to believe how suddenly in one town a large number of people supposedly had violated the law, all of whom also happen to live in an intermarriage." In Frankfurt intermarried Jews, supposedly only Protestant, were also criminalized on false charges and imprisoned in a concentration camp.[37]

The Exception: Releases Due to "Unusually Heavy Protests"

It is striking that Margarete Sommer emphasizes in her contemporaneous report of August 1943 that there was a correlation between "unusually heated protests"[38] and the release (of detainees) from Rosenstrasse. Worth noting are the terms "protest," "dismissal" (*Entlassung*), and "release" (*Freilassung*) which appear in sources from this time period. Sommer even provides an additional piece of evidence that Nazi procedures could only be reversed through a protest. The exact circumstances of this interesting case still have to be investigated but Sommer reports that, "In Innsbruck and other cities of Tyrol non-Aryan spouses were picked up without providing any reason and brought to a concentration camp. Following heavy protests from the Catholics in Vienna, theses spouses from intermarriages were reunited with their families."[39] To support his case, Gruner limits himself to one church document written by Wienken.[40] However, as late as August 1943, the well-informed Sommer is convinced of a link between the release of people from the Rosenstrasse and the protests that occurred. She specifically explains, "the Non-Aryan spouses of intermarriages who had already been torn away from their families by the thousands in February and March of the same year [1943] were released from the detention centers due to . . . vociferous protests by various citizen groups."[41]

Even Dr. Gerhard Lehfeldt,[42] who lived on Düsseldorf Street in Berlin-Wilmersdorf and whose reports were sent to Catholic and Protestant bishops and to Rome,[43] established a direct connection between "public riots" and the release of detained Jews, i.e. people imprisoned at Rosenstrasse released by Gauleiter and Propaganda Minister Goebbels. On Friday, March 5, 1943, as he reports, the wife of a seventy-year-old man was picked up from Münchnerstraße in Berlin-Schöneberg. This must have been one of the cases of a forceful separation of "intermarriages" despite Eichmann's assurance to Wienken on March 4, 1943, that intermarriages would not be affected. Certainly, the age of this arrested wife speaks against Gruner's thesis that "intermarriages" were only "registered" for employment purposes. After the arrest of his wife the seventy-year-old husband allegedly screamed for more than an hour, "Disgrace of our culture (*Kulturschande*)! A bomb on every house, a bomb on every house!" It appears that because of his loud objection public unrest broke out. The old man was subsequently arrested. Lehfeldt who reports about this incident in mid-March 1943, concludes that, "Mr. Goebbels was quite displeased about these riots, therefore on Saturday, March 6 [19]43, a number of those arrested were set free."

Officially it was acknowledged that "violations" had occurred during the massive arrests in Berlin beginning on February 27, 1943, but Eichmann and his representatives obviously remained in office.[44] In her Berlin diary, Ursula von Kardorff reports retrospectively that on March 3 women workers had "banded together at Rosenthaler Platz and loudly protested the deportation of Jews."[45] Therefore during those days, there were several places of public unrest; they were not confined to the Rosenstrasse. Even Goebbels notes in his diary "somewhat disagreeable scenes in front of a Jewish nursing home," i.e. in the former Jewish nursing home on the Große Hamburger Street where "citizens gathered in large numbers and partly even sided a little bit with the Jews."

Even though Goebbels claims to have ordered the secret service to end the evacuations, in the end this seems less pivotal. After all, the RSHA itself was in a position to act flexibly and to call off campaigns especially when—due to public unrest—they proved to be difficult to execute at the moment, only to proceed later with different methods and time schedules.[46] As early as the summer of 1942, Margarete Sommer notes, the Nazis had absolutely no interest in letting these civic disturbances become public knowledge. During transports of old and sick people from nursing homes, boarding houses, and apartments to Terezin, "unrest broke out in Berlin as people expressed sharp disapproval regarding the inhumane treatment of the transport. Arrests also took place as a result of these unrests. The fact that such unrests existed was held in strict secrecy by the authorities."[47]

It is noteworthy that some church leaders claimed credit for the releases and believed that various interventions had won the eventual release of the detainees at Rosenstrasse. None of them ever spoke of mere registration for employment purposes or of the planned replacement of the deported Jewish workforce, in support of Gruner's main argument. *Landesbischof* Wurm of Württemberg came forward hesitantly after the public protests in Berlin had ended and complained in a letter of March 12, 1943, to the Reich Church

Ministry "recently Jews who live in intermarriages with Christian Germans—some of whom are themselves members of the Christian Church—are taken from their home and workplace to be deported to the East." Though, "recently" they are "experiencing better treatment in Berlin." People have been "released." He requests that the alleviation be carried out more uniformly in the entire Reich so that "arbitrary and unequal treatment may be ruled out in the future."[48] Two days later, Wurm wrote to the Reich interior minister that in Berlin "detained people have been set free," and that if because of this, "a change in the policy concerning Jews had been introduced, he would welcome it."[49] Catholic Bishop Wilhelm Berning of Osnabrück writes on April 6, 1943, "Spouses in intermarriages who had been apprehended on February 27 have been released after 8 days [on March 6], as a result of various public offices having advocated for them."[50]

Margarete Sommer's Basis of Information and Conception

Margarete Sommer's contemporaneous opinions and observations about the events on Rosenstrasse carry considerable weight, because she sought to give professional help to people persecuted by the Nazi regime, particularly those who were categorized as "Catholic non-Aryans," "*Mischlinge*," and "couples in intermarriages."[51] Starting in 1941 she oversaw the Relief Organization at the Berlin Bishopric, which was created to assist exactly this group of people. Since 1939 it had been located on the premises of the "Sacred Heart of Jesus" parish at 182 Schönhauser Allee, within walking distance to Rosenstrasse. In August of 1943, when Sommer retrospectively evaluated the "protests that have loudly arisen from within diverse citizens' groups" as having caused the release of "intermarriage partners," her assessment was grounded in her perceptive observations, and detailed information about these events. It is noteworthy that as late as February of 1943 even Margarete Sommer assumed "intermarriages" were "protected." But she changed her assessment in response to the unpredictable and forceful violation by Nazi officials in Berlin. Like Hans Günther Adler, Sommer viewed these RSHA guidelines as "a trial balloon."[52]

Sommer was among the few people who had no illusions about the ultimate goals of Nazi "politics regarding Jews." She had access to information that gave her alarming insights into the intentions of the regime, namely "the preparation of the final solution of the European Jewish question."[53] Recently documents have surfaced that confirm Sommer possessed highly secret information about the Wannsee Conference that had taken place on

January 20, 1942, in Berlin.[54] In this way, information about the Wannsee Conference had been obtained by the Berlin Catholic Relief Organization and was forwarded either by Sommer or by her immediate supervisor Konrad Graf von Preysing, the bishop of Berlin. The report reached the chairman of the Fulda Bishops' Conference, Cardinal Adolf Bertram, the bishop of Breslau, and Pope Pius XII. This discovery means that knowledge of the horrific murder plans and their implementation was not restricted to the NS elite but was available to the head of the Catholic Church and the German bishops.[55] At the time, opinions were split over the appropriate response of the church in light of this knowledge. Preysing and Bertram were on opposite sides in this battle within the episcopacy.[56] As a member of the Committee for the Affairs of Religious Orders (*Ausschuss für Ordensangelegenheiten* or *Ordensausschuss*),[57] which was constituted in 1941, Preysing was betting on public information and public reactions as a way of pressuring the regime. For the *Ordensausschuss* the sermons delivered in summer 1941 by Bishop Clemens August Graf von Galen, a resident of Münster, served as a prime example. Father Odilo Braun OP, a committee member, claimed to have encouraged Galen in a conversation. The committee presented detailed reports and a memorandum to the bishops' conference with the explicit plea: "The seriousness of the hour demands a clear and unambiguous language. . . . The killing of mentally ill people out of economic considerations is and remains murder. . . . While we do not have equal weapons to stand up against armed violence, the rights of justice will eventually prevail over the brutally oppressed. Accountability must unequivocally be identified once and for all before God and all of history."[58] On the other side, Bertram trusted in confidential memorandi (*stille Eingaben*) to the authorities and feared—even in a dictatorship—any disruption in the "harmonious relations between church and state."[59] Like Bishop Preysing, Margarete Sommer pleaded for public measures on the part of the episcopacy as the most effective means in support of the "indisputable rights of all humans." Otherwise the bishops would become guilty of remaining silent "in the face of God and humanity."[60] However, she was only able to convince Bishop Bertram to submit a plea against a law regulating the compulsory separation of intermarriages in November 1942, because Bertram considered this a violation of the sacrament of marriage. As bishop, he did not feel authorized to comment on purely humanitarian and human rights affairs.[61]

Sommer also encouraged Bertram on March 2, 1943, to write to the department representative[62] and to Wienken; it was not until then that the bishops took action. Contrary to the remarks by the historian Rainer Decker, who does not know how to interpret the sources, Wienken did not react "promptly"[63] when he received Bertram's telegram March 2.[64] In fact, he waited two full days, until March 4, before he approached Adolf Eichmann.[65] Sommer, however, had hoped and pleaded for a word of public protest from the bishops as well as an intervention by the pope. Neither occurred.[66]

The Position of the Bishops

Beginning in 1941, Sommer repeatedly urged church officials to protest the discriminatory measures of state authorities and the deportations of "non-Aryans."[67] Therefore it is false to claim, as does the hierarchically-inclined historian Rainer Decker, that the impetus to oppose Nazi policies came from the "elite." The available historical sources do not support such claims.[68] On the contrary, beginning with 1933 the "elite" had not expressed support for people targeted by the Nazi state, neither for German Jews nor for Christians, and especially not for those Catholics considered "Jewish" due to their family ancestry. After the "Nuremberg laws" when "racial intermarriages" were outlawed,[69] there was no outcry from the church, although this certainly violated most fundamental basic rights.[70] Evidently this ban was not altogether inconvenient for the churches. The Catholic Church had always deemed even denominational "intermarriages"—those for instance, between Catholics and Protestants—an unwelcome problem. Catechism instruction warned the faithful against "intermarriage" as the cause of terrible harm.[71] Naturally, the position of the church was that only a marriage formed under ecclesiastic law was officially recognized. Margarete Sommer reprimanded one such intermarried couple, the Holzers, because they were "practically living in a wild marriage and first of all needed to get married,"[72] they were advised to make up for it and have a church wedding. In order to marry her Catholic husband, Elsa Holzer, a Protestant, converted to Catholicism; he, however was considered a "non-Aryan" according to NS racial laws. The priest reportedly requested that Rudi Holzer step before the alter without wearing a "Star of David." It was then agreed to have the ceremony at the priest's private apartment.[73]

According to national socialist definitions, couples were also considered "racially intermarried" when they consisted of two Catholics or two Protestants who had converted before their marriage and had Jewish ancestry. Due to their own anti-Semitism, some bishops even denounced such partners of "racial intermarriages." Bertram's letters, similar to those letters formulated by the Protestant *Landesbishof* Wurm,[74] offered the Nazis an excuse to "justify" their course of actions. Although he supposedly wanted to support people persecuted by Nazi race ideology, the cardinal of Breslau wrote in the fall of 1942 that, "It goes without saying that these convictions of mine do not emanate from a lack of love towards German heritage, nor from a lack of a sense for national dignity, nor even from an underestimation of the harmful impacts of an overgrowth of Jewish influences on German culture and interests of the fatherland."[75] These "harmful impacts" that belonged to the core of anti-Semitic reasoning were directed especially against "intermarriages."[76] Such intercessions offered the Nazis further leverage to proceed against "the Jews." For his part, Bertram was quite receptive towards allegations that "Jews" violated the laws of the state. He did not even see a reason to protest when disproportionate "punishment" for violations of such laws ultimately meant deportation to Auschwitz and inevitable death.[77]

Following the first mass deportations out of the German Reich in October 1941, the church elite, such as the members of the German Bishop's Conference who were holding a meeting in Paderborn, coldly and dispassionately recorded in their minutes, "Even if those Aryans who live in intermarriages with Non-Aryans can currently stay in Germany, it is gravely feared that they will be equated with Jews and evacuated if they do not get a divorce. Whether a *separatio tori, mensae et habitationis*—separation from marital bed, table and residence—by request of an Aryan according to can[on] 1128 and 1131 C[odex] J[uris] C[anonici] can and should be allowed, is to be examined and decided in each individual case by pastoral prudence."[78]

Needless to say, the traditional understanding of Catholic ecclesiastical law maintains unequivocally that a "performed Christian marriage is inseparable." However, as one commentator at the time formulated, this legal understanding can "sometimes become morally impossible." For such cases, the "canon law has created a solution through the institute for the *separatio a toro et mensa*," i.e. the separation of marital bed and table, which, however, does not cancel the "bond of marriage." For instance, a "temporary divorce" is permitted when one partner "endangers the body and soul of the other innocent partner,"[79] which the bishops obviously understood to be the "Aryans." Michael Drummer, the priest from St. Elisabeth in Nuremberg, even recommended that a Catholic woman divorce her husband under state law in order to protect herself and her children. Thomas Breuer comments that "this advice unmistakably combines compassion with the parishioners and mercilessness towards the Jewish man who could only survive the Nazi period because Ms. Kupfer stood by her husband."[80]

The church hierarchy not only failed to defend "non-Aryans" openly, but failed to restrain its own anti-Semitism when negotiating with Nazi officials on behalf of non-Aryans, thereby validating their convictions. Long before the Wannsee Conference, the bishops—in alleged "pastoral wisdom"—were contemplating possibilities to allow divorce that would be supported by the canon law of the church. Such tendencies became even more grievous and grave after the bishops and the pope had learned about the Wannsee Conference and the mass murders following deportations.

Sommer's Conduct in February/March of 1943

Margarete Sommer began her systematic reports on the situation of "intermarriages" and "*Mischlinge*" to Berlin parishes most notably via newsletter on February 17, 1943.[81] On February 11, 1943, the Jesuit priest König noted in his diary not only the names of Bishop Preysing and Father Odilo Braun OP, but also the name of Hans Globke.[82] Globke was one of the informants Sommer listed in regards to the preparation of a divorce law.[83] Sommer commenced a survey carried out by visits to homes.[84] Parallel to Sommer's survey, Gertrud Luckner began to collect information in Southern Germany.[85] Preysing who already on January 17, 1943, had turned to the Pope in response to questions "from Catholics as well as Protestants" concerning an "appeal in favor of the unfortunate,"[86] addressed yet another letter to Pius XII on February 26 with a note about the "compulsory separation of racial intermarriages."[87] On February 27, 1943, the "Factory Action" was launched which included the arrest of intermarried Jews in Berlin and other German cities. Since nothing had come of the proposed compulsory divorce law,[88] a certain significance was attributed to cardinal Bertram's letter in the fall of 1942 which created a false sense of security. On March 2, 1943, Sommer ascertained that: "In strict confidence, one of our men was told by some ministry that just a week ago an appeal had been answered by the SS leadership, stating that the planned raid would not include intermarriages, that they were 'protected.'"[89] With the help of her inquiries Sommer had been able to obtain up-to-date information about the specific targets of the impending raids. She was alarmed and investigated further. On March 2, 1943, she gave Bertram a precise report. Some of the eyewitnesses were surprised when they were visited at home by people unknown to them and told to report to Rosenstrasse 2-4 where intermarried Jews and some "Mischlinge" ("half-Jews") who wore the Jewish Star were being held; there they ended up meeting other family members of "intermarriage partners" who were detained.[90]

Following the inclusion of "intermarriage partners" and Mischlinge in the "Fabrik-Aktion" of February 27, the documents finally allowed Sommer a systematic tracking of personal tragedies. Prior to deportations (in which "non-Aryan" Catholics were also included), Sommer received detailed lists so that she together with her co-workers could actually prepare these people for the path to death.[91] She was familiar with the collection camps as well as with the procedures during such deportations.[92] Since October 1941, Catholics of Jewish descent—who according to NS ideology were classified as "non-Aryans"— had been deported from Berlin without any protests by the bishops or the pope.[93] Nevertheless, some opposition activities were generated on behalf of marriage and family, i.e. "intermarriage partners" and "Mischlinge."

On March 2, Sommer told Cardinal Bertram in Breslau about the developments of which she had become aware immediately after the raid in Berlin, "On Saturday, February 27 an evacuation was initiated of such magnitude and severity as Berlin had not experienced so far. Within two days circa 8,000 non-Aryans were picked up without consideration of whether they had been long baptized, often even for decades. This time no special consideration was given to those persons living in an intermarriage or not; even Christian intermarriages were violently separated in this way." In response to the very first reactions by family members, as Sommer wrote, "All efforts on the part of the Aryan spouses and the half-Aryan children to free the non-Aryan marriage partner or parent are to no avail. They are refused admittance in the harshest of ways and literally chased away. The police blocked off the street where the men and women from the intermarriages are held. Even house keys and food ration cards that were now with the detainees but belonged to all family members were not allowed to be handed over." The rooms were neither prepared nor was there appropriate clothing or food. "This very circumstance, that one is not allowed to care in any way for the future of the thousands who were detained, seems to have fueled the anxiety that they are without future." With "alarming swiftness" 3,500 had already been taken away. In "strict confidence" Sommer relayed that as of Monday evening March 1, the "partners of intermarriages" have not yet been evacuated. Sommer demanded an immediate personal intervention on part of Wienken, the spokesman for the bishop, because Bertram's appeal in November had "neither remained unheard nor been ineffective," as could be seen from "reliable sources." Yet Sommer expected more: for Sunday March 7, she demanded a "clear and accusatory word of protest from all highest spiritual leaders in Germany." Ultimately, Pope Pius XII should transmit "a papal address directed at the conscience of the world via Vatican radio broadcast."[94] Bertram, however, continued to limit his political response to memorandi and behind the scenes negotiations hidden from the public eye. In an identical letter sent to the RSHA, the Reich Chancellery, as well as to the Reich Ministries of the Churches, the Interior, and Justice, he requested "to stop the measures," i.e. to abolish the separation of marriages.[95]

The Bishops and Rosenstrasse

Some people are of the opinion that the step taken by the Catholic Church was a decisive factor in the Rosenstrasse releases and rescue from deportation.[96] However, the *Ordensausschuss* member, Father Odilo Braun OP, assessed the style and content of the memorandi by the chairman of the bishops' conference as "too ineffective due to its soft tone. Everyone dreads a public protest, hence such a step—especially when personally signed by all bishops—will probably save the lives of a lot of parishioners and protect existing marriages. However, this step needs to be taken very soon."[97]

Bertram's confidential communication from November 1942[98] might have been a signal for the Nazis not to go ahead with a compulsory divorce law since this might have provoked trouble with the church. Conversely, this meant the Nazis simply created a fait accompli; at most, the church would react to the regime with confidential memos and polite inquiries from Wienken. In turn, Wienken only received oral responses, which remained noncommittal and even factually wrong information, as in the case from Eichmann. This was entirely consistent with the tactical calculations of the Nazis who did not show much respect in their conduct with the church. Their tactics merely reinforced the standard warnings from the *Ordensausschuss* that "reassuring explanations and denial of such plans from the regime only serve the purpose of making us think we are safe and to prevent public support for these marriages. The Nazis fear the public response to this question."[99] Not until February 1944 did Bertram—unsuccessfully—complain that regarding a response to his memos it is "not satisfactory to receive exclusively oral explanations from the Reich Security Main Office."[100]

In her draft of August 1943 for the episcopacy's memo, Margarete Sommer had included the "loudly raised protests" from the population and the protests "from the bishops" as the reason for the releases on Rosenstrasse.[101] However, a loudly raised protest from the bishops and the pope, such as Sommer had requested immediately on March 2, had never taken place. Similarly the attempts of Father Odilo Braun OP and Bishop Preysing a few days later on March 6 were without avail: Father Braun had demanded a "public protest"[102] in light "of the horrific persecution of Jews" and on the same day Bishop Preysing[103] had requested that Pius XII intervene on behalf of the deported. The Pope remained silent. He left it to the local bishops to find an appropriate response.[104] Bertram's soft memo of November 1942 did not prevent the "trial balloon" (H.G. Adler) in Berlin. Eichmann's supposed comforting promises did not reach Wienken until day six into the protest;

Bertram himself never received a response. None of the steps taken by the bishop reached the public.

Even the preparations of a pastoral letter in April 1943 was simply for the eventuality that an "intermarriage law" should ever come to be; the law never was drafted because the NS refrained from a legal solution for tactical reasons.[105] The pastoral letter was not nearly strong enough to function as a loud protest, because—in the event of compulsory divorces and deportations—bishops were to prosaically declare that "without racial distinction" marriages "performed according to state and church laws" were not to be separated. The "sacramental bond" therefore continues to exist for married couples. However, the reaction to the pastoral letter was not envisioned as a public but as a private-passive one which left the solution to God: "With great sympathy, all Catholic people, its priests and bishops partake in bearing the heavy cross which is about to come over racial intermarriages." The people would lament this and unite in prayer to God that God may avert, lessen or help to bear the affliction.[106]

In the final analysis, it was important to Sommer to show in her draft of August 1943 that the episcopacy should retrospectively emphasize the close connection between the bishops and the protesting public as well as their equally strong and effective rejection of Nazi measures as carried out by government agencies. To urge the church elite toward a proactive measure, Sommer argued that the people were not supportive of government policies. In this, of course, she followed the conception represented by herself and the *Ordensausschuss*, namely that people could be mobilized for certain moral values against those in power. But Sommer's draft remained in the filing cabinets in Breslau because Bertram rejected such a bold statement to the government. Similarly, he did not want to support the joint Decalogue-pastoral letter in summer 1943, which was meant for the education of people, especially in light of the fact that there was a timidity among church leaders in the face of intimation regarding the human rights violations of the regime which he deemed too political.[107] For Sommer and the *Ordensausschuss*, the "loudly raised protests" on Rosenstrasse had been a hopeful sign that the church, which as the only unbroken central organization, could have publicly supported and strengthened the knowledge among the Volk about the crimes of the regime and their possibilities for opposition. This did not happen.[108]

The Dutch Catholic bishops advocated the same maxim as the *Ordensausschuss* and Sommer.[109] Although in 1942, the German occupation forces introduced sanctions which initially only affected Catholics of Jewish heritage—among them the Carmelite nun Edith Stein—the Dutch bishops protested again in 1943. This was preceded by the failure of the Reformed

Church to read the jointly planned protest letter on July 26, 1942, after threats from the occupying forces. In 1943, the Dutch bishops protested nonetheless. In their pastoral letter, read on February 21, 1943, they explained they would not fulfill their obligations, "were we not to publicly raise our voices against the injustices affecting so many of our people." They explicitly referred to Pius XII's Christmas message from 1942 identifying the church as "protector of the natural and supernatural order."[110] The Christmas message encouraged the bishops to protest and stated clearly, "The churches would incur guilt if they neglect to point out the sins committed by those in power while in office, and if they fail to warn them of God's final judgment." The fact that even "Catholic non-Aryans" had been deported—which was also known to the *Ordensausschuss*—did not deter the Dutch bishops from their basic protest.[111] Theo Salemink (Utrecht) debunked the myth that surrounds the 1942 protest in the apologetic secondary literature.[112] Calling upon the facts, he discredited the myth as an argument against the protests—an argument Rainer Decker has made repeatedly.[113] In postwar literature, the number of those deported—it was actually 114—was placed at a highly exaggerated figure. The actual number of victims was to remain uncertain, only to be raised immeasurably in the event of a possible protest by bishops and the pope so that one could justify the previous silence. Nevertheless, the pope was informed of the exact numbers in spring 1943 and was asked to publicly protest, although he refrained.[114]

Helmuth James Graf von Moltke, the main instigator of the "Kreisau Circle," was in close contact with Preysing and members of the *Ordensausschuss* and strongly advocated protests. On March 4, 1943, while Wienken was given an oral explanation by Eichmann, the Jesuit Priest König met with Moltke. The anticipated pastoral letter of protest did not appear, which caused much disappointment.[115] Therefore, it was not the steps taken by the bishops but rather the public street protest that must be considered the deciding factor in the release of the detained in the Rosenstrasse.[116] In his report from mid-March 1943, Gerhard Lehfeldt explicitly states that "intermarriages" had been separated "in spite of a vigorous protest" by Bertram."[117] There is only one passage on "intermarriage" as part of the Decalogue-pastoral letter in the fall of 1943 but no public protest from the Catholic Church, "Inasmuch as they have been performed according to the law of God and the Church, so-called racial intermarriages are fully entitled to God's protection as set down by the sixth commandment with all the values of blessings secured therein: union, sanctity, indissolubility, and the right to procreate. As in every valid Christian marriage, the following commandment of the Lord applies, "What God has joined together, no man shall put asunder' (Mt. 19:6). To this Apostle Paul responded, 'Through faith, you are all God's children in Jesus Christ. All of you who have been baptized in Christ's name, have brought Christ into you' (Gal. 3:26). Human laws can neither disregard nor overrule divine law in this matter."[118]

Since a compulsory divorce law for "intermarriages" was never enacted, all subsequent memos from the bishops remained hidden from public view (i.e. Bertram[119] or Wurm[120]). In some individual cases, bishops would intervene personally, such as by Bishop Albert Stohr in Mainz[121] and Bishop Antonius Hilfrich in Limburg.[122] However, there was clearly not so much concern for the plight of "non-Aryans." Thus in October 1944, Bishop Galen still had not fulfilled the task given to him by the bishops' conference in the spring of 1944.[123] He was supposed to collect information on the situation of "Catholic non-Aryans" remaining in the church communities. By the time he contacted parishes through his clerical relations, most deportations had already been carried out.[124] One witness reported the bitterness: "Those detained said the Church had abandoned them. No priests had come to them."[125]

Protests: Inadequately Investigated Forms of Resistance to Date

The Rosenstrasse protest remained unique; never again were there so many "partners in intermarriages" apprehended so "abruptly" in one place. Already in terms of numbers, Berlin signified quite a unique exception—so that on the streets family members ran into each other during their search for loved ones. Later on, the tactic of the regime shifted from case-to-case decisions to criminalization (accusations of crime), and ultimately in February 1945 to deportations that were camouflaged as "work assignments" (*Arbeitseinsätze*).[126] Before that "*Mischlinge*" and "Aryans who fraternized with Jews (such as non-Aryan marriage partners)" were forced to work with the *Todt* organization. Gerhard Lehfeldt commented on this in saying: "[O]ne obviously [wanted] to render those circles of people harmless, who for themselves could witness the measures taken against the Jews and who, therefore, would confront state leadership with a corresponding disposition . . . After *Mischlinge* and their spouses had been told again and again, they would be accepted into the community of the *Volk* they're being hit from behind now."[127]

Gruner speculates that in February 1945 "intermarriages" remained untouched in Berlin due to a lack of transportation capacity.[128] However, contemporaneous sources from the churches contradict Gruner's main thesis. Those who were actively involved in church assistance to "non-Aryans" and intermarried couples, some of whom were extremely well-informed, observed and noted a connection between the protests and the release of detained "partners in intermarriages." With this single building block removed from Gruner's thesis, his argument is nullified.

That this discussion about the significance of the protest under the Nazi dictatorship has grown into a heated controversy can be attributed to the fact that aside from the levels of resistance such as (1) "non-conformity,"(2) "refusal," and (4) "revolution" there has been little research into (3) the third level of resistance, namely "protest."[129] The foundational study by Nathan Stoltzfus[130] into the events constitutes the first scientific investigation incorporating the protest in the Rosenstrasse into the overall historical context. Aside from this, there are merely a number of other findings for public outcries, such as the removal of crosses in schools[131] or the abolishment of monasteries.[132] The fact that there were several other forms of other public protests in the immediate physical and temporal environment of the Rosenstrasse[133] indicates its centrality in assessing this third level of resistance for its successes and failures to oppose the Nazi dictatorship.[134]

Dr. Antonia Leugers is an expert in Catholic history and theology at the Eberhard-Karls-Universität Tübingen. She is the author of numerous books including *Gegen eine Mauer bischöflichen Schweigens: Der Ausschuss für Ordensangelegenheiten und seine Widerstandskonzeption 1941 bis 1945* (Frankfurt am Main: Knecht, 1996), and *Jesuiten in Hitlers Wehrmacht: Kriegslegitimation und Kriegserfahrung* (Paderborn: Schöningh, 2009).

Notes

This chapter is translated from Antonia Leugers's 2005 edited collection, *Berlin, Rosenstraße 2-4: Protest in der NS-Diktatur; Neue Forschungen zum Frauenprotest in der Rosenstraße 1943* (Annweiler: Plöger, 2005).

1. Wolfgang Benz, "Deutsche gegen Hitler: Widerstand, Verweigerung, Kampf gegen die nationalsozialistische Herrschaft," in his *Herrschaft und Gesellschaft im nationalsozialistischen Staat* (Frankfurt am Main: Fischer, 1990), 180–196, here 190. Cf. "Denkmal Frauenprotest Rosenstraße" in Bundeszentrale für politische Bildung, ed., *Gedenkstätten für die Opfer des Nationalsozialismus: Eine Dokumentation*, vol. 2, (Berlin: Hentrich 1999), 109f.
2. Cf. Beate Meyer. "Geschichte im Film: Judenverfolgung, Mischehen und der Protest in der Rosenstraße 1943," *Zeitschrift für Geschichtswissenschaft* [= ZfG] 52, no 1 (2004): 23–36, here 23; Wolf Gruner, "Die Internierung der Juden aus Mischehen in der Rosenstraße 1943: Das Ereignis, seine Diskussion und seine Geschichte," in ibid. 5–22, here 8. For eyewitness reactions, H. -O. Löwenstein de Witt cf. document 12, in Antonia Leugers, ed., *Berlin, Rosenstraße 2-4: Protest in der NS-Diktatur. Neue Forschungen zum Frauenprotest in der Rosenstraße 1943* (Annweiler: Plöger, 2005).

3. Cf. Wolf Gruner, *Der geschlossene Arbeitseinsatz deutscher Juden: Zur Zwangsarbeit als Element der Verfolgung 1938–1943* (Berlin: Metropol, 1997), 304–321. It is confusing in this text that the print is partially illegible due to the absence of umlauts or rather letters that are replacing punctuation marks. Such as: "Gescheiterte Austauschpl ne und die doppelte ÉFabrik-AktionC (September 1942 bis M rz 1943)" (ibid., 304 and more often). It is also strange that Gruner writes Gernot Jochmann [sic] rather than Jochheim (ibid., 317n. 243).
4. Cf. Claudia Schoppmann, "Rettung von Juden: ein kaum beachteter Widerstand von Frauen," in *Solidarität und Hilfe für Juden während der NS-Zeit*, vol. 5: *Überleben im Untergrund: Hilfe für Juden in Deutschland 1941–1945*, ed. Beate Kosmala and Claudia Schoppmann (Berlin: Metropol, 2002), 113f; Beate Meyer, *"Jüdische Mischlinge": Rassenpolitik und Verfolgungserfahrung 1933–1945* (Hamburg: Dölling und Galitz, 1999), 57; idem, *Geschichte im Film*; idem, "Die Inhaftierungen der 'jüdisch Versippten' in der Berliner Rosenstraße im Spiegel staatsanwaltlicher Zeugenvernehmungen in der DDR," *Jahrbuch für Antisemitismusforschung* [=JfA] 11 (2002): 178–197.
5. Cf. Wolf Gruner, "Die Fabrik-Aktion und die Ereignisse in der Berliner Rosenstraße: Fakten und Fiktionen um den 27. February 1943," *JfA* 11 (2002): 137–177; idem, "Internierung." Gruner's conclusion (ibid., 21): "New sources compel therefore a reinterpretation of the events that occurred at the end of February 1943."
6. Cf. this argument can also be found in Felix Moeller, "Der Protest in der Rosenstraße: Eine Woche im Berlin des Jahres 1943," in *Rosenstraße: Ein Film von Margarethe von Trotta; Die Geschichte: Die Hintergründe: Die Regisseurin,* ed. Thilo Wydra (Berlin: Nicolai, 2003), 25–60, here 54.
7. Cf. Ludwig Volk, "Episkopat und Kirchenkampf im Zweiten Weltkrieg. II: Judenverfolgung und Zusammenbruch des NS-Staates," *Stimmen der Zeit* 198 (1980): 687–702, here 690 and footnote 13 and 14. Contrary to Günther Lewy [*Die katholische Kirche und das Dritte Reich* (Munich: Piper, 1965), 316f] Ludwig Volk states that it cannot be determined as to who should be accredited for the retreat of the authorities: was it due to the women's protest in the Rosenstrasse or because of the intervention of the bishops? Cf. Antonia Leugers, "Widerstand oder pastorale Fürsorge katholischer Frauen im Dritten Reich? Das Beispiel Dr. Margarete Sommer (1893–1965)," in *Frauen unter dem Patriarchat der Kirchen: Katholikinnen und Protestantinnen im 19. und 20. Jahrhundert*, ed. Irmtraud Götz von Olenhusen (Stuttgart: Kohlhammer, 1995), 161–188, here 176–179.
8. Gruner, *Internierung*, 15, 21; idem., *Fabrik-Aktion*, 161.
9. Cf. Martin Höllen, *Heinrich Wienken, der "unpolitische" Kirchenpolitiker: Eine Biographie aus drei Epochen des deutschen Katholizismus* (Mainz: Matthias-Grünewald, 1981).
10. Wienken to Bertram, March 4, 1943, in Ludwig Volk, ed., *Akten deutscher Bischöfe über die Lage der Kirche 1933–1945*, vol. 6: *1943–1945*, (Mainz: Matthias-Grünewald, 1985) (hereafter, Volk 6), 25.
11. Orsenigo to Maglione, March 3, 1943 in Pierre Blet, Robert A. Graham, Angelo Martini, and Burkhart Schneider, eds., *Actes et Documents du Saint Siège relatifs à la Seconde Guerre Mondiale*, vol. 9, *Le Saint Siège et les victimes de la guerre: Janvier/ Décembre 1943* (Città del Vaticano: Libreria editrice vaticana, 1975) [= ADSS IX],

165: "Io ne ho preso occasione, per esprimere ancora una volta al Ministero degli Affari Esteri l'ingrata impressione di tutti i cattolici; fui ascoltato, ma so anche che nessuno qui può opporsi alla forza materiale e sfrenata della così detta,Gestapo', alla cui direzione, dopo l'occasione di Rinaldo [sic] Heydrich, sta ora un efferato viennese."

12. Cf. Nathan Stoltzfus, *Resistance of the Heart: Intermarriage and the Rosenstrasse Protest in Nazi Germany* (New York: W.W. Norton, 1996); German translation: *Widerstand des Herzens: Der Aufstand der Berliner Frauen in der Rosenstraße—1943*, 2nd ed., (Munich: Hansa, 1999), 2002; cf. review: Leugers, "Deutscher Widerstand gegen den Nationalsozialismus," *Neue Politische Literatur* 47, no. 2 (2002): 249–276, here 260f.; Nathan Stoltzfus, "Der 'Versuch, in der Wahrheit zu leben' und die Rettung von jüdischen Angehörigen durch deutsche Frauen im 'Dritten Reich,'" in *Frauen und Widerstand*, ed. Jana Leichsenring (Münster: Lit, 2003), 74–88 and 89–95 (Discussion).
13. Wienken to Bertram, March 4, 1943, in Volk 6, 25. According to Gestapo ordinance in Frankfurt/Oder (Memo from February 24, 1943. Brandenburgisches Landeshauptarchiv Potsdam [Brandenburg State Archive Potsdam]. Rep. 41 Administrative district Großräschen Nr. 272, 84–85) it has been ordered that no Jew who has been arrested in the course of the action (later called the "Fabrik-Aktion") will be permitted to be employed in this or any other factory again. Cf. document 3 in Leugers, *Berlin*. The printing is erroneous in Gruner, *Fabrik-Aktion*, 176f. The following entry is missing: "Vorgang: ohne." (Precedent: None.) The date at the end of the ordinance should be February 27, 1943, instead of 1945. Cf. Gruner, "Die Reichshauptstadt und die Verfolgung der Berliner Juden 1933–1945," in *Jüdische Geschichte in Berlin: Essays und Studien*, ed. Reinhard Rürup (Berlin, 1995), 252.
14. Gruner, *Internierung*, 15; idem., *Fabrik-Aktion*, 161.
15. RSHA guidelines from February 20, 1943. Cf. documents 1 and 2, in Leugers, *Berlin*. Partial citations in Hans Günther Adler, *Der verwaltete Mensch: Studien zur Deportation der Juden aus Deutschland* (Tübingen: Mohr, 1974), 199f.: "intermarriages" are exempted; of the "*Geltungsjuden*" only "single" people should be deported to Terezin, the rest should not be deported. Cf. Gruner, *Fabrik-Aktion*, 158. The file number as given by Gruner for the guidelines is incorrect according to the information provided by the *Bundesarchiv* (to the author, July 7 and August 2, 2004). Wolf Gruner has not been able to verify the file number.
16. In the report written shortly after March 6, 1943 (document reprinted in this volume and also, as Document 5, in Leugers, *Berlin*) it was mentioned in passing that the internees were told that they would be released after their documents had been checked. The writer, however, regarded this as not credible.
17. Cf. Joachim Neander at the Rosenstrasse Conference in Berlin, April 29 and 30, 2004, and at Florida State University, September 11, 2004. Cf. the article by Joachim Neander, in this volume as well as his work in Leugers, *Berlin*.
18. Cf. Gruner, *Internierung*, 16f; idem., *Fabrik-Aktion*, 162–167.
19. Cf. Gruner, *Internierung*, 15, wrote that "According to all the eyewitness reports known to me, there were some teenagers detained at the Rosenstrasse, but no children under 14 years of age. And that was exactly the cut-off point for the compulsory work recruitment."

20. Take for instance the then eight-year-old Evelin-Gisela Weigert who was with her father on the Rosenstrasse and who reported back about other children: Cf. Stoltzfus, *Widerstand*, 296f.; Leichsenring, *Frauen*, 136–140; cf. also Nina Schröder, *Hitlers unbeugsame Gegnerinnen: Der Frauenaufstand in der Rosenstraße* (Munich: W. Heyne, 1998), 173; Diana Schulle, *"Gebt uns unsere Männer frei!,"* in *Juden in Berlin 1938–1945*, ed. Beate Meyer and Hermann Simon (Berlin: Philo, 2000), 164.

21. Cf. Meyer, *Mischlinge*, 58–62; Monica Kingreen, *Gewaltsam verschleppt aus Frankfurt. Die Deportationen der Juden in den Jahren 1941–1945* in idem, ed., *"Nach der Kristallnacht." Jüdisches Leben und antijüdische Politik in Frankfurt am Main 1938–1945* (Frankfurt: Campus, 1999), 357–402, here 383–387; Volker Eichler, "Das 'Judenreferat' der Frankfurter Gestapo," in ibid., 250f.; Margarete Sommer, *Entwurf einer Eingabe des deutschen Episkopats*, August 22/23, 1943, in Volk 6, 217; Sommer's report, August 24, 1943, in ibid., 219; Recording, middle of 1943 in *Landesbischof D. Wurm und der Nationalsozialistische Staat 1940–1945: Eine Dokumentation*, Stuttgart 1968, 165–167, here 166.

22. Cf. Document 3 in Leugers, *Berlin* and in this volume. Also in print in Gruner, *Fabrik-Aktion*, 176f., and in Gernot Jochheim, *Frauenprotest in der Rosenstraße Berlin 1943: Berichte Dokumente Hintergründe*, expanded new edition (Berlin: Hentrich, 2002), 30f.

23. Gruner, *Arbeitseinsatz*, 316n. 236: "Viel würde also von der Willkür vor Ort abhängen, denn die Beamten hatten einen Freibrief erhalten, 'freches Benehmen' von 'geschützten' Juden mit Schutzhaft zu ahnden, wobei Übergriffe vermieden werden sollten." ("Therefore much would depend on the arbitrary behavior of the officers at each location. The officials had received a 'carte blanche' to penalize 'impudent behavior' from 'protected' Jews by taking them into protective custody; however, the officials were also told not to overstep their authority.") In the end, even closed camps, which were supposed to be exempted, were incorporated in the *Fabrik Aktion*. Document printed in this volume and in Leugers, *Berlin*.

24. In print in Gruner, *Fabrik-Aktion*, 176f. Cf. the complete source in Document 3 in Leugers, *Berlin*. Original in Brandenburgisches Landeshauptarchiv Potsdam, Rep. 41 Großräschen Nr. 272, 84f.: The Gestapo ordinance is included in a memo of the Landrat from Calau to police administrators, February 25, 1943:

> Confidential! . . . I am sending this copy for your careful consideration and precise adherence. I am requesting that promptly at the beginning of the workday on February 27, 1943, all Jews (even those living with a German in an intermarriage) be removed inconspicuously from the factories. Impudent behavior from Jews—who live currently in an intermarriage—is to be penalized by taking them into protective custody and by filing a request for placement in a concentration camp. The number of Jews who were removed from factories as well as the number of Jews taken into custody must be reported to me, along with personal information, by 11 o'clock on February 27, 1943. The given deadline must be kept under any circumstance. A nil return (Fehlanzeige) is required. Interrogation records of arrested Jews should be dispatched immediately to me.

25. Documented printed in this volume and as Document 6 in Leugers, *Berlin*, which Gruner neglected to take into account.

26. Cf. Hans-Josef Wollasch, *"Betrifft: Nachrichtenzentrale des Erzbischofs Gröber in Freiburg": Die Ermittlungen der Geheimen Staatspolizei gegen Gertrud Luckner 1942–1944* (Constance: UVK, 1999), 16–82; Angela Borgstedt, "'. . . zu dem Volk Israel in einer geheimnisvollen Weise hingezogen': Der Einsatz von Hermann Maas und Gertrud Luckner für verfolgte Juden" in *Widerstand gegen die Judenverfolgung,* ed. Michael Kißener (Constance: UVK, 1996) 227–259; Angela Borgstedt, "'Bruderring' and 'Lucknerkreis': Rettung im deutschen Südwesten" in Kosmala and Schoppmann, *Solidarität und Hilfe,* vol. 5, 191–203; Ursula Büttner, "Die anderen Christen: Ihr Einsatz für verfolgte Juden und "Nichtarier" im nationalsozialistischen Deutschland," in ibid., 127–150; Michael Phayer and Eva Fleischner, *Cries in the Night: Women Who Challenged the Holocaust* (Kansas City, MO: Sheed & Ward, 1997), 111–135; idem, *The Catholic Church and the Holocaust 1930–1965* (Bloomington: Indiana University Press, 2000), 114–117. About the collaboration of G. Luckner, M. Sommer, and G. Magnis cf. Jana Leichsenring, *Gabriele Gräfin Magnis: Sonderbeauftragte Kardinal Bertrams für die Betreuung der katholischen "Nichtarier" Oberschlesiens: Auftrag—Grenzüberschreitung—Widerstand?* (Stuttgart: Thorbecke, 2000), 75–96. For the most part, Leichsenring follows Leugers's analysis of the actions taken by the church and by Sommer.
27. Report from the secretary for criminal investigations, Hans von Ameln, about the interrogation of J. Stahl, March 6, 1943, in Wollasch, *Nachrichtenzentrale,* 131f.
28. Report from H. von Ameln about the interrogation of J. Baum and I. Schwab, March 7, 1943, in ibid., 133f.
29. Report from the Gestapo headquarters in Düsseldorf to the RSHA IV Vol. 1, March [11th] 1943 in ibid., 140f.
30. Note from March 14, 1943, in Viktor Klemperer, *Ich will Zeugnis ablegen bis zum letzten: Tagebücher 1942–1945,* 3rd ed., ed. Walter Nowojski and Hadwig Klemperer (Berlin: Aufbau, 1995), vol. 2, 343.
31. Cf. to the student resistance group from Munich: Rudolf Lill, ed., *Hochverrat? Neue Forschungen zur "Weißen Rose,"* revised new edition (Constance: UVK, 1999) (with a bibliography, 161–179).
32. Cf. Armin Ziegler, *Eugen Grimminger: Widerständler und Genossenschaftspionier* (Crailsheim: Baier, 2000), 118. Jenny Grimminger (1895–1943) was mentioned on the list that the Württemberg *Landesbischof* Theophil Wurm had already sent to the deanships (*Dekanate*) of his diocese by January 1943: cf. list of the Jews living in intermarriages in Württemberg and Hohenzollern as of June 25, 1942. Landeskirchliches Archiv Stuttgart (LKA, Protestant Church Archive of Stuttgart), A 126/658. There it was noted that her husband was "Aryan" and they lived in a "PME", i.e. "Privilegierte Mischehe" (privileged intermarriage). Wurm wrote to the dean (*Stadtdekan*) of Stuttgart on January 29, 1943 (ibid.), he's sending him the list of "non-Aryan intermarriages, or rather the privileged intermarriages that are currently present in Stuttgart. The list should be confidentially disclosed to the appropriate clergymen in the city. The clergymen are requested to give pastoral guidance to the Protestants who live in intermarriages. As far as they are members of our church, they stand under particular psychological pressure and need our special attention." With this statement, Wurm excluded all those who were not Protestants from church counseling and guidance, which not only meant the

sacramental aspect of it, but the holistic spiritual guidance as well. Therefore, Jenny Grimminger did not belong to the church community.

33. Note in the file of the Limburg Bishopric, June 26, 1943 (in Volk 6, 99) about the information that was delivered by Father Odilo Braun OP. He traveled on behalf of the relief center in Berlin: Braun to the Jewish community in Frankfurt, July 1977 (Antonia Leugers, *Gegen eine Mauer bischöflichen Schweigens: Der Ausschuß für Ordensangelegenheiten und seine Widerstandskonzeption 1941–1945* [Frankfurt am Main: J. Knecht, 1996], 471n. 358). Cf. further examples and a positive assessment of the Rosenstrasse Protest by: Eric A. Johnson. *Der nationalsozialistische Terror: Gestapo, Juden und gewöhnliche Deutsche.* Translated from English by Udo Rennert, (Berlin: Siedler, 2000), 443–463.

34. Cf. Leugers, *Widerstand oder pastorale Fürsorge*; idem, *Gegen eine Mauer*, 214–222; idem, "Sommer, Margarete" in *Lexikon für Theologie und Kirche* (2000) vol. 9, col. 717; Heinrich Herzberg, *Dienst am höheren Gesetz: Dr. Margarete Sommer und das "Hilfswerk beim Bischöflichen Ordinariat Berlin"* (Fredersdorf: SERVI, 2000); Wolfgang Knauft, *Unter Einsatz des Lebens: Das Hilfswerk beim Bischöflichen Ordinariat Berlin für katholische "Nichtarier" 1938–1945* (Berlin: Bischöfliches Ordinariat Berlin [West], 1988); Ursula Pruß, "Margarete Sommer" in *Zeitgeschichte in Lebensbildern*, ed. Jürgen Aretz, et al., (Mainz: Grünewald, 1997), vol. 8, 95–106; Michael Phayer, "The Catholic Resistance Circle in Berlin and German Catholic Bishops during the Holocaust," *Holocaust and Genocide Studies* 7, no. 2 (1993): 216–229; idem, *Protestant and Catholic Women in Nazi Germany* (Detroit, MI: Wayne State University, 1990); Phayer and Fleischner, *Cries in the Night*, 14–41; idem, *The Catholic Church and the Holocaust*, 44f., 68–79, 122–124; Büttner, "Die anderen Christen," 127–150. It is astonishing that Leichsenring does not mention Sommer's explicit assessments of the Rosenstrasse Protest and the context that resulted from the fact that G. Luckner was watched by the Gestapo: J. Leichsenring, "Katholiken in der Rosenstraße: Das 'Hilfswerk beim Bischöflichen Ordinariat Berlin' und die "Mischehen"," *ZfG* 52, no. 1 (2004): 37–49.

35. Draft of a memo from the German Episcopacy [by Margarete Sommer] (I), [August 22/23, 1943], in Volk 6, 217.

36. Sommer's report, August 24, 1943, in Volk 6, 219. For the Hessen case study, Sommer's observations were not taken into consideration by Monica Kingreen, "Verfolgung und Rettung in Frankfurt am Main und der Rhein-Main-Region," in Kosmala and Schoppmann, *Solidarität und Hilfe*, vol. 5, 182–185, Kingreen, *Gewaltsam verschleppt*, 383–390. For the occurrences in Frankfurt cf. also the observations Father Odilo Braun OP made on his trip from Worms via Frankfurt: [Braun] to Bishop [Dietz], March 6, 1943. Print: Antonia Leugers, *Georg Angermaier: Katholischer Jurist zwischen nationalsozialistischem Regime und Kirche: Lebensbild und Tagebücher*, 2nd ed. (Frankfurt am Main: J. Knecht, 1997), 233f. note 9; for the Breslau Archdiocese cf. Leugers, *Widerstand oder pastorale Fürsorge*, 182f.; for Breslau/Beuthen overall: cf. Leichsenring, *Gräfin Magnis*.

37. Notes, middle of 1943, in *Landesbischof D. Wurm und der Nationalsozialistische Staat*, 165–167, here 166f. In the fall 1943 it was reported that people who had been arrested were released and no new people were arrested: cf. Berning to Bertram, November 3, 1943, in Volk 6, 267. Cf. Darmstadt Public Attorney's Office.

Dengler criminal case. Offenses against Jews in 1943 as a Gestapo official, May 11, 1950. *Institut für Zeitgeschichte München* (Munich Institute of Contemporary History), Gd 01.10: Dengler acted in a similar fashion in order to deport "partners in an intermarriage."
38. Sommer's report, August 24, 1943, in Volk 6, 219.
39. Ibid.
40. Cf. Gruner, *Fabrik-Aktion*, 161; idem, *Internierung*, 15.
41. Draft of a memo from the German Episcopacy [by Margarete Sommer] (I), August 22/23, 1943, in Volk 6, 217. Cf. note 101.
42. Gerhard Lehfeldt (1897–1976), LL.D, residence at 60 Düsseldorfer Street, Berlin W 15. In the Berlin city address book 1943, the profession was given as "Syndicus" (message from Jana Leichsenring, December 8, 2004).
43. Notes and reports were found in the literary estate of Bertram, as well as of Wurm and in archives in Rome. Cf. document 6 with comments, in Leugers, *Berlin*, as well as Stoltzfus, *Widerstand*, 277, 279, 397; ADSS IX, 20, 22, 240–242.
44. Quote from: Gerhard Lehfeldt: Report on the Situation of the *"Mischlinge,"* middle of March 1943. Cf. document 6, in Leugers, *Berlin* and in this volume.
45. Note U. v. Kardorff, March 3, 1943, in Ursula von Kardorff, *Berliner Aufzeichnungen 1942 bis 1945: Unter Verwendung der Original-Tagebücher*, 2nd ed. (Munich: dtv, 1997), 72. Since Kardorff's brother was killed in action, she apparently wrote in retrospect on April 2, 1943 in the diary: "In addition, the last eradications of Jews. Driven around in trucks, picked up by SS people in steel helmets, fear on behalf of the Non-Aryans (*die Versippten*), half-breeds (*die Halben*) and one's own helplessness." (ibid., 73 note 2). The note from March 3, 1943, was written in 1947.
46. Goebbels's journal entry, March 6, 1943, quoted in Jochheim, *Frauenprotest*, 180.
47. Sommer's report, [after August 5, 1942] in Ludwig Volk, ed., *Akten deutscher Bischöfe über die Lage der Kirche 1933–1945*, vol. 5: *1940–1942* (Mainz: Matthias-Grünewald, 1983) [= Volk 5], 818.
48. Wurm to the Ministry of the Reich Church, March 12, 1943 in *Landesbischof D. Wurm und der Nationalsozialistische Staat*, 160f. Cf. also note from mid-1943, in ibid., 166: "Already in February 1943, a number of *Mischlinge* of the first degree together with Jews had been brought by the Gestapo in trucks to the Rosenstrasse in Berlin, where they were later released."
49. Wurm to the Reich Interior Ministry, March 14, 1943, in *Landesbischof D. Wurm und der Nationalsozialistische Staat*, 162. Wurm's writings were most likely based on document 5 in Leugers, *Berlin*, that reported about the events on Rosenstrasse. It was only because of this document that the church intervened and called for a release (of the interned *Mischlinge*) at the Rosenstrasse. This means, the reporter did not assume that the church had contributed to the "reversal" from March 6, 1943, rather the concerned Christian circles and families had led to the (change of) believes within "some individuals who were important figures." In the report from mid March (in this volume and document 6, in Leugers, *Berlin*), Goebbels is linked to this, not the heads of church.
50. Notes by Berning, April 6, 1943, in Volk 6, 62f. note 1.
51. Cf. Leugers, *Widerstand oder pastorale Fürsorge*; Herzberg, *Dienst am höheren Gesetz*; Knauft, *Unter Einsatz*; Leichsenring, *Katholiken*. The criteria, which the strict

Catholic woman M. Sommer applied to help the affected people, still need to be more closely analyzed.

52. Adler, *Der verwaltete Mensch*, 202: "At the beginning of 1943 when mass deportations began to near their end, there occurred a push in Berlin to remove all Jewish men who were married to German women. Many were arrested and were supposed to be taken away. Yet, a courageous demonstration by the wives, moved the Gestapo to backpedal exceptionally (*ausnahmsweise*), and the men were released." Cf. also ibid., 307, 340.
53. Minutes of the Wannsee Conference in *Die Grunewald-Rampe: Die Deportation der Berliner Juden*, 2nd corrected ed. (Berlin: Edition Colloquium, 1993), 59.
54. Jana Leichsenring who dealt with this issue in her dissertation (directed by Wolfgang Benz) about Margarete Sommer, introduced this source for the first time at the Rosenstrasse Protest Conference in Berlin, April 29–30, 2004. Cf. the link to the conference report in the online publication of: H-Soz-u-Kult. Regarding the informants cf. also: Leugers, *Gegen eine Mauer*, 471n. 348; idem, *Widerstand oder pastorale Fürsorge*, 175n. 83; Leichsenring, *Katholiken*, 42n. 43, 45n. 72. Cf. Jana Leichsenring's article, in Leugers, *Berlin*.
55. Cf. e.g. the annotation on Sommer's report, after August 5, 1942, in Volk 5, 817: "Went to Rome by messenger." Cf. also in regard to the information: Leugers, *Gegen eine Mauer*, 212–222, 272.
56. Cf. Leugers, "Positionen der Bischöfe zum Nationalsozialismus und zur nationalsozialistischen Staatsautorität" in *Die katholische Schuld? Katholizismus im Dritten Reich- Zwischen Arrangement und Widerstand*, 2nd expanded and revised ed., ed. Rainer Bendel (Münster: Lit, 2004), 122–142. See ibid., 141f.: *Harmoniemodell Kardinal Bertrams, Konfrontationsmodell Bischof Preysings im Ordensausschuss*.
57. Cf. further elaborated by Leugers, *Gegen eine Mauer*. Members were: Bishop Konrad Count Preysing (Berlin), Bishop Johannes B. Dietz (Fulda), Georg Angermaier, Father Odilo Braun OP, Father Laurentius Siemer OP, Father Augustinus Rösch SJ, and Father Lothar König SJ. For more extensive personal biographies of these members: ibid.
58. Regarding the sermons of Galen and Father Odilo Braun OP and the memoir which Galen undoubtedly used to orient himself, see Leugers, *Gegen eine Mauer*, 170, 206–210. Regarding the sermons of Galen, see also Winfried Süß, *Der "Volkskörper" im Krieg: Gesundheitspolitik, Gesundheitsverhältnisse und Krankenmorde im nationalsozialistischen Deutschland 1939–1945* (Munich: Oldenbourg, 2003), 127–151; idem, *"Dann ist keiner von uns seines Lebens mehr sicher:" Bischof Galen, der katholische Protest gegen die "Euthanasie" und der Stopp der "Aktion T 4"* in *Skandal und Öffentlichkeit in der Diktatur*, ed. Martin Sabrow (Göttingen: Wallstein, 2004), 102–124. W. Süß is part of the context for the sermons of Galen—the preliminary work of the *Ordensausschuss* is unknown.
59. Bertram to Muhs, [October 27, 1944], in Volk 6, 436.
60. Draft of a memo from the German Episcopacy [by Margarete Sommer] (II), [August 22/23, 1943], in Volk 6, 220.
61. Cf. Bertram to Thierack, Frick, Muhs, November 11, 1942, in Volk 5, 944f. Cf. Leugers, *Widerstand oder pastorale Fürsorge*, 175f.; idem, "Adolf Kardinal Bertram und die Menschenrechte," *Die Diözese Hildesheim in Vergangenheit und Gegewart: Jahrbuch des Vereins für Geschichte und Kunst im Bistum Hildesheim* 63 (1995):

205–229. Cf. the sermon delivered by Preysing from November 15, 1942, partially printed in Leugers, *Georg Angemaier*, 58.
62. Cf. Bertram to Frick, Muhs, Thierack, Lammers, RSHA, March 2, 1943, in Volk 6, 21–23.
63. Rainer Decker in online publication H-German Forum Rosenstrasse 2004.
64. Cf. Bertram to Wienken, March 2, 1943, in Volk 6, 21n. 3.
65. Cf. Wienken to Bertram, March 4, 1943, in ibid., 25.
66. Report by Sommer, March 2, 1943, in ibid., 19–21.
67. Cf. Leugers, *Widerstand oder pastorale Fürsorge*; Leichsenring, *Katholiken*; cf. also Leugers, *Gegen eine Mauer*.
68. Rainer Decker in online publication H-German Forum Rosenstrasse 2004.
69. Das "Gesetz zum Schutze des deutschen Blutes und der deutschen Ehre" (law for the protection of German blood and German honor) from September 15, 1935. Print: *Reichsgesetzblatt*, part I, 1146f.
70. Cf. Walter Ziegler, "Haben die deutschen Bischöfe im Dritten Reich versagt," in *Festgabe Heinz Hürten zum 60. Geburtstag*, ed. Harald Dickerhof (Frankfurt am Main: P. Lang, 1988), 497–524, here 517–519; Ursula Büttner, "Von der Kirche verlassen: Die deutschen Protestanten und die Verfolgung der Juden und Christen jüdischer Herkunft im 'Dritten Reich.'" in *Die verlassenen Kinder der Kirche: Der Umgang mit Christen jüdischer Herkunft im "Dritten Reich,"* ed. Ursula Büttner and Martin Greschat (Göttingen: Vandenhoeck & Ruprecht, 1998), 15–69.
71. Dekret der Konzilskongregation betr: Die katechetische Unterweisung (Congregation Council Decree concerning catechistic instruction), January 8, 1936, in Bernhard Stasiewski, ed., *Akten deutscher Bischöfe über die Lage der Kirche 1933–1945*, vol. 3: *1935–1936*, (Mainz: Matthias-Grünewald, 1979), 193.
72. Elsa Holzer in Schröder, *Hitlers unbeugsame Gegnerinnen*, 275.
73. Cf. Stoltzfus, *Widerstand*, 200f. Cf. document 11 in Leugers, *Berlin*. Holzer thought this had been Sommers, but she left room for doubt on this point.
74. Cf. Wurm to Reich Interior Ministry, March 14, 1943 in *Landesbischof D. Wurm und der nationalsozialistische Staat*, 162: Allegedly Wurm was happy that the people in Berlin were released again. He welcomes this, "not out of fondness for Judaism. In a time when the press was in favor of the Jews, the Christian side recognized nearly only (*fast nur*) the immense influence of Judaism on the cultural, economic and politic life of the time as fatal." Compare the assessment of Martin Greschat, "Die Haltung der deutschen evangelischen Kirchen zur Verfolgung der Juden im Dritten Reich," in *Die Deutschen und die Judenverfolgung im Dritten Reich*, revised new edition, ed. Ursula Büttner (Frankfurt am Main: Christians, 2003), 330: One of Wurm's memos supposedly "came shamefully close to official Anti-Semitism." Wolfgang Gerlach, *Als die Zeugen schwiegen: Bekennende Kirche und die Juden*, 2nd revised and expanded edition (Berlin: Institut Kirche und Judentum, 1993), 346: "In this note, the paradigmatic Christian and Anti-Semitic double existence of Wurm is finding its expression once more."
75. Bertram to Thierack, Frick, and Muhs, November 11, 1942, in Volk 5, 944. Compare the similar wording still in the writing of Bertram to Frick, Muhs, Thierack, Lammers, RSHA, March 2, 1943, in Volk 5, 22. A further example of anti-Semitic stereotype by a Catholic bishop: In his December, 31 1943 address in the Freiburg

cathedral, the Freiburg Archbishop Conrad Gröber said to believers (Archbishop Archives of Freiburg, Nb8/99): "Even though Judaism was the bearer of divine thoughts, it has proven itself unworthy. The relationship between Christ and the Jews is proven by the cross and the way in which He died. The Jews did it. The fate of Christianity, of the Apostles and of Christians has been consistently threatened by the Jews. They fight it and want to deny it. The history of the Church attests to this. Jews are the leading heads amongst the communists. The most fanatical haters of Christianity are the Jews."

76. Cf. Wolfgang Selig's examples in *Leben unterm Rassenwahn*: *Vom Antisemitismus in der "Hauptstadt der Bewegung"* (Berlin: Metropol, 2001), 178–187. In these examples couples from Munich who live in "intermarriages" were supposedly forced to divorce under such reasoning and if they refused, their stores were to be designated as "Jewish."
77. Cf. the case described in Leugers, *Widerstand oder pastorale Fürsorge*, 183f. As early as October 1941 Bishop Berning (to Bertram, October 27, 1941, in Volk 5, 583) received news from Adolf Eichmann "that Christian non-Aryans were to be evacuated only as an exception, and only if they had already come into conflict with the state police. Non-Aryans who live in intermarriages were not to be affected for the time being."
78. Minutes of the West German Bishop's Conference, November 24 and 25, 1941, in Volk 5, 636.
79. Codex juris canonici; Law Code of the Church. Recounted for the most part with comments provided by Prelate Dr. Anton Perathoner, Emeritus, auditor of the Roman Rota. Cf. *Das kirchliche Gesetzbuch,* 5th corrected and expanded edition. Bressanone 1931, 427–429.
80. Thomas Breuer, *Verordneter Wandel? Der Widerstreit zwischen nationalsozialistischem Herrschaftsanspruch und traditionaler Lebenswelt im Erzbistum Bamberg* (Mainz: Matthias-Grünewald, 1992), 322. Mrs. Kupfer was supposedly refused membership in the Organization of the Catholic Women's Alliance in Nuremberg.
81. Cf. Stoltzfus, *Widerstand*, 281, 447n. 77. Stoltzfus writes that the lists were given either to the Jewish community or to the Gestapo and that he found them in the basement of the Jewish Community on Fasanenstrasse, reported in the community as brought there by someone who bought them at a flea market. I would like to thank Nathan Stoltzfus for copies of the material that he discovered, which Jana Leichsenring has also used in her work including her dissertation. It is important to distinguish on the one side the return of the responses to Sommer's inquiries on part of the priest offices before and shortly after the "*Fabrik-Aktion*" and on the other side the lists which after examination by Jana Leichsenring have older dates (after June 20, 1940, until before the middle of February 1943, with remarks up to 1944). Tip from Jana Leichsenring about revision, October 11, 2004. Leichsenring (about revision December 2, 2004) brings attention to a second connection regarding Sommer's unusual survey from February 17, 1943: In the course of the preparations of the *Fabrik-Aktion*, a platoon of people who were to collect Jews was created on February 15, 1943. The list of this expected 90-man crew was given to the Gestapo official Dobberke in the internment camp on Große Hamburger Street. It is not unlikely that Sommer also heard about this from contact persons such as

Martha Mosse. Cf. Dagmar Hartung-von Doetinchem, "Zerstörte Fortschritte," in *Zerstörte Fortschritte: Das Jüdische Krankenhaus in Berlin, 1756, 1861, 1914, 1989*, ed. Dagmar Hartung-von Doetinchem and Rolf Winau (Berlin: Edition Hentrich, 1989), 75–220, here 189. Compare the expert assessment of the Stoltzfus documents by Jana Leichsenring's article, in Leugers, *Berlin*.
82. See, the journal entries by Father Lothar König SJ, February 11, 1943. *Provinzarchiv* of the Jesuits, Munich.
83. To the informants cf. also Leugers, *Gegen eine Mauer*, 471n. 348; idem, *Widerstand oder pastorale Fürsorge*, 175n. 83; Leichsenring, *Katholiken*, 42n. 43, 45n. 72.
84. This is how the relief organization was answered by the Catholic Church office of St. Marien on March 9, 1943, Sandberger "was still living there on February 26 when he was visited at home." Sommer's material collection (like note 81).
85. Coming from Freiburg, Luckner had been in the following cities: in Stuttgart February 23, 1943, in Würzburg February 24, in the evening to Bamberg, from Bamberg to Nuremberg on February 25, from Nuremberg to Eichstätt, and then to Munich on February 26, in Munich from February 27 to March 2: On March 1 with Cardinal Faulhaber and in St. Michael with Jesuits, back again in Freiburg on March 2. Cf. Surveillance reports in Wollasch, *Nachrichtenzentrale*, 131–145; cf. Adler, *Der verwaltete Mensch*, 825–829.
86. Preysing to Pius XII, January 17, 1943, in ADSS IX, 83.
87. Preysing to Pius XII, January 26, 1943, in ibid., 143.
88. Cf. Meyer, *Mischlinge*, 51f., 70f., 84; Adler, *Der verwaltete Mensch*, 285–292; Stoltzfus, *Widerstand*, 235–237.
89. Sommer's report, March 2, 1943, in Volk 6, 20; cf. Gruner, *Fabrik-Aktion*, 155n. 91. In the Berlin diocese archives (DAB I/1-92) there is a document with the title "Preliminary Help" and a handwritten comment "Miss Luckner Fr[ei]b[ur]g" which gives seven points about steps to be taken in case of deportation (among them: report, determination of the number of people, helpers, baggage, money, provisions, exceptions via help from doctors, etc.). Point 5 states: "Announce: that intermarriages are exempted from the action in order to avoid mix-ups.-Half Aryans or Aryan family members of non-Aryans can come along upon request (this becomes crucial when non-Aryan men are married to Aryan women and there are no children involved, not even illegitimate children) " This refers to the so-called "non-privileged intermarriage". It would be important for future research to determine whether these indications can be applied to the "*Fabrik-Aktion*" or to any following actions, or if they were of older dates.
90. In eyewitness reports of the time it is not uncommon to hear an astonishment that one was informed by an unknown person about the whereabouts of their partners or rather about their appointed release. The question should be looked into further whether this may have been in connection with Sommer's investigations and her relief networks. This is what Leichsenring speculates in regards to the Reis family, Leichsenring, *Katholiken*, 44. The Reis family (couple and son) was listed on Sommer's inquiry list of "privileged intermarriages III" under number 93 and in the list "non-Aryan Catholic heads of households" under number 188 and in the list "privileged marriages" under number 66. Sommer's collected material (see note 81). One of the women working at the detention camp remembered that they

would release people when relatives asked about the detained Jews there: Meyer, *Inhaftierungen*, 188. Cf. the article by Jana Leichsenring, in Leugers, *Berlin*.
91. Cf. Leugers, *Widerstand oder pastorale Fürsorge*, 184–188.
92. M. Sommer also went to the collection camps to give communion to the Catholics; she supposedly succeeded in smuggling children out of one camp. Cf. Herzberg, *Dienst am höheren Gesetz*, 131, 134.
93. Cf. Leugers, *Gegen eine Mauer*, 245–258, for a failed attempt of a pastoral letter in November 1941 that discussed the violations of human rights by the regime.
94. Sommer's report, March 2, 1943, in Volk 6, 19–21. Bertram also received a report on March 1, 1943 "concerning questions about the evacuation of *Geltungsjuden*." Archiwum Archidiecezjalne we Wrocławiu [=AAW], IA25z136. Cf. document 4, in Leugers, *Berlin*.
95. Bertram to Frick, Muhs, Thierack, Lammers, RSHA, March 2, 1943, in Volk 6, 23.
96. Cf. Heinz Hürten, *Deutsche Katholiken 1918 bis 1945* (Paderborn: Schöningh, 1992), 513f., 645f. n 54; Wilhelm Damberg, "Katholiken, Antisemitismus und Ökumene," in *Clemens August Graf von Galen: Menschenrechte- Widerstand, Euthanasie, Neubeginn*, ed. Joachim Kuropka (Münster: Regensberg, 1998), 61f.; Stephan Adam, *Die Auseinandersetzung des Bischofs Konrad von Preysing mit dem Nationalsozialismus in den Jahren 1933–1945* (St. Ottilien: EOS, 1996), 111; Klemens-August Recker, *"Wem wollt ihr glauben?" Bischof Berning im Dritten Reich* (Paderborn: Schöningh, 1998), 347. He evaluates the protest on Rosenstrasse and Bertram´s memo as crucial: see also, Büttner, "Die anderen Christen," 134; the women supposedly pushed for the release: idem, *Von der Kirche verlassen*, 62. Leichsenring, *Katholiken*, 49, phrases this more cautiously and states, one also needs to consider Bertram´s intervention.
97. [Braun] to Bishop [Dietz], March 6, 1943. Print: Leugers, *Georg Angermaier*, 234n. 9.
98. Cf. Bertram to Thierack, Frick, Muhs, November 11, 1942, in Volk 5, 944f.
99. Report [from the Ordensausschuss] for the Fulda Bishops' Conference, August 14, 1943, in Volk 6, 128.
100. Bertram to Wienken, February 21, 1944, in ibid., 293n. 2.
101. Ellipsis in the citation (as note 41): "not only by the bishops, but rather."
102. [Braun] to Bishop [Dietz], March 6, 1943. Print: Leugers, *Georg Angermaier*, 234n. 9.
103. Cf. Preysing to Pius XII, March 6, 1943, in Burkhart Schneider, ed., *Die Briefe Pius' XII: an die Deutschen Bischöfe 1939–1944* (Mainz: Matthias-Grünewald, 1966), 239n. 1.
104. Cf. Pius XII to Preysing, April 30, 1943, in Schneider, *Briefe*, 239; cf. Pius XII's stance: Leugers, *Positionen der Bischöfe*, 139–141.
105. For further development cf. Leugers, *Widerstand oder pastorale Fürsorge*, 179–184.
106. Draft of a pastoral letter, [April 13, 1943] in Volk 6, 64f; cf. Bertram to Preysing, April 13, 1943, in ibid., no. 833a. Gerlach, *Zeugen schwiegen*, 343–345, also suggests that in circles of the *Bekennende Kirche* there seems to have been a prearranged speech from the pulpit during this timeframe. Margarete Sommer supposedly confirmed that a collaboration between Protestant and Catholic representatives had

107. been arranged. Apparently, Pastor Wilhelm Jannasch even traveled for this reason to Breslau Cardinal Bertram on behalf of Berlin's Bishop Preysing.
107. To the Decalogue-pastoral letter cf. Leugers, *Gegen eine Mauer*, 274–289.
108. After 1945 when the church was being criticized for its behavior during the Nazi period, Sommer defended the bishops, although before 1945, she was in favor of a different conception than Cardinal Bertram. Cf. this "loyal work of remembrance": Leugers, *Widerstand oder pastorale Fürsorge*, 186–188.
109. Cf. Joachim Neander's article in Leugers, *Berlin*.
110. Cf. Pope Pius' XII Christmas Eve Radio message, 1942, in *Der Papst spricht: Ansprachen und Botschaften Papst Pius' XII. aus der Kriegs- und Nachkriegszeit*, ed. by the Bishopric of Berlin, (Berlin: 1947) ,18–34.
111. Pastoral letter of the Dutch bishops, February 17, 1943, (in German translation). *Provinzarchiv* of the Jesuits, Munich. Print: *Het verzet van de Nederlandsche Bisschoppen tegen Nationaal-Socialisme en duitsche Tyrannie. Herderlijke Brieven, Instructies en andere Documenten*, Utrecht [1945], no. 64; cf. note by Faulhaber, March 30–31, 1943, in Ludwig Volk, ed., *Akten Kardinal Michael von Faulhabers 1917–1945*, vol. 2: *1935–1945* (Mainz: Matthias-Grünewald, 1984) (= Volk 2), 983: "On February 17, 1943, Dutch bishops issued a pastoral letter against the violent abduction of young men for labor service and the murder of Jews." Bishop Wurm was also informed about the protest in the Netherlands, as is shown in a document translated into German that he had left behind [LKA, D1/108]: "The Synod of the *Nederlandsche Hervormde Kerk* is sending you the attached document for a pulpit announcement on Sunday, February 21, 1943." In this document, attention is brought to "Jewish citizens who are persecuted until their death," as well as protests "against the search, seizure and deportation of thousands of young people. . . . This announcement forbids to encourage participation in acts of injustice, because by participating one will become complicit in this injustice." Cf. also Leugers, *Gegen eine Mauer*, 218f. For protests by bishops in France cf. ibid., 218, 472; Jean-Louis Clément, *Les évêques au temps de Vichy: Loyalisme sans Inféodation; Les relations entre l'Eglise et L'Etat de 1940 à 1944* (Paris: Beauchesne, 1999), 137, 140, 175f. For the examples of France and the Netherlands, see also Joachim Neander's article in Leugers, *Berlin*.
112. For example cf. Hürten, *Deutsche*, 522, 550; Burkhard van Schewick, "Katholische Kirche und nationalsozialistische Rassenpolitik," in *Die Katholiken und das Dritte Reich*, 3rd ed. expanded and revised, ed. Klaus Gotto and Konrad Repgen (Mainz: Matthias-Grünewald, 1990), 169f; Herzberg, *Dienst am Höheren Gesetz*, 20, 89; Andrea Tornielli, *Pio XII: Il papa degli Ebrei* (Casa Monferrato: Piemme, 2001), 200–211, here 206: 40,000 Jews as victims! Cf. also Georg Denzler, *Widerstand ist nicht das richtige Wort: Katholische Priester, Bischöfe und Theologen im Dritten Reich* (Zürich: Pendo, 2003), 39, 43f.
113. Rainer Decker in online publication H-German Forum Rosenstrasse 2004.
114. Cf. Theo Salemink, "Bischöfe protestieren gegen die Deportation der niederländischen Juden 1942: Mythos und Wirklichkeit," in *Zeitschrift für Kirchengeschichte* 116 (2005), 63–77. Against R. Decker's apologetic view on the protests. H-German Forum Rosenstrasse 2004. Jews who live in "intermarriages" remained safe from deportation in the Netherlands.

115. Cf. H.J.v. Moltke to F. Moltke, March 4, 1943 in *Helmuth James von Moltke: Briefe an Freya 1939–1945*, ed. Beate Ruhm von Oppen (Munich: C.H. Beck, 1988), 458: "Die Sache ist im Sande verlaufen und abgefangen. Nun es tut nichts. Ich hatte ja nicht erwartet, daß es eine gewaltige Sache gäbe, aber natürlich ist jede Verlängerung kostbar." ("The matter eventually resolved itself. Well, that is alright. I did not expect that it would turn into a major problem, however, any extension is helpful.") Cf. "intermarriages": ibid., 464f. (April 2, 1943), 508 (July 18, 1943), 522 (August 8, 1943), 531 (August 25, 1943). Cf. the cooperation between resistance and *Ordensausschuss*: Leugers, *Gegen eine Mauer*, 222–240.
116. Consider also Bertram's memo to Thierack, Frick, Muhs, November 11, 1942, in Volk 5, 944f.
117. Cf. document 6 in Leugers, *Berlin*.
118. Pastoral letter by the German Episcopacy (II), August 19, 1943, in Volk 6, 202. To the Decalogue-pastoral letter cf. Leugers, *Gegen eine Mauer*, 274–289.
119. For further developments cf. Leugers, *Widerstand oder pastorale Fürsorge*, 179–184.
120. Cf. Wurm to Hitler, July 16, 1943, in *Landesbischof D. Wurm und der Nationalsozialistische Staat*, 305–307, here 306:
  After non-Aryans were captured by Germans and removed on a large scale, it is now feared that because of several individual events now even the so-called privileged non-Aryans who had been previously safe from deportation are now in danger of being treated in this same manner. In particular, we are strongly raising our objection against those measures that are threatening marriage unions in lawfully indefeasible (*rechtlich unantastbar*) families and the children produced from such marriages. These intentions, as well as the measures to murder other non-Aryans, stand vehemently against God's commandment and violate the basis of Western thought and life: and most of all, the ancient God-given right to life and dignity.
121. Cf. Stohr to Bertram, November 1, 1943. AAW, IA25c60 (1943 letter S). Stohr reports about a Jewish woman from an "intermarriage" who was arrested: "Based on a tip from His Excellency Preysing, I'm informing you, Your Eminence, that the official in Darmstadt expressed his great astonishment about the fact that the Bishop was advocating for a Jewish woman. Other high-profile offices would immediately hesitate if an issue would involve a Jew."
122. An eighteen-year-old woman was set free with the help of the bishop from Limburg, cf. Kingreen, *Verfolgung und Rettung in Frankfurt*, 183.
123. Cf. Minutes of the West German Bishops' Conference, March 13–15, 1944 in Volk 6, 332: Galen and Berning were supposedly asked to attend to the treatment of "*Mischlinge*" and "Aryans related to Jews by marriage."
124. Cf. Memoir from Galen, October 3, 1944 in Peter Löffler, ed., *Bischof Clemens August Graf von Galen, Akten, Briefe und Predigten 1933–1945*, vol. 2 (Mainz: Matthias-Grünewald, 1988) [=Löffler 2], 1070f. Werner Teuber and Gertrud Seelhorst, "'Die christliche Frohbotschaft ist die von Gott den Menschen aller Rassen geschenkte unveränderliche Wahrheit': Der deutsche Episkopat, der Bischof von Münster und die Juden" in *Clemens August Graf von Galen: Neue Forschungen zum Leben und Wirken des Bischofs von Münster*, ed. Joachim Kuropka (Münster:

Regensberg, 1992), 237: He does not mention that Galen had already received the assignment as early as March, but did nothing!

125. Neuß to v. Galen, September 26, 1944, in Löffler 2, 1067. Cf. the survey for parishes in the Fulda diocese from December 1, 1944, and the return (of the survey) with exact details from the middle of December 1944 until January 1945. Fulda Diocese Archives, 270-12.

126. Cf. Gruner, *Arbeitseinsatz*, 328; Meyer, *Mischlinge*, 56; Kingreen, *Gewaltsam verschleppt*, 390; Ursula Büttner, *Die Not der Juden teilen: Christlich-jüdische Familien im Dritten Reich; Beispiel und Zeugnis des Schriftstellers Robert Brendel* (Hamburg: Christians, 1988), 11–71. Cf. also: Peter Cahn, "Tagebuchaufzeichnungen und Briefe von Max L. Cahn und Tilly Cahn aus den Jahren 1933–1943," in *Archiv für Frankfurts Geschichte und Kunst 65*, ed. Rebentisch, Dieter (Frankfurt am Main, 1999), 182–221; Marisa Guiliana and Gabriella Cardosi, *Das Problem der "Mischehe" während der Rassenverfolgung in Italien 1938–1945: Zur Geschichte der Rassengesetzgebung, Briefe der deportierten und in Auschwitz ermordeten Clara Pirani Cardosi aus San Vittore und Fossoli, Dokumente und Zeitzeugnisse*, translated from Italian by Angelika and Armin Burkhardt (Darmstadt: Verl. Darmstädter Blätter, 1985); Dieter Corbach, *6.00 Uhr ab Messe Köln-Deutz: Deportationen 1938–1945; Departure 6.00 a.m. Messe Köln-Deutz: Deportations 1938–1945* (Cologne: Scriba, 1999); Helmut Gatzen, *Befehl zum Abtransport, Juden und "Mischlinge 1. Grades" 1933–1945 in und um Gütersloh* (Gütersloh: Flöttmann, 2001).

127. Gerhard Lehfeldt to Wurm, January 10, 1944. AAW, IA25z136. Cf. Wurm to Lammers regarding measures taken against *Mischlinge* of the first degree, December 20, 1943, in Heinrich Hermelink, ed., *Kirche im Kampf: Dokumente des Widerstands und des Aufbaus in der Evangelischen Kirche Deutschlands von 1933 bis 1945* (Tübingen: R. Wunderlich, 1950), 656–658.

128. Cf. Wolf Gruner, *Judenverfolgung in Berlin 1933–1945: Eine Chronologie der Behördenmaßnahmen in der Reichshauptstadt* (Berlin: Hentrich, 1996), 91: "In Berlin, as in the rest of the Reich territory, all Jews living in a "mixed marriage" as well as Jewish *Mischlinge* were to be deported to Terezin, however this fails due to issues with transportation capacities;" cf. Gruner, *Arbeitseinsatz*, 328.

129. Cf. e.g. "Formen abweichenden Verhaltens im Dritten Reich," in *Alltag unterm Nationalsozialismus (= Beiträge zum Widerstand 17. Gedenk- und Bildungsstätte Stauffenbergstrasse)*, ed. Detlev Peukert (Berlin: Landeszentrale f. polit. Bildung, 1981), 25; "Typen des Widerstandes im totalitären System," in *Katholizismus und Nationalsozialismus—Zeitgeschichtliche Interpretationen und Probleme (= Kirche und Gesellschaft 99)*, ed. Konrad Repgen (Cologne: Bachem, 1983), 11.

130. Cf. Stoltzfus, *Widerstand*. Dipper's opinion that the Rosenstrasse "has long been researched" which he stated in 1995 in response to N. Stoltzfus's article, is refuted by the fact that research is still on-going; cf. Christof Dipper, "Schwierigkeiten mit der Resistenz" in *Geschichte und Gesellschaft (GG)* 3 (1996): 409–416, here 409; Nathan Stoltzfus, *Widerstand des Herzens: Der Protest in der Rosenstrasse und die deutsch-jüdische Mischehe*, in *GG* (1995): 218–247; idem, "*Third Reich History as if the People Mattered*." A reply to Christof Dipper, in *GG* 4 (2000), 672–684; idem, "Der 'Versuch, in der Wahrheit zu leben' und die Rettung von jüdischen Angehörigen durch deutsche Frauen im "Dritten Reich" in Leichsenring, *Frauen*, 74–88,

here 77–79: Verweigerung und öffentlicher Protest als Waffen der institutionell Machtlosen.
131. Cf. Joachim Kuropka, ed., *Zur Sache—Das Kreuz! Untersuchungen zur Geschichte des Konflikts um Kreuz und Lutherbild in den Schulen Oldenburgs, zur Wirkungsgeschichte eines Massenprotests und zum Problem nationalsozialistischer Herrschaft in einer agrarisch-katholischen Region*, 2nd ed. (Vechta: Vechtaer Druckerei und Verlag, 1987); Barbara Möckershoff, "Der Kampf um das Schulkreuz," in *Das Bistum Regensburg im Dritten Reich*, ed. Georg Schwaiger und Paul Mai (Regensburg: Verlag des Vereins für Regensburger Bistumsgeschichte, 1981), 237–255; Christian Will, *Landkreis Würzburg: Unsere Heimat unter Hitlers Gewaltherrschaft in Dokumenten, Erlebnissen und Schicksalen,* ed. Landkreis Würzburg, (Würzburg: Landkreis Würzburg, 1988), 160–165; Johannes Merz, "Der Protest gegen die Schulkreuzentfernungen 1941 in Unterfranken," in *Würzburger Diözesangeschichtsblätter* 52 (1990): 409–437; Th. Breuer, *Verordneter Wandel*, 281–291; Leugers, "Widerstand im Alleingang? Beispiele aus Bambergs Kirchengeschichte während des 'Dritten Reichs,'" *Bericht des Historischen Vereins Bamberg* 131 (1995): 439–451, here 440–442; Roman Bleistein, *Alfred Delp: Geschichte eines Zeugen* (Frankfurt am Main: Knecht, 1989), 202f.; Stoltzfus, *Widerstand*, 39, 202–204; Süß, *Der "Volkskörper,"* 145; idem, *Galen*.
132. Cf. Leugers, *Georg Angermaier*, 112–119; idem, *Gegen eine Mauer*, 152–157, 204–206; Ted Harrison, "The Nazi Dissolution of the Monasteries: A Case-Study," in *The English Review* 431 (April 1994): 323–355; Jonathan Düring, *Wir weichen nur der Gewalt: Die Mönche von Münsterschwarzach im Dritten Reich*, vol. 2, *Münsterschwarzach 1997*, 41–44, secretly taken photos of the demonstrations (!) in front of the abbey: 64f.
133. Cf. also Pascal Prause's article in Leugers, *Berlin*.
134. Cf. also review: Antonia Leugers, *Wolf Gruner: Gedenkort Rosenstraße 2-4; Internierung und Protest im NS-Staat* (= Topographie des Terrors. Notizen, Bd. 6, hg. v. Andreas Nachama), (Berlin: Hentrich, 2013), in *theologie.geschichte* 8 (2013). http://universaar.uni-saarland.de/journals/index.php/tg/article/view/536/575. Idem, "'Mordpläne offen vor der Welt' Gerhard Lehfeldt als Mahner der Kirchen im März 1943", in *theologie.geschichte* 8 (2013). http://universaar.uni-saarland.de/journals/index.php/tg/article/view/534/573. Idem., "'die Kirche soll einschreiten'. Hilferufe von Sinti und Roma angesichts ihrer Deportation 1943", *theologie.geschichte* 8 (2013). http://universaar.uni-saarland.de/journals/index.php/tg/article/view/548/587. Idem., "Widerstand *gegen* die Rosenstraße. Kritische Anmerkungen zu einer Neuerscheinung von Wolf Gruner," in *theologie.geschichte* 1 (2006). http://universaar.uni-saarland.de/journals/index.php/tg/article/view/133/148.

Chapter 9

Protest and Aftermath
Placing Protest in the History of Nazi Germany

Nathan Stoltzfus

At a villa in the Berlin suburb of Wannsee, Rheinhard Heydrich announced plans for the murder of eleven million European Jews.¹ About thirty thousand were German Jews married to non-Jews. Yet they and their Mischlinge children were the main point of contention at the Wannsee Conference on January 20, 1942. Heydrich and the fifteen high ranking officials he had assembled devoted much of their energies at the ninety-minute conference to discussing how to deal with Germany's mixed marriages without drawing unwanted attention to the Holocaust or setting the Volk against the regime.² All hesitations to deport Jews from mixed marriages trace back to the dictatorship's anxiety that the Volk would disapprove strongly enough to unmask the claim that the Nazis had total support from the Volk.

"German blooded" or "Aryan" Germans married to Jews were forced to choose between the dictatorship and their families. From its beginning in 1933, the dictatorship exerted various pressures to dissolve mixed marriages. Germany's intermarried couples were obliged to push back, in order to defend their families. Their defiance escalated and found its strongest expression in a daring street protest in Berlin in early 1943 when "Aryan" wives rescued some two thousand family members. The Reich Security Main Office (RSHA) as well as Reich minister and Berlin Gauleiter Joseph Goebbels altered plans to deport at least the intermarried Berlin Jews wearing the Star. In this interpretation, the dictatorship's concession to protesters was a cold calculation in the vein of a cost-benefit analysis: carrying out plans for a deportation at that time was seen as more costly than temporarily postponing them. By giving way, the dictatorship retained command. This fits within the pattern of decision-making that compelled the regime to control information about the genocide from the start. It also follows a logic along the lines of Hitler's decision to appease rather than punish Bishop August von Galen for his dissent from his pulpit against the "euthanasia" mass murders in August 1941.

In July 1938 the regime rewrote German law to grant divorce at once to any intermarried "Aryan" requesting it (a loosening of legal standards that disturbed many). When this new law, together with increased Gestapo pressures, did not increase divorce rates substantially, the dictatorship divided intermarriages into two parts.[3] In December 1938, following complaints from "Aryans" about the brutal treatment of Jewish family members during the Kristallnacht Pogrom, Hitler secretly granted a "privileged" status to Jews in approximately three-fourths of mixed-marriage couples. Mixed marriages with children baptized as Christians, as well as those in which the wife was Jewish, were "privileged." Other mixed marriages were "simple" or "non-privileged."[4]

With this decree Führer had effectively changed the Nuremberg Laws. The regime tried out this new approach in April 1939 when it ordered Jews from "non-privileged" intermarriages to move into "Jewish Houses." This might have caused gentiles in these mixed marriages to divorce instead of moving, but this did not happen in many cases.[5] On August 20, 1941, by agreeing to require only Jews from the category of "non-privileged" mixed marriages to wear the Star, Hitler indicated his intention to remove at least that minority from Germany along with other persons also marked as "Jews." As Goebbels said, persons wearing the Star were marked as criminals—enemies of the Volk—slated for removal. "In the first days after the introduction of the Jewish star, newspaper sales in Berlin skyrocketed," Goebbels wrote:[6]

> Each Jew who had to cross the street got a newspaper to coyly conceal his mark of Cain. When this was banned, one began to see Jews parading around with non-Jewish foreigners on the streets of western Berlin. These Jewish flunkeys would have actually also required their own Jewish Star. The argument they make for their provocative conduct is always the same: the Jews are in fact human beings too—as if we had ever claimed anything different. The same is also true of robbers, murderers, child molesters, thieves and pimps—except that one never wanted to stroll down the Kurfürstendamm with them! ... Whoever wears a Jewish Star is marked as an "enemy of the Volk. Whoever still goes around with [a Jew] privately in everyday life belongs to him and must be valued and treated as a Jew. He earns the contempt of the entire Volk, whom he abandons in base cowardice at the hardest moment, by putting himself at the side of his despiser.

However, the regime and its ideology, as Goebbels voiced it here, bowed to political expediency temporarily: as the regime began the systematic deportation of German Jews wearing the Star in October 1941, "Aryans" married to Jews were not treated as Jews; instead their Jewish partners were deferred from the mass murder deportations—on a "temporary" basis. Accompanying this deferment to intermarried Jews as a category was a policy of deporting them one by one, as soon as their gentile partners either died or agreed to a divorce, to Theresienstadt.[7]

On November 22, 1941, Hitler relayed to Goebbels the basic principle regarding Germany's mixed marriages. "The Führer wants a forceful policy against the Jews," Goebbels wrote, "although one that does not cause us unnecessary difficulties. Concerning the mixed marriages, especially those in artist's circles, the Führer recommends that I follow a somewhat reserved course of action." Intermarried Jews would "die out bit by bit"; they must be eliminated, but circumspectly rather than all at once.[8]

Three weeks after telling Goebbels to exercise caution regarding mixed marriages, Hitler told the assembled Gauleiters—the party officials responsible for clearing their respective regions of Jews—that if any European Jews survived, the war would prove only partially successful. Goebbels wrote that the Führer had decided to "clear the table."[9] But no new orders were given; the Gauleiter still faced the same challenge of clearing their regions of Jews without drawing unwanted attention to the genocide and to intermarried couples.[10] In early October 1941, Reinhard Heydrich and Adolf Eichmann proposed that non-Jewish ("Aryan") partners who refused to divorce their Jewish spouses should also be deported to the East. But Hitler would not approve this. Instead, he maintained a clear line between those who were slated for deportation, and those who were not.[11] Thus the Volk remained certain that it was clearly exempted from the persecution of German Jews.

However, the great majority of these mixed couples remained together, so that the Führer's principle of deporting this group of Jews circumspectly conflicted with his equally firm principle that no German Jew could survive the war. The policy of deporting an intermarried Jew at the moment of separation, by divorce or death of the gentile partner, exemplified the official drive to remove intermarried Jews as quickly as possible, while also illustrating that the exemption from deportation for intermarried Jews depended upon their partners.[12]

The Wannsee Conferees determined on January 20, 1942 that this must change: in the interest of the "definitive settlement" of the Jewish problem, Heydrich said, Jews from mixed marriages would be murdered. In specific cases, "in consideration of the effects of such a measure on the German relatives," an intermarried Jew could be sent to Theresienstadt rather than Auschwitz.[13] Interior Ministry Deputy Secretary Wilhelm Stuckart noted that the deportation of one partner was not possible until the couple was legally divorced, and proposed a law that would declare all mixed marriages annulled. But at a follow-up meeting on March 6, 1942, Goebbels's propaganda ministry objected.[14] Legal measures annoyed Himmler. On June 9, 1942, he announced his determination to exterminate Europe's Jews within the coming year, and in July he impatiently proscribed such laws about Germany's intermarried couples because they limited his ability to strike without warning at the opportune moment. "With all these silly commitments we are only binding our own hands!" he said.[15] In general, as he stated six years earlier, he was "totally indifferent as to whether a legal clause opposes our actions."[16]

Himmler was not able to sidestep the regime's anxiety about mixed marriages, however. The regime avoided forcibly separating partners in mixed marriages fearing that the Volk would notice and disapprove. When a gentile man came to the train station to see his Jewish wife one last time before her deportation to Auschwitz, a Gestapo agent in Darmstadt hissed at him to leave as quickly as possible and to do so without drawing any attention to the fact that a husband of a Jew being deported was there.[17] In 1942 Vienna, Gauleiter Baldur von Schirach and his accomplices "clearly intended" to clear Vienna of non-privileged Jews, those who wore the Jewish Star.[18]

Indicating that intermarried Jews had been "temporarily deferred" from deportations only so long as this did not cause unrest or draw attention to the genocide, the RSHA began deporting them as criminals. As the population of German Jews rapidly dwindled during 1942, pressures mounted to end the RSHA's temporary exemption of intermarried Jews wearing the Star. By late 1942, by some accounts, the RSHA was preparing to deport German Jews in "non-privileged" mixed marriages.[19] The RSHA began to murder some intermarried Jews in some places by charging them as criminals and sending them off to their deaths; intermarried Jews wearing the Star of David were falsely accused and criminalized, as part of an effort to make the city of Darmstadt, near Frankfurt/Main, "Judenfrei." This was an effort to draw them into the Holocaust while reducing the risk that this would attract widespread attention or appear as an effort to deport all mixed-marriage Jews, according to a postwar court in West Germany.[20]

Intermarried Jews made up a considerable portion of German Jews employed to manufacture weapons, which the war industry had protected by designating as irreplaceable. But in a meeting from September 20 to 22, Hitler ordered Director of Forced Labor Fritz Sauckel "to deport all Jews still at work in armament factories located in the East." According to Armaments Minister Albert Speer, Hitler was referring to "mostly the Berlin Jews." Goebbels wrote on September 30, 1942, that Hitler had voiced "firm determination, to remove the Jews at least from Berlin."[21]

At the Interior Ministry, reports began to circulate in September 1942 that the RSHA was now preparing to deport the Mischlinge—rumors that Adolf Eichmann did not deny.[22.] The historians Raul Hilberg and Uwe Adams concluded that the RSHA was making preparations to deport Jews in mixed marriages by early 1943.[23] In late 1942, Himmler issued decrees for the *Entjudung* (elimination) of Jews from Reich territory: even German Mischlinge were to be deported as Jews—at least those in camps.[24] With Hitler and Goebbels's focus on Berlin, deportation expert Alois Brunner was transferred from Vienna to the Reich capital in November 1942 to make quick work of deporting Berlin's last Jews. His men began arresting anyone from the streets who appeared to be Jewish. This included non-Jews whose outraged protests forced him to refer to the Gestapo's registry before making arrests.[25]

With the determination to clear the Reich of Jews, authorities in Berlin were double-checking its registry of Jews. On November 27, 1942, the German Central Jewish Organization required anyone defined by the Nuremberg Laws to register. Berlin Jews in intermarriages *and* their partners were required to register at the Jewish Community.[26] On February 17, the Relief Office of Berlin's Catholic bishop wrote to the city's parishes, requesting each to identify its intermarried couples, and their children. Most parishes replied to the Relief Office by February 27, with lists of names and addresses identified in categories of "Privileged Intermarriages" and "Non-privileged Intermarriages."[27]

At this same time, the push from Berlin to deport the city's Jews was magnified by a pull from Auschwitz for laborers. Anticipating a massive movement of slave labor from factories in the Reich to the camps in the East, Himmler had begun to relocate armaments production factories within the concentration camp structure. At Auschwitz, after Himmler promised to supply the camp with thousands of skilled laborers, German armaments producer IG Farben built a prisoner camp known as "Buna." Nevertheless, the labor supply at Auschwitz-Buna had remained a fraction of what Farben wanted. On February 10, Oberstrumführer Gerhard Maurer, the boss at the SS Economic and Administrative Department (WVHA), promised "to make sure" the labor force would soon increase several fold; he requested and received permission from the RSHA to take laborers directly from the massive freight cars packed with German Jews arriving at Auschwitz.[28]

For early 1943, the RSHA planned what it called the "Aktion zu Entjudung des Reichsgebietes" arrests (Action for the Elimination of Jews from the Reich).[29] In the Reich capital, "at the beginning of 1943, as the mass deportations drew to a close, there followed a thrust (*Vorstoss*) to push out the Jewish men in Berlin who were married to German women," wrote historian H.G. Adler.[30] These arrests were scheduled for early 1943, in conjunction with the tenth anniversary of Nazi rule, according to one senior Jewish Community authority.[31] Coinciding with that same anniversary, however, was the Wehrmacht's debacle at Stalingrad, just as the Allies greatly increased the firepower of their bombing raids over German cities. On February 2, 1943, as Berlin received definitive news of the Wehrmacht surrender at Stalingrad, Goebbels received an offer from Sepp Dietrich, the leader of the elite SS Division, the Leibstandarte Hitler. Dietrich proposed to "place a company of the Leibstandarte at my disposal," Goebbels wrote, "so that I can reach my goal with brute force—which is not exactly the appropriate means by which to prevail, under the current circumstances."[32]

In the propagandist's calculations, brute force could be deployed more effectively to control the Volk at moments when the regime was riding high in popular acclaim. Thus on August 13, 1940, following Germany's crushing defeat of France, Goebbels instructed the Gauleiters that such a victory allowed leaders an increased latitude for using force to work their will on the home front.[33] Following this calculus, Goebbels worried on February 2 that the new nadir of morale in Germany caused by recent defeats did not provide the right "circumstances" for prevailing at home through intimidating squads of SS men, if another 1918-style defeat was to be avoided. Goebbels had just convinced Hitler to declare a "total war" mobilization of resources on the home front, and he now had to show, in the face of his powerful adversaries, that it was the right step for the Reich.

As Berlin's Gauleiter, Goebbels was contemplating a separation of intermarried partners on an unprecedented scale, and the SS-Leibstandarte represented a means for intimidating objections.[34] He had just convinced Hitler to declare a "total war" mobilization of resources on the home front, and in the face of his powerful adversaries, did not want to be accused of stirring another rebellious "stab in the back" which the Nazis had blamed for Germany's loss of World War I. On February 18 Goebbels recorded his intention to make his city free of Jews[35]: "The Jews in Berlin will now once and for all be pushed out. With the final deadline of February 28 they are supposed to be first brought to collection centers and deported, up to 2,000, batch-by-batch, day-by-day. I have set for myself a goal to make Berlin entirely free of Jews by the middle or end of March at the latest."[36]

Well-informed Germans now suspected that intermarried Jews would be deported. Gertrud Luckner, who worked for the Berlin Relief Office directed by Catholic Bishop von Preysing, warned an associate on February 24, 1943, that a "Schluss" or "final" arrest "was about to take place in Berlin." This was according to the Gestapo's report on its interrogation of Luckner, who was sent to the Ravensbrück camp in late February on charges of being pro-Jewish. The Gestapo's report emphasized that Luckner had many points of contact throughout "the entire Reich," and had been particularly active in warning intermarried Jews and their children of "impending actions" (arrests). Luckner worked for Preysing's Relief Office and reported that she had been collecting lists of intermarriages and Mischlinge ordered on February 17. Luckner's information was that the "intermarriage law" that had previously protected Jews has now been postponed, and "measures against intermarriages and Mischlinge" were now pending. Her warnings that these persons must avoid all unlawful actions shows she that had good sources of information, in light of Nazi efforts to murder intermarried Jews one by one after first criminalizing them.[37]

A Gestapo order from Frankfurt/Oder dated February 24 underscores the regime's desire to avoid drawing attention to the intermarried problem, while also deporting some on criminal charges. The decree (printed in full in the appendix) instructed officers to proceed inconspicuously, even in this small city where Jews were relatively sparse: "Impudent behavior by Jews who still live in existing mixed marriages is to be punished by taking the Jews into protective custody and filing an order to bring them to a concentration camp. These actions can be carried out unsparingly, although the impression must be avoided that this action is a means to fundamentally solve the mixed marriage problem once and for all. If there are no reasons to justify the arrest of Jewish marriage partners, they are to be dismissed to their homes."[38]

This authorization to make arrests was underscored by the administrator of the Frankfurt/Oder district of Calau: when he forwarded this decree to police administrators of his district he underscored the point that officers had authority to arrest "impudent" intermarried Jews. The encouragement for officers to press charges "generously" while avoiding the appearance that *all* intermarried Jews were being deported at that moment indicates that the RSHA wished to deport some intermarried Jews even in this hinterland. Impudence was a common charge against Jews, and local officers now had wide latitude for using it.[39]

Arresting intermarried Jews after charging them with crimes was a tactic the RSHA was already employing elsewhere in the Reich. In cities around the Frankfurt am Main region, Gauleiter Sprenger deported such Jews after falsely indicting them.[40] By early 1943 some two hundred intermarried Jews had been criminalized in this way and sent to camps to die or be killed, a method the RSHA used to draw intermarried Jews into the genocide while provoking little dissent.[41]

Struggling to meet Hitler's imperatives of removing intermarried Jews during the war without drawing public outrage, the RSHA issued contrasting orders. Even as it authorized the removal of intermarried Jews on criminal charges, it also, on February 20, 1943, issued an order temporarily deferring intermarried Jews from deportations. Of course there may have been little contradiction, considering that any "temporary" deferment could be ended at any moment the regime considered opportune. Meanwhile the order could also be used to reassure those who expressed concern about these Jews.

This method of gradually deporting mixed-marriage Jews by criminalizing them could work in regions with smaller Jewish populations like Frankfurt/Oder, but could not be effective in Berlin with almost nine thousand intermarried Jews. Taking account of variations from region to region, Hitler gave regional party chiefs, the Gauleiters, leeway in clearing their territories of Jews; the Führer's mandate for the deportation of German Jews threw the doors open to a range of initiatives, from officials at the local level on up.[42] If the number of Jews expected to fill a deportation could not be found among those whom the directives designated, then those who were supposed to have been held back were pushed forward to fill the train.[43] Gauleiter Arthur Greiser had a free hand in his Wartheland region, like the carte blanche Hitler granted Gauleiter Baldur von Schirach in Vienna.[44]

On February 27, the Gestapo launched the RSHA's "Elimination of Jews from Reich Territory" in German cities. The focus was on Berlin, where the Gestapo's codename for the arrests was the *Schlussaktion,* or Final Roundup, of Berlin Jews.[45] Sometime after the war this arrest in Berlin was renamed the "Factory Action."

The Rosenstrasse Protest Interrupts Plans for the Deportation of Intermarried Jews

Orders for Frankfurt/Oder did not resemble those for Berlin, or did not hold sway. The Frankfurt/Oder order authorized something that could describe a "Factory Action," but it does not reflect what happened in Berlin. The sheer numbers of persons arrested in Berlin, not to mention the presence of the most elite SS division, made the circumspection ordered for Frankfurt/Oder impossible.[46] The SS were highly visible, as three hundred trucks fanned out across Berlin, and incarceration of the city's Jews continued for a week.[47] This phalanx of trucks storming through traffic as some ten thousand Berlin Jews were grabbed from their jobs and homes was shocking. Persons seen wearing the Star were chased down, and thrown onto the Gestapo's covered furniture trucks headed for collection centers. Even out-of-town Jews who were visiting Berlin were arrested and carted away. The SS tossed and shoved Jews; dozens suffered broken bones and scores of children were separated from their parents. Many sought escape in suicide: "People plunged through windows, threw themselves under cars, or took poison . . . which particularly cautious persons always had with them."⁴⁸ Based on identifications that those arrested carried with them, and which did not have to be verified, some of the mixed marriage Jews and Mischlinge were released.

Most of these arrested Jews ended up in the Auschwitz machinery of death over the course of the following days. About two thousand, however, were sorted out and imprisoned at a Jewish Community welfare office on Rosenstrasse 2-4. The overwhelming majority of imprisoned Jews were men whose wives arrived on the street to receive information. Some arrived as early as the evening of February 27, and already by the following morning voices of the wives could be heard calling in unison, "Give us our husbands back!"⁴⁹ The women held their vigil day and night for a week. From time to time, the police scattered them with threats to shoot them, but each time the women advanced again, and their solidarity grew. "You went there in the first place just because you had heard the rumor: 'they are there!'" remembered Ruth Gross, a Mischling whose father was imprisoned at Rosenstrasse. "So you naturally went there, and returned there: Did anyone hear anything? Could you meet someone? Can anyone say something or other, were there any reports? Someone called out, and then the others joined into the group, and into the chorus of voices . . . it was always the case that one was never supposed to be very noticeable—always. Conspicuous it certainly was." The protests on Rosenstrasse drew attention to thousands of mixed-marriage couples in the Reich capital where many Germans as well as foreign journalists and diplomats could observe, and were noted in the diaries of two Berliners.⁵⁰

Corresponding with Hitler's priorities, Berlin Jews were targeted first in the RSHA's 'Elimination of Reich' arrests beginning February 27, 1943. "In Berlin there was an "evacuation of a magnitude and severity never before seen," wrote Dr. Margaret Sommer on March 2. Sommer was the director of Bishop Preysing's Catholic Relief Office whose co-worker Gertrud Luckner had just been thrown into Gestapo custody. One week earlier, Sommer had been told that "the mixed marriages would not be affected by the planned raid." Now, she realized, "the opposite is the case." Sommer was convinced already on March 2 that the Jews at Rosenstrasse were about to be deported since, as she wrote, contrary to earlier practices at the collection camps for the Jews who were awaiting deportation, no one was allowed to bring "useful or comforting" items. "Instead those who tried were refused harshly and chased away." This had the effect of changing fears that the imprisoned intermarried Jews had no future, into a "certainty" that they would perish. "This time no special consideration was given to those persons living in an intermarriage," Sommer wrote, "this time partners were separated."⁵¹

Also on March 2 the SS in Auschwitz received a telegram from the WVHA Berlin headquarters stating that "On March 1, 1943, the transports of Jews from Berlin will begin . . . [including] about 15,000 healthy Jews fit for work."[52] Fifteen thousand Jews fit for work could not be supplied from Berlin without including intermarried Jews.[53] As of February 27, 1943, there were just eleven thousand Berlin Jews in armaments work, and of these, seven thousand were from intermarriages.[54] Two-thirds of Berlin's Jews most eligible for work in Auschwitz were intermarried; to send the number of laborers Auschwitz was expecting from Berlin, the temporary ban on deporting intermarried Jews would have to lifted, at least for the moment, in Berlin.

In a report, dated March 3, 1943, Nuncio Cesare Orsenigo reported that when he expressed concern about the arrest of Jews at the Ministry of Foreign Affairs, he was told that nobody was able to defy the "tangible and rampant violence" of the Gestapo."[55] However, on March 4, the sixth day of street protests, Bishop Heinrich Wienken heard from Adolf Eichmann that "the non-Aryan Catholics in racially mixed marriages who were arrested in Berlin . . . will be *released*, and also put to work again in the armaments industry."[56] Eichmann told Wienken that this applied to mixed-marriage Jews without children as well to those with children. Importantly, this communication also reveals the regime's plan at this time to deal with intermarried Jews segment by segment; those without children were in the most danger.

Despite Eichmann's information, on March 6 1943, twenty-five intermarried men were not released but sent from the collection center at Rosenstrasse to Auschwitz. A Jewish woman was arrested in central Berlin, while her seventy-year-old gentile husband began protesting loudly on the street.[57] An explanation for this confusion within the RSHA may lie in divisions that developed about how to respond to the protest. Erwin Sartorious, who drove a Gestapo truck that transported Jews, told the postwar German judiciary that he had heard rumors that rivaling factions had arisen within the RSHA about how to handle the situation, resulting in "conflicting orders." This also coincides with the recollection of Goebbels's deputy, State Secretary Leopold Gutterer, after the war.[58]

Indeed, some intermarried Jews were deported. Also on March 4, Eichmann said that mixed-marriage Jews without children would also be returned to armaments work. However, Walter Stock, the director of the Berlin's Gestapo's "Jewish Bureau" selected twenty-five Jews without children for deportation from Rosenstrasse 2-4, directly to the Buna labor camp (without the usual "selection") at Auschwitz, in line with the RSHA plan a month earlier to direct prisoners straight from arriving deportations, to slave labor camps. Stock, who was also the head of the Berlin Gestapo's "Sabotage Office," recalled for his trial six years after the war, that he had in fact sent twenty-five Jews incarcerated at Rosenstrasse to Auschwitz-Buna.[59] "You will be neither shot nor hanged," these intermarried Jews were told. "You will be employed there where we need you more urgently." Dr. Gerhard Lehfeldt, whose dispatches were sent to the Vatican and to Catholic and Protestant bishops, reported in mid-March 1943 that Eichmann's explanation for the treatment of these Berlin Jews was "not a case of deportation, but of employment for work."[60]

On the street, the protests and the regime's efforts to intimidate them continued. Foreign news sources reportedly said there were four to five hundred protesters, although historians now cite the figure of several hundred as the likely number gathered on the street at any given time.[61] With conditions now causing some Germans to seriously question whether Germany could prevail in the war, the Rosenstrasse protest brought Hitler and Goebbels's plans to make Berlin "free of Jews" into conflict with the regime's will to repress public dissent, and avoid drawing attention to Germany's mixed marriages. For Nazi authorities, the Rosenstrasse events signaled that forcibly separating thousands of mixed-marriage couples all at once and holding them for a week and more, caused an unusual spectacle. Protesting for Jews was extraordinarily dangerous, but the Nazis had evoked a willingness from some of the Volk to sacrifice everything they had.

On March 6, when most of the Jews imprisoned at Rosenstrasse were released,[62] Reichminister and Berlin Gauleiter Goebbels recorded his decision to release the Jews at a time when the regime had just declared "total war" and wanted to raise morale, depressed by Germany's defeat at Stalingrad and rapidly increasing air attacks:

> The people gathered together in large throngs and even sided with the Jews to some extent. I will commission the security police not to continue the evacuations of Jews during such a critical time. Rather we want to put that off for a few weeks; then we can carry it out all the more thoroughly. One has to intervene all over the place, to ward off damages. The efforts of certain offices are so lacking in savvy that one cannot leave them on their own for ten minutes. The basic malady of our leadership and above all of our administration consists in operating according to Schema F [rote attention to orders without adapting appropriately to circumstances].[63]

In his report to church officials that month Dr. Lehfeldt also identifies Goebbels as the authority who made the decision to release the Jews, and public protest as his motivation.[64] From his prodigiously informed perspective on the regime and familiarity with its documents, Adler concluded that Jewish men married to German women "were supposed to be sent away, but a courageous demonstration of women caused the Gestapo, in an exception, to give in, and the husbands were released."[65] On March 9, the second workday after he ordered the Jews released, Goebbels visited Hitler, and the Führer agreed that Goebbels had responded correctly to the "psychological" challenges of clearing Berlin of Jews, but reiterated that Goebbels would nevertheless still have to make Berlin "Judenfrei." Two days later, Goebbels regretted that Jews from "privileged" intermarriages had been among the first Berlin Jews arrested—at the same time as intermarried Jews whose marriages were not privileged. The attempt to arrest the Jews all at once "proved to be a fiasco," Goebbels wrote. "Particularly in artist circles, the arrest of Jews and Jewesses from privileged marriages caused a great sensation," although he could not "take undue regard for this at the present moment."[66]

Goebbels was clear about the difference for his plans that intermarried Jews in "non-privileged" intermarriages made, in contrast to those he referred to here in "privileged" intermarriage, as he wrote in his diary: "A whole collection of . . . Jews from privileged intermarriages and also Jews from [non-privileged] intermarriages are still to be found in Berlin. . . . I do not want Jews with the Jewish star running around the Reich capital. Either one must take the Jewish star away and privilege them, or on the other hand once and for all evacuate them from the Reich capital." From this we can infer that the definition of clearing Berlin of Jews—which Goebbels had vowed to achieve by mid-March 1943—would have at a minimum removed intermarried "non-privileged" Jews, because they wore the Star.

This was also the opinion at the time of well-informed government ministers as well as church bishops. On March 8, Ernst Kaltenbrunner, the new head of the RSHA following Heydrich's assassination, informed Interior Minister Wilhelm Frick that the deportations had been limited to Jews who did not live in "mixed marriages,"[67] indicating that their fate had been in question. This was true among the highest church officials as well: Bishop Theophil Wurm of Württemberg did not doubt that the intermarried Jews had been snatched from deportation. On March 12 he complained to the Reich Ministry of Churches that "the Jews who live in intermarriages with Christian Germans—some of whom are themselves members of the Christian Church—were taken from their home and workplace to be deported to the East." Those same Jews, he continued were *"released."*[68] Two days later, Bishop Wurm wrote to the Reich interior minister that if their release signaled "a change in policy . . . he would welcome it."[69] On April 6, 1943, Catholic Bishop Wilhelm Berning of Osnabrück wrote that "spouses in intermarriages who had been arrested on February 27 have been *released* after 8 days [on March 6], as a result of various public offices having advocated for them."[70]

In the course of the Berlin arrests, 120 intermarried Jews had been deported to Auschwitz, including the 25 imprisoned at Rosenstrasse. For them—like hundreds and hundreds of other intermarried Jews the regime had deported before this—the "temporary" exemption from deportations proclaimed for them in the RSHA directives of February 20, 1943, had ended, just as it would have ended for thousands more, had no Germans objected so forcefully as the protesters did.

Sometime around March 22, the twenty-five men sent from Rosenstrasse to Auschwitz-Buna returned to Berlin, where as Stock admitted in testimony, he met them at the train station. Upon arriving in Auschwitz, the intermarried Jews were sent to work at the Buna work camp, where the SS expected to receive up to fifteen thousand Berlin Jews. On the morning of their twelfth day an SS man informed these men that on the order of "high authorities," they were to prepare to return to Berlin. The men were sent back on a normal passenger express train. "They couldn't get rid of us fast enough," remembered one. At Auschwitz, rumors of a release of prisoners spread like wildfire among the Auschwitz prisoners, recalled Johnny Huttner, a communist Jew who had been in various concentration camps since 1936. "We turned it over in our minds whether it was a true 'release.' It could have been a special 'Human Experiment' we thought."[71] In Berlin, Nazi authorities wished to make it seem impossible that a protest had shifted their plans: when a surprised Gestapo secretary wondered why Jews were released from Auschwitz, she was told that overzealous underlings had transgressed their orders.[72] This makes little sense, considering the Nazi drive to annihilate all Jews and also the fact that the large majority of Berlin's intermarried Jews sent to Auschwitz at the same time were not returned.

Like Dr. Lehfeldt and top church and government officials in Germany, the U.S. Secret Service also received intelligence that protests had interfered with a deportation the Nazis had planned. On April 1, an American OSS dispatch from Leland Harrison in Bern, Switzerland, stated that. "[A] source which is considered trustworthy has reported that actions against Jewish wives and husbands on the part of the Gestapo, reported in my telegram no. 1597 dated March tenth, had to be discontinued some time ago because of the protest which such action aroused."[73]

Four months later Dr. Margarete Sommer of Preying's Relief Office was still convinced that the protest had rescued Jews at Rosenstrasse from deportation. In August 1943 Sommer reiterated her conclusion that there had been a direct connection between "unusually heated protests" and the "release" of those imprisoned at Rosenstrasse. In the same report she backed up her judgment about the Rosenstrasse events by reporting the results of another protest: "In Innsbruck and other cities of Tyrol, non-Aryan spouses were apprehended without any stated reason, and brought to a concentration camp. Following extensive protests from the Catholics in Vienna, these spouses from intermarriages were reunited with their families."[74] Even protesters demanding the repression of fundamental regime policy, as it affected their families, were not punished.

New Critics

After the war a number of persons in a position to know told a similar story, including Leopold Gutterer, the deputy of Propaganda Minister and Gauleiter Goebbels and Herbert Titze, the Gestapo officer who was charged with preparing the lists for each deportation of Berlin Jews. Jewish Community authorities Martha Mosse and Siegbert Kleemann also said that, because of the protest, the regime did not deport the Jews to the East as it had intended.[75] Over the decades, the judgment of a variety of experts, historians as well as German prosecutors and judges, has also been that the protest influenced the regime to release rather than deport these Jews.[76]

No one has ever seriously proposed that during the Nazi dictatorship Germans could get together, decide what they wanted, and then take to the streets in protest to get it. But meeting and planning were not a prerequisite for this protest (or the others examined in this book). Rather these wives were motivated by their expectations of private-sphere rights and responsibilities; each acted individually but discovered others who were also motivated by a sense of their rights and responsibilities to stand up in defense of them. The more these displays of dissent reflected popular opinion, or had the chance of influencing opinion, the more likely the regime was to postpone its action or use other means, particularly if the protest was directing popular scrutiny toward policies it preferred to mask.

Nor does anyone seriously deny that the regime's goal was to remove from Germany anyone wearing the Star of David, and it is hard to imagine any reason why Hitler—as well as the RSHA and not just Goebbels—would have preferred to wait to deport the Jews imprisoned at Rosenstrasse until some later point. "In every question" concerning the "fate of Jews," recalled Hitler's confidant and Armaments Minister Albert Speer, "no regard was taken; it was hardly ever possible to implement exemptions."[77] Following the Reich's *Entjudung* decision in late 1942 to eliminate remaining Jews from German territory, there was no longer any question of whether Jews would be killed but only why they would not be killed.[78]

Nevertheless, some historians have now made a concerted effort to do that, which requires excising the longstanding perspective. In recent years, as the protest become more widely known, it became less possible to ignore interpreting it. In 2003, during a peak of controversy about this protest, historian Kurt Pätzold sought to explain this. Any argument that the protest had influence, he wrote, "strikes at the center of the historical perception of the character of the Nazi regime and the way it functioned, and weighs on judgments about the possibilities for resistance."[79]

This was articulated as the heart of the matter in the earliest attacks on the established view of the protest. Beginning with his dissertation in 1994, Wolf Gruner has argued that the Frankfurt/Oder decree (printed in full in appendix 2) provides definitive evidence for his revisions. Cited as corollary evidence are two ambiguous Gestapo orders along with the February 20, 1943, RSHA directive that intermarried Jews were to be exempted on a "temporary" basis from the deportations.[80] Gruner grounded his initial opposition in an assessment of the basic nature of Nazi power: protests were "obviously not the cause for the release of the Jews," he wrote in 1995, since "interpretations that such demonstrations could have hindered the deportation plans of the RSHA certainly do not hold up within the historical context."[81] In a scholarly exchange in 2004, Gruner identified this apprehension further: considering the protest as influential carries "a danger of dramatically underestimating the supremacy [*Herrschaft*] of the Nazi regime." The historian Beate Meyer added in that same exchange that seeing the protest as influential leaves us with the question of "how the murder of Jews could actually happen, if it really only took seven days of standing fast (*Standhaftigkeit*) to hinder it."[82]

This work sought to show that the Gestapo worked around the protesters to fastidiously carry out their orders. Because the Gestapo intended no harm to their imprisoned Jewish loved ones, the protesters were "running through an open door.".[83] In his book from 2005, Gruner wrote that despite the efforts of historians including his dissertation advisor historian Wolfgang Benz, "the story of the success of the protest . . . lived on . . . unhindered."[84] Accounts before his, he wrote were "almost completely based on the statements of survivors." He went on to conclude that "in light of the facts and history presented here [his 2005 book], the notion that at the end of February 1943 there was a deportation plan for the Jews in intermarriage and that this was abandoned by the Gestapo as a consequence of the protest, can hardly still be convincing."[85] Notions that public protests had rescued intermarried Jews were postwar inventions, Gruner wrote, "legends based on reports from survivors and subjective impressions."[86] The Gestapo had merely intended, "very explicitly," to confirm the "racial" status of the Jews imprisoned, and also to select 225 Jews to replace workers from the Jewish administration who had just been deported.[87] Gruner's most recent work, a book published in 2013 with eighty-eight generously illustrated pages, continues to rely on the evidence in his dissertation, to reiterate the claims he made then.[88]

Because those who oppose the long-acknowledged interpretation now simply cite Gruner's work to support their position, it is possible to challenge them by critiquing his arguments.[89] They repeat the claim that the conventional interpretation is a legend, but leave to his critics any intensive engagement with the entire record of sources and arguments.[90] If in this interpretation, ordinary Germans could have had no impact on Nazi decision making, at least not in early 1943 under the circumstances at Rosenstrasse. If on the other hand, the long-held postwar interpretation is correct, uncomfortable questions are raised that impinge on the unifying national narrative about the Nazi past, in which all public opposition was immediately slapped down.

Given the pressures from Hitler and Goebbels, not to mention the RSHA and the SS in Auschwitz, the burden of proof is high indeed for any argument that the regime did not wish to deport Jews wearing the Star that it arrested and incarcerated for a week at Rosenstrasse. Yet the key argument for revising this history is that the Gestapo never intended to deport the Jews imprisoned at Rosenstrasse.

In fact there is no compelling evidence to suggest that Nazi leaders wished to keep these Jews in Berlin rather than deporting them at once, although the Frankfurt/Oder decree is cited as conclusive evidence[91]: "As is apparent in a decree of the Frankfurt/Oder Gestapo of February 24, 1943, which the RSHA had ordered: 'all Jews still working in factories are to be collected' for removal from their workplace. This directive applies also to 'the Jews living in mixed marriages.' Their forced labor was supposed to be reorganized, but their deportation was not allowed."

The position that the Gestapo planned to register and employ the Jews rather than deport them leaves pressing questions unexplained. Given its commitment to not draw attention to its mass murder and to intermarried couples, why did the authorities not inform the women immediately that their family members were going to be released, rather than attempting repeatedly to intimidate their protest with weapons and threats? Why would the regime release these Jews once it had imprisoned them in the course of making Berlin free of Jews? Why didn't the regime punish the protesters for publicly protesting on behalf of Jews? Who was responsible for the regime's decision to defer the deportation temporarily in the first place, if not the "Aryans" married to Jews?

During the arrests, Gestapo agents had released a number of persons arrested on the basis of the identification they carried, who apparently did not fit the profile of persons intended for incarceration at Rosenstrasse. How could the "racial status" of these persons—who were employed in "Jewish task forces" in the factories and taken from the street if wearing the Star—have been in doubt at all?[92] If the Gestapo had wished to check the "race" status of Berlin's intermarried Jews, why would it have checked only those it imprisoned—some two thousand—which was less than one quarter of the nearly nine thousand intermarried Jews living in Berlin?

The replacement of Jewish workers after deportations was hardly the reason for a massive arrest and weeklong detention in horrible conditions that spurred a street protest; rather this was a routine matter handled by the Jewish authorities themselves, deportation after deportation, and pressure was on these authorities to reduce their Jewish employees.[93] There is neither any precedent for—nor later examples of—Jews arrested during deportation roundups who were held for a week or more before being released, in such large numbers.[94] If imprisoning thousands at Rosenstrasse was the "simplest" way to select 225 persons for work, as the revised history states,[95] why was this not done every time replacements were needed at the Jewish Community? Why were children and elderly kept so long in the suffocating misery at Rosenstrasse, if the regime was carefully searching out the best workers?[96]

Significantly, the documents showing that prisoners from Rosenstrasse were employed by the Jewish Community are only descriptive; neither they nor any other documents show that the regime intended to imprison Jews for a week in order to check their status and select a fraction for different jobs. They simply describe what happened rather than saying this is what the regime intended. The job reassignments make more sense as an improvised response to circumstances, especially considering Goebbels's criticism on March 6, 1943, that those pressing for their deportation, despite the protest, were slavishly following orders [*Schema F*] rather than adapting pragmatically to circumstances.

Again basic interpretations of the regime are in play: the new version of the events sees the regime as driven by pre-existing plans written into orders and carried through flawlessly. Official documents are viewed as reflecting the authentic intentions of a regime infamous for exploiting deception as a primary means to achieve its ends.[97] But Himmler specifically scorned laws and regulations if they got in the way of his ultimate objectives, and the "temporary" deferment of the RSHA directive of February 20, 1943, was lifted at least hundreds of times (including 106 intermarried Jews from Berlin deported during the "Factory Action" Final Roundup arrests). Nazi trickery specifically within deportation directives are reflected in euphemisms as well as specific attempts to deceive, reflected for example by Heydrich's decision to order decorated Jewish veterans sent not to Auschwitz but to

Theresienstadt, and the regime did take the effort to send them there first, before sending them post haste to Auschwitz.[98]

The demand that history fit the close reading of a document bearing a Gestapo stamp is narrow. Rather than evaluating in context, H.G. Adler's judgment that on Rosenstrasse "a courageous protest caused the Gestapo, in an exception, to give in,"[99] the criticism ties Adler's judgment to this specific source, and then disparages that source as "too vague."[100] But Adler was not blindly following this or that source, but rather making a judgment from his vast knowledge about what was the most likely reason that these Jews were released rather than deported. Adler's broad understanding of how the regime released the intermarried Berlin Jews would not be changed by any document discovered since he wrote.

At the same time, the perspective revealed by a succession of documents long available is sometimes ignored. One example is the identification of all intermarried Jews as "privileged."[101] But the regime "privileged" the majority so that it could focus on the "non-privileged" minority wearing the Star. This intention is obfuscated by the identification of a list of various groups as "privileged," including: "decorated war veterans, officers, doctors."[102] Due to sensitivity about morale within the Reich, Nazi leaders agreed that the deportation of German Jews would proceed in stages.[103] Wanting to draw intermarried Jews circumspectly into the Holocaust, the dictatorship intended to deport them one group at a time.[104] Goebbels wrote that during the arrests to clear Berlin of Jews, some "from privileged marriages were arrested too at first, which led to great fear and confusion." But considering the way Goebbels was using that term in his diaries on April 18, he regretted that some "privileged" as well as "non-privileged" Jews from mixed marriages had been arrested during the "Factory Action."[105] The regime had wished to assuage dissent by making it appear as though not all intermarried Jews were being deported, but the initial arrest of some Jews from "privileged "intermarriages had caused confusion about this, according to Goebbels.

If the "legend" that the Gestapo had planned to deport the Jews was fabricated after the war, as the critics say,[106] what are we to make of the reports which did this in 1943, including Goebbels, not to mention Frick, Wurm, Sommers, Lehfeldt, and the OSS? Of course no serious historian has made a case about the Gestapo's intentions based on the reports of protesters. Yet we ignore eyewitness reports at the expense of important histories that the regime did not wish to be known—the Sonderkommando uprising at Auschwitz in 1944, or day-to-day life in the slave-labor camp at Starachowice, Poland.[107]

Neither the fact that the protest was not repressed nor the dearth of surviving documents about it indicate that it was unimportant. The regime did not repress protest, but it did repress reports about it, and we no longer have its documents on the Rosenstrasse events. The regime kept records assiduously on every possible offender, including matters of much less importance such as "wandering speakers;"[108] the high degree of interest that leaders from Hitler on down had in intermarried Jews and their families is registered in the prodigious amount of time devoted to considering how to handle them. Indeed the debates culminating in late 1942 show the regime's overwhelming drive to really finalize the "Final Solution."[109] Hitler had given his directive on the matter and it remained in place: remove the Jews but do not cause unrest. In Berlin authorities were constrained to try to find a method to deport intermarried Jews that would not overstep the boundaries of what the Volk would accept.[110] The protests were important to executors of the Final Solution since they helped to determine the line between what was feasible and what not, in Hitler's calculus requiring an energetic deportation of Jews while avoiding "unnecessary difficulties" in the case of intermarried Jews.

There are no doubt a variety of reasons for the long postwar silence about the protest. Represented by their marriages, the protesters personify a sense of self that rejects fixed institutional boundaries. They were intermarried, and they were women, Germans who moved back and forth between institutions, crossing boundaries between secular and sacred, Jewish and Christian spheres. Their voice represents a tiny fraction, and moreover their story may seem to form a rebuke to the vast majority who were complicit in trying to intimidate them, or failed to struggle at all.

Yet recognizing mixed marriage couples for the rescue of German Jews need not represent a sharp reproach. Germans were most likely to protest and had the most chance of success, when the regime violated the private sphere in ways that received customs could not accept. The regime was continuously testing the boundaries of how far it could interfere, and at what pace, but it could stop short of intruding on the private sphere when Volk dissent arose from official intrusions on spheres, which they continued to see as under private jurisdiction.

Still the Rosenstrasse history faces another challenge, that of transgressing normative perspectives. After all, any survivor who claims that the protest on Rosenstrasse made a difference flies in the face of millions of contradictory testimonies—all those who have grown up hearing that such a thing was impossible. Dr. Gerhard Lehfeldt's report in March 1943, connecting protest with the disruption of Nazi plans for Berlin's Jews, for example was welcomed neither in 1943 nor in the intervening decades, languishing in Vatican archives for decades.[111] A clue to the fate of Lehfeldt's report appears already in 1946 when Lehfeldt wrote a letter to Bishop

Theophil Wurm, dated September 9, pointing out the dire situation in postwar Germany of church members who during the war had been persecuted as "non-Aryan" Christians. Six days later, Bishop Wurm reacted with a letter to Eugen Gerstenmaier saying Lehfeldt was to be handled with care ("mit vorsicht zu geniessen").[112]

Lehfeldt was avoided while Gerstenmeier soon became president of the West German Parliament. Lehfeldt's report apparently did not fit into the way prevailing interests interpreted Nazi power and dealt with the history of intermarriages. In a 2013 book published under Germany's Topography of Terror memorial, Managing Director Rabbi Andreas Nachama, wrote that his great aunt had also protested on Rosenstrasse and had also believed, wrongly given the "newer research," that protesters had rescued their Jewish family members. He writes that non-Jews married to Jews who "allowed themselves to be pressured into a divorce by the Gestapo," allowed their Jewish partners to be deported, an acknowledgement that the fate of these Jews was held in the hands of their mates—alone. But Nachama apparently precludes the possibility that the arrest and internment of Jewish family members at Rosenstrasse was one more form of pressure, under a yet more heightened and imminent threat, to see whether these wives would finally relent and abandon their Jewish family members. This suggests that the interpretation of events at Rosenstrasse are a subject of contention so significant it must be taken under the wing of a public site of memory, dedicated to a "decidedly German collective memory based on notions of national peculiarity."[113]

But why at this point would scholars and memorials strain to limit the discussion of the Rosenstrasse events in Nazi history?[114] There is in fact a plurality of understandings among Germans about the Rosenstrasse events; German historians Antonia Leugers and Joachim Neander, along with many others, have for years argued compellingly for a different approach, and many Germans agree. So it remains to be seen whether the view that the exclusive, no-room-for-disagreements view from Berlin's Topography of Terror will become mainstream opinion in Germany.[115] To paraphrase the German philosopher Karl Jaspers speaking in 1946 of the Nazi past, it is best to regard our differences as starting points of conversation rather than as "finalities."[116]

Tony Judt, the historian of post–World War II Europe, wrote that "the first postwar Europe was built upon deliberate mismemory—upon forgetting as a way of life." Claims that the vast majority were neither implicated nor capable of resisting helped restore a sense of community. Europe's "moral reconstruction" required "a highly stylized story," as Tony Judt points out. However, historians must now redress the "sea of mismemories."[117]

Nathan Stoltzfus is Rintels Professor of Holocaust Studies at Florida State University and the author or editor of numerous books and articles on modern German history and environmental activism, including *Resistance of the Heart* (New York: Norton, 1996) and *Nazi Crimes and the Law*, co-edited with Henry Friedlander (New York: Cambridge, 2009).

Notes

1. Nuremberg Trials Document NG-2586 (G), "Memorandum of Conference on the Final Solution of the Jews Problem, Berlin, January 20, 1942."
2. In 1939 there were about 30,000 intermarried Jews—one out of every ten in the Reich. At the end of 1942 there were still 27,744—more than one in three Jews in the Reich area. Korherr report of March 23, 1943, Nuremberg Trials Document NO-5195. Raul Hilberg, *Destruction of the European Jews* (New Haven, CT, 2003), vol. 1, 169, 169n 35.
3. Of intermarried couples in Vienna only "5 to 7 percent divorced" during the Nazi years. Evan Burr Bukey, *Jews and Intermarriage in Nazi Austria* (New York: Cambridge University Press, 2011), 94n 40, 191. Ursula Büttner estimated that some 7 percent of German intermarried couples divorced during the Nazi years. Büttner, *Die Not der Juden teilen: Christlich-judische Familien im Dritten Reich* (Hamburg, 1988), 57. Paul Sauer estimated that 7.2 percent of intermarried couples divorced in Baden Württemberg while Leo Lippmann concluded that in Hamburg less than 10 percent had divorced by 1942. Ursula Büttner and Martin Greschat, *Die verlassenen Kinder der Kirche: Der Umgang mit Christen jüdischer Herkunft im 'Dritten Reich'* (Göttingen: Vandenhoeck & Ruprecht, 1998), 25n 18. Cf. Beate Meyer, *"Jüdische Mischlinge:" Rassenpolitik und Verfolgungserfahrung 1933–1945* (Hamburg: Dilling und Galitz, 1999), 73, who estimated the divorce rate in Hamburg above 20 percent. Marion Kaplan, *Between Dignity and Despair: Jewish Life in Nazi Germany* (Oxford: Oxford University Press, 1998), 93.
4. Hermann Göring to ministry of the interior, December 28, 1938. Hilberg, *Destruction*, vol. 2, 443–444; Nathan Stoltzfus, *Resistance of the Heart: Intermarriage and the Rosenstrasse Protest in Nazi Germany* (New York: Norton, 1996), 102, Meyer, *Jüdische Mischlinge*, 30.
5. Stenographic Report for a Meeting on the Jewish Question under Goering at the Reich Aviation Ministry on November 12, 1938. International Military Tribunal document 1816-PS. Victor Klemperer moved to a "Jews' house" with his "Aryan" wife, Eva; Klemperer, *I Will Bear Witness: A Diary of the Nazi Years, 1933–1941* (New York: Random House, 2001), 339, diary entry of May 26, 1940.
6. Joseph Goebbels, "Die Juden Sind Schuld!," in *Das Eherne Herz* (Munich: Eher Verlag, 1943), 85–91, here 87, 91.
7. Kaplan, *Dignity and Despair*, 190; Victor Klemperer, *I Shall Bear Witness: The Diaries of Victor Klemperer*, vol. 2 (London: Weidenfeld & Nicolson, 1998), 91. Jews who did not wear the Star of David, and whose partner died or divorced were exempted according to directives from May 1942. Hans Günther Adler, *Der*

verwaltete Mensch: Studien zur Deportation der Juden aus Deutschland (Tübingen: J.C.B. Mohr, 1974), 197.
8. Joseph Goebbels, *Die Tagebücher von Joseph Goebbels*, ed. Elke Fröhlich part II, vol. 2 (Munich: K. G. Saur Verlag, 1996), November 22, 1941.
9. Peter Longerich, *Holocaust: The Nazi Persecution and Murder of the Jews* (Oxford: Oxford University Press, 2010), 305; Kershaw, *Hitler: Nemesis*, 491; Goebbels, *Tagebücher*, pt. 2, vol. 2, December 13, 1941.
10. Longerich, *Holocaust: The Nazi Persecution and Murder of the Jews* (New York: Oxford University Press, 2010), 305; Kershaw, *Hitler:Nemesis*, 491.
11. Bukey, *Jews and Intermarriage*, 142. Just a few months earlier Bishop Galen had raised a public furor by warning the Volk from the pulpit that any one of them could become victims of the euthanasia program, since no one could perceive a clear line defining who was being victimized, and who not, that guaranteed safety.
12. Kaplan, *Dignity and Despair*, 190. Ursula Büttner, *Die Not der Juden*, 57. Victor Klemperer survived because his wife was not Jewish. See in particular, *I Will Bear Witness*, vol. 2, 91.
13. NG-2586 (G), Minutes of the Wannsee Meeting. For the overall significance of this conference see Mark Roseman, *The Wannsee Conference and the Final Solution: A Reconsideration* (New York: McMillan, 2003).
14. Nuremberg Trials Document NG-2586 (H), "Record, Conference on the Final Solution of the Jewish Problem, Berlin, March 6, 1942."
15. Christian Gerlach, "The Wannsee Conference, the Fate of German Jews, and Hitler's Decision in Principle to Exterminate All European Jews," *The Journal of Modern History* 70, no. 4 (December 1998): 759–812, here 791. Wolf Kaiser, "Die Wannsee-Konferenz," in *Täter, Opfer, Folgen: Der Holocaust in Geschichte und Gegenwart*, ed. Heiner Lichtenstein and Otto R. Romberg (Bonn: Bundeszentrale für Politische Bildung, 1995), 24–37, here 29.
16. As quoted in Michael Burleigh, *The Third Reich: A New History* (New York: Hill & Wang, 2000), 192.
17. Antonia Leugers, ed., *Berlin, Rosenstrasse 2-4: Protest in der NS-Diktatur; Neue Forschungen zum Frauenprotest in der Rosenstrasse 1943*. (Annweiler: Plöger, 2005), 11.
18. Bukey, Jews and Intermarriage, 152, 153. Hitler ruled in January 1944 that further discussions of intermarried Jews "should be avoided, but this "directive seems to have been ignored or taken lightly." (Bukey, 164). Hitler's subordinates could act independently, and the codified law was no more secure than Hitler's orders, because the Nazis used the law opportunistically. as another tactic among many used to move most expeditiously toward larger Nazi goals. Protesters were appeased despite the fact that they slowed this progress. Cf. Nicholas Stargardt, *The German War: A Nation Under Arms, 1939-1943* (New York: Basic Books, 2015), 406.
19. Büttner, *Die Not der Juden*, 57, writes that this was beginning in the summer of 1942. Hilberg, *Destruction*, vol. 2, 447. See also Uwe Adams, *Judenpolitik im dritten Reich* (Düsseldorf: *Droste* Verlag, 1972), 17, 29, 316.
20. Judgment against Georg Albert Dengler (2a Ks 1/49), 26, Hessisches Hauptstaatsarchiv, Wiesbaden. The judgment is also printed in Irene Sage-Grande, et al., eds., *Justiz und NS-Verbrechen: Sammlung deutscher Strafurteile wegen*

nationalsozialistischer Tötungsverbrechen 1945–1966 (Amsterdam: Amsterdam University, 1981), vol. 22, 658–682.
21. Albert Speer, *Der Sklavenstaat: Meine Auseinandersetzungen mit der SS* (Stuttgart: Deutsche Verlags-Anstalt, 1981), 346. Goebbels, *Tagebücher*, pt. 2, vol. 5, September 30, 1942. Goebbels added that Hitler rejected industrialists' claims that they could not do without the work of Jews they employed.
22. Bernhard Lösener, "Als Rassereferent in Reichsministerium des Innern," *Die Vierteljahrshefte für Zeitgeschichte* 9, no 3 (1961): 264–313, here 298. In September of 1942 new rumors began to circulate in the Interior Ministry that the RSHA was preparing to deport Mischlinge. Hilberg, *Destruction*, 423. This corresponds with Gerhard Lehfeldt's report of mid-March 1943, printed in appendix 1.
23. Raul Hilberg, *Destruction*, vol. 2, 447; Uwe Adams, *Judenpolitik im dritten Reich*, 17, 29, 316. Compare also Wolf Gruner, *Jewish Forced Labor Under the Nazis: Economic Needs and Racial Aims, 1938–1944* (New York: Cambridge University Press, 2006), 87. Concern expressed for the Mischlinge by the Deputy Secretary for the Interior Department, Wilhelm Stuckart, in September 1942 did not change the plans of those far above him; in any case, Mischlinge were "half Jews" not "full Jews" like intermarried Jews, whom Stuckart had been trying to deport. Stuckart had just been brushed aside when he proposed a law to forcibly annul intermarriages.
24. BArch, R 58/276, 348, Fernschrieben, RSHA an alle Staatspolizei(leit)stellen, Berlin 5.11.1942, gez. Müller.
25. Georg Zivier, "Aufstand der Frauen" *Sie: Frauenszeitung für Menschenrecht*, December 1945. Alexandra Przyrembel, *Rassenschande: Reinheitsmythos und Vernichtungslegitimation im Nationalsozialismus* (Göttingen: Vandenhoeck & Ruprecht, 2003), 125; Hildegard Henschel, "Aus der Arbeit der judischen Gemeinde Berlin während 1941–1943 [1946], Zeitschrift für die Geschichte der Juden [Tel Aviv] 9, no. 1–2 [1972]: 43–44. Mary Felstiner, "Alois Brunner: 'Eichmann's Best Tool,'" *Simon Wiesenthal Centre Annual* 3 (1986): 1–46. Statement of Max Reschke, May 4, 1959, StA Landegericht Berlin (LB) I Js 5/65 supporting documents file 30.
26. Statement of Max Reschke, June 1, l959, (LB) I Js 5/65 supporting documents file 30.
27. This is an unmarked folder from the Berlin Jewish Community, titled "Lists Due to the Forced-Deportations" containing correspondence between Catholic offices. Stoltzfus, *Resistance*, 206, 207. Jana Leichsenring, *Die Katholische Kirche und "Ihre Juden": Das "Hilfswerk Beim Bischöflichen Ordinariat Berlin" 1938–1945* (Berlin: Metropol-Verlag, 2007), 204.
28. See Joachim Neander, chapter 7, 195-201.
29. The Gestapo in Dortmund as well as the county administrative office (Landsamt) in Meschede identified the arrests there in late February and early March 1943 as the "Entjudung des Reichsgebietes." Werner Jacob, et al., eds., *Ich Trage Die Nummer 104953: Ein Letztes Zeugnis*, (Der Oberkreisdirektor des Kreises Olpe: Kreisarchiv, 1997), 145; Leugers, *Berlin,* 182–183; A telegraph of January 25, 1943, from the RSHA to all Inspectors of the Security Police and the SD, pertaining to the "Entjudung des Reichsgebietes—Arbeitseinsatz" ordered all Inspectors to report, by February 3, the number and nationality of Jews who were employed in

armaments production as of January 15, 1943. NA, Stapost Nuernberg Item no. OCC-110, Roll 657, Frame 1.
30. Speer, *Sklavenstaat,* 202, 346; Adler, *Der verwaltete Mensch,* 202.
31. Ronny Loewy and Katharina Rauschenberger, eds., *"Der Letzte der Ungerechten": der Judenälteste Benjamin Murmelstein in Filmen 1942–1975* (Frankfurt: Campus, 2011), 16. On Murmelstein's connections to Adolf Eichmann and Karl Rahm see Anna Hájková's article in the same book, 75–100.
32. Goebbels *Tagebücher,* pt. 2, vol. 7, February 2, 1943.
33. Bundesarchiv, NS 18/112, Goebbels to Gauleiters, August 13, 1940. Goebbels was concerned that the Churches, by holding ceremonies for Germans who died on the war front, were winning converts Guenter Lewy, *The Catholic Church and Nazi Germany* [Boston: Da Capo Press, 2000 [orig. 1964]], 391n 141.
34. On March 9, Goebbels clarified that the SS *Leibstandarte-Hitler* would be ready to put down any revolt in Berlin by Jews joining forces with foreign workers. "That's why I shall have to get the Jews out of Berlin as fast as possible, despite the fact that this involves psychological problems." Goebbels, *Tagebücher,* pt. 2, vol. 7, March 9, 1943.
35. Goebbels, *Tagebücher,* pt. 2, vol. 7, March 11, 1943.
36. Goebbels *Tagebücher,* pt. 2, vol. 7, February 18 and April 18, 1943.
37. See Antonia Leugers, chapter 8, 221-222.
38. See the full decree in appendix 2, and Leugers, chapter 8, 220.
39. See Wolf Gruner, *Der Geschlossene Arbeitseinsatz deutscher Juden: Zur Zwangsarbeit als Element der Verfolgung 1938–1943* (Berlin: Metropol Verlag, 1997), 316n 236.
40. Kaplan, *Dignity and Despair,* 190; Stoltzfus, *Resistance,* 204. This led at least one person to question why intermarried couples were "separated" in Frankfurt and not in Berlin. Michael Grüttner, "Hochschulpolitik zwishen Gau und Reich," in *Die NS-Gaue: Rregionale Mittelinstanzen im zentralistischen "Führerstaat"?,* ed. Jürgen John, et. al., (Munich: R. Oldenbourg, 2007), 183.
41. Judgment against Georg Albert Dengler (2a Ks 1/49), 26, Hessisches Hauptstaatsarchiv, Wiesbaden. The judgment is also printed in Sage-Grande, et al., *Justiz und NS-Verbrechen*: Sammlung deutscher Strafurteile wegen nationalsozialistischer Tötungsverbrechen 1945–1966, vol. 22, Irene Sage-Grande, et. al. eds. (Amsterdam: Amsterdam University, 1981), vol. 22, 658–682. Monica Kingreen, ed., *Nach der Kristallnacht: Jjüdisches Leben und antijüdische Politik,* ed. Monica Kingreen (Frankfurt: Campus,, 1999), p. 250; Fritz Bauer, et al., eds., *Justiz und NS-Verbrechen: Sammlung deutscher Strafurteile wegen sozialistischer Tötungsverbrechen 1945–1966,* Vol. 6, eds. Fritz Bauer, et. al. (Amsterdam: University Press Amsterdam, 1971), vol. 6, 380. On Hamburg see Joachim Neander, "Die Rosenstrasse von aussen gesehen," in Leugers, ed., *Berlin, Rosenstrasse 2-4,* 182. Reports that Alois Brunner, in late 1942, deported intermarried Jews and Mischlinge—falsifying documents at will—illustrate initiative by lower ranking officials. Hildegard Henschel, "Aus der Arbeit der Jüdischen Gemeinde Berlin während der Jahre 1941-1943: Gemeindearbeit und Evakuierung von Berlin, 16. Oktober 1941–16 Juni 1943," in *Zeitschrift für die Geschichte der Juden,* 9 (1972): 33–52, here 43–44. Stoltzfus, *Resistance,* 185–186; Bukey, *Jews and Intermarried Jews,* 141-162.
42. Kershaw, *Hitler: Nemesis,* 481. Kaplan, *Dignity and Despair,* 190.

43. This was true in France and accounts for the deportations of some German mixed marriage Jews. Serge Klarsfeld, *Memorial to the Jews Deported from France, 1942–1944: Documentation of the Deportation of the Victims of the Final Solution in France* (Paris: B. Klarsfeld Foundation), 1983), 431, 440–446.
44. Hans-Ulrich Wehler, *Deutsche Gesellschaftsgeschichte vol. 4: Vom Beginn des Ersten Weltkriegs bis zur Gründung der beiden deutschen Staaten, 1914–1949* (Munich: C.H. Beck Verlag, 2003), 895; Longerich, *Holocaust*, 291; Kershaw, *Hitler: Nemesis*, 351, 478–479,
45. In 1951, Walter Stock, former director of the Berlin Gestapo's Jewish Desk, recalled the name of the massive arrests of around ten thousand Berlin Jews including those interned at Rosenstrasse 2-4 as the *Schlußaktion* (final roundup). Statement of Walter Stock B Rep 058 vol. 464 kt. 646, 1PK LS 3/52, Strafsache gegen Walter Stock, Stock deposition, August 13, 1951.
46. In the 1955 trial of the Leibstandarte leader Sepp Dietrich, who had offered the use of his SS to Goebbels, reported that the SS men arresting Jews in Berlin "wore a small band with the script 'Leibstandarte SS Adolf Hitler.' Two were officers wearing war medals." Statement of Karl Hefter, October 28, 1955, in the trial against Josef (Sepp) Dietrich, I P Js 3767.65, Staatsanwaltschaft Berlin. In his report dated mid-March 1943, Dr. Gerhard Lehfeldt identified the Leibstandarte with the plans for intermarried Jews and Mischlinge. Lehfeldt, "Bericht über die Lage von 'Mischlingen,' Mitte März 1943," in Leugers, *Berlin*, 237f; The SS, a driver for a truck transporting Jews testified, made arrests in working-class neighborhoods where the chance of uprising was considered highest. Statement of Erwin Sartorious, December 13, 1965. Eyewitness Martha Mosse as well as H.G. Adler identified the SS present as the Leibstandarte. Adler, *Der verwaltete Mensch*, 226–227, 340. Wolf Gruner, *Widerstand in der Rosenstraße: Die Fabrik-Action und die Verfolgung der "Mischehen" 1943* (Frankfurt a.M.: Fischer. 2005), 61, writes that Adler is wrong because he relies on Mosse, but his citation of Mosse is backed by his formidable knowledge of Nazi documents and the regime's administration of the Holocaust.
47. Statement of Else Hannach (who escaped Germany in July 1944), July 26 and 31, 1944, LB I Js 5/65 supporting documents file 30. Stoltzfus, *Resistance*, xv.
48. Stoltzfus, *Resistance*, xvi–xvii.
49. During the first week of March, groups of protesters also took to the streets outside a Jewish old peoples' home on Berlin's nearby Große Hamburgerstr, after their Jewish family members were imprisoned there. Eberhard Röhm and Jörg Thierfelder, *Juden-Christen-Deutsche*, vol. 1, *1933–1945*, part 4, issue 2 (Stuttgart: Calwer, 2007), 192 ff.; Stoltzfus, *Resistance*, 242.
50. Ursula von Kardorff wrote that on March 3, 1943, women workers banded together and "loudly protested the deportation of Jews." Ruth Andreas-Friedrich, another diarist in Berlin wrote of women crying and screaming for their husbands. Kardorff, *Berliner Aufzeichnungen 1942 bis 1945: Unter Verwendung der Original-Tagebücher*, 2nd ed. (Munich: Dt. Taschenbuch-Verl., 1997), 72. Kardorff wrote this in 1947; Ruth Andreas-Friedrich, *Der Schattenmann* (Berlin: Suhrkamp, 1947), February 28 and March 7, 1943, 108–110.
51. Sommer's report, March 2, 1943, in Ludwig Volk, ed., *Akten deutscher Bischöfe*, vol. 6, *1943–1945* (Mainz: Matthias-Grünewald-Verl., 1985), 19–21. Bertram also

received a report on March 1, 1943 concerning the deportation of Geltungsjuden. See Leugers, chapter 8, 150-152.
52. See Neander, chapter 7, 200.
53. One third of Germany's Jews lived in Berlin. Goebbels proposed to Hitler their removal in May 1942, particularly the Jewish armaments workers. In October 1941, 18,700 Berlin Jews worked for this industry. Adler, *Der verwaltete Mensch*, 223. Neander, chapter 7, 199, shows that they needed at least nine thousand (although expecting fifteen thousand) and points out that this is the number of Jews Eichmann planned to send to the East, according to Lehfeldt.
54. Neander, chapter 7, 201, and Wolf Gruner, "Die Fabrik-Aktion und die Ereignisse in der Berliner Rosenstraße: Fakten und Fiktionen um den 27. Februar 1943," *Jahrbuch für Antisemitismusforschung* 11 (2002): 137–177, 154, 158.
55. "Orsenigo an Maglione, March 3, 1943" in Pierre Blet, Robert A. Graham, Angelo Martini, and Burkhart Schneider, eds., *Actes et Documents du Saint Siège relatifs à la Seconde Guerre Mondiale*, vol. 9: *Le Saint Siège et les victimes de la guerre: Janvier/Décembre 1943, Città del Vaticano 1975*, 165; Leugers, chapter 8, 217.
56. Wienken to Bertram, March 4, 1943, Volk, *Akten deutscher Bischöfe*, vol. 6, 25. Antonia Leugers, "Widerstand gegen die Rosenstrasse," *theologie.geschichte* 1 (2006): 152, writes that Gruner incorrectly dates Wienken's consultation with Eichmann as March 3, in Gruner, *Widerstand*, 115; Eichmann's stated plan to return Berlin's intermarried Jews to armaments work contradicts the interpretation Gruner gives to the February 24 Frankfurt/Oder decree. But Gruner has omitted this part of Wienken's report —that Berlin's Jews would be put back to work in the armaments industry. Wolf Gruner, "The Factory Action and the Events at the Rosenstrasse in Berlin: Facts and Fictions about 27 February 1943: Sixty Years Later," *Central European History* 36, no. 2 (2003): 179–208, here 197; Antonia Leugers, review of Wolf Gruner, *Gedenkort Rosenstraße 2-4: Internierung und Protest im NS-Staat* (Berlin: Topographie des Terrors, 2013), *theologie.geschichte* 8 (2013). http://universaar.uni-saarland.de/journals/index.php/tg/article/viewArticle/536/575.
57. See Lehfeldt's report (appendix 1).
58. Statement of Erwin Sartorious, December 13, 1965, Strafsache *gegen Bovensiepen u. a*; Stoltzfus, *Resistance*, xx, xxi.
59. Statement of Walter Stock B Rep 058 vol. 464 kt. 646, 1PK LS 3/52, Strafsache gegen Walter Stock, Stock deposition, August 13, 1951.
60. Neander, chapter 7, 202; Lehfeldt's report (see appendix 1), also identified the Leibstandarte with the plans for intermarried Jews and Mischlinge.
61. In the East German Communist Party newspaper Inge Unikower wrote that "foreign news sources reported at the time of 400 to 600 . . . including London Radio." Although she titled the article "Silent Protest," Unikowever reported that protesters called out together, "Give us our husbands back. We want to have our husbands again." Unikower, "Stummer Protest," *Neues Deutschland* no. 46, November 14, 1964.
62. See Leugers, chapter 8, 150.
63. Goebbels, *Tagebücher*, pt. 2, vol. 7, March 6, 1943.
64. Lehfeldt described a public "Krawall" on March 5, 1943, elsewhere in Berlin and concluded that public protests led Goebbels to release the Jews on March 6. See appendix 1.

65. Speer, *Sklavenstaat,* 202, 346; Adler, *Der verwaltete Mensch,* 202.
66. This references the basic instructions Hitler had given Goebbels on November 22, 1941, on the deportation of intermarried Jews, particularly in artist's circles, as well as the regime's efforts to deport intermarried Jews in phases, avoiding the appearance that all intermarried Jews were being deported at this time. Goebbels, *Tagebücher,* pt. 2, vol. 7, March 9 and 11, 1943.
67. Leugers, "Widerstand gegen die Rosenstrasse," 199.
68. Bishop Wurm to the Ministry of the Reich Church, March 12, 1943, in *Landesbischof D. Wurm und der Nationalsozialistische Staat,* 160ff; page 166 notes that "Already in February 1943, a number of *Mischlinge* of the first degree together with Jews had been brought by the Gestapo in trucks to the Rosenstrasse in Berlin, where they were later released."
69. See Leugers, chapter 8, 227.
70. Notes by Berning, April 6, 1943, in Volk, *Akten deutscher Bischöfe,* vol. 6, 62n 1.
71. Interview with Johnny Hüttner, December 27, 1985, (East) Berlin in Stoltzfus, *Resistance,* 253. One of the twenty-five remained behind because he was sick. Eleven other Berlin Jews from intermarriage were returned from Auschwitz to Berlin on the same train. For Hüttner's story see Len Crome, *Unbroken: Resistance and Survival in the Concentration Camps* (New York: Schocken Books, 1988). See Neander, chapter 7, 205f. .
72. These Jews had been deported by "mistake" (*Fehlgriffes, versehentlich*) and were returned to Berlin on orders of a "high Reich official." Statement of Johanna Heym in the Trial against Otto Bovensiepen, Stoltzfus, *Resistance,* 340–341n 65. Gruner has also posited this—even though only 35 of the 120 intermarried Jews deported to Auschwitz were released. Wolf Gruner, "Ein Historikerstreit? Die Internierung der Juden aus Mischehen in der Rosenstraße 1943: Das Ereignis, seine Diskussion und seine Geschichte," *Zeitschrift für Geschichtswissenschaft* 1 (2004): 5–22, here 20.
73. Harrison to Donovan, Office of Strategic Services, April 1, 1943, National Archives, Washington, DC, RG 226 (OSS) Entry 134: Washington Registry Office Radio & Cable Files, Box 171, Folder 1079.
74. Margarete Sommer, August 22–24, 1943, in Volk, *Akten deutscher Bischöfe,* vol. 6, 217–219.
75. Titze testified that: "The mixed marriage partners sent to the Rosenstrasse Collection Center were released a little later. The Aryan wives of these Jews got together back then to protest in front of the center." Herbert Titze Statement, August 1, 1966, LAB B Rep. 058, Supporting Document 22, 1 JS 9/65; Mosse's testimony from 1958 is cited in Adler, *Der verwaltete Mensch,* 782–785, here 785. For the statements of Kleemann and Gutterer see Stoltzfus, *Resistance,* 213, 244–245, 260–261.
76. The postwar judiciary as well as scholars have agreed. Christof Dipper wrote in 1996 that up until this point only a few historians had doubted that the protest had caused the Gestapo to release the Jewish prisoners at Rosenstrasse. Dipper, "Schwierigkeiten mit der Resistenz," *Geschichte und Gesellschaft* 22 (1996): 409–416. Some who have made this interpretation include: Kurt Jakob Ball-Kaduri, "Berlin wird Judenfrei: Die Juden in Berlin in den Jahren 1942/1943," *Jahrbuch*

für die Geschichte Mittel- und Ostdeutschlands 22 (1973): 212–214; Doris L. Bergen, *War and Genocide: A Concise History of the Holocaust* (Lanham: Rowman & Littlefield Publishers, Inc., 2009), 202; Heinz Boberach, *Aemter, Abkuerzungen, Aktionen des NS-Staates: Handbuch für die Benutzung von Quellen der Nationalsozialistischen Zeit* (Munich: Saur, 1997), 379; Paul Bookbinder, "Confronting Resistance in Nazi Germany: An Overview," in *Confront!: Resistance in Nazi Germany,* ed. John Michalczyk (New York: Peter Lang, 2004), 8; Helmut Eschwege and Konrad Kwiet, *Selbstbehauptung und Widerstand deutsche Juden im Kampf um Existenz und Menschewuerde 1933–1945* (Hamburg: Christians, 1984), 43; Raul Hilberg, *Perpetrators, Victims, Bystanders: The Jewish Catastrophe, 1933–1945* (New York: Aaron Asher Books, 1992), 132; Eric A. Johnson, *Nazi Terror: The Gestapo, Jews, and Ordinary Germans* (New York: Basic Books, 1999), 25; Kaplan, *Dignity and Despair*, 193; Kershaw, *Hitler: Nemesis*, 963n 115; Claudia Koonz, *Mothers in the Fatherland: Women, the Family, and Nazi Politics* (New York: St. Martin's Press, 1987), 337; Sybil Milton, "Women and the Holocaust: The Case of German and German-Jewish Women," in *When Biology Became Destiny: Women in Weimar and Nazi Germany*, ed. Renate Bridenthal, Atina Grossmann, and Marion A. Kaplan (New York: Monthly Review Press, 1984), 319; Monika Richarz, *Jüdisches Leben in Deutschland: Selbstzeugnisse zur Sozialgeschichte*, vol. 3, 1918–1945 (Stuttgart: Dt. Verl.-Anst., 1982), 64; Wolfgang Scheffler, *Judenverfolgung im Dritten Reich 1933 bis 1945* (Frankfurt am Main: Büchergilde Gutenberg, 1965), 44, 69; Marlis G. Steinert, *Hitler's War and the Germans: Public Mood and Attitude During the Second World War*, trans. T.E.J. de Witt (Athens: Ohio University Press, 1977), 142; Gerhard Weinberg, Jill Stephenson, Julia Torrie, Katharina von Kellenbach, Antonia Leugers, and Joachim Neander in this book (and elsewhere) also see the street protest as causing the regime to release rather than deport the Jews held at Rosenstrasse 2-4.

A court judgment rationale of 1969 for the regional court of Berlin stated that: "There developed in front of the collection center [Rosenstrasse] an overt protest (Protestkundgebung) of 'Aryan' marriage partners, which led to the result that a part of those arrested were set free again, while others [Jews in intermarriage], by contrast, had to make their way to Auschwitz . . . from which they were, however, returned to Berlin a couple of weeks later." *Urteilsgründe*, Trial against Kurt Venter and Max Graustueck [(500) 1 Ks 2/69 (10/69)] 79,80. In its charges against a former head of the Berlin Gestapo a postwar German prosecutor made the same conclusion. Trial against Otto Bovensiepen et al., Landesarchiv Berlin, B Rep 058, 1 Js 9/65.

77. Speer, *Sklavenstaat*, 346.
78. Christopher R. Browning with Jürgen Matthäus, *The Origins of the Final Solution: The Evolution of Nazi Jewish Policy, September 1939–March 1942* (Lincoln: University of Nebraska Press, 2004), 297.
79. Kurt Pätzold, "Der eigentliche Streitwert: Zur Kontroverse um die Rosenstraße," *Neues Deutschland*, September 27, 2003.
80. Gruner, *Widerstand*, 54–55, 95. As additional evidence for his interpretation of the Frankfurt/Oder decree Gruner referred in several sentences to two additional documents, one from the Bielefeld Gestapo he cites only on the basis of Margit

Naarmann's book on the Paderborn Jews (although Naarmann neither reproduces the document nor quotes it in full). From a document of the Dortmund Gestapo dated February 24, 1943, Gruner cites only the following: "In the course of the scheduled Removal of Jews partially from the Reich Territory" and effective February 27 throughout the administrative district of Arnsberg, Jews found in the process of working are to be removed with the goal of evacuating them to the East." This is hardly sufficient evidence to rebut the clear presumption that authorities at this moment wanted to deport all persons wearing the Star of David from Berlin.

81. Wolf Gruner, "Die Reichhauptstadt und die Verfolgung der Berliner Juden 1933–1945," in *Jüdische Geschichte in Berlin: Essaays und Studien*, ed. Reinhard Rürup (Berlin: Edition Hentrich, 1995), 253.
82. H-German sponsored an online forum that ran from July through September 2004 with scores of opinions exchanged under the heading "Rosenstrasse Forum," and posted until 2015: http://www.h-net.org/~german/discuss/Rosenstrasse/Rosenstrasse_index.htm. As of September 2015 it had disappeared, although the entries for the Rosenstrasse Forum can be viewed, one by one rather than as a unit, under the discussion logs of H-German at: http://h-net.msu.edu/cgi-bin/logbrowse.pl?trx=lm&list=h-german, where entries are listed in the order that they were originally published. The separate entries in this forum can be viewed in the months of July, August, and September of 2004. Beatte Meyer's entry is at: http://h-net.msu.edu/cgi-bin/logbrowse.pl?trx=vx&list=H-German&month=0407&week=d&msg=oN6p2xHv/wqg9q2hC75dFw&user=&pw=; Wolf Gruner's is at: http://h-net.msu.edu/cgi-bin/logbrowse.pl?trx=vx&list=H-German&month=0409&week=b&msg=UMAIiJE0RcI%2bCD0y5xkAyA&user=&pw=; Nathan Stoltzfus is at: http://h-net.msu.edu/cgi-bin/logbrowse.pl?trx=vx&list=H-German&month=0409&week=d&msg=xcSwqBWaTwMa%2bf0Y%2bz4HTg&user=&pw=.
83. Meyer, *Jüdische Mischlinge*, 57.
84. Gruner, *Widerstand*, 18.
85. Gruner, *Widerstand*, 10, 165.
86. Gruner, *Widerstand*, 32, 202.
87. Gruner, *Widerstand*, 55, 110, 119, 128.
88. Leugers, "Widerstand Gegen die Rosenstrasse," 177; Antonia Leugers, review of Gruner, *Gedenkort Rosenstraße 2-4*.
89. Benz wrote that Gruner's work "reconstructed the real history of Rosenstrasse," and also apparently sees no reason for further discussion. Wolfgang Benz, "Kitsch as Kitsch can," *Die Süddeutsche Zeitung*, September 20, 2003 (See the response, Nathan Stoltzfus, "Die Wahrheit jenseits der Akten," *Die Zeit*, October 30, 2003). In his latest book, Benz writes off the customary interpretation as legend without citing any source. Wolfgang Benz, *Der deutsche Widerstand gegen Hitler* (Munich: Beck, 2014), 65–66. However, this indicates that Benz now sees it as necessary to include "Rosenstrasse" in a book on resistance, although his earlier treatments do not (i.e., Wolfgang Benz and Walter H. Pehle, eds., *Encyclopedia of German Resistance to the Nazi Movement* (New York: Continuum, 1997). Reflecting treatments of the Rosenstrasse events in professional history at the time, Benz covered the history in several sentences, in his voluminous book on Jews in Nazi Germany published in 1989. He placed the events under a heading

of "Survival in the Underground, 1943–1945" rather than under "resistance." Wolfgang Benz, ed., *Die Juden in Deutschland: Leben unter Nationalsozialistisher Herrschaft* (Munich: C.H. Beck Verlag, 1989), 688. Still missing from these overviews on resistance are other important acts of public protest including the Witten protest examined by Julia Torrie and others. See Torrie's study in this book and "The Witten Protest and German Civilian Evacuations," *German Studies Review* 29, no. 2 (2006): 347–366.

90. Gruner, *Gedenkort Rosenstraße 2-4*. See Antonia Leugers' review at http://universaar.uni-saarland.de/journals/index.php/tg/article/viewArticle/536/575. Examples of the criticisms of his 2005 book are in Evan Burr Bukey, *Holocaust and Genocide Studies* 21, no. 2 (Fall 2007): 308–312; Leugers, "Widerstand gegen die Rosenstrasse"; Joachim Neander, review of "Gruner, Wolf: *Widerstand in der Rosenstrasse*," March 2, 2006, http://hsozkult.geschichte.hu-berlin.de/rezensionen/2006-1-145; Nathan Stoltzfus, *American Historical Review* 1 (2007): 1628–1629.

91. Gruner, *Widerstand*, 52–55. For arguments about the definitiveness of this single document for this school see also Gruner, "Ein Historikerstreit?" 5–22. Antonia Leugers points out that Gruner has entirely misinterpreted the heading of this document, "Vorgang: ohne" which is a matter of internal communication and not a comment on the nature of the arrests, as Gruner writes. Leugers has found a variety of serious errors in Gruner's account, and his unwillingness to debate his position. Leugers, "Widerstand gegen die Rosenstraße: Kritische Anmerkungen zu einer Neuerscheinung von Wolf Gruner," *theologie.geschichte: Zeitschrift für Theologie und Kulturgeschichte* 1 (2006), Münster 2008, 131-205, here 177–181, 190; Gruner, "Ein Historikerstreit?" 10–12.

92. In November 1942, the deportation expert Alois Brunner had arrested everyone he suspected of being Jewish, and even though he checked their identification on this spot, this led to such an uproar of protest among non-Jews that Brunner was forced to begin working from the Gestapo's card file to find out where Jews lived, before arresting anyone. Hildegard Henschel, "Aus der Arbeit der Jüdischen Gemeinde Berlin während der Jahre 1941–1943: Gemeindearbeit und Evakuierung von Berlin, 16. Oktober 1941–16 Juni 1943" *Zeitschrift für die Geschichte der Juden* 9 (1972): 33–52, here 43–44.

93. In an effort to reduce what the SS considered to be an overgrown number of Jews protected by their employment with the Berlin Jewish Community, Eichmann's deputy Rolf Günther had asked the Berlin Community authorities to select some five hundred Berlin Jews employed by the community for deportation to Auschwitz on October 26, 1942. Elisabeth Kraus, *Die Familie Mosse: deutsch-jüdisches Bürgertum im 19. und 20. Jahrhundert* (Munich: C.H.Beck Verlag, 1999), 580; ed., Annagrette Ehmann, et al., eds., *Die Grunewald-Rampe: die Deportation der Berliner Juden* (Berlin: Berlin: Landesbildstelle Berlin, 1993), 39.

94. The words "set free" and "released" which RSHA and other officials used to describe the fate of those at Rosenstrasse, are better suited to captives than to persons who are having their identities checked or being reviewed for a job selection.

95. Gruner, *Widerstand*, 121.

96. Gruner explained that the Gestapo had taken children from their homes and locked them up at Rosenstrasse "so they would not be left alone at home when

their parents were arrested." Gruner, *Widerstand*, 109. See Leugers, *Widerstand*, 188. Already during the 1980s there were reports on the Weigert child imprisoned at Rosenstrasse, who in turn had remembered seeing other children held there as well. Stoltzfus, *Resistance*, 219.

97. Gruner, *Widerstand*, 194.
98. Hilberg, *Destruction*, vol. 2, 448–449. Peter Fritzsche, *Life and Death in the Third Reich* (Cambridge, Ma.: Harvard University Press, 2008), 207.
99. Adler, *Der verwaltete Mensch*, 202, Adler makes the same judgment on page 340, and in his *Theresienstadt 1941–1945: Das Antlitz einer Zwangsgemeinschaft* (Tübingen: Mohr, 1955), 775.
100. Gruner, *Widerstand*, 61.
101. Longerich, *Holocaust*, 562n 37.
102. Gruner, *Widerstand*, 135.
103. Kershaw, *Hitler: Nemesis*, 480.
104. Meyer also concludes that the regime intended to deport intermarried Jews, one group at a time. Meyer, *Jüdische Mischlinge*, 58.
105. *Goebbels diary*, part II, vol, 8, entry for April 18, 1943. The reason that the overwhelming number of Jews imprisoned at Rosenstrasse were men, rather than women, was that men in mixed marriages were much more likely to be non-privileged, and thus wear the Star; German Jewish women married to Gentile men were almost all "privileged."
106. Gruner, *Widerstand*, 202. Gruner sees the "legend" originating in a single article printed in a Berlin newspaper for women and human rights: Georg Zivier, "Aufstand der Frauen," *Sie*, December 1945.
107. Christopher R. Browning, *Remembering Survival: Inside a Nazi Slave Labor Camp* (New York: Norton, 2010), 8–12, reports on the importance of using oral history to write a history otherwise inaccessible.
108. "Wanderredner," 38 0396, in *Regimekritik, Widerstand und Verfolgung in Deutschland und den besetzten Gebieten: Meldungen und Berichte aus dem Geheimen Staatspolizeiamt, dem SD-Hauptamt der SS und dem Reichssicherheitshauptamt 1933–1945*, ed. Heinz Boberach, in cooperation with the Bundesarchiv, K.G. Saur, 2003 (microfiche edition). This recent enormous collection of police reports (Gestapo and SD), pairing resistance with persecution under one title, does identify some incidents of popular "protest" and "demonstrations," although only in other countries. Under these categories for Germany, incidents of public protest and demonstrations are taken from what the regime categorized as "Enemy Propaganda." But, of course, not all the records of public protests in Germany can be attributed to "enemy propaganda." An SD secret police account of November 18, 1943, for example, covers a public protest staged by three hundred women in Witten on October 11, 1943, in considerable detail, within a report titled "Contemporary Events and the Impact on the Morale and Behavior of Women." Curiously, although this collection includes many SD reports, it apparently does not include this one on public protests by women in the Ruhr area in October 1943 that caused regime leaders to make concessions rather than punish the protesters. The original index makes no reference to it that I could find.
109. Hilberg, *Destruction*, vol. 2, 443.

110. This effort to influence the Volk to comply without upsetting the Volk was mirrored in Nazi policy throughout the war regarding the wartime evacuation of civilians from cities under attack from the Allied air forces as well. See Julia Torrie, *For Their Own Good: Civilian Evacuations in France and Germany* (New York: Berghahn Books, 2010).
111. Robert Graham, S.J., sent me Lehfeldt's report immediately after I published "'Jemand war für mich da': Der Aufstand der Frauen in der Rosenstrasse," Dossier, *Die Zeit*, no. 30, July 21, 1989 (International edition, July 28, 1989).
112. Antonia Leugers, "Mordpläne offen vor der Welt: Gerhard Lehfeldt als Mahner der Kirchen im März 1943," *theologie.geschichte* 8 (2013). http://universaar.uni-saarland.de/journals/index.php/tg/article/view/534/573.
113. Andreas Nachama, "Vorwort," Wolf Gruner, *Gedenkort Rosenstraße 2 - 4. Internierung und Protest im NS-Staat* (Berlin: Hentrich & Hentrich, 7 - 8). Rudy Koshar, *From Monuments to Traces: Artifacts of German Memory, 1870–1990* (Berkeley: University of California, 2000), 266.
114. Herbert Marcuse, writing for an H-German Forum discussion on Rosenstrasse, said that: "Now we really need to ask why German historians so utterly beyond reproach would stubbornly minimize the impact of public protest . . . I would suggest that what I call a legacy of the "myth of resistance" may be at work here . . . the postwar claim by many Germans that, inasmuch as they knew about Nazi crimes, and within the limits of acceptable risk, they had attempted to resist the regime. Many websites show that her opinion is widely shared by other Germans, including http://www.rosenstrasse-protest.de/, and http://www.h-net.org/~german/discuss/Rosenstrasse/Rosenstrasse_index.htm.
115. For years before this 2013 publication, Topographie's website had taken the same position, stating despite all the German experts who disagree and have provided evidence for disagreement that the Gestapo never intended to deport any of the Jews at Rosenstrasse ("die aufgrund ihres "geschützten" Status nicht in diese Deportationen eingeschlossen waren"). http://www.topographie.de/en/rosen.htm, accessed October 21, 2008. Topographie does not acknowledge the opinions of other accomplished German historians, such as Joachim Neander and Antonia Leugers, who wrote in 2013 that as a site of public memory Topographie des Terrors has a responsibility to "inform the public of the complexity of the Rosenstrasse events rather than declaring them settled in a one-sided way, and off-bounds to discussion." Antonia Leugers, review of Gruner, *Gedenkort Rosenstraße 2-4*. Although it is fully publicly funded, and in that sense represents official history, history the way Germans are supposed to know it, many concerned Germans disagree. See for example Professor Gerhard Schumm's website, www.rosenstrasse-protest.de.
116. Karl Jaspers, *The Question of German Guilt* (New York: Fordham University Press, 2001) 12.
117. Tony Judt, *Postwar: A History of Europe Since 1945* (New York: Penguin, 2005), 799, 829. Ernst Renan, quoted in Judt, *Postwar,* 803; Tony Judt, "The Past is another Country: Myth and Memory in Postwar Europe," in *The Politics of Retribution in Europe: World War II and Its Aftermath*, ed. István Deák, Jan T. Gross, and Tony Judt (Princeton, NJ: Princeton University Press, 2000), 315.

Afterword
Protest and Resistance

David Clay Large

Some twenty years ago a British journalist reviewing an essay collection on resistance within Germany to the Nazi regime opined that this topic merited only a very short book, because the "resistance" in question had been inconsequential at best.[1] (Interestingly, this assessment echoed the attitude toward domestic opposition to Hitler held by British political and military leaders during World War II).[2] German resistance to the Nazi regime may indeed have been inconsequential in the sense that, as we all know, none of the homegrown efforts to overthrow or even substantially weaken Hitler's dictatorship succeeded, and Nazism had to be crushed by military conquest. But the failure in this case certainly did not translate into insignificance—at least not for anyone who wants to know how the Third Reich functioned and how Hitler retained his hold on power. Moreover, the leaders of the Third Reich themselves certainly did not consider opposition to their rule in all its multifarious forms—from attempts to kill the Führer or spying for the enemy through public acts of group defiance down to simple individual non-conformism—as matters of little consequence. Ever vigilant regarding *any* threats to its aspiration for total control, the Hitler regime defined itself, at least in the domestic realm, largely through its efforts to deal with these threats.

Historians of the Third Reich have long been aware of the importance of internal opposition to Nazism, and over the years a small mountain of literature on this subject has grown up. Considering that our scholarly scrutiny of the Hitler era has gone on far longer than the Third Reich itself, even the historiography focused on domestic anti-Nazi opposition has developed a complicated internal history of its own, replete with intriguing twists and turns, and populated by factions and stakeholders with their own theories to push and scholarly turf to defend.[3] The sheer mass of this resistance literature is perhaps yet another reason to be thankful that the would-be "Thousand Year Reich" lasted only twelve.

This is hardly the place for a comprehensive re-navigation of the currents of resistance historiography, but one recent channel needs to be noted here, because it threatens to carry us away from some hard-won research terrain that warrants further, not reduced, exploration. In brief, this recent interpretive direction calls into question earlier arguments that the Nazi regime could be, and sometimes was, significantly influenced by bottom-up popular opposition to official policy. Falling back on yet earlier views of the Hitler government as a top-down, single-minded bureaucratic apparatus, and mindful of the undeniable fact that the regime enjoyed widespread backing from the national population, this line of thinking tends to dismiss examples of spontaneous group protest as ineffective and peripheral to the master narrative of popularly sanctioned control. In marginalizing localized, single-issue dissent on grounds of a purported lack of efficacy, this interpretive perspective is reminiscent of the above-mentioned denigration of homegrown anti-Nazi resistance as a whole.[4]

The purpose of this latest collection of original essays on domestic German protest in the Third Reich is not to defend an endangered patch of scholarly turf. Yet there has been sufficient muddying of interpretive waters to suggest the need for a thorough re-examination of the role of popular opposition during the Hitler era. Apart from calling, or re-calling, our attention to the signal importance of this issue, the essays collected here should help us better understand the specific character and dimensions of popular "resistance" within Germany to the Nazi tyranny.

At stake in this argument is not just our assessment of certain forms of domestic opposition in the Third Reich—namely, spontaneous non-violent civilian dissent focused on specific issues or grievances—but our appreciation of how the Nazi dictatorship worked and how it responded to internal challenges. We all know that the Hitler regime struck fear (and also awe) into the hearts of ordinary Germans, but much less appreciated is the extent to which the regime was itself running in fear of the very populace it so wanted, and needed, to control. This was especially true during the almost six-year period of war, when, with memories of breakdowns in the "Civil Truce" during World War I still vivid, maintaining home-front morale was perceived as absolutely crucial. Until that new war was won—or, just as crucially, until victory no longer seemed at all possible—the Nazi regime was prepared to make tactical concessions to certain kinds of popular protest, even at the cost of compromising cardinal tenants of ideology.

The body politic of the Third Reich can be said to have suffered from "raw nerves" in several places—sensitive regions where the regime was particularly vulnerable to critical prodding from malcontented citizens, provided the citizens in question were "Aryans" and their prodding was both non-violent and limited in scope. Timing was important too: opposition that might be tolerated, even accommodated, at one point could yield harsh retaliation at another.

Although, as the essays appearing in this volume suggest, the Nazi regime was most vulnerable to popular pressure during wartime, there was never a moment when the Hitler government was free of anxiety regarding its level of public support, and that anxiety could yield sudden reversals of policy when factors of timing and location conjoined to make manifestations of popular discontent seem particularly dangerous. The regime's embarrassing flip-flop in its treatment of Hans Meiser, a state bishop in the Bavarian branch of Germany's Evangelical (Protestant) Church, is a case in point. The Meiser affair, as Christiane Kuller explores it here, constituted the earliest example of a "successful" public protest action against an impolitic and deeply unpopular Nazi policy. Unlike better-known Protestant dissidents such as Martin Niemöller and Dietrich Bonhoffer, Bishop Meiser did not challenge the very fundaments of Nazi ideology and practice, but his insistence on clerical independence in doctrinal and organizational matters made him anathema to hyper-conformists in the so-called Reichskirche, above all Reichsbishof Ludwig Müller and his coterie of backers in Bavaria who favored the complete "coordination" of that state's Protestant institutions under the central authority in Berlin. In October 1934 Meiser suddenly found himself under house arrest, conveniently sidelined while one of this subordinates attempted to restructure the state church so as to make it more compliant with Berlin. It quickly became apparent, however, that Bavaria's Protestants were on the whole no more inclined to kowtow to this kind of bullying than their more numerous Catholic neighbors. Angry Bavarian Evangelicals not only disseminated written protests against the Meiser arrest; hundreds also traveled from Protestant enclaves in Franconia down to Munich to parade their grievances before the clerical and secular authorities. Faced with a "furor protestanticus" that showed no signs of abating, even Nazi zealots like Julius Streicher, the thuggish Gauleiter of Franconia, hastily backed away from the campaign against Meiser. Moreover, what may have seemed initially like a tempest in a teapot soon gained international resonance when Protestant luminaries from abroad, even the archbishop of Canterbury, weighed in on the matter. The Meiser affair took on such significance that Hitler himself had to get involved. Tellingly, after two weeks of policy-limbo he saw to it that Meiser was not only released from house arrest but fully rehabilitated.

In analyzing the motivation behind the Nazi regime's behavior in the Meiser case, Kuller emphasizes several factors: confusion and ambivalence on the part of the authorities regarding their handling of the Bavarian Evangelical Church and its prickly state bishop; solid patriotic and loyalist credentials on the part of the protesters; alarm among top Nazi officials that the protest could, if not placated, turn into a full-scale revolt; worry, too, that the affair could have repercussions outside its immediate environs—above all in the impending referendum in the Saar state regarding that border entity's relationship with the Reich. Yet Kuller insists, in my view rightly, that the regime's precipitous back down in the Meiser case should not be dismissed as a minor clerical kerfuffle. It constituted, she maintains, a massive loss of prestige and power for the embryonic Reichskirche and a genuine setback for Nazi efforts at full *Gleichschaltung* in religious affairs. And, as will become apparent from other examples of "successful" public protest discussed in this volume, the Meiser case might be seen as a kind of template for the whole phenomenon of limited or single-issue domestic opposition to governmental policy during the Third Reich.

As we know, after some rocky patches during his first years of rule Hitler managed effectively to consolidate his hold and power and achieve some astonishing successes in the domestic and foreign spheres, such as curbing mass unemployment via public works projects and rearmament; remilitarizing the Rhineland; staging the 1936 Olympic Games; and integrating his former homeland of Austria into the German Reich. But although all these triumphs were achieved peacefully, the Nazi state from the outset was oriented toward war, and Hitler would indeed launch the military crusade that segued into World War II less than seven years after taking power—and, arguably, well before the country was ready for sustained global warfare. Of course, the onset of war in 1939 brought added pressures on citizens of the Reich to conform to governmental dicta; but, by the same token, the stresses of prolonged military conflict also made maintaining strong morale at home all the more imperative. And as the rigors of war grew evermore stressful, the Nazi regime's "raw nerves," those parts of the body politic especially susceptible to painful irritation, became increasingly exposed.

One of those highly sensitive policy regions involved state-mandated euthanasia: the killing off of all those whom the Nazi authorities dismissed as "*lebens-unwertes Leben*" (life unworthy of life). As Winfried Süß points out in his contribution to this volume, the Hitler regime's programs of forced sterilization and euthanasia, though meant to be clandestine, had generated domestic criticism, especially from German Catholics, as soon as they became known. Yet it was the pressure of a long war, with its imperatives of solid support from the home front, which gradually empowered clerical critics of this murderous policy and finally yielded major revisions in the ways in which Hitler's medical minions dealt with those the state considered unfit to live.

Before the war, and even in its earliest stage, the German Catholic hierarchy, while opposed to Nazi policies like forced sterilization, abortion, and above all euthanasia, had been somewhat indecisive and largely ineffective in its criticism. As Süß makes clear, the major reason for this was the church's reluctance to make its opposition public for fear of losing its central and (to it) valuable position within the German public health system. Yet where the Catholic hierarchy failed—and indeed continued to fail even after war broke out—to exercise its moral authority vis-à-vis the regime, some individual priests, supported by a tenaciously resilient Catholic lay community, showed that traditions of decency and humanity had not entirely given way to the dictates of clerical Realpolitik. The key figure here was Clemens August Count von Galen, bishop of Münster, whose impassioned public denunciation of euthanasia in August 1941 ignited a firestorm of public opposition to this loathsome policy. Tellingly, as Süß reminds us, Galen was a relatively young cleric—and one his elders tended to dismiss as a "theological lightweight." Yet there was nothing shallow or lightweight about the three seminal sermons he delivered in the summer of 1941—jeremiads that began with protests against regime harassment of Catholic institutions and culminated with a full-throated denunciation of euthanasia. Galen's voice might not have resonated so loudly, however, had it not been for two factors: growing popular frustration with the regime for its failure to protect civilians from Allied bombing; and the willingness, indeed anxiousness, of individual Catholic laypeople (and later non-Catholics as well) to duplicate and disseminate copies of Galen's firebrand sermons. It was the tenacity and breadth of this Samizdat-like campaign that saved it, and Galen himself, from effective countermeasures by the authorities. On the advice of Goebbels, Hitler decided not to punish Galen for fear that doing so might spark an open revolt among German Catholics. Crucially, in the wake of Galen's attacks, Hitler even ordered the suspension of the Reich's main euthanasia program, codenamed "T4" after the district in Berlin where it was headquartered. The Galen case should remind us, once again, that a regime that lived by popular acclamation persistently feared that it might just as easily die from a lack of same. Better then, to put off the "Galen problem" until after the war, when it might also be possible to resume getting rid of all that accumulated "life unworthy of life."

Euthanasia policy also figures prominently in Gerhard Weinberg's meditation on the practices and procedures of Nazi mass murder during the Holocaust—and the public opposition these policies engendered. Systematic killing of the sort that Hitler advocated from the outset of his political career could not proceed in earnest until the world war, when mass slaughter on the battlefield offered a rationale (and, for a time, a cover) for mass slaughter of pre-selected victim groups at home. Before the Nazis embarked on their campaign to exterminate Europe's Jews, they honed their killing procedures by practicing on "defective" newborn infants, as well as physically or mentally handicapped children and adults. As the war began generating large numbers of badly wounded soldiers, some of these helpless creatures, too, found themselves in the discard bin. Like Christiane Kuller and Winfried Süß, Weinberg notes that the Nazi euthanasia program had generated considerable popular opposition from the outset, when its victims were all "civilians." Thus it is hardly surprising that the extension of this program to badly maimed veterans sparked outcries of indignation. Soon even the Nazis had to recognize that clearing the decks of armless and legless heroes was not the best morale booster in time of war, when of course the list of the maimed was growing longer by the day. In the interest of averting possible public protest, the government halted its centralized soldier-euthanasia program—although some killing apparently continued on an ad hoc basis under the cover of strict secrecy. It is Weinberg's contention that considerations of home-front morale were so crucial in this case that the mere *prospect* of public opposition, not necessarily actual manifestations of popular protest, yielded the change in policy.

According to Weinberg, fears of a negative impact on wartime morale seem also to have played a role in another area of high "sensitivity" for the Nazi regime: its treatment of *Mischlinge* (partial Jews) and Jews married to "Aryan" spouses. Why, he asks, didn't the Hitler government ghettoize, deport, and execute these people wholesale the way it did full Jews or Jews without marital ties to the non-Jewish community?

Yet another patch of wartime policy-terrain requiring some delicate maneuvering (never, it must be said, a strong suit of the Nazis) had to do with the evacuation of women and children from industrial regions subject to heavy bombing by the British (and later) Americans. The Ruhr District town of Witten certainly fell into this category. After the city had come under repeated attack in 1942 and early 1943, the Gauleiter responsible for the area ordered the wholesale evacuation of civilian dependents to rural regions in Baden, Pomerania, and the Sudetenland. While the policy of moving vulnerable dependents out of harm's way made good sense (the British government pursued a similar policy during the Blitz), it generated considerable resentment among the evacuees because it typically entailed splitting up families (husbands employed in war-related industries stayed behind) and required extended billeting among strangers whose customs seemed alien and whose welcome for the newcomers was anything but warm. (The sense of dislocation experienced by citified Ruhr District folk forced to live among the farmers of Baden reminds one of Thomas Mann's fictional "Toni" Buddenbrook, a proud daughter of Lübeck who cannot adjust to the weird ways of her new husband's rustic relatives in Bavaria.) In an ill-advised effort to prevent malcontented evacuees from returning to their homes, Nazi officials often tied food-ration privileges to the assigned places of evacuation, thus effectively denying sustenance to people, mainly women and their children, who chose to go back to their home regions. But since this draconian rationing policy was likely to add to the growing disgruntlement on the home front, some Nazi officials elected not to apply it at all, while others did so selectively. Such inconsistency, of course, only compounded the sense of grievance among those who did not benefit from the ad hoc leniency.

The Hitler regime's problematic evacuation and rationing policies provided the immediate backdrop for one of the most significant (albeit least known) instances of successful civilian protest during the Third Reich: the Witten women's demonstration of October 11, 1943. In her contribution to our volume, Julia S. Torrie puts this seminal moment in proper historical context, revealing how a wartime protest of some three hundred Witten women forced one of Hitler's regional satraps to alter prevailing policy regarding food rationing for evacuees who had defied the law by returning home. Crucially, the police called in to break up the women's demonstration refused to do so because they sympathized with the women's cause and were disinclined to use force against fellow townsfolk. Smaller scenes of protest over evacuation/rationing policy took place in other Ruhr towns, leading a shocked SS security officer to report, "The abuse of official and leading persons was on the agenda."[5]

As Torrie makes clear, the Witten episode had several features in common with other successful civilian protests, including the opposition to the government euthanasia programs, public campaigns against the removal of crucifixes from schoolrooms in Bavaria, and, most famously, the protest in Berlin's Rosenstrasse by "Aryan" wives against the incarceration and possible deportation of their Jewish husbands. In all these cases, the actors were racially approved members of the German Volk; the actions took place in the public domain and in full view of other citizens; the demonstrations were largely spontaneous and focused on single, relatively easily resolvable issues; the grievances in question were rooted in readily understandable religious and/or family concerns that allowed the protestors, in effect, to hoist the Nazi regime on its own "family values" petard; the policies under attack were confused and did not enjoy consistent or unqualified support even among their sponsors and supposed enforcers; and the actions occurred in a time of war when maintaining home-front morale seemed more crucial than ever.

While the limited nature and scope of these protest actions helps explain why they could be successful, these conditioning factors do not significantly reduce the protests' historical importance. After all, public group-protest of any sort was strictly illegal, and the very appearance of such demonstrations, let alone their efficacy, compromised the Nazi regime's cherished principle of full control over popular behavior. This is why the government took them so seriously. To the historian, these episodes reveal with especial clarity how a regime that made so much of operating according to the "will of the people" simply could not afford to thwart manifestations of popular will. We see too, that the protests had the additional effect of exacerbating internal divisions within the Nazi leadership, thereby rendering consistent or "total" control even less likely. In such instances of internal dispute, the regime typically fell back on its primary default mechanism: i.e., a "final" decision by the Führer himself. Obsessed with memories of breakdowns in home-front morale during World War I, Hitler tended to take an accommodationist way out. It was certainly a bad sign for the Third Reich when Adolf Hitler became the chief voice of reason. Yet of course Hitler's relative "leniency" was motivated exclusively by short-term tactical calculations. The timing considerations that helped condition these protests' successes also pointed up their limitations in the longer run. Once the prospects for victory had dimmed so far that morale boosting was no longer a priority, any willingness to turn a blind eye to civilian dissidence evaporated.

While the Witten women's protest has largely slipped under the radar of historians of the Third Reich, the Rosenstrasse protest certainly has not. After a long silence about this seminal episode on the German home front during World War II, historians, most notably Nathan Stoltzfus, turned the Rosenstrasse demonstration into exhibit number one for the argument that such acts of popular protest were crucial moments in the history of National Socialism. With Stoltzfus's widely read and highly regarded study, *Resistance of the Heart: Intermarriage and the Rosenstrasse Protest in Nazi Germany*,[6] appreciation for the importance of this particular act of public protest, and for public opposition to Nazism in general, took on among historians of Nazi Germany what lawyers like to call "stare decisis"—settled law.

But the very prominence and apparent consensus-quality of this new perspective made it an attractive target for contrarians on the lookout for an established "myth" to puncture. Puncturing myths, of course, is not only the professional historian's right but also his/her duty, so it's certainly not acceptable to take issue with the project of subjecting the arguments by Stoltzfus and others to rigorous scrutiny. But does the scrutiny in this case stand up to similar scrutiny applied toward *it*? This is the question investigated by two contributors to this volume: Antonia Leugers and Joachim Neander.

Without going into the details of Leugers and Neander's dissection of the historian Wolf Gruner's critique of Stoltzfus' central thesis (that's best left up to the contributors themselves), some general points need to be made here. As with their regulations on evacuation and food rationing, the Nazi authorities' policies regarding "racial" intermarriage—that is, full Jews married to gentiles—showed ample signs of indecision, confusion, and inconsistency. As we know, according to governmental plans, Jews married to "Aryans" were not supposed to be deported to camps in the East, at least during the early phases of the war. But if the Jewish husband's "German" wife had converted to Judaism, and the man himself had technical expertise that might be of use in one of the camps, deportation was not only possible but likely, even early on.[7] By the time of the so-called Fabrik-Aktion of February 1943, the regime was apparently prepared to remove all Jews, including those with gentile wives, from war-related work in Berlin and send them to the East. Joachim Neander's essay argues persuasively that in the "push-pull" calculus surrounding the deportation of Jews from the Reich, the "pull" of Auschwitz was decisive given that camp's chronic need for labor. But even in the unlikely event that the authorities did not intend to deport the Jewish men interned in the Rosenstrasse collection center, the protest by these men's wives would be of signal importance. The willingness of hundreds of gentile women to break the law by openly and loudly protesting day after day in the street tells us something important about popular attitudes toward authority at this time and place, while the authorities' unwillingness to use violence to end a public act of defiance is just as revealing regarding the mindset of the putative enforcers. In the immediate wake of the bitter loss at Stalingrad, the regime seems not to have been willing to risk further eroding home-front morale by using violence against "Aryan" women whose only "crime" was to be married to a Jew, and whose only purpose in demonstrating was to get their men back into the bosom of hearth and home. Although, as with Witten and other acts of single-issue protest, the limited purpose and scope of the Rosenstrasse demonstration was absolutely critical to its very existence, not to mention its success, this action *did* constitute a notable challenge to Nazi authority. It is hard to imagine a similar protest being allowed in Stalin's Moscow in the middle of the war. And when a similarly non-violent protest action against Chinese governmental policy materialized some forty-six years later at Beijing's Tiananmen Square, we know what happened. For that matter, we might also reflect on what happened to peaceful demonstrators in countries like Egypt, Libya, and (especially) Syria during the so-called Arab Spring. Of course, Nazi Germany never experienced a "spring" of any kind, not even a "Springtime for Hitler."

The fact that it was *women*, or mainly women, who took the risk of mounting public protests against various Nazi policies, is itself a matter of genuine importance. Of course, we cannot conclude from this that German women as a whole were disinclined to back Nazi authority and to support official doctrine, however noxious. We have long known that women played important roles in the Third Reich and even in the workings of the

Holocaust. Recent research, focusing on thousands of ordinary German women who willingly went out to the occupied eastern territories during the war, suggests that the female contribution to Nazi genocide might have been even greater than previously thought.[8] Yet in the end, women were more likely than men to be on the front lines of whatever public protest activity materialized during the Third Reich. Although, as Jill Stephenson points out in her contribution to this volume, all such protest was "political" in Nazi eyes, it was easier for women to come across as less politicized in their motives and actions than their male counterparts. After all, women, especially in the National Socialist perspective, were thought to be slaves to their emotions, animated preeminently by "private" feelings connected to home, family, and faith. Thus, even when openly defying the regime, they might be dismissed as relatively non-threatening.

This of course did not mean that women who stood up to the regime in a serious way were necessarily spared the grim punishment typically meted out to male resisters. Most famously, Sophie Scholl met the same fate as her brother Hans—execution by guillotine—for distributing anti-Nazi leaflets over several months between summer 1942 and early 1943 in the city of Munich, the "Capital of the [Nazi] Movement." Toward the end of the war, as major German cities like Munich were being overrun by Allied troops, women who waved the white flag of surrender in defiance of governmental orders were sometimes shot or hanged. But even in less desperate times, women who in any way took public stances against Reich policy risked serious punishment because of the Nazi system's essential unpredictability.

If women dominated the ranks of public protest in the Third Reich, this was not unusual: over the ages, and especially during time of war, it has been the womenfolk in any given polity who typically have been foremost in decrying the brutalities and privations they and their loved ones were forced to endure. There is good reason for this: when wars break out the menfolk get to go off and kill and rape and pillage, while the womenfolk and their children are obliged to stay home to be killed, raped, and pillaged.

It has also been women's fate, as Katharina von Kellenbach reminds us in her contribution, to have their oppositional activities marginalized or forgotten by the men who have kept the record books. This marginalization is all the easier because, whether we are speaking of the female followers of Jesus, the Argentine mothers at the Plaza de Mayo protesting the fate of their "disappeared" sons and daughters, or the gentiles wives of the Rosenstrasse Jews, women's actions can be relegated to the private or family sphere, regions long ignored in the annals of official historiography. The argument that women's resistance might have been as "political" as any other form of public opposition, and also just as efficacious, just as capable of generating significant change in state policy, runs so counter to traditional notions of the proper female place in the body politic that it has spawned considerable resistance of its own.

The fact that single-issue protest of the sort investigated in this volume is now threatened with renewed scholarly marginalization brings to mind an earlier tendency among some students of German anti-Nazi resistance to admit only those actors determined to destroy the Third Reich—and to risk their lives trying to do so—into their sacred canon of "Resistance." As Klemens von Klemperer once wrote, individuals or groups who practiced partial "refusal" or opposition while generally conforming to the mandates of the Hitler regime must not be confused with the "real" practitioners of resistance. Historians, he wrote, must not allow the "weed" of partial opposition "to take over and to smother . . . that precious plant in our garden, true resistance to tyranny."[9] No doubt there *are* important distinctions to be made when we examine the phenomenon of opposition to the Third Reich, or, for that matter, to any dictatorship. Yet it is also useful to remember, as the contributors to this volume would have us do, that, just as the Nazis defined who was a Jew, it was *they* who defined who was a resister.

In my view, moreover, the Nazis were on to something here. Hitler and his satraps knew that the greatest danger to their kind of "consensual dictatorship" came not from the few extraordinarily courageous individuals who were determined to topple the entire system, but from those whose more limited opposition challenged the vision, the mystique, of a movement enjoying unqualified popular support. Paradoxically, the Nazi regime's huge investment in the ideal of consensual control made it especially vulnerable to actions with a potential to disrupt that ideal. This is why one of the great tragedies of the Third Reich is that there were not a lot more Rosenstrasses, a lot more Wittens. Yet it would be unhistorical to argue that there should have been more of these actions. On the one hand, the regime *did* enjoy widespread popular support, even in time of war; on the other, as we emphasized above, *all* opposition was risky, and it was impossible to know how the authorities would respond in any given case. No one disputes that what Colonel Count Claus von Stauffenberg, the Wehrmacht officer who tried unsuccessfully to kill Hitler with a time bomb on July 20, 1944, did was "resistance."[10] Most of us would be equally *disinclined* to employ that term for what General Kurt von Hammerstein did—bitch about the Nazis in private but keep his mouth shut in public. On the other hand, the activities of Hammerstein's two daughters, who secretly recorded Hitler's plans for dictatorship and sent them on to Moscow, surely qualifies as resistance.[11] Was the defiance displayed by the Rosenstrasse and Witten women also resistance? And what about the drunken Parisienne who, seeing bemedaled

German officers feasting at Fouquet's, yelled at them, "Eh, bien, moi, je vous dis MERDE!"[12]

In the end, perhaps, it doesn't matter so much what *we* call all those thousands of daily acts of defiance, or, for that matter, the relatively few larger-scale demonstrations of public opposition of the kind examined in this book. What matters is what the Nazi regime thought of them, and how it responded to the challenge they represented.

David Clay Large is professor emeritus in the Department of History at Montana State University and a prolific historian. His most notable books include *Where Ghosts Walked: Munich's Road to the Third Reich* (New York: WW Norton, 1997), *Nazi Games: The Olympics of 1936* (New York, WW Norton: 2007), and *Berlin* (New York: Basic Books, 2000).

Notes

1. Review of David Clay Large, ed., *Contending With Hitler: Varieties of German Resistance in the Third Reich* (New York, 1991). The review in question appeared in *The Economist* in 1991.
2. Eugen Gerstenmeier, *Streit und Friede hat seine Zeit: Ein Lebensbild* (Frankfurt, 1981), 322.
3. For a recent assessment of some of the relevant resistance literature, see Jill Stephenson, "Resistance and the Third Reich," *Journal of Contemporary History* 36, no. 1 (2001): 507–516; Gerd R. Ueberschär, *Für ein anderes Deutschland: Der deutsche Widerstand gegen den NS-Staat 1933–1945* (Frankfurt, 2006).
4. For references to this literature, see the notes in the contribution to this volume by Antonia Leugers.
5. Heinz Boberach, ed., *Meldungen aus dem Reich: Die geheime Lageberichte des Sicherheitsdienstes der SS*, 17 vols. (Hersching, 1984), vol. 15, 6,030.
6. Nathan Stoltzfus, *Resistance of the Heart: Intermarriage and the Rosenstrasse Protest in Nazi Germany* (New York, 1996).
7. Such was the case with a talented chemist named Dr. Max Schohl, whose "Aryan" wife, having converted to Judaism after their marriage, was unable to prevent his deportation to Auschwitz in summer 1942. He died there in December 1943. See David Clay Large, *And the World Closed Its Doors: The Story of One Family Abandoned to the Holocaust* (New York, 2003).
8. See "Women's Role in Holocaust May Exceed Old Notions," *New York Times*, July 18, 2010, 8. This article focuses primarily on recent work by the American historian Wendy Lower.
9. Klemens von Klemperer, "The Solitary Witness: No Mere Footnote to Resistance Studies," in Large, *Contending With Hitler*, 135.
10. On Stauffenberg and his brothers, see Peter Hoffmann, *Stauffenberg: A Family History, 1905–1944* (Cambridge, 1995).

11. On Kurt von Hammerstein and his daughters, see Hans Magnus Enzensberger, *The Silences of Hammerstein: A German Story* (New York, 2010).
12. Charles S. Glass, *Americans in Paris: Life and Death Under Nazi Occupation* (New York, 2010), 113.

Appendix 1

The Situation of the "*Mischlinge*" in Germany, Mid-March 1943*

[A report written in mid March 1943 by Gerhard Lehfeldt[1]].

The endangered non-Aryans can be divided into four groups:[2]

1. Religious Jews and full Jews baptized as Christians who are also married to full Jews. (Wear the Star [of David])
2. Full Jews baptized as Christians who are married to an Aryan spouse and live in a mixed marriage without children. (Men wear the Star)
3. Full Jews baptized as Christians who live in a mixed marriage with an Aryan spouse and share children (privileged mixed marriages).
4. *Mischlinge* of the first degree (Christian-raised offspring from a mixed marriage) (children of mixed parentage raised Jewish qualify as "Jews")

According to the Nuremberg laws, Non-Aryans #1-3 [from the above list] are considered "Jewish" without regard to their religion or whether they are married to an Aryan. Like the Aryans, *"Mischlinge* of the first degree" also own so-called temporary national civil rights. According to law, they are only *supposed* to be expelled from some occupations and are permitted to marry an Aryan only with special permission. Otherwise, they should be treated like Aryans.

While the group of Jews identified under #1 (aside from few exceptions), were already deported towards the end of 1942, in regard to groups #2 and #3 considerations were given because of the Aryan spouse. Towards the end of the previous year, radicals under the leadership of Dr. Goebbels[3] insisted on a termination [forced divorce] of mixed marriages and—despite a forceful protest[4] by the Cardinal-Archbishop Bertram[5] in Breslau—the Aryan spouse was, in many cases, snatched away from their partner, driven through the city like a criminal and interned in the synagogue in preparation for deportation. Initially, this only happened in childless mixed marriages. According to a statement made by Minister Director Gritzback[6] (adjutant of

Göring⁷), at the end of December 1942, mixed marriages without children should be initially separated while the privileged mixed marriages should not be affected. However, as the Reich's military situation worsened considerably in January 1943,[8] the radicals once again insisted on the separation of the privileged mixed marriages as well and the deportation (*i.e. murder*— emphasis added) of the Jewish spouse. In the meantime, the plan was made to ship the *"Mischlinge* of the first degree" to labor assignments –undoubtedly as well for the purpose of extermination. The *Mischling* law in question,[9] which had already been written, is a draft made by the Ob[er]sturmbannführer Eichmann, Director of the Resettlement Department of the Reich Main Security Office on the Kurfürstenstraße in Berlin. Eichmann is also the director of the deportation of the Jews. This *Mischling* law was justified with the claim that it was necessary to make sexual intercourse impossible between those of mixed parentage and, especially, between *Mischlinge* and Aryans. The intent was also even to separate marriages between *Mischlinge* and Aryans, even though 75% of their blood was of pure Ayran descent and the marriage could only produce children who would be admitted into German society as 75% Aryans anyway. At the beginning of December 1942, Eichmann stated that the *Mischling* law has been "delayed by three months."

Directly after the fevered speech made by Dr. Goebbels on 1.30.1943,[10] mass *Judenaktionen*[11] began in Berlin, in which thousands of Jews from privileged mixed marriages were arrested and taken from their spouse by the armed SS—and were publicly evacuated on trucks. There were heart-rending sights happening everywhere. In many cases, even though many Jews were being abused in other places, the people publicly took the Jews' side.[12] Occasionally, in connection with this action, the persons of mixed blood of the first degree were also suddenly arrested and were transported along with the Jews on the trucks like felons. Eichmann commented on this that the *Mischlinge* would not be placed together with the Jews at the same gathering place, but rather brought to a place on Rosenstaße in Berlin. From this statement it appears that the arrest of the *Mischlinge* cannot have been a matter of [someone] overreaching authority, but rather it occurred as a result of a planned action. Indeed, it had already been suspected that boisterous protests against this terror, especially against the separation of married couples, would occur. For this reason, attempts were made to cover up the action in the following way:

Eichmann reported that from the Eastern front, 9000 men had been requested with great urgency to build an embankment. Thus he had arrested the remaining Jew, and because this was not sufficient, he had to fall back on the *Mischlinge* of the first degree. Thus [according to Eichmann] this was not a matter of deportation but rather a matter of deploying workers.[13]

This is a poor subterfuge considering the fact that the action precisely matched the law drawn up by Eichmann in December 1942. Through this law, he wanted to separate the male *Mischlinge* from their Aryan wives. In addition, the Gestapo has nothing to do with the deployment of workers. However, even if the laborers had been needed, it would have been sufficient to order the presence of the workers at the employment office via postcard rather than having them publicly driven through the city on trucks by armed SS people like felons. For those who were affected, it is a blessing from God that actions were taken since otherwise the Mischlinge would have been sent in the usual way to forced labor in Poland. Then they would have been discretely exterminated there, and their advocates would have never been able to convince the public of the seriousness of the situation. But as it turned out, fate was in their favor and the murderous plans were publicly spread across the globe.

On Friday, March 5, 1943, public riots broke out on Münchenerstraße in Berlin as someone snatched the wife of a seventy year old man from the couple's apartment. The seventy year old man screamed for an entire hour, "This is a cultural disgrace! Bomb every house, bomb every house!" He was then arrested and it is doubtful whether he is still alive. These riots were, to be sure, quite unpleasant for Mr. Goebbels.[14] As a result, quite a few of the arrested were released on Saturday, 6 March 1943. As expected, this was then explained as a matter of overreaching authority. Equally predictable, Eichmann and his deputy remained in office. It is to be feared that the campaign will now be continued in secrecy, posing great danger for those affected.

The explanation that this entire sequence of events happened only due to the overreaching authority was also issued by the Ministry of the Interior; there it was also claimed that Minister Dr. Frick[15] had personally arranged the termination of the actions. A few weeks ago, a meeting was said to have taken place for the SS unit *Leibstandarte*[16] in Berlin's Pharus Hall, where the rallying cry was sounded that the Jews are to be killed. The SS was then said to have acted on its own authority and initiated the campaign of its own accord. The *Mischlinge* who had been captured and transported to concentration camps were those types of persons who had been reported to the SS or Gestapo for having behaved in a subversive manner or were termed particularly disagreeable elements. This was the extent of the given explanation!

Here is a short summary of the rebuttal:
1. If the action had been a matter of overreaching authority, then the wrongdoers would have had to be removed from office.
2. If the SS had acted on its own without further authority, then the Gestapo would not have been present at each and every arrest.

3. If on the other hand the Gestapo had acted on its own authority, then the *Obersturmbannführer* Eichmann would not have had announced this beforehand.
4. If it had not been intended that *Mischlinge* be arrested, then there would not have been a need to provide a special building for their accommodation (Rosenstrasse).
5. Even mixed Jews from other cities who by chance happened to be visiting Berlin were arrested. Hence, mixed Jews who were described (by whom, by the way?) to the Gestapo as having a somewhat disagreeable character were by no means the only ones arrested,
6. All of the editors from the Swedish press received a phone call from the Propaganda Ministry before the beginning of the campaign, and told that if they should notice particular actions taking place in Berlin during the next few days, it would be forbidden for them to print anything about it in their pages!!

Notes

*Copy in private archives of Nathan Stoltzfus, from the late Robert A. Graham SJ. Rome. The footnotes here have been added. A *Mischling* is a person with both Jewish and non-Jewish ancestry.

1. Gerhard Julius Eugen Lehfeldt was born on December 31, 1897, in Magdeburg, Germany, and died in Schöneberg, West Berlin, in 1976. His parents were Jewish. On August 16, 1915, he joined the Infantry Regiment 82 Göttingen. A war injury in July 1917 paralyzed his right arm. On October 10, 1918, he was matriculated at the Georg-August-University in Göttingen where he studied for seven semesters. On March 31, 1920, he received honorable discharge as a Lieutenant. In 1920 he was married in Magdeburg; Lehfeldt indicates that he is Protestant. He received his doctorate of law degree on May 28, 1923, with a dissertation on law and political science. In a report of 1945, Lehfeldt indicates that he had been expelled from his work in Magdeburg eight years earlier (in 1937). At some point he moved to Berlin; according to the 1943 Berlin city address book he lived at Düsseldorfer Str. 60 in Berlin Wilmersdorf and is identified as a "legal adviser." In June 1945, he was temporarily appointed as *Head of Civil Service* of Magdeburg. In a letter to the regional Bishop Wurm from September 20, 1946, Lehfeldt called the imprisoned Nazis the "murderers of our relatives." His father's brother, the dentist Dr. Michael Lehfeldt of Magdeburg, was murdered in Auschwitz. See Antonia Leugers, ed., *Berlin, Rosenstraße 2-4: Protest in der NS-Diktatur: Neue Forschungen zum Frauenprotest in der Rosenstraße 1943* (Annweiler.: Plöger, 2005) 233.
2. Regarding the racial ideological categorization, this report is somewhat imprecise.
3. Joseph Goebbels (1897–1945): as of 1926 the head of the NSDAP administrative district, or Gauleiter, in Berlin-Brandenburg; as of 1933 the Reich Minister for the People's Enlightenment and Propaganda.

4. For the evaluation of the role of the churches in these events see the article by Antonia Leugers in this volume.
5. Aldolf Bertram (1859–1945), 1906 Bishop of Hildesheim, 1914 prince-bishop of Breslau, 1916–1919 cardinal, 1930 archbishop, chairman of the Bishops' Conference in Fulda since 1920.
6. Dr. Erich Gritzbach (born 1896) ministerial advisor in the Prussian Secretary of State Department, Prussian State Councilor, head of the policy department of Göring and his personal advisors.
7. Hermann Göring (1893–1946), 1933 Prussian minister-president, 1935 commander-in-chief of the air force, 1940 Reichsmarschall.
8. The Soviet offensive brought the Battle of Stalingrad to an end on February 2, 1943, where the 6th German Army had been surrounded since November 22, 1942.
9. Not determined. Concerning the plans for a *Mischling* law cf. *Sommer an Bertram*, November 10, 1942, in: *Volk*, vol. 5, p. 939f.
10. Goebbels gave a speech in the *Sportpalast* for the tenth anniversary of coming into power (*Machtergreifung*), on January 30, 1943 in which he initially delivered a statement explaining the absence of the Führer. On February 18, 1943 he gave his infamous *Sportpalast* speech, in which he called out repeatedly, "Do you want the total war?"
11. There were deportations of Jews went from Berlin to Theresienstadt and Auschwitz on February 2 and 3, 1943 and then again on February 19 and 26; immediately after the mass arrests in Berlin on February 27, more deportations followed from March 1 through March 4 and on March 6, 1943.
12. See Leugers's contribution in this anthology.
13. Joachim Neander in this volume calculates a substitution of six thousand people for the assigned Polish people from Auschwitz and three thousand for the agreed increase of Buna. However, since only a maximum of four thousand so-called armament Jews were available in Berlin, authorities had to fall back on the arrest for their purposes of two thousand other Jews.
14. See the journal entry by Goebbels from March 6, 1943.
15. Wilhelm Frick (1877–1946), 1933–1943 Reich's Minister of the Interior, 1943–1945 Reich's Protectorate of Bohemia and Moravia.
16. *Leibstandarte-SS Adolf Hitler (Personal Security for Hitler)*, sworn to protect Hitler's person since November 9, 1933, integrated in the Waffen-SS since 1939; in the military division since 1942.

Appendix 2

Decree Regarding the Removal of Jews from Frankfurt/Oder Factories, February 24, 1943

Beginning with his dissertation, Wolf Gruner has cited the following Frankfurt/Oder document as decisive evidence that authorities never intended to deport the Jews they arrested during the massive "Removal of All Jews from the Reich Territory" (Entjudung des Reichgebietes) arrest actions in German cities beginning February 27, 1943. In his book Widerstand in der Rosenstrasse (2005), Gruner briefly referenced two other documents to support his dependence on this Frankfurt/Oder document. The first is from the Bielefeld Gestapo. Gruner cites it on the basis of Margit Naarmann's book on the Paderborn Jews (although Naarmann neither reproduces the document nor quotes it in full) that dates the document in the text from February 25, 1943 (but in the footnote from January 26, 1943). Gruner gives no archival reference for the document and writes only that it ordered a "work ban for all Jewish-German forced laborers in multiple [mehrere] cities and counties." The second document Gruner uses to support the Frankfurt/Oder decree is from the Dortmund Gestapo and is dated February 24, 1943. He cites it briefly: "In the course of the scheduled Removal of Jews from the Reich Territory and effective February 27 throughout the administrative district of Arnsberg, Jews found in the process of working (Arbeitsprozess) are to be removed with the goal of partially evacuating them to the East." No archival source for this Dortmund document is provided. Summing up, Gruner writes that "therewith lie three regional Gestapo orders, which in fact appear in differing shapes (Gestalt), that on the whole come to a concurrence about the RSHA instructions distributed to local officials for the Fabrik-Aktion. From these documents the double goal of the Great Raid emerges very clearly: the deportation of 'unprotected' Jews as well as the removal from businesses of still 'protected' Jews from 'mixed marriages,' and this indeed was not just in Berlin but rather in the entire Reich territory."

Public Decree of the State District Administrator of the Calau District
Calau, February 25, 1943
Copy.

Secret state police	Frankfurt/Oder, February 24, 1943
State police office	Secret!
Frankfurt/Oder	Urgent! Present Immediately!

B. No. II B 4 – 1958/42
Re.: Evacuation—Or as the Case May be [bzw]—Removal of Jews from factories
Precedent: None.

Since the Jews—with the exception of those living in mixed marriages who were residing in the local community —have all been almost completely resettled, the Reich Main Security Office in Berlin has ordered that all Jews still working in factories are to be removed from their workplace and assembled. This action pertains to the Jews living in mixed marriages. Any objections from managers are to be politely rejected with the comment that this measure is being carried out with the agreement of the armaments command center as well as the offices responsible for labor employment and production.

The managers of factories will be informed by the local employment office, which will also handle questions concerning the replacement of workers. The assembly of the Jews working in factories is to take place without attracting attention, possibly with the involvement of factory security personnel. However, attention must be given so that disturbances by Jews and attempts to escape are avoided. Indeed, under no circumstances may there be any overstepping boundaries of authority on the side of officials or the men assigned to keep guard, especially not in public or within the business area itself. Impudent behavior by Jews who still live in existing mixed marriages is to be punished by taking the Jews into protective custody and filing an order to bring them to a concentration camp. These actions can be carried out very generously, although the impression must be avoided that this action is a means to fundamentally solve the mixed marriage problem once and for all. If there are no reasons to justify the arrest of Jewish marriage partners, they are to be dismissed to their homes. Under no circumstance are they allowed to be employed in this or any other factory again. Further directives on their future utilization will follow.

Jews who are already working in factories that are kept in enclosed camps, such as in Neuendorf i[m] S[ande], the forest camps, etc., are not to be arrested in this action. Also the Polish Jews who are employed as a group in various factories within the Frankfurt/Oder district and are in enclosed camps are not to be arrested. Provided that Jews living in mixed marriages have been dismissed from the factories after their removal, they may not be placed in the workforce again. By orders of the Reich Main Security Office, this action is to be conducted promptly on February 27, 1943 at the beginning of work hours. Authorized officials are to be given a written notice, as needed, to be shown to the factory manager, that state something to the effect that the official has the authorization to remove all the Jews employed in the factory for the purposes of registering them. The number of the Jews removed from the factory and the number of Jews taken into custody must be reported, along with personal information, by telephone to the Frankfurt/Oder Secret State Police, telephone 2870/71 by 4 pm. The given deadline must be kept under any circumstance.

> A Nil Return is Required (Fehlanzeige ist erforderlich)
> As for Jews living in mixed marriages taken into custody, they may be placed in a concentration camp; their interrogation records should be dispatched immediately to the local office so that the further remaining steps can be arranged.
> Signed: Wolff

I dispatch the copy for careful attention and exact consideration. I request that all Jews (even those who are living in a mixed marriage with a German) be promptly and inconspicuously removed from the factories starting at the beginning of the workday on 27 February 1943. Jews behaving impudently who are still living in existing mixed marriages are to be punished. They should be taken into custody with a request for their placement in a concentration camp.

In accordance with the particulars, on February 27, 1943 by 11 a.m. the number of Jews removed from the factory and the number of Jews taken into custody are to be reported to me over the phone. The given deadline is to be kept. A nil return is required (Fehlanzeige ist erforderlich).

As for Jews taken into custody, interrogation reports are to be sent to me at once.

By proxy
Signed Richter
(District Administrator's seal)   Certified:
< . . . >
Government Secretary

Notes

1. Wolf Gruner, *Widerstand in der Rosenstraße: Die Fabrik-Action und die Verfolgung der "Mischehen" 1943* (Frankfurt a.M.: Fischer, 2005), 54, 55.
2. Gruner, *Widerstand*, 55
3. Brandenburgisches Landeshauptarchiv Potsdam, *Rep. 41 administrative district Großräschen no. 272, pg. 84-85. Heading: State District Administrator. File reference: File Ref. I 5/15 g. Note:* Secret! *With address at end:* to the police administrator or office representative in (handwritten) Vetschau. *Postmark:* Secret! The Bureau Chief as the local police authority in Großräschen, Lower Lausitz, February 27, 1943. (*Handwritten note at end*): 1. *Fehlanzeige* may be reported by telephone. This decree is partially printed in Wolf Gruner and Ursula Marcum, "The Factory Action and the Events at the Rosenstrasse in Berlin: Facts and Fictions about 27 February 1943: Sixty Years Later," *Central European History* 36, no. 2 (2003): 179–208, the English version of Wolf Gruner, "Die Fabrik-Aktion und die Ereignisse in der Berliner Rosenstraße," in *Jahrbuch für Antisemitismus-Forschung*, ed. Wolfgang Benz (Berlin: Metropol Verlag, 2002), 137–177. The annotations here are from the document and annotations printed in Antonia Leugers, ed., *Berlin, Rosenstraße 2-4: Protest in der NS-Diktatur: Neue Forschungen zum Frauenprotest in der Rosenstraße 1943* (Annweiler: Plöger, 2005), 221–224. Dr. Friedrich Haas was State District Administrator of the Calau District 1939–1945. See Hass: personal file of the court's junior judge Haas: Geheimes Staatsarchiv Preußischer Kulturbesitz (GStAPK), I HA Rep. 184 higher administrative court, Pers.- no. 951 as well as GStAPK, I HA Rep. 77, Interior Ministry, no. 4647. It is possible that the letter intended for Vetschau was swapped with that of Großräschen.
4. Wolf Gruner, *Der Geschlossene Arbeitseinsatz deutscher Juden. Zur Zwangsarbeit als Element der Verfolgung 1938–1943 (*Berlin: Metropol, 1997), 268, 69, draws attention to the fact that, despite the different RSHA-mandate, the enclosed camps of Gut Winkel and Skaby in the course of the massive arrests of Jews on February 27 were evacuated and shut down. The inmates who were initially spared deportation were deported between April and June 1943.
5. Reinhard Wolff born 1909, April 1941 to March 1943 head of the Stapoleitstelle Frankfurt/Oder. See Gruner, "Die Fabrik-Aktion," 177n. 205.
6. District Administrator Haas or his representative, Richter.

Appendix 3

April 1, 1943, OSS Document Identifying Protest in Berlin with the Interruption of Deportation of Jews

OFFICE OF STRATEGIC SERVICES
OFFICIAL DISPATCH

DATE: April 1, 1943, 5 p.m.
FROM: AMERICAN LEGATION, BERN
TO: SECRETARY OF STATE, WASHINGTON
OFFICE OF STRATEGIC SERVICES

CD 16981

DISTRIBUTION
(FOR ACTION) SI
(FOR INFORMATION) DONOVAN, SECRETARIAT, SO, GEN. MAGRUDER

RECEIVED

SECRET

#2045.

A source which is considered trustworthy has reported that action against Jewish wives and husbands on the part of the Gestapo, reported in my telegram no. 1597 dated March tenth, had to be discontinued some time ago because of the protest which such action aroused.

HARRISON

NARA-CP
RG 226
Entry 134
Box 171
Folder 1079

STATE DEPARTMENT PARAPHRASE

TOR 4/7/43 9:30 am

SECRET

Appendix 4

Translated Excerpts from the Diaries of Joseph Goebbels

Die Tagebücher von Joseph Goebbels, ed. Elke Frölich (Munich: K.G. Saur)

"Also concerning the Jewish Question the Führer is fully in agreement with my points of view. He wants a forceful policy against the Jews, though one that does not cause us unnecessary difficulties. The evacuation of the Jews is to be conducted city by city. It is therefore still unclear when it will be Berlin's turn; but when it has its turn, then the evacuation should also be carried out as quickly as possible. Concerning the Jewish mixed marriages, especially those in artist's circles, the Führer recommends that I follow a somewhat reserved course of action since he is of the opinion that these marriages in any case will die out bit by bit, and one shouldn't get any gray hair over this."
Goebbels Diary, November 22, 1941

"I am reading an extensive memorandum from the SD and Police about the Final Solution of the Jewish Question. From it arise a vast array of new considerations. The Jewish question has to be solved in the entire European context. In Europe there are still more than 11 million Jews. They must later first of all be concentrated in the East; perhaps one could allot them an island, for example Madagascar, after the war. In any case there will be no peace and quiet in Europe if the Jews are not entirely pushed out of the European territory. That raises a gazillion questions of extraordinary delicacy. What happens to the half-Jews, what happens to those related to Jews, their in-laws, those married to Jews? We will thus be having a few things to do and in the context of solving this problem a whole lot of personal tragedies will play out. But that is unavoidable. Now the situation is ripe to apply a final solution to the Jewish question. Later generations will no longer possess the drive and also no longer have the alertness of instinct. That's why we are doing well to proceed radically and consistently here. What today saddles us as a burden will be a fortune and advantage for those who come after us." *Goebbels Diary, March 7, 1942*

"It is astonishing how strongly indeed the English Volk, above all those in the highest circles, have been corrupted by Jewry (verjudet) and hardly show English character any longer. That can in fact be traced back mainly to the fact that the top ten thousand are so strongly infected by Jewish marriages that they can barely still think like English." *Goebbels Diary, March 12, 1942*

"The Führer once again gives voice to his firm determination, to remove the Jews from Berlin at any rate. The claims of our economic advisors and manufacturers that they could not do without the so-called fine work of the Jews, also does not impress him." *Goebbels Diary, September 30, 1942*

(Compare with Speer's record of the same week:
  "In the meeting of 20 to 22 September, Hitler ordered Saukel to deport all Jews who are still working in armament factories in eastern locations. By this, [Hitler] meant mostly the Berlin Jews." Albert Speer, *Der Sklavenstaat* [Stuttgart, 1981], 346)

[Sepp Dietrich] "even offers to possibly place a company of the [SS] Leibstandarte [Hitler] at my disposal once, so that I can reach my goal with brute force, which is not exactly the appropriate means by which to prevail, under the current circumstances." [particularly the German defeat at Stalingrad] *Goebbels Diary, February 2, 1943*

"The Jews in Berlin will now once and for all be pushed out. With the final deadline of February 28 they are supposed to be first collected in camps and then deported, up to 2,000, batch-by-batch, day-by-day. I have set for myself a goal to make Berlin entirely free of Jews by the middle or end of March at the latest." *Goebbels Diary, February 18, 1943*

"We are pushing the Jews once and for all out of Berlin. This past Saturday they were collected without warning and will now be pushed off to the East very shortly. Unfortunately in this case too it turned out that the better classes, in particular the intellectuals, do not understand our Jewish policies and in some measure take sides with the Jews. As a consequence news of our action was prematurely betrayed, so that a whole lot of Jews has slipped through our hands. But we will nevertheless still get ahold of them. In any case, I will not rest until the Reich capital at least has become totally free of Jews." *Goebbels Diary, March 2, 1943*

"The SD considers this exact moment to be right for proceeding with the evacuation of the Jews. Unfortunately some disagreeable scenes have played out in front of a Jewish Old People's Home. The people gathered together in large throngs and even sided with the Jews to some extent. I will commission the security police not to continue the Jewish evacuations during such a critical time. Rather we want to put that off for a few weeks; then we can carry it out all the more thoroughly. One has to intervene all over the place, to ward off damages. The efforts of certain offices are so lacking in savvy that one cannot leave them on their own for ten minutes. The basic malady of our leadership and above all of our administration consists in operating according to Schema F [incapable of adapting orders to circumstances]. One has the impression that these people, who carry out this or that measure, don't reflect a wit, but rather hang to the written word, whose main value to them is that they thus have their actions covered by orders from above." *Goebbels Diary, March 6, 1943.*

"I discuss the news about Berlin with Gutterer [Goebbels' Deputy for the Greater Berlin Gau/region]. There is nothing essentially new to report . . . The Führer has the greatest understanding for the psychological questions of the war and expressed himself very sharply about the tactical imprudence of prominent persons as well as their wives . . . In the Jewish question he approves of my actions and specifically gives me the mandate to render Berlin free of Jews . . . I describe my actions to the Führer as generous toward the people, hard toward the wrong doers. The Führer also considers this completely correct." *Goebbels Diary, 9 March 1943*

[Gutterer confirmed in interviews in August 1986 at his home in Aachen with Nathan Stoltzfus that Goebbels did make the decision to release rather than deport the intermarried Jews imprisoned at Rosenstrasse, because this was the easiest way to get rid of the street protests, and that Goebbels reviewed this decision with Hitler on March 9]

"The evacuation of the Jews from Berlin did in fact lead to some disagreements. Unfortunately the Jews and Jewesses from privileged marriages were arrested too at first, which led to great fear and confusion. Because of the short-sightedness of industrialists, who warned the Jews in time, the supposed arrest of Jews on one day was a flop. In total, 4,000 Jews evaded us. They are now going around unregistered and without housing in Berlin and comprise, of course, a great danger for the public. I order the police, army and party to put everything into settling up with these Jews as fast as possible.

The arrest of Jews and Jewesses from privileged marriages had a particularly strong, sensational affect on artist circles. Because precisely among actors these privileged marriages exist in a certain number. But in the moment I can't pay overly much attention to that. If a German man can still even now manage to live in a legal marriage with a Jewess, then that speaks against him absolutely, and during war there is no longer time to be all too sentimental in judging this question." *Goebbels Diary, March 11, 1943*

[Goebbels's diary entry for April 18, below, shows that in referring here to Jews from "privileged marriages" he was not designating all Jews in intermarriage but only those who did not wear the Star, because they were privileged.]

"The Jewish question in Berlin is still not yet completely solved. A whole collection of so-called 'Geltungsjuden' ['half-Jewish' 'Mischlinge' who are considered Jews and wear the Star of David], Jews from privileged intermarriages ["full Jews" according to the Nuremberg Laws but exempted from wearing the Star of David], and also Jews from intermarriages ["full Jews" required to wear the Star of David, who comprised the vast majority interned on Rosenstrasse] are still to be found in Berlin. A lot of extraordinarily difficult problems arise from this. In any case I authorize that all Jews who still find themselves in Berlin, will undergo a further inspection. I do not want Jews with the Jewish star running around the Reich capital. Either one must take the Jewish star away and privilege them, or on the other hand once and for all evacuate them from the Reich capital. I am convinced that with the freeing of Berlin of the Jews, I have completed one of my greatest political achievements. " *Goebbels Diary, April 18, 1943*

"One dare not bend to the will of the people in this point [evacuations] since the people of course have no overview of the coming probable developments in the air war." The shuffling back and forth of German masses between evacuation sites and their bombed home cities puts an undue strain on the train system, Goebbels wrote, and "we must therefore try to dam up this reverse current with appropriate measures. If this is not to be achieved through friendly cajoling, "then one must use force. It is not true that force does not lead to results. Of course it leads to results if is explained to the public with the necessary specificity, and then is actually deployed. Up until now, one has not sensed any of this, and the people know just exactly where the soft spot of the leadership is, and will always exploit this. Should we make this spot hard where we have been soft up until now, then the will of the people will bend to the will of the state. Currently we're on the best path to bending the will of the state to the will of the people. I consider that to be extraordinarily cataclysmic, not only from the objective perspective but also from the standpoint of leadership in general. The state may never, against its better insight, give in to the pressure of the street. If it does this the second time, it will be still less strong than it was the first time, and gradually lose its entire authority." *Goebbels Diary, November 2, 1943* [Goebbels wrote this after the Witten Protest examined here by Julia Torrie.]

Appendix 5

Excerpts from testimonies of women who protested for their Jewish husbands in response to a request from the Berlin Bureau of Reparations, 1955.

Front Page, Jüdische Allgemeine (Jewish Weekly) *February 18, 1955*

REPARATIONS FOR STERNTRÄGER: THOSE REMAINING PLEASE REGISTER

The Office of Reparations urgently requests the registration of persons whose relatives were members of resistance groups against National Socialism and were sentenced to death or died in a concentration camp . . . Also the participants of the demonstration-march of the 'Aryan' wives on Rosenstrasse should please register at the Berlin office of Reparations.

In response, more than sixty participants wrote in. Many of the testimonies, from persons who no doubt did not know each other, rendered similar descriptions: women arrived at Rosenstrasse 2-4 to confirm that their family members were imprisoned there and to bring them small items of comfort; as they grew in numbers they began calling out together for the release of their husbands in a chorus over and over; armed guards repeatedly threatened to shoot them if they did not disperse; the protesters fled in fear but soon regrouped and continued their protest. These details were confirmed during the following decade by additional testimony from other participants given to the German prosecution in the Bovensiepen and Graustück cases.

Reparations were not forthcoming, although an official response to these eyewitness reports has not yet been found. These testimonies of the protesters instead made it into the Leo Baeck Institute (Wiener Library microfilm, AR 7187/Reel 600). Examples include:

Gertrud Cohen Berlin-Neukölln 14 March 55
Neé Vanselow
Emserstrasse 6

On Saturday evening, the 27th of February, my husband Dr. Jur. Hans Cohen, as a full Jew and wearer of the star . . . was arrested by the SS . . . Searching for the whereabouts of my husband I discovered that arrested Jews were being held in the house of the Jewish Community in the Rosenstrasse, and went there, where already many (zahlreiche) wives had gathered together. Although the posted police commanded us to move on, we called out together in a chorus: "We want to have our husbands back!"

Gertrud Blumenthal Berlin-Steglitz, the 6th of March 1955
  Kühlebornweg 24

After we demonstrators were threatened with pistols by the Gestapo we first quickly dispersed but then a short while later gathered together again and protested more.

Else Putzrath geb. Lingne Berlin-Wilmersdorf den 24.2.1955
  Mansfelderstr. 34

I hereby state that I as an Aryan (Christian) wife of the Star-wearer-Jew Herbert Putzrath took part every day in the demonstration in the period between February 28 until March 3. I could name witnesses for this.

Appendix 6

Excerpts of Individual Sections and Paragraphs from Legal Texts and Ordinances (1933–1941)

I.
First Ordinance for the execution of the law
for the restoration of the civil service system.
From 11 April 1933. RGBl (*Reichsgesetzblatt*) 1 p. 195.

§ 3

(1) One is considered non-Aryan if one is descended from non-Aryan, especially Jewish parents or grandparents. It suffices if one parent or one grandparent is non-Aryan, especially if one parent or one grandparent has belonged to the Jewish religion.
(3) If Aryan descent is questionable, an expert opinion has to be obtained by an appointed specialist on race research at the Ministry of the Interior.

II.
Reich Citizenship Law.
From 15 September 1935. RGBl I p. 1146.

§ 1

(1) A German citizen is one who belongs to the Association of the German Reich and is especially committed to it because of this membership in the association.

§ 2

(1) A citizen of the Reich is that person only who is of German or kindred blood and who, through his conduct, shows that he is both desirous and fit to serve the German people and Reich faithfully.
(2) Citizens of the Reich are the sole bearers of full political rights in accordance with the law.

III.
Law for the Protection of German Blood and German Honor
From 15 September 1935. RGBl I S. 1146–1147.

§ 1
(1) Marriages between Jews and German citizens or kindred blood are forbidden. Marriages concluded in defiance of this law are void, even if, for the purpose of evading this law, they were concluded abroad.

§ 2
Sexual relations outside marriage between Jews and citizens of German or kindred blood are forbidden.

§ 5
(1) Whoever violates the ban imposed by § 1 will be jailed.
(2) Any man who violates the ban imposed by § 2 will be punished by incarceration in prison or jail.

IV.
First Ordinance of the Reich Citizenship Law
From 14 November 1935. RGBl I p. 1333–1334

§ 2
(2) A Jewish *Mischling* is anyone who, according to race, is descended from one or two Jewish grandparents, as long as he is not considered a Jew according to § 5 para. 2. A grandparent is considered fully Jewish without more ado if he had enrolled as a member of a Jewish religious community.

§ 4
(1) A Jew cannot be a citizen of the Reich. He is not entitled to suffrage in political affairs; he cannot hold a public office.

§ 5
(1) A Jew is anyone descended from at least three Jewish grandparents. § 2 para. 2 clause 2 is to be applied.
(2) A person is also considered a Jew if he is descended from two Jewish grandparents and is a citizen and Jewish *Mischling*,
a) who was a member of a Jewish religious community at the time of the enactment of the law or will be admitted to one thereafter,
b) who was married to a Jew at the time of the enactment of the law or will be married to one thereafter,

c) who, in terms of paragraph 1, was born into a marriage with a Jew that was contracted after the Law for the Protection of German Blood and German Honor of 15 September 1935 *(Reichsgesetzbl[att]* I p. 1146) came into effect,
d) who was born from sexual relations with a Jew outside of marriage in terms of paragraph 1 and was born out of wedlock after 31 July 1936.

V.

First Ordinance for the Implementation of the Law
for the Protection of German Blood and German Honor.
From 14 November 1935. RGBl I p. 1334–1336.

§ 2

Also falling under the forbidden marriage act according to § 1 of the law are marriages concluded between Jews and German citizens who are Jewish *Mischlinge* who have only one Jewish grandparent.

§ 12

(1) A household is Jewish [. . .] if a Jewish man is the head of the household or belongs to the household community.

§ 16

The *Führer* and Reich Chancellor can grant exemptions from the provisions of the laws and regulations.

VI.

Police Ordinance in Regard to the Marking of Jews
From 1 September 1941. RGBl I p. 547.

§ 1

(1) Jews (§ 5 of the First Ordinance of the Reich Citizenship Law of 14 November 1935—*Reichsgesetzbl[att]* I p. 1333) who have completed their sixth year of life are forbidden to show themselves in public without a Jewish star.
(2) The Jewish star consists of a palm-sized, six-pointed star outlined in black and made out of yellow material with the black inscription *"Jude"* (Jew). It is to be worn visibly sewn onto the upper left side of one's clothing.

§ 2

Jews are forbidden
(a) to leave the area of their residential community without carrying written permission from the local police authority;
(b) to wear medals, decorations and other insignia.

§ 3

§§ 1 and 2 do not apply[3]
a) to Jewish spouses living in a mixed marriage, as long as the marriage bore descendents and these descendents are not considered Jews, even if the marriage no longer exists or the only son has died in the present war;
b) to the Jewish wife in a childless mixed marriage for the duration of the marriage.

§ 4

(1) Whoever violates the ban in §§ 1 and 2 intentionally or negligently will be fined up to 153 *Reichsmark* or imprisoned for up to six weeks.
(2) Additional safety measures and penal provisions by the police will remain in effect.

Notes

1. A *Mischling* according to Nazi usage was a person of Jewish as well as "Aryan" or "German-blooded" ancestry.
2. This provision referred to as the "privileged" and "non-privileged mixed marriages" had been established in *Geheimer Schnellbrief Görings an das Reichsinnenministerium vom 28.12.1938 (Göring's Secret Express Letter to the Reich Ministry of the Interior of 28 December 1938)*. Privileged mixed marriages were those with: 1) a child baptized as a Christian; 2) a Jewish wife without children. The Jewish partner in these marriages was "privileged." Mixed marriages were *not* privileged if 1) there were children classified as Jewish according to the 1935 Nuremberg Laws; 2) the husband was Jewish and there were no children. In these cases the Jewish partner was not "privileged." Hilberg, *Destruction*, vol. 2, 443–44; Stoltzfus, *Resistance of the Heart*, 102; Meyer, *Mischlinge*, 30.

Appendix 7

RSHA Guidelines for Deportation to Auschwitz, Berlin, February 20, 1943

Institute for Contemporary History, Eichmann Trial documents of proof, No. 1282. With heading: Reich Security Main Office IV B 4 a. *Reference number:* 2093/42 g (391). *Title: Guidelines* for the technical implementation of the evacuation of Jews *to the East (KL* [concentration camp] *Auschwitz). Underlining and date in the original. Handwritten comments and notes in the margins were not recorded. Partial quotations or excerpts:* H.G. Adler, p. 199; J. v. Lang, document facsimile, not paginated; Topography of Terror, p. 118f.

For the evacuation of Jews[1] from the territory of the Reich and Bohemia and Moravia to the East, the following guidelines, which are to be observed exactly at all points, have been established under the reversal of orders enacted up until now.

I. Authorized agencies.
The implementation is the responsibility of the State Police Headquarters (in Vienna, as before, the settlement center of the Central Office for Jewish Emigration in collaboration with the Special Branch Headquarters in Vienna, in the Protectorate the commander of the security police and the SD *[Sicherheitsdienst* (Security Service)], Central Office for the Regulation of the Jewish Question in Bohemia and Moravia, Prague).

The role of these agencies, in addition to gathering the group of individuals to be evacuated in a designated place and collecting their personal information for written records, is the removal of these Jews on chartered German State Railroad trains in accordance with the railway schedule created by the Reich Security Main Office after consultation with the Imperial Ministry for Transport, and the regulation of proprietary issues.

II. Ordinance for the group of persons to be evacuated
In the course of this evacuation initiative, all Jews can be captured (§ 5 of the 1st enactment of the Law of the Reich Citizen of 14 November 1935, RGBl. *[Reichsgesetzblatt]* I, p. 1333) apart from the following provisional exceptions:

1./ Jews living in German-Jewish mixed marriages as well as a/ Jewish spouses from a no longer existing German-Jewish marriage, who, in compliance with § 3, para. a) of the police regulations of 1 September [19]41 (RGBl I, p. 547) are exempt from the law requiring Jews to wear identifying marks, b/ Persons of partial Jewish ancestry who are classified as Jews[2] according to § 5 (2) of the 1st ordinance of the Civil Code of the Reich Citizen of 14 November [19]35 (RGBl. I, p. 1333) provided they are not married to a Jew.

2./ Jews who are to be temporarily deferred from evacuation on account of particular decrees of the Reich Security Main Office IV B 4.

3./ Jews over 65 years of age. In the case of Jewish marriages in which one spouse is under 65 years and the other over 65 years of age, both spouses can be evacuated.

4./ Bearers of the Wound Badge[3] and of high decorations for bravery (EK I[4], Golden Bravery Medal[5], etc.)

5./ According to a petition of the Reich Ministry of the Interior presently at hand, Jews and *Geltungsjuden* affected by hereinafter called cases of hardship (further handling and/or examination is scheduled in due time): a/ Resignation from the Jewish religious community can ensue only after the effective date (15 September 1935) but before the reunification of Austria with the German Reich[6]. (Valid only for former Austrian citizens). b/ It has been substantiated that the half-Jew would have resigned from the Jewish religious community in due time, i.e. before the reunification of Austria with the German Reich, if this had not been forbidden by the Austrian law of 25 May 1868 on Interdenominational Relations of Citizens (RGBl. for Austria 1868 p. 99) because the law forbade a change in denomination between one's completed 7th and 14th years of life. (Valid only for former Austrian citizens). c/ The intention of an *actual resignation* from the Jewish religious community was *proven* before the effective date (15 September 1935), but the official resignation from the Jewish religious community as prescribed by governmental laws was not executed or not executed in due form for *excusable* reasons.

7./ A separation of spouses and of children up to 14 years of age from their parents is to be
   avoided if possible.[7]

Separate instructions apply concerning the treatment of *Jews with foreign citizenship*.

Notes

1. Cf. the legal provisions underlying this document and the others, the law excerpts in Document 1a.

2. Because § 5 para. 2 begins with the phrase *"Als Jude gilt"* ("The following are classified as Jews"), this group of persons is also signified as *Geltungsjuden.*
3. Wound Badges in black (one to two times), silver (three to four times), and gold (more frequent injuries), established September 1, 1939.
4. *Eisernes Kreuz Erster Klasse* (Iron Cross First Class).
5. The name *"Tapferkeitsmedaille"* (Bravery Medal) for the Bavarian Army's *"Militär-Verdienst-Medaille"* (Military Service Medal) established by Elector Karl Theodor in 1794 (awarded in gold or silver) was officially introduced in March 1918. In the Bavarian Army it was the highest decoration for enlisted men and non-commissioned officers. Its Prussian counterparts were the *Goldenes Militärverdienstkreuz* (Golden Military Service Cross) and the *Pour le mérite*. I would like to thank Dr. Achim Fuchs, Bavarian Main State Archive—War Archive—Munich for this information.
6. March 13, 1938.
7. A sixth item is missing in the original.

Appendix 8

Documents of the SS at Auschwitz from early March 1943 indicating their "pull" for workers from Berlin and their expectation that more working Jews (intermarried) would be sent from Berlin

2 March 1943 Telex No. 1298 Time 9:59 p.m. Recorded by Rissler
   Oranienburg No. 1298 2. 3. 43. Time 9:40 p.m. — Z5D—
Top Secret!
To the
Camp Commander Concentration Camp Auschwitz
*SS-Obersturmbannführer Höss*_____
Subject: Evacuation of Jews.
Reference: Known.
   As it is known there, the transports of Jews from Berlin begin on 1 March 1943. It will be brought to your attention once more that on these transports there will be 15,000 healthy Jews, fully able to work, who previously worked in the Berlin arms industry. Their further ability to work is of great importance.
   Responsible for the Accuracy of Statement Chairman of Central
   Administrative Bureau
   Sgd. Liebahenschel
   SS-Obersturmbannführer
   a. B. i. V.
   SS-Untersturmführer
   This document is in the Auschwitz Museum's archives: D-AUI-3a/85a nr inw. 172841 (hand-written notation).
   Transcription of a letter from the Chairman of Central Administrative Bureau of Office D I of the SS Economic and Administrative Main Office to the Concentration Camp Commander Rudolf Höss with the message that

among the transports arriving from Berlin there are about 15,000 healthy Jews who are able to work. APMO [Auschwitz Museum]: D-AuI-3a, Letters and Telegrams about the Prisoners' Employment of Labor, Bl.392.

Concentration Camp Auschwitz Telex Service.

Received Sent
Day Month Year Time Space for Receipt Stamp Day Month Year Time
2 March 1943 9:59 p.m. 3 March 1943
by delivered on III-a
through (—) podpis nieczyteiny through

Telex No. 1290

Oranienburg 1290 2.3.43. 2140—ZED—

To the Commander SS-Obersturmbannführer Höss Concentration Camp Auschwitz.
Subject: Evacuation of Jewish armaments workers out of Berlin. I am bringing to your attention once more that the Jewish armaments workers from Berlin, whose transport began yesterday, must absolutely be kept in a state in which they are able to work. Because they have worked in the armaments industry in Berlin, their employability is to be recognized. First of all, the camp Buna must be brought into the best possible condition.

In doing so, I am asking you to please take care that the Jewish workers absolutely not be unloaded in the usual location, but directly at the Buna factory, which would be more advantageous. Therefore, I expect a significant increase in inventory at the Buna factory.

Sgd. Maurer, SS-Obersturmbannführer.
M.P. Concentration Camp Auschwitz
Department Head: Employment of Labor
3 March 1943
(—) podpis nieczyteiny

Message—Telex—Radiogram—Flash Message
   No. 7749 5 March 1943

To: Economic and Administrative Main Office
Office D II

Oranienburg

Subject: Evacuation of Jewish armaments workers

Reference: There: Telex from 2 March 1943 No. 1290
1750 Jews arrived on 4 March 1943 from Berlin.
Out of these, 200 women sent to employment of labor and 918 women and children sent to special treatment.
The rest 1118 women and children.
Out of these, 200 women sent to employment of labor and 918 women and children to special treatment. Average age of male prisoners arriving for employment of labor: 50-60 years.
If the transports from Berlin continue to arrive with so many women and children alongside older Jews, it does not look very promising in regard to the employment of labor. What Buna needs most of all are strong or younger workers.

Sgd. Schwarz
SS-Obersturmführer (—) podpis nieczyteiny

Message.
WV Hauptamt
Office D II 8 March 1943
Oranienburg.

Subject: Evacuation of Jewish armaments workers.
On 5 and 7 March the following Jewish prisoner transports arrived.
Transport from Berlin, entry 5 March 1943, size of the transport was 1128 Jews. 389 men (Buna) and 96 women were sent to employment of labor. 151 men and 492 women and children received special treatment. Transport from Breslau, entry 5 March 1943, size of the transport was 1405 Jews. 406 men (Buna) and 190 women were sent to employment of labor. 125 men and 684 women and children received special treatment.
Transport from Berlin, entry 7 March 1943, size of the transport was 690 including 25 protective custody prisoners. 153 men and 25 protective custody prisoners (Buna) and 65 women were sent to employment of labor. 30 men and 417 women and children received special treatment.

Sgd. Schwarz
(—) Obersturmführer

Concentration Camp Auschwitz Telex Service.
Received Sent
Day Month Year Time Space for Receipt Stamp
7 Nov. 1942 8:43 a.m. Entry: 7 Nov. 1942 (—) podpis nieczytelny through (—) podpis nieczytelny Telex No. 8885
1834

KGL.D.W. SS Lublin 8885 7.11.42 0840—SP
To the Commander's Office of the Concentration Camp Auschwitz.
Subject:—Transfer of Jewish prisoner clockmakers.
Reference:—Ordinance ORBG—D- 11/1 23 SO./F. of 28 October 1942.

In accordance with the O.A. Ordinance, the 48 Jewish prisoner clockmakers announced in the letter of 9 September 1942 are to be transferred to the concentration camp Auschwitz. From these announced 48 Jewish prisoners, 23 are now deceased, which means that now only 25 prisoners can be transferred. The transfer will take place on 7 November 1942—3:02 p.m. from the train station Lublin to Warsaw.

Sgd. Kögel SS-Obersturmbannführer and Commander.
MP Concentration Camp Auschwitz 9 November 1942.
(—) podpis nieczytelny.
Must be intercepted, sealed, to Bohl. Wentsl.!
Completed on 12 November 1942 (—) podpis nieczyteiny.

Appendix 9

Documents in response to the Witten Protest and from 1944 indicating Hitler's continuing refusal to use force against "racial" civilians who refused to follow regime guidelines for evacuating bombed areas.

1) Circular Nr. 6, Gau liaison officer Spratte, November 20, 1944
"As I already informed you, the Gauleiter [Albert Hoffmann, Westphalia-South] also wants to prevent our evacuees' many return trips by not handing out ration cards for food provisioning to any evacuee who returns to the air emergency region without permission."

2) SD-report on "contemporary events and their effects on the morale and behavior of women," November 18, 1943
"Women stand behind the Führer . . . in general women always take the view that the Führer certainly would put things right, if he knew everything. . . . In Witten [Westphalia-South region] . . . The women in question had indeed tried to *force* [italics original] the delivery of food ration cards in order to take a public stand against the measures that led to prohibitions on the dispensation of food ration cards. Shameful scenes developed so that the city administration of Witten found itself forced to call on the police so as to restore order. They refused to get involved however since the demands of the women were fair and there was no legal basis for not handing out food ration cards to German people who had returned [home]. Also in Hamm, Lünen, and Bochum wild scenes reportedly played out in front of the food offices. Agitated crowds of people waited in line for the distribution [of rations]. Because some of the women brought with them small children and nursing infants and the miners in some cases showed up in the place of their wives, those waiting began to exchange accounts of their experiences in the

places they had been evacuated to, and the craziest (tollste) statements were made. Miners declared that they would not return to the mines before they had received the necessary food ration cards for their families. Women announced that they would rather suffer bombs here than to once again return to the quarters assigned to them. The publication in the newspaper as well as at the distribution center on October 12, 1943 that food ration cards would not only be denied to those who had returned but also to all children required to attend school, even if they had not yet been evacuated, led to *a firsthand rebellion among the women* [italics original], who had been capable of anything, without exercise of the least restraint or caution about consequences. Friendly persuasion had the opposite effect. Insults of official and high-ranking persons were the order of the day."

3) 18.1.44—Reich Minister for People's Enlightenment and Propaganda Pro LK Nr. 27/43 g (1) 2580 a to all Gauleiter regarding Reich Inspection for the Implementation of Civilian Air War Measures
"In carrying out measures to prevent the undesirable return of evacuees, particular difficulties have arisen from the fact that this question is not dealt with in a unified way across the Reich. Individual Gaue have defended themselves against returns by blocking ration tickets. But because town limits often run right through developed areas, different practices have often arisen in the same communities. The Führer has therefore ordered that you refrain from blocking ration cards. Similarly, the Führer does not wish parents who have not evacuated their children to be fined for every day children miss school if, because of the school closures, the children are not sent to school. The Führer is of the opinion that other ways and means must be found to move these members of the community, too, to evacuate their children."

4) Section from the Ministerial Gazette for the Baden domestic administration Nr. 32 of 25 August 1944: "Evacuation due to air raid danger and bomb damage." Circular of the Minister of the Interior and Head of Civil Government in Alsace, Government and Political Department, 21 August 1944 Nr. 48541
"With an order of July 29, 1944 –II RV 1724/44—220 U—the Plenipotentiary for Reich Administration [Heinrich Himmler], in agreement with the Director of the Party Chancellery [Martin Bormann], has taken a position as follows: 'The use of measures of force in the preventative evacuations continues to be considered inexpedient.'"

5) 12.10.44—Reich Leader M. Bormann to Assistant Gauleiter Schlessmann, Essen. Regarding: returns of women and children from the evacuated areas to the

major cities. Your teletype message of 9.10.44. Reichsleitung NSV—Rundschreiben Nr. 139/44 of 13.11.44
"Dear Party Comrade Schlessmann, At the beginning of this year, the Führer refused to apply compulsory measures against evacuees who returned [home to bombed cities]. The grounds upon which he based his decision at that time are still relevant today. In order to dam the flood of evacuees returning to major cities, I asked the Reich Minister of the Interior to inform his subordinate offices to exercise the utmost restraint in issuing travel documents, and a similar instruction is going to the National Socialist Welfare Organization. Through appropriate presentations in the reception areas, the party will inform evacuees about the difficulties and dangers that await those who return to the cities. I hope that these measures will suffice to keep the flood of returning evacuees within tolerable limits."

6) *28.09.44 Reich Inspection of Civilian Air War Measures Goebbels to Gauleiter, R 55/447 Verhinderung der Rückkehr von Umquartierten*
"The Führer has ordered that blocking of food ration cards must be stopped . . . The Führer believes that the aspired goal [to stop evacuees from returning home] can be reached in particular through propaganda actions that vividly present parents with the dangers facing their children."

Appendix 10

Excerpts from the recent German press representing controversies about public protest by ordinary Germans in the Third Reich

"Kitsch as Kitsch can"
Wolfgang Benz
Süddeutsche Zeitung, September 18, 2003
www.sueddeutsche.de/kultur/218/405995/text/

"In the opening to Margarethe von Trotta's film "Rosenstrasse" we read that the events have actually taken place in Berlin as the end of February/beginning of March 1943. In fact it is knitted together with legends . . . that only the defiance of women moved the Nazis to relent. Through such false representations of history, is the resistance of the women at Rosenstrasse not mocked and devalued (because Goebbels hat nothing to do with Rosenstrasse and couldn't have had any influence there)? . . . [It] stands history on its head and invents new myths that are dishonest and make nonsense of clear understanding."

"Wunder und Wahrheit"
Christian Habbe
Der Spiegel, December 12, 2002

"The release of 2,000 Berlin Jews from Nazi imprisonment was long considered a miracle. As recent research shows, this is not quite right. . . . After extensive studies of the files of the Reich Security Main Office (RSHA), the Berlin historian Wolf Gruner comes to the conclusion that the release of the imprisoned Jews was planned from the outset . . . Gruner proves that Hitler's willing executioners were not intimidated, but proceeded according to an elaborate plan . . . SS Jewish Affairs Expert Adolf Eichmann even personally confirmed this to Church authorities."

"Gebt uns unsere Männer zurück!"
Neue Studien im "kleinen Historikerstreit": Aber es bleibt unbelegt, ob die Frauen-Proteste in der Rosenstraße 1943 zur Freilassung führten
Sven Felix Kellerhoff
Berliner Morgenpost, July 3, 2005
http://www.morgenpost.de/content/2005/07/03/feuilleton/764157.html

"Goebbels and the Gestapo gave in to a few hundred Berlin women. Due to their vociferous protest the Propaganda Minister and the Gestapo released about 2000 "Jews related to Aryans" at the beginning of March 1943 . . . Experts [*Fachleute*] have been arguing violently about Stoltzfus' interpretation of the protests at Rosenstrasse and Trotta's film now for more than two years, sometimes with personal attacks . . . The Berlin historian Wolf Gruner . . . can now claim to have provided the only coherent interpretation . . . If Goebbels had in fact ordered the release of the arrested Jews because of public pressure, it would cast doubt on virtually all attempts to explain the Nazi state."

Email excerpt from a member of the Technical University of Dortmund faculty, June 13, 2007:
"I have never, whether in private or public, seen anything reported on or heard anyone speak of the protests [by 300 women in Witten] in October 1943. There have been discussions of everything possible: about the conditions of the evacuation reception areas, about the air raids, about the separation of families due to the war. Even in interviews that I have had with women [in Witten] this topic was never raised. Because I myself first heard of it about four years ago in "Meldungen aus dem Reich" [the collection of SD reports published in 1984], I could also not have asked them about it specifically."

"Helden ohne Namen"
Nathan Stoltzfus
Der Spiegel, EINESTAGES, November 10, 2008
http://einestages.spiegel.de/static/topicalbumbackground/1477/1/helden_ohne_namen.html

"'The thesis may be daring but it is defensible: the regime, dependent on compliance especially during war, responded carefully to open and half-open criticism of its Jewish policies and may have even had to react by pulling back,' wrote German historian Ekkehard Klausa in 2005. This is what 'it actually did in response to Galen's sermons and the women's protest on

Rosenstrasse.' Such an interpretation is "daring" because interpretations of Hitler's power have built up and become established over the decades that Hitler held everything in his grip without regard to other forces. . . . A "documentation" published in 1990 by the Workshop for Witten Women's History is painfully modest, neglecting even to mention that the women got what they demanded by protesting. The Workshop's call for eyewitnesses or information about the protest has not returned a single echo. Perhaps still today, in a world where the archetypal story of resistance suggests that public resistance was always futile, it is too 'daring' to claim to have protested openly in Hitler's Germany in late 1943."

Selected Bibliography

Arnault, Lynn S. "Cruelty, Horror and the Will to Redemption." *Hypatia* 18, no. 2 (2003): 155–188.
Baier, Helmut. *Die Deutschen Christen Bayerns im Rahmen des bayerischen Kirchenkampfes.* Nuremberg: Verein für Bayerische Kirchengeschichte, 1968.
Blank, Ralf, and Jörg Echternkamp, Karola Fings, Jürgen Forster, Winfried Heinemann, Tobias Jersak, Armin Nolzen, Christoph Rass, Derry Cook-Radmore. *Germany and the Second World War.* Vol. 9/1, *German Wartime Society, 1939–1945: Politicization, Disintegration, and the Struggle for Survival.* New York: Oxford University Press, 2008.
Blumental, Nachman, ed. *Dokumenty i materiały—tom I—obozy.* Łódź: Wydawnictwo Centralnej Żydowskiej Komisji Historicznej przy C.K. Żydów w Polsce, 1946.
Broszat, Martin, Elke Fröhlich, and Falk Wiesemann, eds. "Bayern in der NS-Zeit." In *Soziale Lage und politisches Verhalten der Bevölkerung im Spiegel vertraulicher Berichte.* Munich: Oldenbourg, 1977.
Corner, Paul, ed. *Popular Opinion in Totalitarian Regimes: Fascism, Nazism, Communism.* Oxford: Oxford University Press, 2009.
Czech, Danuta. *Kalendarz wydarzeń w KL Auschwitz.* Oświęcim: Wydawnictwo Państwowego Muzeum w Oświęcimiu-Brzezince, 1992.
Fisher, Jo. *Mothers of the Disappeared.* Boston: South End Press, 1989.
Flammer, Thomas, Barbara Schüler, and Hubert Wolf, eds. *Clemens August von Galen: Ein Kirchenfürst im Nationalsozialismus.* Darmstadt: Wissenschaftliche Buchgesellschaft, 2007.
Fork Films., Abigail E. Disney, Gini Reticker. *Pray the Devil Back to Hell.* Sausalito, CA: Roco Films Educational, 2008.
Friedlander, Henry. *The Origins of Nazi Genocide: From Euthanasia to the Final Solution.* Chapel Hill: University of North Carolina Press, 1995.
Fritz, Stephen G. *Endkampf: Soldiers, Civilians, and the Death of the Third Reich.* Lexington, KY: University Press of Kentucky, 2004.
Gellately, Robert. *Backing Hitler: Consent and Coercion in Nazi Germany.* Oxford: Oxford University Press, 2001.
Gerstenmaier, Eugen. *Streit und Friede hat seine Zeit: Ein Lebensbild.* Frankfurt: Propyläen Verlag, 1981.
Glass, Charles S. *Americans in Paris: Life and Death under Nazi Occupation.* New York: Penguin Books, 2010.
Gregor, Neil. "Politics, Culture and Political Culture: Recent Work on the Third Reich and its Aftermath." *Journal of Modern History* 78, no. 3 (2006): 643–683.
Griech-Polelle, Beth A. *Bishop von Galen: German Catholicism and National Socialism.* New Haven, CT: Yale University Press, 2002.
Gruner, Wolf. *Gedenkort Rosenstraße 2–4: Internierung und Protest im NS-Staat.* Berlin: Topographie des Terrors, 2013.

———. *Widerstand in der Rosenstraße: Die Fabrik-Aktion und die Verfolgung der "Mischehen" 1943*. Frankfurt am Main: Fischer, 2005.

Guzman Bouvard, Marguerite. *Revolutionizing Motherhood: The Mothers of the Plaza de Mayo*. Wilmington, DE: Scholarly Resource Book, 1994.

Hagemann, Karen. "Frauenprotest und Männerdemonstrationen: Zum geschlechtsspezifischen Aktionsverhalten im großstädtischen Arbeitermilieu der Weimarer Republik." In *Massenmedium Straße: Zur Kulturgeschichte der Demonstration*, edited by Bernd Jürgen Warneken, 202–230. Frankfurt: Campus, 1991.

Hanisch, Ernst. "Peasants and Workers in their Environment: Nonconformity and Opposition to National Socialism in the Austrian Alps." In *Germans Against Nazism: Essays in Honour of Peter Hoffmann; Nonconformity, Opposition and Resistance in the Third Reich*, edited by Francis R. Nicosia and Lawrence D. Stokes. Oxford: Berg, 1990.

Henke, Klaus-Dietmar. *Die amerikanische Besetzung Deutschlands*. Munich: Oldenbourg, 1996.

Hamm, Berndt, Harry Oelke, and Gury Schneider-Ludorff, eds. *Spielräume des Handelns und der Erinnerung: Die Evangelisch-Lutherische Kirche in Bayern und der Nationalsozialismus*. Göttingen: Vandenhoeck & Ruprecht, 2010.

Heyen, Franz Josef. *Nationalsozialismus im Alltag: Quellen zur Geschichte des Nationalsozialismus vornehmlich im Raum Mainz-Koblenz-Trier*. Boppard: Boldt, 1967.

Höß, Rudolf. *Kommandant in Auschwitz: Autobiographische Aufzeichnungen des Rudolf Höß*, edited by Martin Broszat. Munich: DTV, 1963.

Hummel, Karl-Joseph, and Michael Kißener, eds. *Die Katholiken und das Dritte Reich. Kontroversen und Debatten*. 2nd ed. Paderborn: Schöningh, 2010.

Hummel, Karl-Joseph, and Christoph Kösters, eds. *Kirchen im Krieg: Europa 1939–1945*. Paderborn: Schöningh, 2007.

Jaspers, Karl. *The Question of German Guilt*. New York: Fordham University Press, 2001.

Jäckel, Eberhard, ed. *Hitler: Sämtliche Aufzeichnungen 1905–1924*. Stuttgart: Deutsche Verlags-Anstalt, 1980.

Jochheim, Gernot. *Frauenprotest in der Rosenstraße Berlin 1943: Berichte Dokumente Hintergründe*. Berlin: Hentrich, 2002.

Judt, Tony. *Postwar: A History of Europe Since 1945*. New York: Penguin, 2005.

Kaplan, Marion A. *Between Dignity and Despair: Jewish Life in Nazi Germany*. Oxford: Oxford University Press, 1998.

Kershaw, Ian. *Hitler*. Vol. 1, *Herkunft—Aufstieg—Machtentfaltung 1889–1936*. Munich: Taschenbuchverlag DTV, 2002.

———. *The Nazi Dictatorship: Problems and Perspectives of Interpretation*. 3rd ed. New York: Routledge, 1993.

———, ed. *Popular Opinion and Political Dissent in the Third Reich: Bavaria 1933–1945*. Oxford: Oxford University Press, 1983.

Kiernan, Ben. *Blood and Soil: A World History of Genocide and Extermination from Sparta to Darfur*. New Haven, CT: Yale University Press, 2007.

Klemperer, Victor Klemperer. *I Will Bear Witness: A Diary of the Nazi Years 1942–1945*. New York: Random House, 1999.

Kock, Gerhard. *"Der Führer sorgt für unsere Kinder . . .": Die Kinderlandverschickung im Zweiten Weltkrieg*. Paderborn: Schöningh, 1997.

Kösters, Christoph, and Mark Edward Ruff, eds. *Die katholische Kirche im Dritten Reich: Eine Einführung.* Freiburg i. Br.: Herder, 2011.

Kremmel, Paul. *Pfarrer und Gemeinden im evangelischen Kirchenkampf in Bayern bis 1939: Mit besonderer Berücksichtigung der Ereignisse im Bereich des Bezirksamts Weißenburg in Bayern.* Lichtenfels: Kommissionsverlag Schulze, 1987.

Kroener, Bernhard R. *"Der starke Mann im Heimatkriegsgebiet," Generaloberst Friedrich Fromm: Eine Biographie.* Paderborn: Schöningh, 2005.

Kuropka, Joachim, ed. *Streitfall Galen: Studien und Dokumente.* Münster: Aschendorff, 2007.

Langer, Lawrence. *Preempting the Holocaust.* New Haven, CT: Yale University Press, 1998.

———. *Holocaust Testimonies: The Ruins of Memory.* New Haven, CT: Yale University Press, 1991.

Large, David Clay. *And the World Closed Its Door: The Story of One Family Abandoned to the Holocaust.* New York: Basic Books, 2003.

———, ed. *Contending With Hitler: Varieties of German Resistance in the Third Reich.* New York: Cambridge University Press, 1991.

Lee, Everett S. "A Theory of Migration." *Demography* 3, no. 1 (1966): 47–57.

Leichsenring, Jana. *Die Katholische Kirche und "ihre Juden": Das "Hilfswerk beim Bischöflichen Ordinariat Berlin" 1938–1945.* Berlin: Metropol-Verlag, 2007.

Lerner, Gerda. *The Creation of Feminist Consciousness: From the Middle Ages to 1870.* New York: Oxford University Press, 1994.

Leugers, Antonia, ed. *Berlin, Rosenstraße 2–4: Protest in der NS-Diktatur: Neue Forschungen zum Frauenprotest in der Rosenstraße 1943.* Annweiler: Plöger, 2005.

———. "Widerstand *gegen* die Rosenstraße. Kritische Anmerkungen zu einer Neuerscheinung von Wolf Gruner." *theologie.geschichte* 1 (2006). http://universaar.uni-saarland.de/journals/index.php/tg/article/view/133/148.

———. Review: Wolf Gruner: *Gedenkort Rosenstraße 2–4: Internierung und Protest im NS-Staat* Topographie des Terrors. Notizen. Vol. 6. Andreas Nachama, ed. Berlin, 2013. *theologie.geschichte* 8 (2013). http://universaar.uni-saarland.de/journals/index.php/tg/article/view/536/575.

Mason, Tim. "The Legacy of 1918 for National Socialism." In *German Democracy and the Triumph of Hitler: Essays in Recent German History*, edited by Anthony Nicholls and Erich Matthias. London: Allen and Unwin, 1971.

Mason, Tim, and Jane Caplan. *Social Policy in the Third Reich: The Working Class and the National Community.* Providence, RI: Berg, 1993.

Meier, Kurt. *Kreuz und Hakenkreuz: Die evangelische Kirche im Dritten Reich.* Munich: Deutscher Taschenbuch Verlag, 2001.

Meiser, Hans. *Kirche, Kampf und Christusglaube: Anfechtungen und Antworten eines Lutheraners*, edited by Fritz and Gertrude Meiser. Munich: Claudius-Verlag, 1982.

Neliba, Günter. *Der Legalist des Unrechtsstaates Wilhelm Frick: Eine politische Biographie.* Paderborn: Schöningh, 1992.

Peukert, Detlev. *Volksgenossen und Gemeinschaftsfremde: Anpassung, Ausmerze und Aufbegehren unter dem Nationalsozialismus.* Cologne: Bund Verlag, 1982.

Piper, Franciszek. *Arbeitseinsatz der Häftlinge aus dem KL Auschwitz.* Oświęcim: Verlag Staatliches Museum in Oświęcim, 1995.

Röhm, Eberhard, and Jörg Thierfelder. "Gebt uns unsere Männer frei"—Der Aufstand der Frauen in der Rosenstraße im Rahmen der "Fabrikaktion." In *Juden-Christen-Deutsche*. Vol. 4/2, *1941–1945: Vernichtet*, edited by Eberhard Röhm and Jörg Thierfelder, 188–203. Stuttgart: Calwer, 2007.

Ruddick, Sara. *Maternal Thinking: Toward a Politics of Peace*. Boston: Beacon Press, 1989.

Schmid, Heinrich. *Apokalyptisches Wetterleuchten: Ein Beitrag der evangelischen Kirche zum Kampf im "Dritten Reich."* Munich: Verlag der Evangelisch-lutherischen Kirche in Bayern, 1947.

Scholder, Klaus. *Die Kirchen und das Dritte Reich*. Vol. 2. Berlin: Ullstein, 1985.

Schröder, Nina. *Hitlers unbeugsame Gegnerinnen: Der Frauenaufstand in der Rosenstraße*. Munich: W. Heyne, 1998.

Schüssler Fiorenza, Elisabeth. *In Memory of Her: A Feminist Theological Reconstruction of Christian Origins*. New York: Crossroad Publishing, 1994.

Stephenson, Jill. *Hitler's Home Front: Württemberg under the Nazis*. London: Hambledon Continuum, 2006.

Stoltzfus, Nathan. *Resistance of the Heart: Intermarriage and the Rosenstrasse Protest in Nazi Germany*. New York: W.W. Norton, 1996.

Süß, Winfried. *Der "Volkskörper" im Krieg: Gesundheitspolitik, medizinische Versorgung und Krankenmord im nationalsozialistischen Deutschland 1939–1945*. Munich: Oldenbourg Wissenschaftsverlag, 2003.

Tent, James F. *In the Shadow of the Holocaust: Nazi Persecution of Jewish-Christian Germans*. Lawrence: University Press of Kansas, 2003.

Torrie, Julia S. *For Their Own Good: Civilian Evacuations in Germany and France, 1939–1945*. New York: Berghahn Books, 2010.

Volk, Ludwig, ed. *Akten deutscher Bischöfe über die Lage der Kirche 1933–1945*. Vol. 5. *1940–1942*. Mainz: Matthias-Grünewald-Verlag, 1983.

Weinberg, Gerhard L. *Germany, Hitler, and World War II: Essays in Modern German and World History*. Cambridge: Cambridge University Press, 1995.

Westerfield, Leigh. *This Anguish, Like a Kind of Intimate Song: Resistance in Women's Literature of World War II*. Amsterdam: Rodopi, 2004.

Wolf, Hubert. *Clemens August Graf von Galen: Gehorsam und Gewissen*. Freiburg i. Br.: Herder, 2006.

Index

abortion, 58, 212
Adams, Uwe, 181
Adenauer, Konrad, 8
Adler, Hans Günther, 134, 151, 157, 181, 187, 194, 201n46, 247
Aktion T4, 67, 69, 213. *See also* euthanasia
Allies, 10, 13, 15–16, 31, 62–63, 218. *See also* bombings
Ameln, Hans von, 147
Arab Spring, 217
Argentina Mothers of the Plaza de Mayo, 108–09, 117–18, 218
Auschwitz, 120, 141n37, 148, 154, 179–81, 192–94, 206n93, 217, 220n7, 226n1, 227n11, 247, 251–54
    Buna Camp, 127–35, 138n11, 139n25, 181, 186, 189, 227n13, 252–53
    gas chambers, 126
    Polish labor, 129–31, 139n25, 140n27, 140n32, 227n13
    Rosenstrasse Deportations, 96, 116, 125–37, 140n32, 140n34, 185–86, 189, 192, 203nn71–72, 204n76
    Stalingrad, 129–30, 141n37
    Transport, 35a, 134–36, 142n51, 252–54
Arnsberg, 205n80, 229
Austria, 28–30, 212, 248

Bad Kreuznach, 28
Bad Windsheim, 32
Baden, 25–26, 28–29, 79–80, 82, 88, 94, 99n21, 99n26, 101nn44–46, 197n3, 214
Bamberg, 147
Baum, Justin, 147

Bavaria, 3, 6–7, 24, 27–32, 38–51, 52n4, 72n22, 77, 94–96, 211, 214–15, 249n5
Bavarian Provincial Church, 38–51
    See also crucifix campaign
Beck, Jakob, 44
Beijing, 217
Bekennende Kirche (Confessing Church), 28, 46, 49, 172n106
Bell, George (Bishop), 43
Benz, Wolfgang, 110, 143, 191, 205n89, 259
Berlin, v, 6, 23, 26, 38, 82, 84, 96, 104n100, 108–09, 112–13, 118, 133–34, 155, 177–78, 185
    armaments industry in, 14, 131–33, 140, 144, 180–81, 186, 202, 227n13, 230, 236, 252–53
    Berlin Catholic Relief Organization, 137, 148, 151–52, 181–83, 185, 189
    bishops, 60, 137, 148, 151–52, 156, 173n106
    bombing of, 89, 93, 104n100, 137, 156
    Bureau of Reparations, ix, 113–14, 241–42
    evacuation of Jews from, x, 23, 122n20, 126, 132–37, 140n34, 141n38, 143, 146–51, 156, 168n52, 177, 180–81, 188, 237
    evacuation of non-Jews from, 26, 80, 82, 86, 131, 156
    Nazi leaders in, 6, 23, 46, 93, 134, 141, 146, 151, 177
    Protests, 14, 22, 84, 150.
    See also Rosenstrasse Protest; *Fabrik-Aktion*

Berning, Wilhelm, 61, 65, 151, 170n77, 188
Bertram, Adolf (Catholic Bishop), 58–59, 61, 113, 152–60, 223, 226n5
Bielefeld, 204n80, 229
Birkenau. *See* Auschwitz
Black Forest, 80, 83–84
Blumenthal, Gertrud, 242
Bochum, 4, 26, 76, 79, 82, 85, 117, 255
Bohemia, 227, 247
bombings, 4–5, 15, 24–25, 27, 31–32, 78–81, 83–84, 89–94, 99n21, 103n87, 104n100, 126, 150, 182, 207n110, 213–14, 238, 255–57
Bonhoeffer, Dietrich, 211
Bormann, Martin, 5, 9n7, 68, 88–91, 94, 104n108, 256
Braun Odilo, 148, 152, 155, 157, 166n33, 168n57
Braunes Haus, 40, 44
Breit, Thomas, 41
Breslau, 140n34, 152–54, 156, 158, 223, 253
Brunner, Alois, 181, 206n92
Buchenwald, 128, 130
Bulgaria, 12
Buna Camp. *See* Auschwitz: Buna Camp
Bürckel, Josef, 47

Calau, 145, 183, 230. *See also* Frankfurt am Oder
Casti Conubii, 57
Catholic Church, 6–7, 11, 18, 25, 28–29, 33, 42, 55–69, 82, 117, 137, 147, 149, 152–55, 171n90, 173n106, 190, 211, 212–13
  bishops, 3, 7, 11, 55–67, 113, 149, 151–52, 158, 170n75, 181–82, 187–88
  Catholic Relief Office, 181–82, 185
  Catholic Youth, 5
  intermarriage, 137, 144, 151, 153
  Jewish heritage, 144, 147, 151, 153, 155–56, 158–60, 171n90, 186
  nuns, 58–59, 158
  Rosenstrasse Protest and the, 157–59
  See also crucifix campaign; Fulda Bishops' Conference; Vatican
China, 217
Church Conflict, 45, 47–51
Cohen, Gertrud and Hans, 242
Cologne, 24–25, 91–92
communism, 20, 45, 57, 119, 170n75, 189
Communist Party (KPD), 20, 45, 82, 100n39, 109
concentration camps, 12, 14–15, 126–30, 135, 189, 225. *See also* Auschwitz
Confessing Church. *See* Bekennende Kirche
crucifix campaign, 6, 28–29, 61, 77, 94–96, 107, 215

Dachau, 128
Dahlem, 46, 49
Daimler, 32
Darmstadt, 180
Deaneries, 62
Decker, Rainer, 137, 152–53, 159
Denmark, 21
Deutsche Tafelglas (DETAG), 78
Deutschen Christen (German Christians), 42, 44, 49
Dietrich, Sepp, 182, 201n46, 236
Dipper, Christof, 175n130, 203n76
Donaueschingen, 83–84, 101n46
Dortmund, 21, 79, 85, 205n80, 229, 260
Dresden, 15, 148
Drummer, Michael, 154
Düsseldorf, 147, 149, 226n1
Dutch Reform Church, 158–59

East Germany, 1, 142n54, 202n61
Eastern Front, 3, 11–12, 66, 70, 90, 133, 141n37, 224
Ebermannstadt, 28–30
Egypt, 217
Eichmann, Adolf, 129, 132–33, 135, 141n37, 144, 150, 153, 157, 159, 179, 181, 186, 202, 224–26, 247, 259
Eichstätt, 147
Einsatzgruppen, 11

Entjudung des Reichgebietes Aktion ("Elimination of Jews from German Territory"). *See Fabrik-Aktion*
Episcopal Church, 62, 66
Epp, Franz Ritter von, 6–7, 39–40, 44, 50
Erbach, 29
Essen, 9n7, 25, 94, 101n45
euthanasia, v, 3, 7, 10–11, 55–70, 88, 103n72, 177, 198n11, 212–15
evacuations,
 Jews, 23, 125, 147–48, 150, 156, 187, 230, 235, 237, 247, 251–253
 non-Jews, 4–5, 24, 26–27, 30, 33, 76–82, 84–87, 89–94, 99n17, 101n47, 207n110, 214–16, 238, 256, 260
Evans, Richard, 33, 97n3, 97–98n5, 102n51, 104n100, 106, 110–11, 116–17, 122n20

Fabrik-Aktion, ix, 7, 116, 125–37, 141n38, 142n54, 155, 163n13, 170n81, 171n89, 181–82, 184–85, 190, 193, 199n29, 217, 229
Factory Action. *See Fabrik-Aktion*
Faulhaber, Michael von, 58, 72n22
Final Roundup (*Schlussaktion*). *See Fabrik-Aktion*
Finland, 12
Flossenbürg, 128
Food Office, 26–27, 76, 82, 84, 87, 90, 255
France, 21, 31, 43, 103n87, 141n36, 182
Franconia, 39–43, 46, 50, 211
Frankfurt am Main, 145, 148–49, 180, 183
Frankfurt am Oder, 183–84, 200n40, 229–31
 Frankfurt am Oder Decree, 145, 163n13, 183–85, 191–92, 202n56, 204n80, 229–32
Freiburg, 147, 169n75
Frick, Wilhelm, 44, 47–48, 51, 188, 194, 225
Friedlander, Benjamin, v

Friedlander, Henry, v
Friedländer, Saul, 106, 111–12, 116, 119–20
Fromm, Friedrich, 13
Fulda Bishops' Conference, 59–61, 144, 152, 157, 160

Galen, August von, 3, 7, 11, 57, 59–70, 72n22, 152, 160, 177, 198n10, 213, 260
Galilee, 107
Geltungsjuden, x, 144, 146, 163n15, 238, 248. *See also Mischlinge*
genocide, 9n3, 177, 179–80, 183, 218
German Labor Front, 19
Gestapo, 2, 20, 30, 57, 106, 113, 132, 144, 178, 186, 196, 225–26, 242, 260
 Auschwitz, 130, 134–37, 180, 189
 Catholics, 61–64, 68, 70, 185–86
 Fabrik-Aktion, ix, 116, 134, 137, 180–84, 229
 communists, 20
 Rosenstrasse, 4, 106, 110, 123n48, 125–26, 134, 137, 144–47, 149, 167n48, 168n52, 170n81, 185–86, 188–94, 201n45, 203n68, 203n76, 204n80, 206n92, 206n96, 208n115,
Gerstenmaier, Eugen, 196
Gleichschaltung, 38, 42, 47, 212
Globke, Hans, 155
Goebbels, Joseph, ix–x, 4–5, 14, 21, 23, 30, 33, 66, 77, 79, 96, 104n100, 115, 200n34, 201n46, 202n53, 226n3, 227n10, 235–39
 euthanasia protests, 66–69, 167n49, 200n33, 213
 Rosenstrasse Protest, 23, 96, 126, 134, 141n38, 146, 149–50, 177–82, 186–88, 190, 192–94, 199n21, 202n64, 203n66, 223–25, 237–38, 259–60
 Witten protests, 4–5, 27, 33, 79, 83, 86–94, 238–39, 257
Golgotha, 108
Gomaringen, 32
Göring, Hermann, 14, 93, 127, 224

Great Britain, 11, 62, 209, 214, 236
Greece, 12
Greiser, Arthur, 184
Grimminger, Eugen, 148, 165n32
Gritzbach, Erich, 223
Grohé, Josef, 91–92
Groß-Beeren, 136
Gruner, Wolf, 106, 110–13, 116–17, 125–26, 133–37, 143–45, 149–50, 160–61, 191–92, 204n80, 216, 229, 259–60
Günther, Rolf, 206n93
Gunzenhausen, 39
Gürtner, Franz, 47
Gutterer, Leopold, ix, 115, 186, 190, 237

Hamburg, 20, 24, 78, 145, 197n3
Hamm, 4, 26, 76, 82, 85, 87, 117, 255
Hammerstein, Kurt von, 219
Hannover, 47–49
Harrison, Leland, 189, 234
Hess, Rudolf, 44, 50
Hesse, 148
Hilberg, Raul, 181
Hildmann, Gerhard, 40
Hilfrich, Antonius, 160
Himmler, Heinrich, 5, 9n7, 15–16, 30, 61, 66–68, 88–91, 93–94, 126–28, 131, 180–81, 193, 198n18, 256
Hitler, Adolf, 3–4, 77, 96, 219, 227n16
  certainty of victory, 4, 31, 59
  euthanasia and the Church, 3, 38–39, 43–50, 59, 67–70, 177, 211–13
  evacuations and the Witten Protest, 5, 76, 79, 86–87, 92, 94, 215, 255
  foreign opinion, 9n3, 43, 46
  German home front, 3–4, 182
  intermarriages, 178–83, 187, 190, 192, 195, 203n66, 214, 237
  Nazi Party leadership, 5, 28, 30–31, 44, 46, 50, 68, 90, 92–93, 126, 182, 184, 190, 195, 210, 212, 219
  "Nero decree", 31
  popular support, 1, 3, 5, 69, 77, 84, 86, 187, 209–11, 216
  racial policies, xi, 2, 10–12, 30, 126, 178–95, 199n21, 202n53, 236, 255, 259
  rationing, 5, 90, 92, 94, 215
  Rosenstrasse Protest, 187, 190, 192, 237, 261
  World War I, 2, 216
Hitler Youth, 5, 19, 34
Hoffmann, Albert, 25–27, 30, 81, 87–88, 91, 94, 99n29, 103n87, 255
Holocaust, v, 9–11, 15, 116, 119–21, 177, 180, 194, 201n46, 213, 218
Holz, Karl, 42–43, 50
Holzer, Elsa and Rudi, 153
Höss, Rudolf, 127, 131, 251–52
Hungary, 12
Hunzinger, Ingeborg, v
Huttner, Johnny, 189, 203n71

IG Farben, 127–29, 131, 181
Intermarriage (Jewish/non-Jewish mixed marriages), 13–15, 33, 95, 140nn34–35, 141n36, 141n38, 141n42, 148, 164n24, 170nn76–77, 171n89, 175n128, 177, 196, 197n2, 201n46, 202n56, 203n66, 216–17, 220n7, 229–31, 235
  and Catholic Churches, 7, 113, 137, 144, 147–49, 151–60, 171n90, 174n120–21, 181–83, 185–90, 223
  divorce, 33, 136, 148–50, 152, 154–60, 170nn76–77, 177–80, 182, 196, 197n3, 197n7, 199n23, 200n40, 223–24
  intermarriage laws, 147, 149, 152–55, 157–60, 178–80, 183, 199n23, 244–47
  "non-privileged" intermarriage, x, 7, 15, 141n38, 145–46, 171n89, 177–78, 180–81, 188, 194, 197n7, 207n105, 223, 246n2. See also Star of David
  "privileged" intermarriage, ix–x, 15, 23, 146, 165n32, 171n90, 174n120, 178, 181, 188, 194, 207n105, 223–24, 237–38, 246n2

and Protestant Churches, 7, 23,
113, 133, 141n36, 145, 148–51,
153, 155, 157, 159–60, 165n32,
167nn48–49, 169n74, 174n120,
187–89, 196, 201n46, 202, 223–26
Rosenstrasse, ix-x, 14–15, 23, 95,
97n3, 106, 108, 110, 113, 122n20,
125–26, 134–37, 142n54, 143–61,
168n52, 174n121, 185–94, 203n71,
203n75, 204n76, 207n105, 237–38
See also Mischehen
Innsbruck, 149, 189
Interministerial Air War Damages
Committee, 94
Italy, 12

Jäger, August, 38–42, 44, 50
Jaspers, Karl, 8, 196
Jehovah's Witnesses, 5, 18–19
Jerusalem, 107–08
Jesus of Nazareth, 107–08, 160, 218
Jüdische Allgemeine, ix, 113–14, 241

Kardorff, Ursula von, 150
Kellenbach, Katharina von, 7, 121,
204n76, 218
Kerrl, Hanns, 23
killing centers. *See* concentration camps
Klausa, Ekkehard, 260
Kleemann, Siegbert, 190
Klemperer, Klemens von, 219
Klemperer, Victor, 15, 148, 219
Kliner-Lintzen, Martina, 97n5, 102n51
KPD. *See* Communist Party
Kommandostab Reichsführer-SS, 11
Kögel, Otto Max, 254
König, Lothar, 155, 159
Kreisführer, 28
Kristallnacht Pogrom, 178
Kuller, Christiane, 3, 6, 51, 211–12, 214
Kulturkampf, 68
Kurhessen, 29
Kursk, battle of, 3

Lamberti Church, 60, 64
Lammers, Heinrich, 69

Landeskirchenamt, 39–42, 47, 50
Lang, Cosmo, 43
Langer, Lawrence, 120
Lehfeldt, Gerhardt, 113, 133, 135, 141,
145, 149–50, 159–60, 187, 189,
194–96, 201n46, 202n53, 223, 226n1
Leibstandarte Hitler. *See* SS-Leibstandarte
Leugers, Antonia, 4, 6–7, 23, 124n48,
161, 196, 204n76, 206n91, 208n115,
216
Leutershausen, 31
Liberia, 117–18
Libya, 217
Liebehenschel, Arthur, 131–33, 251
Limburg, 160
Lolling, Enno, 130
London, 43
Luckner, Gertrud, 147, 155, 171n89,
182–83, 185
Lünen, 4, 26, 76, 82, 85, 117, 255
Lutherans, 3, 43–44

Mainz, 160
Mannesmann, 78
Marahrens, August, 44, 47–48
Marienthal Mental Institution, 60
Mary Magdalene, 107–08
Maurer, Gerhard, 127–29, 131, 138n11,
140n32, 181, 252
Mauthausen, 128, 139n25
Meiser, Hans, 6, 38–50, 52n15, 211–12
Mergenthaler, Christian, 30
Meyer, Alfred, 27, 89
Meyer, Beate, 118–19, 191
Meyer-Erlach, Wolf, 42
Milton, Sybil, v, 97n5, 102n51
Mischehen. *See* Intermarriage
Mischlinge, x, 13–14, 23, 133, 136,
140n34, 146–47, 155–56, 171n89,
181, 183, 185, 199n23, 203n68, 214,
235, 238, 244–45, 248
Mischling Law, 223–26
See also Geltungsjuden
Moltke, Helmuth James Graf von, 159
Monowice, 128
Monowitz. *See* Monowice

Moravia, 227, 247
Moscow, 217
Mosse, Martha, 190
Müller, Ludwig, 38, 43–50, 211
Munich, 6, 10, 38–45, 47, 52n4, 58, 147, 170n76, 211, 218
Munich University, 20
Münster, 27, 57, 59–62, 64–65, 67–70, 89, 104n108, 152, 213
Murr, Wilhelm, 24

Nachama, Andreas, 196
NS-Frauenschaft, 19, 28–29, 65
NS-Lehrerbund, 19
NS-Volkswohlfahrt, 19, 22, 26, 99n21, 101n44
National Welfare Organization, 4
Natzweiler, 128
Neander, Joachim, 4, 7, 124n48, 137, 145, 196, 202n53, 204n76, 208n115, 216–17, 227n13
Netherlands, 158–59, 173n111, 173n114
Neuburg, 40
Neuwied, 28
New Testament, 107–08
Niedermirsberg, 29
Niemöller, Martin, 47, 62, 211
Nuremberg, 40, 42–43, 52n4, 147, 154
Nuremberg Laws, x, 125, 146, 153, 178, 181, 223, 238, 246

Ochsenfurt, 32
Oldenburg, 27, 61
Olympic Games (1936), 212
"Operation Gomorrah", 24
Oranienburg, 127–28, 136, 251, 253
Order Police, 11
Orsenigo, Cesare, 144, 186
Osnabrück, 61, 65, 151, 188
OSS (Office of Strategic Services), 123n48, 189, 194, 233–34

Pacelli, Eugenio, 61. *See also* Pope Pius XII
Paderborn, 66, 154, 205, 229
Palatinate, 47

Pätzold, Kurt, 191
Peter (Saint), 107
Petersberg (Petrograd), 27, 29
Peukert, Detlev, 6, 97n5
Pfeffer, Franz van, 44, 47, 50
Pfullingen, 32
Poland, 14, 122n20, 129–31, 133, 137, 139, 140n32, 194, 225, 227n13, 230
police, 15, 22–23, 32, 108, 137, 148–49, 207n108, 242, 245–48
  and the crucifix campaign, 28–29
  Bishop Meiser protests, 38–40, 42, 44, 52n15
  general roundups of Jews, 15, 235, 237–38
  Rosenstrasse, 15, 23, 110, 112, 122n20, 135, 145, 156, 170n77, 183, 185, 187, 230–31
  Witten, 25, 27, 33, 76, 81, 87, 102n61, 117, 215
  See also Order Police; SD
Pomerania, 79–80, 214
Pope Pius XII, 152–53, 155–57, 159
Press, 18, 24, 40–41, 47, 51, 102n61, 113, 169n74, 183, 259
Preysing, Konrad von, 60, 152, 155, 157, 159, 173n106, 174n121, 182–83, 185
Protestant Burial Society (*Begräbnisverein*), 41
Protestant Church, 3, 6, 11, 18, 25, 28–29, 38–51, 56, 82, 84, 86, 113, 148, 155, 211
  clergy, 11, 62, 113, 149, 153, 187, 211
  and Euthanasia, 62
  intermarriage, 149, 153, 165n32
  Jewish Protestants, 149, 153, 226n1
  resistance, 6, 211
  See also Wurm, Theophil
Provincial Church. *See* Bavarian Provincial Church
Putzrath, Else and Herbert, 242

rationing, 5, 22, 24–27, 33, 76, 81–92, 94–95, 99n29, 102n57, 102n67, 103n87, 104n108, 156, 215–16, 255–57

Ravensbrück, 147–48, 182
Red Cross, 19
Reeswinkel, Wilhelm, 83–84, 95,
    101nn46–48
Reich Association for Physical Exercise, 19
Reich Chancellery, 30, 68–69, 156, 256
Reich Church (*Reichskirche*), 3, 23, 38–40,
    42–44, 46–50, 150–51, 188, 211–12
Reich Defense Council, 127
Reich Food Estate, 19
Reich Inspection of Civilian Air War
    Measures, 91, 93, 257
Reich Party Congress, 45
Reich Security Main Office (RSHA),
    117, 125, 129–33, 135, 137, 140n34,
    144–45, 147, 150–51, 156, 177,
    180–81, 183–86, 188–93, 199n22,
    206n94, 224, 229–31, 247, 259
Reichstag Fire, 18
Reichsverteidigungskommissare (RVK),
    24–26
Reutlingen, 32
Rhine River, 24
Rhineland, 28, 212
Roman Empire, 107
Rome, 144, 149
Roosevelt, Franklin, 62
Rosenheim, 41
Rosenstrasse (film), 118, 143, 259–60
Rosenstrasse Memorial, v
Rosenstrasse Protest,
    Deportations to Auschwitz, 96, 116,
        125–37, 140n32, 140n34, 185–86,
        189, 192, 203nn71–72, 204n76
    reports during the war, 101n48,
        123n48, 148–53, 155–58, 166n34,
        168n54, 170n81, 171n90, 172n106,
        185, 188–89, 194, 233–34
Ruhrgebiet, 4, 23, 25–27, 76, 78–81,
    83–86, 89, 94, 117, 207, 214–15
Ruhrstahl AG, 78
Russia. *See* Soviet Union

Saar, 47, 212
Sachsenhausen, 128
Salzburg, 29, 83

Sartorious, Erwin, 186
Sauckel, Fritz, 180, 236
Schellenberg, Walter, 16
Schemm, Hans, 42
Schirach, Baldur von, 180
Schlessmann, Fritz, 104n108, 256–57
Scholder, Klaus, 38
Scholl, Hans, 218
Scholl, Sophie, 20, 218
Schutzpolizei, 87
Schwab, Ivan, 147
Schwarz, Heinrich, 127–29, 131,
    134–36, 254
SD (Sicherheitsdienst), 3–4, 23, 26, 29,
    67, 76–77, 81–89, 102n59, 207n108,
    235, 237, 247, 255, 260
Siebert, Ludwig, 40, 44, 46, 50
Sindelfingen, 32
Sirleaf, Ellen Johnson, 118
Social Democrats Party (SPD), 20, 22,
    45, 51, 82, 100n39
Sommer, Margarethe, 101n48, 148–53,
    155–58, 166n34, 168n54, 170n81,
    171n90, 172n106, 185, 189, 194
Soviet Union, 28, 33, 64, 69, 82, 217
    commissars, 3
    invasion of, 7, 11, 69, 129
    Jews in, 11
    prisoners of war, 13
    Revolution, 27
    See also, Stalingrad
South German League of Evangelical
    Christians, 42
Speer, Albert, 10, 180, 190, 236
Sprenger, Jakob, 184
Spratte (Head liaison officer, Westfalen-
    Süd), 80–81, 85, 99n29
SS (Schutzstaffel), 11, 23, 30–32, 110,
    112, 127–28, 136, 155, 182, 185, 189,
    192, 215, 224–25, 242, 251
SS-Leibstandarte, 182, 184, 200n34,
    201n46, 206n93, 225, 236
SS-WVHA (Economic and
    Administrative Department), 127–28,
    130–34, 140n34, 181, 185, 251
Waffen-SS, 30, 227

"Stab in the back" myth, 2, 11, 22–23, 33, 67, 182
Stahl, Johanna, 147
Stalin, Joseph, 217
Stalingrad, 3, 14, 23, 129–30, 137, 139n23, 141n37, 182, 187, 217, 236
Star of David, ix-x, 7, 141n38, 145–46, 153, 180, 190, 197n7, 205n80, 238, 242. *See also* "non-privileged" intermarriage
Starachowice, 194
Stauffenberg, Claus von, 219
Stein, Edith, 158
Stephenson, Jill, 2, 34, 204n76, 218
Stock, Walter, 186, 189, 201n45
Stohr, Albert, 160, 174n121
Stoltzfus, Nathan, xi, 7–8, 14, 91, 95, 99n20, 106, 110, 145, 161, 170–71n81, 175n130, 197, 216, 237, 260
Streicher, Julius, 41–43, 50, 211
Stuckart, Wilhelm, 79, 90–91, 179, 199n23
Sturmabteilung (SA), 19
Stuttgart, 24–25, 147–48, 165n32, 236
Sudetenland, 79–80, 214
Süß, Winfried, 3, 7, 70, 168n58, 212–14
Swabia, 39–41, 101
Schwarz, Heinrich, 127–28, 131, 134, 136, 253
Sweden, 113, 226
Switzerland, 189
Syria, 217

T4 Program. *See euthanasia*
Taylor, Charles, 118
teachers, 19, 25, 28–29
Terezin, 150, 175n128
Theresienstadt, 129, 144, 179, 194, 227n11
Titze, Herbert, 190, 203n75
Topography of Terror memorial, Berlin, 196, 247
Torrie, Julia, 4–5, 27, 96, 204n76, 205n89, 215, 239
Trier, 28

Trotta, Margarethe von, 118, 148, 259–60
Tübingen, 32

Ukraine, 21
Ulm, 29
Unikower, Inge, 202n61
United States, 31–32, 109, 120, 189, 198n18, 214
USSR. *See* Soviet Union

Vatican, 57, 61, 187, 195. *See also* Pope Pius XII
Vienna, 5, 180–81, 184, 190, 247
Vistula River, 127
Volk, 1–6, 8, 62, 88, 91, 158, 160, 177–80, 182, 187, 195, 198n11, 207n110, 215, 236
Volksgemeinschaft, xi, 2–3, 45, 57, 60, 62, 66, 86, 96
Volkssturm, 31–32

Wagner, Adolf, 6–7, 28, 30, 44, 96
Waibstadt, 28
Wannsee Conference, 12, 151–55, 177, 179
Wartheland, 184
Wehrmacht, 3–4, 11, 13, 27, 33, 57, 63–64, 182, 219
Sixth Army, 14
Weimar Republic, 84
Weinberg, Gerhard, 4, 16, 204n76, 213–14
Werner, Wolfgang, 97n5
West Germany, 8, 64, 66, 119, 180, 196
Westerstetten, 29
Westfalen-Nord, 27, 83, 89. *See also* Westphalia
Westfalen-Süd, 25, 30, 79–81, 84, 87, 91, 99n26, 99n29, 101nn46–47, 255. *See also* Westphalia
Westfälische Landeszeitung (WLZ), 81, 83
Westphalia, 60, 62–63, 68. *See also* Westfalen-Süd; Westfalen-Nord

White Rose, 5, 20, 148
Wienken, Heinrich, 144–45, 149–50, 152, 156–57, 159, 186
Witten, 4–5, 23, 25–27, 33, 76–102, 117, 205n89, 207n108, 214–17, 219, 239, 255, 260–61
World War I, 2, 7, 11, 13, 22, 27, 33, 57, 84, 102n61, 116, 182, 210, 216

Wurm, Theophil (Protestant Bishop), 23, 44, 47–48, 113, 148, 150–51, 153, 160, 165n32, 167n49, 169n74, 173n111, 188, 194–96, 226n1
Württemberg, 23–24, 29–30, 32, 34, 47–49, 150, 165n32, 188, 197n3
Würzburg, 147

Yugoslavia, 12

Protest, Culture and Society

General editors:
Kathrin Fahlenbrach, Institute for Media and Communication, University of Hamburg
Martin Klimke, New York University Abu Dhabi
Joachim Scharloth, Technical University Dresden, Germany

Protest movements have been recognized as significant contributors to processes of political participation and transformations of culture and value systems, as well as to the development of both a national and transnational civil society.

This series brings together the various innovative approaches to phenomena of social change, protest and dissent which have emerged in recent years, from an interdisciplinary perspective. It contextualizes social protest and cultures of dissent in larger political processes and socio-cultural transformations by examining the influence of historical trajectories and the response of various segments of society, political and legal institutions on a national and international level. In doing so, the series offers a more comprehensive and multi-dimensional view of historical and cultural change in the twentieth and twenty-first centuries.

Volume 1
Voices of the Valley, Voices of the Straits: How Protest Creates Communities
Donatella della Porta and Gianni Piazza

Volume 2
Transformations and Crises: The Left and the Nation in Denmark and Sweden, 1956–1980
Thomas Ekman Jørgensen

Volume 3
Changing the World, Changing Oneself: Political Protest and Collective Identities in West Germany and the U.S. in the 1960s and 1970s
Edited by Belinda Davis, Wilfried Mausbach, Martin Klimke, and Carla MacDougall

Volume 4
The Transnational Condition: Protest Dynamics in an Entangled Europe
Edited by Simon Teune

Volume 5
Protest Beyond Borders: Contentious Politics in Europe since 1945
Edited by Hara Kouki and Eduardo Romanos

Volume 6
Between the Avant-Garde and the Everyday: Subversive Politics in Europe from 1957 to the Present
Edited by Timothy Brown and Lorena Anton

Volume 7
Between Prague Spring and French May: Opposition and Revolt in Europe, 1960–1980
Edited by Martin Klimke, Jacco Pekelder, and Joachim Scharloth

Volume 8
The Third World in the Global 1960s
Edited by Samantha Christiansen and Zachary A. Scarlett

Volume 9
The German Student Movement and the Literary Imagination: Transnational Memories of Protest and Dissent
Susanne Rinner

Volume 10
Children of the Dictatorship: Student Resistance, Cultural Politics, and the 'Long 1960s' in Greece
Kostis Kornetis

Volume 11
Media and Revolt: Strategies and Performances from the 1960s to the Present
Edited by Kathrin Fahlenbrach, Erling Sivertsen, and Rolf Werenskjold

Volume 12
Europeanizing Contention: The Protest Against 'Fortress Europe' in France and Germany
Pierre Monforte

Volume 13
Militant Around the Clock? Left-Wing Youth Politics, Leisure, and Sexuality in Post-Dictatorship Greece, 1974–1981
Nikolaos Papadogiannis

Volume 14
Protest in Hitler's 'National Community': Popular Unrest and the Nazi Response
Edited by Nathan Stoltzfus and Birgit Maier-Katkin

Volume 15
Comrades of Color: East Germany in the Cold War World
Edited by Quinn Slobodian

Volume 16
Social Movement Studies in Europe: The State of the Art
Edited by Olivier Fillieule and Guya Accornero

Volume 17
Protest Cultures: A Companion
Edited by Kathrin Fahlenbrach, Martin Klimke, and Joachim Scharloth

Volume 18
The Revolution before the Revolution: Late Authoritarianism and Student Protest in Portugal
By Guya Accornero

Volume 19
The Nuclear Crisis: The Arms Race, Cold War Anxiety, and the German Peace Movement of the 1980s
Edited by Christoph Becker-Schaum, Philipp Gassert, Wilfried Mausbach, Martin Klimke, and Marianne Zepp

Volume 20
A Fragmented Landscape: Abortion Governance and Protest Logics in Europe
Edited by Silvia De Zordo, Joanna Mishtal, and Lorena Anton

Volume 21
Hairy Hippies and Bloody Butchers: The Greenpeace Anti-Whaling Campaign in Norway
Juliane Riese

Volume 22
The Women's Liberation Movement: Impacts and Outcomes
Edited by Kristina Schulz